HOTEL FRONT OFFICE MANAGEMENT

FIFTH EDITION

JAMES A. BARDI, EdD, CHA
THE PENNSYLVANIA STATE UNIVERSITY

John Wiley & Sons, Inc.

Copyright © 2011, 2007, 2003 by John Wiley & Sons, Inc. All rights reserved.

Published by John Wiley & Sons, Inc., Hoboken, New Jersey.
Published simultaneously in Canada.

For general information on our other products and services, or technical support, please contact our Customer Care Department within the United States at 800-762-2974, outside the United States at 317-572-3993 or fax 317-572-4002.

Wiley also publishes its books in a variety of electronic formats. Some content that appears in print may not be available in electronic books. For more information about Wiley products, visit our web site at www.wiley.com.

Library of Congress Cataloging-in-Publication Data

Bardi, James A., 1947-
  Hotel front office management /James A. Bardi.–5th ed.
    p. cm.
  Includes bibliographical references and index.
  ISBN 978-0-470-63752-4 (acid-free paper)
  1. Hotel management. I. Title.
  TX911.3.M27B35 2011
  647.94'068–dc22
                                             2010039007

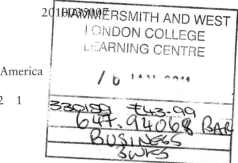

Printed in the United States of America

10 9 8 7 6 5 4 3 2 1

To Linda
Your love, patience, and encouragement made this book possible.

and

To Maria & Rob, Ryan & Jenni, and David
The joy of sharing this book with you makes it all worthwhile.
And now, the special delight in sharing this book with my grandchildren,
Ben and Sophia, and all my future grandchildren will provide much joy for this grandfather.

Contents

Preface

The *Fifth Edition* of *Hotel Front Office Management* remains one of the leading texts in addressing the demands for instructing future leaders of the hotel industry. Educators who are preparing professionals for roles as front office managers and general managers in hotels are required to meet the challenges of operations, technology, training, empowerment, and international applications. This latest edition of *Hotel Front Office Management* continues to encourage students to take an active part in applying these concepts to the exciting world of hotel operations.

To the Student

The emphasis on management continues to play a central role in *Hotel Front Office Management, Fifth Edition.* The text's structure will assist you as you prepare for positions as entry-level managers. The logical presentation of chapters in order of operations—overview of lodging hospitality; tour of the front office, review of the guest cycle, and analysis of guest services—allows you to gain insight into a front office manager's role in the hotel. Reviews and analysis of other departments and how they relate to the front office include security and housekeeping.

To the Instructor

Instructors will find text material presented in a logical manner to develop lesson plans. Features include Chapter Focus Points; Opening Dilemmas to encourage students to relate to practical information; figures, tables, and photos that represent current industry trends; International Highlights, which encourage diversity; End-of-Chapter Questions that support content presented in the text; and three well-developed Case Studies per chapter to facilitate student discussion.

A list of Key Words can be found at the end of each chapter, and an excellent Glossary at the end of the text is provided to assist instructors as they develop classroom activities and exams. Faculty will also find PowerPoint Slides and a well-developed **Instructor's Manual with Test Bank** on the web site.

Text Features

The *Fifth Edition* of *Hotel Front Office Management* has maintained its high standards of pedagogical features, including:

- **Opening Dilemmas** present students with a mini-case-study problem to solve with the help of subsequent chapter presentations; a **Solution to the Opening Dilemma** is included at the end of each chapter.

OPENING DILEMMA

The group leader of a busload of tourists approaches the front desk for check-in. The front desk clerk acknowledges the group leader and begins the check-in procedure, only to realize no clean rooms are available. The desk clerk mutters, "It's 4:00 P.M., and you would think someone in housekeeping would have released those rooms by now." The group leader asks, "What's holding up the process?"

- **Hospitality Profiles** feature selected commentaries from hotel front office managers, general managers, and other hotel department managers; these contribute a human relations element to the text.

HOSPITALITY PROFILE

Eric O. Long, general manager of the Waldorf=Astoria in New York City, has been employed by Hilton Corporation for 30 years. He has served in various management positions at the Hilton Short Hills, Chicago Hilton and Towers, Hilton Walt Disney Village, Fontainebleau Hilton Resort, and the Palmer House.

- **International Highlights** include articles of interest that accentuate the international workforce and international career opportunities for hospitality graduates. Additionally, they provide a forum for instructors and students to discuss this aspect of hotel management.

INTERNATIONAL HIGHLIGHTS

International translation cards, which assist foreign guests in translating travel phrases of their native language into English, are frequently kept at front desks. International visitors and hotel desk clerks find these cue cards helpful.

■ **Front-line Realities** present unexpected yet realistic situations. Students are asked to discuss a method of handling these situations.

FRONT-LINE REALITIES

A future guest has called the hotel and wants to arrange a small dinner party for his guests on the first day of his visit. The marketing and sales office is closed for the day, and the banquet manager has left the property for a few hours. What would you suggest the front desk clerk do to assist this future guest?

■ There are now three **Case Studies** at the end of each chapter.
■ A **Glossary,** which appears at the end of the book, summarizes terms introduced in each chapter (and appearing in italics in the text).

What's New and Revised in This Fifth Edition

Chapter 1 Introduction to Hotel Management

■ "Select-service" lodging terminology is introduced to reflect current usage; "limited-service lodging" was used previously.
■ Technological advances, including social media, guest room technology, IT infrastructure, surviving a tough economy with help from technology, and demystifying Web 2.0 are now included in the technological list of advances of the lodging industry.
■ The importance of the Internet is emphasized for its role in marketing.
■ A section on the economic downturn of the late 2000s is included to encourage students to address this challenge as they face their career and future management horizons.
■ Additional metrics allow students to maintain their currency in the lodging market GOPPAR (Gross Operating Profit per Available Room).

Chapter 2 Hotel Organization and the Front Office Manager

■ Updates include organizational charts of a large, full-service hotel, a medium-sized lodging property, and a select-service lodging property.

Chapter 3 Effective Interdepartmental Communications

- New information on social media and its use by the marketing and sales departments is presented and discussed.

Chapter 4 Property Management Systems

- Updates now include social media terminology (Facebook, Twitter, LinkedIn®, YouTube) where applicable to emphasize its appropriateness to reservations as well as to marketing and sales.
- A brief listing of property management system vendors is now included, encouraging students to go beyond the text to seek information they will need in their future careers.

Chapter 5 Systemwide Reservations

- New facts about social media applications including Facebook, Twitter, and LinkedIn are integrated throughout the chapter.
- Information on the central reservation systems for Choice Hotels®, Hilton Hotels®, and Marriott International, Inc., is updated.
- The effect of the Internet on pricing rooms is updated.
- Discussion of the global distribution system and its counterpart, customer relationship management, is expanded.

Chapter 6 Revenue Management

- A discussion of the Star Report is now included.
- The section on channel management now covers current technology that allows users to alter rates, inventory, and reservations in connection with third-party web sites.
- Other features include multilingual and international currency capability.

Chapter 7 Guest Registration

- The section on self-check-in is updated.

Chapter 9 Guest Checkout

- Foreign currency transactions are exemplified by the exchange of Euros to U.S. dollars.

Chapter 10 Preparation and Review of the Night Audit

- Figures on Case Studies (Night Audits) were updated.

Chapter 11 Managing Hospitality

- Information on social media and the impact of technology on managing hospitality is refreshed.

Chapter 13 Promoting In-House Sales

- The figures in the sales budget for the example Planning a Point-of-sale Front Office are updated.

Chapter 14 Security

- The effects of international terrorism on hotel security are discussed.
- Information on electronic locks is expanded to included contactless electronic locks such as wristbands, key fobs, and key cards that use radio frequency identification (RFID).

Chapter 15 Executive Housekeeping

- New emphasis is placed on technology used to assign room attendants.
- The management concept of outsourcing housekeeping activities is presented.
- A new section addresses the chief engineer's responsibilities, including role in a lodging property, managing maintenance, interdepartmental communications, energy management, and the greening of the lodging industry.

Additional Resources

An **Instructor's Manual** to accompany the textbook is available to qualified adopters and may be downloaded from www.wiley.com/college/bardi. It contains materials to assist in the classroom. An updated Test Bank is also included.

The **Test Bank** for this textbook has been specifically formatted for **Respondus**, an easy-to-use software program for creating and managing exams that can be printed to paper or published directly to Blackboard, WebCT, Desire2Learn, eCollege, ANGEL, and other eLearning systems. Instructors who adopt *Hotel Front Office Management* can download the **Respondus Test Bank** for free. Additional Wiley resources also can be uploaded into your LMS course at no charge.

PowerPoint Slides are available for download at the text's website (www.wiley.com/college/bardi). Each set of slides contains the chapter focus points and key discussion points of the main topics of the chapter.

I think you will enjoy this new *Fifth Edition* of *Hotel Front Office Management*. I always appreciate hearing your comments (jxb21@psu.edu or james_bardi@yahoo.com).

My very best to the future professionals of the hotel industry!

Acknowledgments

I wish to acknowledge the following professors, who provided insightful reviews of individual chapters of this and previous editions; without their concern and thoughtful commentary, this effort for our students would not have been possible: Barbara Dexter-Smith, Middlesex Community College; Raphael Thomas George, The Ohio State University; Danna Gildersleeve, Anne Arundel Community College; Chad M. Gruhl, Metropolitan State College of Denver; Terry Jones, Community College of Southern Nevada; Thomas Jones, University of Nevada at Las Vegas, Robert McMullin, East Stroudsburg State University; Amanda Micheel, Purdue University; and James Reid, New York City Technical College.

I would like to express my appreciation to the following hospitality professionals, who provided commentary for the Hospitality Profiles included in this *Fifth Edition:* Gary Budge, Algonquin Hotel, New York City; Marti Cannon, former executive housekeeper, Sheraton Reading Hotel, Wyomissing, Pennsylvania; James Heale, corporate controller for Meyer Jabara Hotels; Lee Johnson, director of corporate sales at Pier 5 Hotel and Brookshire Suites at Baltimore, Maryland's Inner Harbor; John Juliano, director of safety and security, Royal Sonesta Hotel, Cambridge, Massachusetts; Debra Kelly, revenue manager, The Sheraton Parsippany Hotel, Parsippany, New Jersey; Kevin Corprew, director of rooms operation at the Marriott in St. Louis, Missouri; Eric Long, general manager, Waldorf=Astoria, New York City; Joseph Longo, general manager, The Jefferson, Richmond, Virginia; and Patrick Mene, former vice president of quality for the former Ritz-Carlton Hotel Company, LLC.

Special thanks are also extended to Gary Budge and Debra Kelly for their time in discussing the operations of room reservations and revenue management, and to Marti Cannon for her countless hours in explaining the management of the housekeeping department. Their insights provided a framework that will help future generations of hoteliers understand the business.

One additional acknowledgment is offered to Dr. Trish Welch of Southern Illinois University, who was instrumental in developing the *First Edition* of *Hotel Front Office Management.* Her words of support to Van Nostrand Reinhold for the initial prospectus and sample chapter are still greatly appreciated.

CHAPTER 1

Introduction to Hotel Management

OPENING DILEMMA

A hospitality career fair is scheduled at the end of the week at your college or university. Your recent review of this chapter has enticed you to explore the career opportunities in select-service and full-service hotels. Your instructor has asked you to prepare a list of possible questions to ask the recruiter. What would you include in that list?

CHAPTER FOCUS POINTS

- Historical overview of the hotel industry
- Hotel classification system
- Trends that foster growth and employment in the hotel industry
- Career development

The mere mention of the word *hotel* conjures up exciting images: a busy lobby filled with international dignitaries, celebrities, community leaders, attendees of conventions and large receptions, businesspeople, and family vacationers. The excitement you feel in a hotel lobby is something you will have forever in your career. Savor it and enjoy it. It is the beginning of understanding the concept of providing hospitality to guests. As you begin to grasp the principles of a well-operated hotel, you will discover the important role the front office plays in keeping this excitement intact.

The *front office* is the nerve center of a hotel property. Communications and accounting are two of the most important functions of a front desk operation. Effective communications—with guests, employees, and other departments of the hotel—are paramount in projecting a hospitable image. Answering guest inquiries about hotel services and other guests, marketing and sales department requests for information on guest room availability, and housekeeping department inquiries concerning guest reservations are but a few of the routine tasks performed almost constantly by a hotel front desk in its role as communications hub.

Accounting procedures involving charges to registered and nonregistered hotel guest accounts are also important in the hospitality field. Itemized charges are necessary to show a breakdown of charges if a guest questions a bill.

Services for which fees are charged are available 24 hours a day in a hotel property. Moreover, because guests may want to settle their accounts at any time of the day or night, accounts must be current and accurate at all times. Keeping this data organized is a top priority of good front office management.

Founders of the Hotel Industry

A history of the founders of the hotel industry provides an opportunity to reflect on our heritage. Learning about the founding giants such as Statler, Hilton, Marriott, Wilson, and Schultz, to name a few, allows a student of the industry to discover the interesting lineage of hoteliers. Studying the efforts of the innovators who carved out the modern hotel industry may help future professionals with their own career planning.

E. M. Statler

To begin to understand the history of the modern hotel industry, let's look at its early entrepreneurs, who were motivated by wealth and fame on a grand scale.[1] Ellsworth M. Statler (1863–1928) developed the chain of hotels that were known as Statlers, beginning with a hotel in Buffalo, New York, built for the 1901 Pan-American Exposition. Eventually there were Statler hotels in Boston, Cleveland, Detroit, New York City, St. Louis, and other locations. In 1954, Statler sold this chain to Conrad Hilton.[2]

Statler devised a scheme to open an incredible two-story, rectangular wood structure that would contain 2084 rooms and accommodate 5000 guests. It was to be a temporary structure, covered with a thin layer of plaster to make it appear substantial, although simple to tear down after the fair closed.[3]

Conrad Hilton

Conrad Hilton (1887–1979) became a successful hotelier after World War I, when he purchased several properties in Texas during its oil boom. In 1919, he bought the Mobley Hotel in Cisco, Texas. In 1925, he built the Hilton Hotel in Dallas, Texas.[4] His acquisitions during and after World War II included the 3000-room Stevens Hotel (now the Chicago Hilton), the Palmer House in Chicago, and the Plaza and Waldorf=Astoria in New York City. In 1946, he formed the Hilton Hotels Corporation, and in 1948, he formed the Hilton International Company, which came to number more than 125 hotels.[5] With the purchase of the Statler chain in 1954, Hilton created the first major chain of modern American hotels—that is, a group of hotels that follow standard operating procedures in marketing, reservations, quality of service, food and beverage operations, housekeeping, and accounting. Hilton Hotels now includes Hilton Garden Inns, Doubletree, Embassy Suites, Hampton Inns, Harrison Conference Centers, Homewood Suites by Hilton, Red Lion Hotels and Inns, and Conrad International.

Cesar Ritz

Cesar Ritz was a hotelier at the Grand National Hotel in Lucerne, Switzerland. Because of his management abilities, "the hotel became one of the most popular in Europe and Cesar Ritz became one of the most respected hoteliers in Europe."[6]

William Waldorf Astor and John Jacob Astor IV

In 1893, William Waldorf Astor launched the 13-story Waldorf Hotel at Fifth Avenue near Thirty-fourth Street in New York City. The Waldorf was the embodiment of Astor's vision of a New York hostelry that would appeal to his wealthy friends by combining the opulence of a European mansion with the warmth and homey qualities of a private residence.

Four years later, the Waldorf was joined by the 17-story Astoria Hotel, erected on an adjacent site by William Waldorf Astor's cousin, John Jacob Astor IV. The cousins built a corridor connecting the two hotels, which together became known by a single hyphenated name, the Waldorf=Astoria. In 1929, after decades of hosting distinguished visitors from around the world, the Waldorf-Astoria closed its doors to make room for the Empire State Building.

Today's 2200-room, 42-floor Waldorf=Astoria Hotel was built at Park and Lexington avenues between Forty-ninth and Fiftieth streets. Upon the hotel's opening, President Herbert Hoover delivered a message of congratulations. Hoover later became a permanent resident of the Waldorf Towers, the luxurious "hotel within a hotel" that occupies the twenty-eighth through the forty-second floors. Conrad N. Hilton purchased the hotel in 1949 and then the land it stands on in 1977. In 1988, the hotel underwent a $150 million restoration. It was designated a New York City landmark in January 1993.[7]

Kemmons Wilson

Kemmons Wilson started the Holiday Inn chain in the early 1950s, opening the first in Memphis, Tennessee. He wanted to build a chain of hotels for the traveling family and later expanded his marketing plan to include business travelers. His accomplishments in real estate development coupled with his hotel management skills proved a highly successful combination.

Wilson blazed a formidable path, innovating with amenities and high-rise architecture, including a successful round building concept featuring surprisingly functional pie-shaped rooms. Wilson also introduced the in-house Holidex central reservation system, which set the industry standard due to both the volume of business it produced and the important byproduct data it generated (for example, it made it possible to determine feasibility for new locations with cunning accuracy).[8]

Wilson died in February 2003 at the age of 90. His legacy to the lodging industry is serving the traveling public with comfortable, safe accommodations while making a profit for investors.

J. W. Marriott and J. W. Marriott Jr.

J. W. Marriott (1900–1985) founded his hotel empire in 1957 with the Twin Bridges Marriott Motor Hotel in Virginia, near Washington, DC. By the time he died in 1985, Marriott Hotels and Resorts had grown to include Courtyard by Marriott and American Resorts Group. At this point, J. W. Marriott Jr. acquired the Howard Johnson Company; he sold the hotels to Prime Motor Inns but retained 350 restaurants and 68 turnpike units. In 1987, the Marriott company completed expansion of its Worldwide Reservation Center in Omaha, Nebraska, making it the largest single-site reservations operation in U.S. hotel history. Also in 1987, Marriott acquired the Residence Inn Company, an all-suite hotel chain targeted at extended-stay travelers. With the introduction of limited-service hotels—hotels built with guest room accommodations and limited food service and meeting space—Marriott entered the economy lodging segment, opening the first Fairfield Inn in Atlanta, Georgia, in 1987.[9]

Ernest Henderson and Robert Moore

Ernest Henderson and Robert Moore started the Sheraton chain in 1937, when they acquired their first hotel, the Stonehaven, in Springfield, Massachusetts. Within two years, they purchased three hotels in Boston and soon expanded their holdings to include properties from Maine to Florida. At the end of its first decade, Sheraton was the first hotel chain listed on the New York Stock Exchange. In 1968, Sheraton was acquired by ITT Corporation as a wholly owned subsidiary, and ambitious development plans were put into place to create a global network of properties. In the 1980s, under the leadership of John Kapi-oltas, Sheraton's chairman, president, and chief executive officer, the company received international recognition as an industry innovator in modern hotel accommodations.[10] The Sheraton chain is currently owned by Starwood Hotels & Resorts Worldwide.

Ray Schultz

In the early 1980s, Ray Schultz founded the Hampton Inn hotels, a former company in the Holiday Inn Corporation. These hotels were tagged as *limited-service* (now referred to as *select-service*), meeting the needs of cost-conscious business travelers and pleasure travelers alike. Schultz's pioneering efforts in developing a product and service for these market segments have proved a substantial contribution to the history of the hotel industry.

At a 1998 celebration of the expansion of the Hampton Inn hotel corporation to more than 800 properties, Schultz said:

We started the Hampton Inn chain in 1984 to provide guests with a quality room and special amenities, like a free continental breakfast and free local phone calls, all at an exceptional value. The opening of this hotel today tells us that we understood our guests' needs and that price/value is still a viable concept nearly 15 years later. Hampton Inn has been, and is committed to remaining, the standard against which all midpriced, limited-service hotel brands are measured.[11]

Historical Developments

The history of the hotel industry is filled with concepts that shaped the products and services offered.

The atrium concept design, limited-service hotels, and technology were notable innovations. Management concepts such as marketing and total quality management (TQM) offered managers a new way to do business in hotels. The major U.S. economic reorganization in the late 1980s shaped the way hotels could be profitable. Also, in the 1990s, a new financial approach—real estate investment trusts (REITs)—changed the financial structuring and operation of hotels.

The terrorist events of September 11, 2001, continue to affect how hotels market their products and services and deliver hospitality. The economic upheaval of the recession of the late 2000s has challenged marketing practices and operational practices in the hotel world.

Atrium Concept

The hotel industry has seen many notable developments over the past years. The *atrium concept,* an architectural design in which guest rooms overlook the lobby from the first floor to the roof, was first used in the 1960s by Hyatt Hotels.

FIGURE 1-1 **Atriums are a common site in today's hotels. Courtesy of the Bellevue Hilton, Bellevue, Washington.**

The dramatic approach to hotel style was exemplified by the Hyatt Regency in Atlanta. Designed by architect John Portman and featuring a striking and impressive atrium soaring up its 21 stories, the hotel changed the course of upscale hotel design. As a result, hotels became more than a place to rest one's head. They became hubs for excitement, fun, relaxation, and entertainment.[12]

This 1260-room hotel "is now one of the nation's premier convention and trade show facilities, with 180,000 square feet of ballroom, exhibit, meeting, and hospitality space."[13]

Select-Service Hotels

The movement of hotel construction from the downtown, center-city area to the suburbs in the 1950s coincided with the development of the U.S. highway system. The *select-service* concept—hotels built with guest room accommodations and limited food service and meeting space—became prominent in the early 1980s, when many of the major chains adopted this way to serve business travelers and travelers on a limited budget. Hampton Inn revolutionized the hotel industry as the first national brand targeted to the new select-service hotel segment. The hotels featured spacious, comfortable rooms but eliminated or reduced other elements common to hotels at that time, such as restaurants, lounges, and meeting and lobby space, passing on the resulting cost savings to guests in the form of lower rates.

The company pioneered a number of ideas, including the mounting of the first site by a hotel brand on the Internet. In 1989, Hampton Inn became the first national brand to offer guests an unconditional 100 percent satisfaction guarantee, which today is the cornerstone of all Promus brands and a testament to the company's commitment to quality.[14]

Technological Advances

Technology has played a major role in developing the products and services offered to guests. Reservations systems, property management systems, and in-room guest checkout are only the most obvious advances. Impressive firsts in the adaptation of technology to the hotel industry are shown in Figure 1-2. Note how many of the developments we call technology are recent adaptations.

Recent additions to the list include applications of wireless technology that allow front office staff to alert others on VIP check-ins, housekeeping staff to report guest room cleaning and release, marketing staff to maintain guest profiles, and bell staff to process baggage handling. Guests have also found technology in the 2000s to increase their ability to work and play at the same time; they can check email and print documents as needed from so-called hot spots, or designated wireless transmission and reception areas in the hotel.

Marketing Emphasis

An emphasis on niche marketing to guests was the theme in the 1970s. This technique surveyed potential guest markets and built systems around the needs of identified segments.

FIGURE 1-2	Introduction of technological advances to the hotel industry.
1846	Central heating
1859	Elevator
1881	Electric lights
1907	In-room telephone
1927	In-room radio
1940	Air conditioning
1950	Electric elevator
1958	Free television
1964	Holiday Inn reservation system with centralized computer
1965	Message lights on telephone
	Initial front office computer systems introduced followed by room status capability
1970s	Electric cash register
	POS (point of sale) systems and keyless locks
	Color television standard
1973	Free in-room movies (Sheraton)
1980s	Property management systems
	In-room guest checkout
1983	In-room personal computers
	Call accounting
1990s	On Command Video (on-demand movies)
	LodgeNet Entertainment (interactive video games)
	Interactive guest room shopping, interactive visitor's guide, fax delivery on TV, interactive guide to hotel's facilities and activities, reservations from the guest room for other hotels within the same organization, and interactive weather reports
	Internet reservations
	Introduction of legislation that monitored hotel ownership through real estate investment trusts (REITs)
2000s	Wireless technology—Wireless technology VIP check-in, housekeeping guest room clean and release status, marketing guest profile, bell staff baggage handling; guest "hot spot" centers in hotels for wireless transmission and reception of emails and documents. Social media, guest room technology, IT infrastructure, surviving a tough economy with help from technology, and demystifying Web 2.0

Sources: Sources: American Hotel & Motel Association; Madelin Schneider, "20th Anniversary," *Hotels & Restaurants International* 20, no. 8 (August 1986): 40 (copyright *Hotels* magazine, a division of Reed USA); Larry Chervenak, "Top 10 Tech Trends: 1975–1995," *Hotel & Motel Management* 210, no. 14 (August 14, 1995): 45; www.hotel-online.com/News/PR2009_2nd/Apr09_HITECTechTrends.html.

The larger hotel-management and franchise companies also were discovering the advantages of forging strong reservations and marketing systems. For a guest, this meant that by calling a single phone number, he or she could be assured of a reservation and feel confident of the quality of accommodations expected.[15]

The marketing emphasis continues in the 2000s through the routine use of the Internet to place guest reservations.

Surveys show that up to 84 percent of travel research and planning in the United States is conducted via the Web (eMarketer/TIA). The Internet has become the single most important travel planning and distribution channel in hospitality. In 2009, over 40 percent of all revenues in hospitality will be generated by the Internet, and another third of hotel bookings will be influenced by the Internet but done offline. Each year since 2004, Internet hotel bookings have surpassed GDS hotel bookings.[16]

Total Quality Management

Total quality management (TQM), a technique that helps managers critique processes used to create products and services with an eye to improving those processes, is practiced in hotels today. This emphasis on analyzing the delivery of services and products, with decision making at the front lines, began in the 1990s and continues today under terms such as *quality assurance* and *service quality.* These concepts are discussed in more detail in chapter 11.

Major Reorganization, 1987–1988

The economic period of 1987 to 1988 saw a major reorganization of the hotel industry. In 1986, Congress unraveled what it had stitched together in 1981. The revised Tax Act made it clear that passive losses on real estate were no longer deductible. Hotels that were previously economically viable suddenly were not. At this time, there were plenty of Japanese investors who seemed intent on buying up, at astronomical prices, any piece of U.S. property with a hotel or golf course on it. As a result, the value of American hotel properties continued to increase. Between 1990 and 1995, the recession began and ended, and the full impact of the 1986 law and overbuilding were experienced. Some investors who had built properties in the early 1980s found those properties' sales or replacement value had fallen to 50 percent or less of original cost. Some owners simply abandoned their properties to their mortgage holders—which in many cases turned out to be Uncle Sam, because of the simultaneous savings and loan debacle.[17]

Hotel Investment

Real estate investment trusts (REITs) provide an investment opportunity for hoteliers. In the Spring 2000 *Virginia Hospitality and Leisure Executive Report*, P. Anthony Brown of Arthur Andersen wrote the following about the U.S. Tax Relief Extension Act of 1999. This information will be useful as you plan your career.

The most significant provision… creation of a new type of corporation—a "Taxable REIT Subsidiary" (effective January 1, 2001)—which will allow REITs to create new incremental income streams. With new growth opportunities, shareholders should be rewarded with higher stock prices since companies with increased growth rates typically trade in the market at higher earnings multiples.

Under the terms of the 1999 legislation, Taxable REIT Subsidiaries can provide non-customary services to tenants through their subsidiaries. This legislation should enable REITs to provide better customer service, create stronger customer loyalty and sell new, non-customary services to tenants. In addition these new subsidiaries can lease lodging facilities from REITs. However, the lodging facilities must be managed by an independent contractor that is actively engaged in the trade or business of operating lodging facilities for any person other than the REIT.

With these changes, hotel REITs will be able to reorganize their structure in order to retain more of the income generated by their hotels. For example, FelCor Lodging Trust Inc., a hotel REIT based in Irving, Texas, in 2000 leased its hotels to two tenants: (1) a company owned by its executives and directors and (2) Bristol Hotels and Resorts, a publicly traded company. With the new legislation, FelCor will be able to form a new taxable REIT subsidiary and transfer the leases of its hotels to this new subsidiary. Accordingly, the net income of the existing lessee would be transferred to the new taxable REIT subsidiary. However, a management company (not owned by FelCor) must manage the hotels and must be actively engaged in the trade or business of operating lodging facilities for any person other than the REIT.[18]

September 11, 2001

The terrorist events of September 11, 2001, will have a lasting effect on how a hotel markets its products and services and delivers hospitality. The immediate impact of the terrorist attacks on the industry was a decrease in the number of people willing to fly and, thus, a decrease in demand for hotel rooms. Hotels (as well as restaurants, tourist attractions, government agencies, and the like) and the federal, regional, and state tourism associations continue to cooperate to address the issue of fear as it relates to travel and tourism.

Hoteliers reviewed their marketing plans and determined how to attract the post 9/11 corporate traveler. The huge corporate guest market can no longer be taken for granted. Corporate executives, travel planners, and traffic managers now must be greeted personally by hotel staff and asked when business might be expected. New methods of attracting markets such as local and regional residents are being developed. These efforts include special packages emphasizing local history and culture, businesses, sporting events, and natural attractions and are combined with the products and services of an individual hotel. Is this an easy challenge? Indeed no, yet it is one that hoteliers had to grasp with eagerness and enthusiasm in order to succeed.

R. Mark Woodworth reports that this effort is indeed a formidable task in light of the data revealed in *Trends in the Hotel Industry—USA*, published by PKF Consulting and the Hospitality Research Group (HRG). The 2003 edition reported that "the operating profit for the average U.S. hotel dropped 9.6 percent in 2002, this after a 19.4 percent decline in profits in 2001."[19]

Rick Swig of RSBA & Associates notes that although hotel revenues increased by 2 percent from 2003 to 2004, "other issues such as supply of hotel rooms of 4.4% since June 2001 versus average number of rooms sold increas[ed] only by 3.3%." He urges, "Hotel operators should focus on pricing power for the next 24 months until occupancy returns to pre-2001 levels and compression begins to build...National consortium and high volume travel contracts are being finalized for 2005. Hotels will have to be successful in achieving significant rate hikes through these conduits, since the past two years of negotiations have yielded little or no rate increase as operating expense inflated."[20]

Further insight into the challenge facing hoteliers is expressed by Tom Belden of the *Philadelphia Inquirer*, who relates that 94 percent of the 112 corporations surveyed by the Business Travel Coalition of Radnor, Pennsylvania, cut their travel spending over a three-year period. He reports that one participant increased its use of web-based meeting software by 50 percent in one particular year.[21]

The delivery of hospitality in hotels has also come under review. For example, hoteliers are reviewing security plans to include the front-line employee who must take immediate action based on observations at the front desk, in the dining room and recreational areas, and on guest and public floors. The front-line employee who sees uncommon activities must know the importance of reporting concerns to supervisors. Special training in what to look for in guest interactions in public areas and on guest floors assists the front-line person in becoming proactive.

Hoteliers must also be concerned with how to support hospitality as part of responsible community citizenship. Hotel general managers should develop emergency plans that allow immediately offering public space to medical personnel and disaster victims. Short-term concerns, such as feeding disaster victims and emergency personnel, and long-term commitments, such as housing displaced members of the community, are among the many issues faced by the hotel industry.

Liability implications for the owner, management contractor, or lessee with respect to repair of facilities have arisen, as have concerns for the safety of guests resulting from terrorism. Andrew MacGeoch, reporting in *Hotel*, notes:

> The obligation of an owner to repair the hotel under a management agreement usually depends on the extent of the damage. In general, if the costs of repair do not exceed a certain threshold specified in the management agreement [which is usually a certain percentage of the replacement costs of the hotel], the owner will be obliged to return it to its condition prior to the destruction. However, if the costs of repair exceed the specified threshold, the owner will have the right to choose not to undertake the repair and to terminate the management agreement.

MacGeoch continues with a note on liability toward guests by acts of terrorism.

Generally, neither the operator nor the owner would be held liable for any injury or death caused by terrorist activities, unless the owner or operator has failed to exercise reasonable care for the safety and security of their guests. Therefore, to make sure that the reasonable-care standard is met, it is necessary and advisable for owners and operators to take reasonable and necessary steps to protect the safety of guests, including implementing appropriate security policies and measures and providing crisis-management training to all employees.[22]

Economic Downturn of the Late 2000s

PKF Hospitality Research (PKF-HR) prepared a statement in June 2009 concerning the effects of economic impact upon the U.S. hotel economy.

Given the forecast 17.5 percent decline in RevPAR for 2009, PKF-HR is projecting total hotel revenues to decrease 16.0 percent for the year [2009]. U.S. hotel managers, as they have in the past, will cut costs by 7.5 percent, but that will not be enough to avoid a decline in the typical hotel's net operating income (NOI) (before deductions for capital reserve, rent, interest, income taxes, depreciation, and amortization). PKF-HR is forecasting that the typical U.S. hotel will suffer a 37.8 percent decline in NOI in 2009 and an additional 9.2 percent in 2010. It should be noted that U.S. hotels will continue to generate a positive NOI. However, given the projected declines in NOI, hotel profit margins are forecast to be well below the long-term average of 25.7 percent.

The article continues with a quote from Professor Robert C. Baker of Cornell University.

"Fewer guests paying lower prices is a recipe for evaporating profits," said John B. (Jack) Corgel, the Robert C. Baker professor of real estate at the Cornell University School of Hotel Administration and senior advisor to PKF-HR. "Add to that the potential for an increase in fixed charges such as utility costs, insurance, and property taxes and the situation could get ugly quickly. Not many current industry participants were around 72 years ago, the last time PKF-HR recorded a unit-level profit decline in excess of 20 percent. Needless to say, profit declines in excess of 30 percent have a wide-ranging impact on hotel values, debt coverage, default covenants, and solvency."

However, the forecast for the future looks brighter with the following quote from the same article.

While the cumulative declines in revenue and profits during the current industry recession exceed those of previous industry downturns, the magnitude of forecast recovery will be exceptionally robust. In 2011 and 2012, PKF-HR forecasts that RevPAR will increase on an average annual basis of 9.2 percent, while profits will rise at a 17.8 percent pace. "If you are an owner, investor, or lender that can weather this year and next, the return to prosperity should be strong and quick," Woodworth added.[23]

The economic downturn of the late 2000s had its effect on marketing effort and operations in hotels. Marketing is a vital planning tool that hotels rely on to determine customers, to determine customers' needs, and to make a profit. Activities related to business include advertising (newspapers, radio, television, Internet); public relations and publicity; and promotions (coupons). Concerns for hotel-operations cost include labor and product.

Carol Verret, in her article "Selling Into a Bad Economy: Overcoming Fear and Stealing Share," says the following about hotel sales in tough economic times.

Pull way back if not eliminate expensive hard copy print advertising in favor of Internet-based strategies. How do you buy things, how do you research your options for a purchase? Consumer buying behavior has changed and this also applies to the business and leisure consumer—accessing information on the web. Take calculated risks—try platforms that you haven't tried before or increase your presence on those that you are already on. Some of these will represent "electronic billboards" that consumers will use for research prior to making direct contact.[24]

At the eighth annual Americas Lodging Investment Summit (ALIS), "2009: Industry Looks to the Long Term, Leaders, and Innovation," Frits van Paasschen, president and CEO of Starwood Hotels and Resorts Worldwide, commented, "Focus on operations, watch costs and prepare for a turnaround and growth. You must have an enormous amount of will to ask how we can be internally more efficient and reach out to our guests and stakeholders.[25]

These issues—marketing, delivering hospitality, the possibility of terrorism, and the economic recession of the late 2000s—are ongoing concerns hoteliers must continue to discuss. They must focus on goals and subsequent planning for implementation of a safe environment for guests and employees.

Overview of the Hotel Industry

A working knowledge of the classifications used in the hotel industry is important to understanding its organization. The types of properties, their market orientation and location, sales indicators, occupancy, and revenues as they relate to levels of service and types of business affiliation are all means of classifying hotel properties. Figure 1-3 serves as a reference point throughout this discussion.

FIGURE 1-3   Hotel industry overview.

I.   Types of hotel properties
   a. Hotels
   b. Motels
   c. All-suites
   d. Select-service hotels
   e. Extended-stay hotels
II. Market orientation/location
   a. Residential
      i. Center-city
         1. Hotels
         2. All-suites
         3. Select-service
         4. Extended-stay
      ii. Suburban
         1. All-suites
         2. Select-service
         3. Extended-stay
   b. Commercial
      i. Center-city
         1. Hotels
         2. All-suites
         3. Select-service
         4. Extended-stay
      ii. Suburban
         1. Hotels
         2. Motels
         3. All-suites
         4. Select-service
         5. Extended-stay
      iii. Airport
         1. Hotels
         2. Motels
         3. All-suites
         4. Select-service
      iv. Highway
         1. Motels
         2. All-suites
         3. Select-service
         4. Extended-stay
III. Sales indicators
   a. Occupancy
   b. Average daily rate (ADR)
   c. Yield percentage
   d. Revenue per available room (RevPAR)
   e. Gross Operating Profit per Available Room (GOPPAR)
   f. Revenue per Available Customer (RevPAC)
IV. Levels of service
   a. Full-service
   b. All-suites
   c. Select-service
   d. Extended-stay
V.   Affiliation
   a. Chain
      i. Franchise
      ii. Company-owned
      iii. Referral
      iv. Management contract
   b. Independent

Types of Lodging Facilities

Classification of hotel facilities is not based on rigid criteria. Definitions can change depending on market forces, legal criteria, location, function, and, in some cases, personal preference, but the definitions that follow are generally accepted and are the ones intended for these classifications throughout this text.

Hotels

A hotel usually offers guests a full range of accommodations and services, which may include reservations, suites, public dining and banquet facilities, lounge and entertainment areas, room service, cable television, personal computers, business services, meeting rooms, specialty shops, personal services, valet, laundry, hair care, swimming pool and other recreational activities, gaming/casino operations, ground transportation to and from an airport, and concierge services. The size of the property can range from 20 to more than 2000 rooms. Hotels are found in center-city, suburban, and airport locations. Guest stays can be overnight or long term—as long as several weeks. Properties sometimes specialize in catering to particular markets, such as conventions or gambling. Casino hotels usually take a secondary role to the casino operation, where the emphasis is on profitable gaming operations. Marriott's hotels operated as JW Marriott Hotels & Resorts and Renaissance Hotels & Resorts, as well as Hyatt brands operated as Hyatt Regency Hotels, Grand Hyatt Hotels, and Park Hyatt Hotels, are examples in this category.

FIGURE 1-4

Photo courtesy of Waldorf=Astoria Hotel, New York City.

Motels

Motels offer guests a limited range of services, which may include reservations, vending machines, swimming pools, and cable television. The size of these properties averages from 10 to 50 units. Motels are usually in suburban highway and airport locations. Guests typically stay overnight or for a few days. Motels may be located near a freestanding restaurant.

All-suites

The all-suites concept was developed in the 1980s as a separate marketing concept. These hotels offer guests a wide range of services that may include reservations, living room and separate bedroom, kitchenette, optional public dining room and room service, cable television, videocassette players and recorders, specialty shops, personal services, valet and laundry, swimming pool, and ground transportation to and from an airport. The size of the operation can range from 50 to more than 100 units. This type of property is usually found in center-city, suburban, and airport locations. The length of guest stay can be overnight, several days, or long term.

Although this type of hotel may seem relatively new, many downtown center-city hotels have offered accommodations with in-room kitchenette and sitting room since the

HOSPITALITY PROFILE

Joseph Longo is the general manager of The Jefferson Hotel, a 265-room historic property in Richmond, Virginia. One of only 17 hotels in North America to receive both the Mobil Five Star and AAA Five Diamond ratings, The Jefferson Hotel offers guests the highest level of products and services available, with a strong commitment to warm, genuine, and gracious service.

Mr. Longo obtained B.S. degrees in business administration and communication from Saint John's University in New York. While in college, he worked at the front desk at The Saint Regis Hotel in New York City and began his professional career at the Sheraton-Carlton Hotel in Washington, DC, as the rooms division manager. He then became general manager of The River Inn hotel in Washington, DC, and then the regional director of operations for the Potomac Hotel Group. Prior to becoming general manager of The Jefferson Hotel, Mr. Longo was regional director of operations for the Field Hotel Association in Valley Forge, Pennsylvania.

The sales and marketing effort for this independently owned property requires aggressive sales and public relations strategies. Focus is placed not only on the guest rooms but also on the 26,000 square feet of function space and the two restaurants, one an AAA Five Diamond Award winner.

Mr. Longo encourages students who are pursuing a hospitality management career to remember that, as innkeepers, the hotel is like your home, where all of your guests are made to feel welcome. This means providing all guests with the basics of hospitality: a comfortable room, exceptional food, and a friendly staff to serve them. He adds that hospitality is a diverse business, offering a unique work experience each day.

early 1900s. Now, with *mass marketing*—advertising products and services through mass communications such as television, radio, and the Internet—this type of hotel is considered "new." Examples of the all-suite concept include Hilton's Embassy Suites Hotels and InterContinental Hotels' Candlewood Suites.

Select-service Hotels

Select-service hotels appeared in the mid-1980s. Hampton Inn and Marriott were among the first organizations to offer select service properties.

The concept of select service was developed for a specific segment of the market: business and cost-conscious travelers. The range of accommodations and services may include reservations, minimal public dining and meeting facilities, cable television, personal computers, personal services (valet and laundry), and ground transportation to and from an airport. The size of the property can range from 100 to more than 200 rooms. Select-service hotels are found in center-city, suburban, and airport locations. They are usually located near restaurants for guest convenience. Guest stays can be overnight or long term. These properties sometimes specialize in catering to the business traveler and offer special business technology centers. Select-service hotel properties include Holiday Inn Express, operated by InterContinental Hotels Group; Comfort Inn, by Choice Hotels International; and Marriott's Fairfield Inn.

Extended-stay Hotels

Extended-stay properties were designed to offer guests a home-away-from-home atmosphere over long stays precipitated by business, leisure, or personal necessity. For example, a person may have to attend to a business project for several days or weeks; another may want to visit with relatives whose home does not have adequate accommodations for visitors; a third may be accompanying a relative or friend receiving an extended health treatment at a medical center and require overnight accommodations. The patient himself may appreciate the homelike atmosphere of the extended-stay hotel in which to recover between treatments.

Leon Stafford of the *Atlanta Journal-Constitution* writes, "The big, fancy hotels... have struggled to get 60 percent of their rooms filled since 2001. Meanwhile, extended stays...have remained at least 70 percent filled." He adds an interesting idea for your career development consideration: "About three extended-stay lodges were built for every traditional hotel constructed between 2001 and 2004."[26]

At Hilton's Homewood Suites, the following room amenities are included: king-size bed or two double beds in the bedroom and foldout sofa in the living room; two remote-controlled color televisions; fully equipped kitchen with a microwave, refrigerator with ice maker, coffeemaker, twin-burner stove, and kitchen utensils; a spacious, well-lit dining area; ceiling fans; iron and ironing board. Additional hotel services include a business center, an exercise room, and a pool. This hotel concept also structures its room rates to attract the long-term guest.

Market Orientation

Market orientation in the hotel industry is categorized into two segments: (1) *residential hotels*, which provide guest accommodations for the long term; and (2) *commercial hotels*, which provide short-term accommodations for traveling guests. Residential properties include hotels, all-suites, select-service, and extended-stay properties. Services may include (but are not limited to) public dining, recreational facilities, social activities, and personal services. These hotels are usually located in center-city and suburban areas where other activities (shopping, arts and entertainment, business services, public transportation) are available to round out the living experience.

Commercial properties service the short-term transient guest. Services include (but are not limited to) computerized reservation systems, public dining, banquet service, lounge and entertainment areas, personal services, and shuttle transportation to airports. These hotels may be located almost anywhere.

It is essential to note that these two categories overlap. A commercial lodging establishment may have a certain percentage of permanent residents. Likewise, a residential hotel may have nightly rentals available. Owners and general managers must exhibit a great deal of flexibility in meeting the needs of the available markets.

Sales Indicators

Sales indicators, including hotel occupancy and average daily rate, are another way of describing hotels. This information is necessary for business investors to estimate the profitability of a hotel.

Six factors measure a hotel's degree of financial success:

1. *Occupancy percentage* is the number of rooms sold divided by the number of rooms available.

2. *Average daily rate (ADR)* is the total room revenue divided by the number of rooms sold.

3. *Yield percentage*, the effectiveness of a hotel at selling its rooms at the highest rate available to the most profitable guest, reveals a facility's success in selling its room inventory on a daily basis.

4. *Revenue per available room (RevPAR)* is used to indicate the ability of each guest room to produce a profit. Once the daily sales opportunity has presented itself, it cannot be repeated (excluding the opportunity to sell a room at a half-day rate). (Note: See below for computation of RevPAR.)

5. Gross operating profit per available room (GOPPAR) is defined as total gross operating profit (GOP) per available room per day, where GOP equals total

revenue less the total departmental and operating expenses. GOPPAR does not indicate the revenue mix of a hotel property and, therefore, does not allow an accurate evaluation of the rooms' revenue department; however, it does provide a clear indication of a hotel's profit potential. It can reflect the profitability, managerial efficiency, and underlying value of hotel properties as a whole.[27]

6. Revenue per available customer (RevPAC) reflects the customer as the fundamental driver of value in the hospitality industry. Cline reports lodging entrepreneurs should look at the guest's needs as the driving force in developing the bottom line for profits in hotels. Examples included technology in the guest room or in the social area of the business center and perhaps "collecting experiences" of themed restaurants that have been leased to a third party will be in order.[28]

Occupancy

Occupancy percentages measure the effectiveness of the marketing and sales department as well as the external and internal marketing efforts of the front office. Occupancy percentage is also used by investors to determine the *potential gross income*, or the amount of sales a hotel might obtain at a given level of occupancy, average daily rate, and anticipated yield. However, it is important not to assume that occupancy is standard each night. Variations occur daily and seasonally.

$$\frac{\text{Number of Rooms Sold} \times 100}{\text{Number of Rooms Available}} = \text{Single Occupancy \%}$$

Average Daily Rate (Average Room Rate)

The average daily rate (sometimes referred to as *average room rate*, or ADR), is also used in projecting *room revenues*—the amount of room sales received—for a hotel. However, this figure also affects guests' expectations of their hotel experience. Guests expect higher room rates to correlate with higher levels of service; the hotel with a rate of $175 per night is expected to offer more services than a hotel in the same geographic area with a rate of $85 per night. These expectations are extensively capitalized on by major hotel chains, which develop different properties to meet the expectations of different segments of the hotel market.

$$\frac{\text{Total Room Sales}}{\text{Number of Rooms Sold}} = \text{ADR}$$

Yield Percentage

Yield percentage measures a hotel manager's efforts to achieve maximum occupancy at the highest room rate possible. This term is discussed more fully in chapter 6. It is sufficient to note here that this concept is relatively new in the hotel industry. Prior to the

1990s, hotel managers relied on occupancy and average daily rate as indicators of meeting financial goals. Yield percentage forces managers to think in more active terms.

$$\text{Yield} = \frac{\text{Revenue Realized (number of rooms sold} \times \text{number actual rate)}}{\text{Revenue Potential (number of rooms available for sale} \times \text{rack rate)}}$$

RevPAR (Revenue per Available Room)

RevPAR is determined by dividing room revenue received for a specific day by the number of rooms available in the hotel for that day. The formulas for determining RevPAR are as follows:

$$\frac{\text{Room Revenue}}{\text{Number of Available Rooms}}$$

or

Hotel Occupancy × Average Daily Rate

For example, RevPAR for a hotel that has $10,000 in room revenue for the night of September 15 with 200 rooms available equals $50 ($10,000 ÷ 200 = $50).

If one considers further operating statistics of this same hotel on September 15, with 200 rooms, room revenue of $10,000, 125 rooms sold at an average daily rate of $80 ($10,000 ÷ 125 − $80), and with hotel occupancy of 62.5 percent (125 rooms sold ÷ 200 rooms available × 100 = 62.5 percent), it produces the same RevPAR (0.625 × $80 = $50).

RevPAR is used in hotels to determine the amount of dollars each hotel room produces for the overall financial success of the hotel. The profit from the sale of a hotel room is much greater than that from a similar food and beverage sale. However, the food and beverage aspect of the hotel industry is essential in attracting some categories of guests who want conference services. Chapter 6, "Revenue Management," discusses the importance of considering the potential income from room and food and beverage sales.

Consider the following article by Mark Woodworth, president of PKF Hospitality Research, on how hotel financial experts regard RevPAR.

ATLANTA, June 11, 2009—PKF Hospitality Research (PKF-HR) today announced that, according to its June 2009 edition of Hotel Horizons®, rooms revenue per available room (RevPAR) will reach its cyclical low point in the third quarter of 2009. This will bring to a close the escalating trend of declines in RevPAR that began in the third quarter of 2008, according to Smith Travel Research (STR). In May 2009, Moody's Economy.com downgraded its outlook of a 2.9 percent national employment decline to 3.8 percent, causing PKF-HR to revise its RevPAR forecast for the year. Given the correlation between employment and lodging demand, the new expectation is for RevPAR to decline 17.5 percent in 2009, followed by another 3.5 percent decline in 2010.[29]

Levels of Service

The four commonly used *market segments*—identifiable groups of customers with similar needs for products and services—are full service, all-suites, select service, and extended stay. There is a great deal of overlap among these divisions, and much confusion, some of which occurs because leaders in the hotel industry do not agree on terminology.

Some industry leaders avoid the "budget" tag because of its connotations of cheapness and poor quality. Others welcome the label because it appeals to travelers looking for basic accommodations at inexpensive rates. Nevertheless, the following definitions provide some idea of what is offered at each level of service. *Full service* is a level that provides a wide range of conveniences for the guest. These services include, but are not limited to, reservations, on-premises dining, banquet and meeting facilities, and recreational facilities. Examples of full-service hotels include Marriott Hotels & Resorts, Renaissance Hotels & Resorts, and Hilton.

As discussed earlier, the *all-suites* category indicates a level of service appropriate for guests who desire an at-home atmosphere. Services include separate sleeping and living areas or working areas, kitchenette facilities, wet bars, and other amenities at the mid-price level. This concept appeals to the business traveler as well as to families. Marriott's and Hilton's Embassy Suites Hotels are examples of all-suite hotels. It is interesting to note that this concept is also employed in older center-city commercial hotels, in which rooms adjoining the bedroom and bath have been remodeled as living rooms and kitchenettes to create suites.

Select service emphasizes basic room accommodations, guest amenities, and minimal public areas. A continental breakfast and/or an evening cocktail is often included in the price of the room. Guests have the opportunity to trade the public meeting room for free in-room movies, the dining room for free local phone calls. Hampton and aloft are examples of select-service hotels. In an article describing the new aloft, several new ideas to respond to this market segment:

- a colorful, sloping signature carport cover and building roof-line, and colorful glowing linear light sources on the building facade inspired by the notion of travel and motion.
- a mix lobby, a flexible space that lends itself to both daytime and evening socialization, featuring a sunken living room with a two-sided glass fireplace which opens to an outdoor patio, a customized pool table and a 24/7 grab 'n' go gourmet pantry influenced by a New York deli (re:fuel by aloft).
- two guest rooms options, [including] a 275-square-foot room with a king-size bed and a 325-square-foot room with two double beds. Both are loft-like spaces with 9-foot-high ceilings and oversized windows. The rooms exhibit a calming palette with touches of blue and purple, an abundance of natural light, and a selection of custom furniture such as a multifunctional headboard which serves as a wall partition, built-in storage space, nightstand, and a place for artwork. The bathrooms are simple, serene, and cleanly designed, with oversized walk-in showers with glass doors.

a circular aloha desk [that] serves as a stylish alternative to the traditional check-in desk and sits in the center of the lobby entry to welcome guests and be part of the experience. Equipped with check-in capabilities, a staff member to assist with guests' needs, and a register for guests to pay for items purchased from the re:fuel by aloft pantry and the sundries shop. Here design meets function. A custom mirror, located in front of the desk and compris[ing] numerous small panels arranged to create a kaleidoscopic effect, serves as a way for staff members to see the entire area of the lobby. Guests can also check in via high-tech kiosks which allow guests to select floors and rooms, much like selecting seats on aircrafts.[30]

Extended stay is a level of service that offers a home-away-from-home atmosphere for business executives, visitors, and families who are planning to visit an area for an extended period. A fully equipped kitchenette allows international guests to prepare comforting foods in a new environment. The spacious bedrooms and living areas provide space for work and recreation. Light breakfast and evening meals are included. Examples of this level of service include Homewood Suites by Hilton, InterContinental's Staybridge Suites, and Choice Hotels International's MainStay Suites.

Business Affiliations

Business affiliations, which indicate either chain or independent ownership of hotels, also categorize the hotel industry. These classifications are the most easily recognizable by consumers with regard to such features as brand name, structural appearance, and ambiance. Long-lasting marketing effects develop a brand loyalty and acceptance that are most important to the long-term profitability for a hotel.

Chain Affiliation

When asked to name several *chain* operations (a group of hotels that follow standard operating procedures such as marketing, reservations, quality of service, food and beverage operations, housekeeping, and accounting), most people would probably mention Holiday Inn, Marriott, Sheraton, Days Inn, Hyatt, Hilton, or Econo Lodge. Students should stay up to date with acquisitions, restructuring, and other changes in these organizations. This information, important to know when making career decisions, can be obtained from trade journals such as *Hotels* (published by Reed Business Information, a division of Reed Elsevier Inc., Highlands Ranch, CO), whose annual July issue includes a listing of hotel chains, addresses, and number of rooms; the *Wall Street Journal*; and other newspapers, magazines, and websites.

Chain affiliations, which include hotels that purchase operational and marketing services from a corporation, are further divided into franchisee, referral, company-owned properties, and management contract companies. Franchise corporations offer support to the franchisee, who is the owner of the land and building, in the form of reservation systems, advertising, operations management, and management development. In return for these services, the franchisee pays fees for items such as initial startup, rental of signs and other equipment, use of the corporation's reservation referral system, and national advertising.[31]

Anyone wishing to enter the hotel business by investing personal funds wants to be sure of realizing a profit. Perhaps due to lack of experience in operating a hotel or motel, a lack of business acumen, a poor credit rating, or limited knowledge of real estate development, this type of entrepreneur may need to seek the guidance of others. He or she can receive direction from a corporation, such as Days Inn, Sheraton, or Hilton, concerning land, building, and management development.

Referral Property

Sometimes a hotel organization chooses to become a *referral property*—that is, to operate as an independent in association with a certain chain. Because the property is already physically developed, the entrepreneur may want assistance only with management, marketing and advertising, or reservation referral. Likewise, the fees are based on services required. The chain's quality assurance standards must, however, be met by the referral property.

Company-owned Property

A *company-owned property*, a hotel that is owned and operated by a chain organization, allows the hotel company developer to act as an independent entrepreneur. The hotel company developer operates the hotel property in competition with all other properties in the area. It uses its own expertise in site selection, property development, marketing and advertising, and operations management. The hotel company developer recruits talented professionals to manage such properties. It uses the chain's reservation system. The hotel company developer may set a limit on the number of franchises so a majority of the properties remain company-owned.

Management Contract Property

A *management contract property*, a hotel operated by a consulting company that provides operational and marketing expertise and a professional staff, is similar to a referral property. Several management contract organizations develop business relationships with existing hotels and operate the hotels as their own. Their business relationship requires financial accountability and profitability. Management contract companies may choose to operate each hotel as a member of a franchise or as an independent.

Brands

Hotel brands are an important part of the lodging industry, especially in consumer marketing. Branding allows a hotel company to create a concept in the mind of a consumer. This mind-concept helps the consumer classify a hotel's offerings. For example, a fictitious brand such as the Hotel Flower Chain may have three distinct offerings in its portfolio of lodgings: the Lilac Extended Stay, the Rose Select Inn, and the Violet All-Suites. Another fictitious brand such as the Timber Chain may have seven more brands in their chain with similar facilities, such as the Pine All-Suites, the Maple All-Suites, the Sunset Extended-Stay Suites, the Timber Express, the Timber Grand Hotels, the Timber Falls, and the Pine Select Service. Each of these brands has distinct product and service offerings such as communication via website, reservation service, a reservation reward point program, room accommodations, food service, personal fitness and business equipment, and meeting and convention facilities. Therefore, when guests have certain needs for business or pleasure traveling, they can match them to a certain brand.

An interesting article by Bryan E. Young sheds light on the importance of viewing the brand as a financial safeguard during tough economic times.

"In most cases," according to Greg Kennealey, a senior asset manager with Strategic Hotels & Resorts in Chicago, Illinois, "the major hotel brands provide owners with significant advantages versus independent operators, and this is especially true during economic downturns. These organizations have the tremendous sales and marketing resources which help insure that every possible business opportunity is aggressively pursued. In addition, their expense management systems are comprehensive and very responsive to changes in business demand. This enables owners to aggressively cut costs in a declining market to preserve profit margins."

However, a study was conducted by Northwestern University Kellogg School of Management to determine the importance of branding during varying economic times to hotels without a brand. Some of the results included the following:

The luxury segment, both branded and unbranded, has a higher level of volatility in RevPAR, resulting in underperformance in periods of economic distress.

The results showed that transient demand has fallen by a significantly larger percentage recently relative to other segments. Despite testimonials by various players in the industry, there is no evidence to suggest that the statistical measurements of the highly volatile transient demand segment are mitigated when attributed to branded lodging facilities, versus non-branded or boutique assets.

The intent of this study is to illustrate that brands do not always offer fiscal resilience. Could the lack of such resilience in this study be due to the proliferation of online bookings, which are generally impartial between branded and non-branded hotels in reservation queries? Or the improving perception that luxury boutique properties offer significant value relative to their competitive branded counterparts?

Whatever the battle plan might be, it is clear that no matter the shape, size, color, or affiliation of a property hotel owners cannot simply use the franchise badge as a crutch when times are bad or defer operational responsibilities to the franchise corporation in lieu of managing the asset properly.

Most importantly, one cannot underestimate the value of property-level service as part of front-line defensiveness in economic swings.[32]

The following is a list of major hotel brands. Further information can be accessed on each of the hotel companies on the Internet.

MARRIOTT	STARWOOD
Marriott Hotels & Resorts	Sheraton
JW Marriott Hotels & Resorts	Westin
Renaissance Hotels & Resorts	Four Points
Courtyard	St. Regis
Residence Inn	The Luxury Collection
Fairfield Inn	W Hotels
Marriott Conference Centers	Le Méridien
TownePlace Suites	aloft
SpringHill Suites	Element
Marriott Vacation Club International	
The Ritz-Carlton	
Marriott ExecuStay	
Marriott Executive Apartments	

HYATT
Park Hyatt Hotels Regency
Andaz
Grand Hyatt Hotels
Hyatt Regency Hotels
Hyatt Resorts
Hyatt Place
Hyatt Summerfield Suites
Hyatt Vacation Club
Park Hyatt

INTERCONTINENTAL HOTELS GROUP	CARLSON COMPANIES
InterContinental Hotels & Resorts	Park Inn
Crowne Plaza Hotels & Resorts	Country Inns & Suites by Carlson
Hotel Indigo	Plaza Hotels & Resorts

Holiday Inn Hotels & Resorts

Holiday Inn Select

Holiday Inn SunSpree Resort

Holiday Inn Garden Court

Holiday Inn Express

Staybridge Suites

Candlewood Suites

Forum Hotels & Resorts

Parkroyal Hotels & Resorts

CentraHotels & Resorts

Regent Hotels & Resorts

Radisson Hotels & Resorts

CHOICE HOTELS INTERNATIONAL

Comfort Inn

Comfort Suites

Quality

Sleep Inn

Cambria Suites

MainStay Suites

Suburban

Econo Lodge

Rodeway Inn

HILTON

Hilton

Conrad Hotels & Resorts

Doubletree

Embassy Suites Hotels

Hampton

Hilton Grand Vacations

Home2 Suites by Hilton

Hilton Garden Inn

Homewood Suites by Hilton

Waldorf=Astoria Collection

WYNDHAM HOTELS & RESORTS

Wyndham Hotels

Wyndham Grand Collection

Wyndham Resorts

Viva Wyndham Resorts

Wyndham Historic Hotels

Wyndham Garden Hotels

Wingate by Wyndham

Wyndham Mayan Resorts

Wyndham Vacation Resorts

Independent Properties

An *independent hotel* is one not associated with a franchise. It provides a greater sense of warmth and individuality than does a property associated with a chain. Independent hotel characteristics include an owner who functions as a manager, room rates similar to those of chain properties, rooms decorated in different styles, and inviting dining rooms. These hotels may be residential or commercial, with locations in the center city, suburbia, along the highway, or near an airport. The number of rooms can range from 50 to 1000. They may offer full services to guests, including suites, dining room, room service, banquets, gift shop, beauty shop, athletic facilities, swimming pool, theaters, valet services, concierge, and airport shuttle service. Some older independent hotels have refurbished their suites to capture a share of the all-suites market.

With all of these advantages, why aren't all lodging properties independent? The answer lies with the U.S. economy. The development of large chains and of smaller properties often brings tax advantages and improved profits to investors. Millions of dollars in capital are required to develop a 2000-room full-service property. Business, financial, and managerial expertise is more readily available in a company with a pool of skilled experts. Large corporations can also offset financial losses in certain fiscal years or from certain properties against financial gains of other companies or properties in their diversified portfolios.

The independent entrepreneur operates his or her business without the advantages of consultation and assistance. This person may have worked for a large chain or gained a great deal of operations and development experience in the industry. He or she may also purchase a hotel property to balance an investment portfolio. As for any financial investment, the entrepreneur seeks a professional to manage and operate the establishment. The person chosen for this job must manage all aspects of the business: room, food and beverage, housekeeping, security, maintenance, parking, the controller's office, and marketing and sales. All business decisions on expenditures must be coordinated with a profit-and-loss statement and a balance sheet. Every sale of a guest room, every guest purchase of food and beverage, occurs because the management of that property has been able to market and manage the property effectively. The challenge of managing an independent property can be overwhelming. It can, however, also offer enormous satisfaction and financial independence.

Trends That Foster Growth

Future professionals in the hotel industry must be able to analyze who their customers will be and why those customers will exist. Marketing classes teach how to determine the buyers of a particular product—who the potential guests of a particular hotel property are. Such courses show how to evaluate *demographic data* (the size, density, distribution, and vital statistics of a population broken down into, for example, age, sex, marital status, and occupation categories) and *psychographic data* (emotional and motivational forces that affect a service or product) for potential markets.

The second question—why those customers will exist—is an important one. Students will explore this question many times during their career in the lodging industry. A manager must plan for profitable results. This plan must take into account the reasons customers purchase a product. What trends will increase or decrease the need for hotel facilities? Factors include the growth of leisure time, the development of the me/pleasure concept, increases in discretionary income, the trend toward smaller families, changes in business travel, and expansion of the travel experience. Other economics and political trends—such as public liability, insurance costs, overbuilding, the value of the U.S. dollar overseas, gasoline prices, safety from random danger while traveling, and legislation—affect commerce; labor and the airline industry also have an impact on current sales as well as growth in the lodging industry.

Leisure Time

The trend toward increased leisure time—in the form of three-day weekends, paid vacations and personal days, a workweek of 40 hours or less, and early retirement—sets the stage for the growth of the lodging industry. As more people have available leisure time to explore new geographical areas, try new hobbies, sample culinary trends, participate in sporting events, and just relax, the customer base of the hotel industry expands.

Workers are spending fewer years in the labor force as the concept of early retirement becomes more popular. As the population segment known as the baby boom ages, the number of retirees is projected to soar. Many of them will take on a second career, but part-time jobs will likely be more common. With the two prime ingredients for using hotel facilities—time and money—readily at hand, these people will be a primary market for the hotel industry.

The Me/Pleasure Concept

The idea of deserving recreation away from the job to restore mental acuity and improve attitude has evolved over the years. The work ethic of the eighteenth and nineteenth centuries strongly influenced the way Americans played, as recreation and leisure were considered privileges reserved for the wealthy. Today, most workers enjoy vacations and the feeling of getting away from it all. This trend toward fulfilling personal needs continues in the twenty-first century.

The isolated nature of many jobs increases the need for respite. As more and more people find themselves spending more time communicating via computer and other machinery rather than face to face, social needs continue to grow. Workers need the away-from-job experience to balance their social and mental needs with their daily life demands. Travel helps satisfy these needs, and the hotel industry benefits as a result.

Discretionary Income

Discretionary income, the money remaining from wages after paying for necessities such as food, clothing, and shelter, is the most important of all the trends that support the growth of the hospitality industry. One of the main reasons for the increase in discretionary income of American families is the emergence of the two-income family. An almost double-income family unit has emerged over the years as more married women join or stay in the labor force. The strong growth in this labor segment will undoubtedly continue. As more income becomes available to pay for the necessities of life, more discretionary income for leisure time and corresponding goods and services also becomes available.

Discretionary income is not a constant. It is strongly affected by economic factors; an economic downturn with increased unemployment reduces discretionary income, for example. Different economic conditions tend to favor different ways of spending discretionary income; for example, low interest rates, which make the purchase of high-ticket items (such as homes, cars, boats, and aircraft) more desirable, make less discretionary income available for short vacations or quick day trips. Students of the U.S. economy need only review the effects of recessions, the energy crisis of the 1970s, and September 11, 2001, to see how quickly discretionary income formerly directed to the hospitality industry can evaporate.

Family Size/Household Size

The current trend toward smaller families also indicates growth for the hospitality industry. The discretionary income available for a family with two children is greater than that for a family with five children when total incomes are equal. Household size—the number of persons in a home—has decreased over the years. Like the trend toward smaller families, the increased number of small households indicates that more discretionary income is available. The costs associated with a one- or two-person household are less than those for a household of four or more people. Moreover, people who live in smaller households are more likely to dine out, travel, and participate in leisure-time activities.

Business Travel

Corporate business travel should not be taken for granted by hotel managers in today's world of high energy prices and speedy communication. Oil prices significantly affect business travel; as the cost of fuel oil rises, higher prices for air travel and other means of transportation result. A business is not always willing or able to increase its travel budget. When travel costs increase, less travel is undertaken and the necessity for any business travel is reviewed. Executives no longer hop the next plane to clinch a deal if the same task can be accomplished via a phone call (either a *conference call*, in which three or more persons are linked by telephone, or *PictureTel*, which is the use of telephone lines to send and receive video and audio impressions). Online *social networking*, or personal and professional groupings of people with a common interest in communicating, offers opportunities for more frequent informal meetings and, thus, less need for official gatherings. Examples include Facebook, Twitter, and LinkedIn. Shorter trips (day trips or one-night stays) are another response to the increased cost of travel.

Business travel often represents the largest portion of the regular income of a hotel property. This prime market must be constantly reviewed for economic details that affect its viability.

Female Business Travel

Female business travelers represent an increasing segment of the corporate travel market. As previously discussed, their travel is affected by energy prices and speedy communication. This particular market segment requires close attention to fulfilling special needs. Female travelers request particular amenities and demand close attention to safety. Marketing and sales managers must develop products and services to capture this growing market segment.

Andrea Newell reports the following on special needs of women:

Forty-three percent of business travelers worldwide were women; women will spend $125 billion on travel in the next year (2010); and while traveling, women's needs are different from men's. These needs are met by offering women's only floors (more common in hotels in Asia) and instructing hotel staff to give women their room assignment on a folded paper with keys that don't show their room number to maintain their privacy. Along with deadbolts and door peepholes, better lighting in hallways and parking lots, keycard access to floors and jogging escorts, among other things—safety even affects things like room service menus.[33]

Travel as Experience

At one time, people traveled primarily out of necessity; business and family visits were the usual reasons for traveling. Today, people travel for many reasons, including education, culture, and personal development. Many people want to learn more about the society in which they live. They have studied American or world history and want to see the places they have read about. Cultural pursuits—art, theater, music, opera, ballet, and museums—can attract a constant flow of visitors. Sports and nature attract travelers who want to enjoy the great outdoors as well as those who prefer to watch their favorite teams. The push for lifelong learning has provided an incentive for many to take personal

FIGURE 1-5

Photo courtesy of Waldorf=Astoria Hotel, New York City.

development or enrichment courses, whether to update professional skills or to increase knowledge of a particular hobby. *Ecotourists*, people who plan vacations to study the culture and environment of a particular area, want to enjoy nature in its unblemished and unsullied form.

Career Development

An introductory chapter on hotel management would not be complete without attention to career development. People planning a career in the hotel industry need to review the fundamentals of career development, which revolve around five important concepts: educational reparation, practical experience, membership in professional organizations, ports of entry, and growth areas for the industry.

Educational Preparation

The educational base you build now will serve you well over time. The classes you are taking in your major course of study—including management and supervision, cost control, human resources management, quantity food production, hotel management, purchasing, sanitation, layout and design, accounting, and marketing—constitute a strong foundation for your continued development of technical skills. Courses outside your major—such as English, speech communication, computer training, arts, economics, psychology, sociology, nutrition, science, and math—will help develop the skills you need to cope in the professional world. The formal education you receive in your classroom study will be enhanced by extracurricular activities such as clubs, student government, sports, and other areas of special interest. These activities are a microcosm of the environment in which you will apply your technical, liberal arts, and science courses. Clubs associated with your major, in particular, allow you to apply theoretical concepts learned in class to a real-life business environment.

Your educational experience will open the door to your career. You must apply your skills and knowledge after graduation to be an effective, successful employee in the hotel industry. Use your degree as a starting point for an exciting career in hospitality.

Your current endeavor for a higher education must be nurtured beyond graduation day. There are many opportunities for *inservice education*, which are courses that update a professional's educational background for use in current practice; these are offered by professional organizations, sponsors of trade shows, community colleges and universities, technical schools, correspondence schools, trade journals, and other industry groups. Inservice education provides the professional an opportunity to stay current in industry practices.

Just as professionals in other industries take classes to refresh their skills and learn new concepts and procedures, so must professionals in the hotel industry maintain awareness of industry advances. One particularly relevant area is computer training. Professionals who attended school before the early 1980s had little exposure to computers and their ever-changing technology; even some recent graduates are not always aware of the most current trends and advances. The professional has the choice of overlooking this need or enrolling in computer applications courses. The next choice is to determine whether these new procedures and equipment are applicable to a particular establishment.

Professional organizations—such as the *American Hotel & Lodging Association*, the Hospitality Sales & Marketing Association International, and the National Restaurant

Association—offer professionals continuing education opportunities through correspondence courses and seminars. The American Hotel & Lodging Association offers opportunities for hotel employees to become a Certified Hotel Administrator (CHA) and Certified Rooms Division Executive (CRDE), among other certifications. Trade shows sponsored by these organizations promote the latest concepts in technology, products, and supplies as well as provide mini seminars on how to use current technology in human resources management, food production, marketing, and general management. Community colleges and technical schools offer special-interest courses in management and skills application to keep you and your staff abreast of new areas and to review basic concepts. Attending these courses can provide new insight into operational problems. Each of these professional organizations sponsors a website and provides opportunities to access the abovementioned career information.

Correspondence courses are another way to learn new skills and understand new areas. *Distance learning*—classes offered via satellite broadcasts, cable, PictureTel, or online computer interaction—are offered by colleges, universities, and professional groups.

Trade journals are also extremely helpful in keeping professionals up to date with new management concepts, technical applications, marketing principles, equipment innovations, and the like. The isolation experienced by managers in out-of-the-way hotel establishments can be alleviated by reading trade journals. Such journals help all managers feel connected to the community of hotel industry professionals, perhaps providing insight into solving technical problems as well as boosting morale. Some trade journals are offered free on the Internet.

Education is a lifelong venture; it does not stop with the attainment of a degree from a university or community college. The degree is only the beginning of a commitment to nurturing your career.

Work Experience

The practical experience you obtain from entry-level hotel jobs—whether you are a desk clerk, waiter/waitress, host/hostess, maid/houseman/room attendant, bellhop, or groundskeeper—will be invaluable as you plan and develop your career in the hotel industry. It will give you an opportunity to learn what hotel employees do and how departments interact, and it will expose you to the momentum of a hotel—the time frame of service available for the guest, management applications, and service concept applications, to name just a few.

Your work experience will enable you to evaluate theoretical concepts offered in the classroom. You will have a basis for comparing your work experiences with those of other students. You will also develop your own beliefs and behaviors, which can be applied to other hotel properties throughout your career. At times, you will have to think on your feet in order to resolve a guest complaint, evaluate equipment proposals, reorganize work areas for efficiency, or achieve cost-effective spending. Your work experience provides you with the proper foundation on which to base a successful career.

Professional Memberships

A professional trade organization is a group of people who voluntarily pool their efforts to achieve a set of goals. These goals may have a political nature, such as lobbying legislators or providing certification of achievement.

Professional trade organizations in the hospitality industry serve members in many ways. First and foremost, they are a political voice in government. Through use of membership fees, trade organizations are able to lobby local, state, and federal legislators to be sure the entrepreneur's views are recognized. (Members can opt not to have their membership fee used to support legislators they don't politically support on personal issues.) These organizations also offer significant opportunities for continuing education by sponsoring seminars and trade shows. They offer group plans for insurance and other programs that can be cost-efficient to the entrepreneur. Professional trade associations also allow you to interact with others in the industry on both a professional and a social level. Valuable advice and rewarding friendships often result.

Ports of Entry

A review of the organizational structure of a hotel shows many departmental managers in a large organization. Which area is the best for you to enter to develop your career goals? Four of the ports of entry are marketing and sales, front office, food and beverage, and controller. It is impossible to say which the best port of entry is; all are avenues for career development.

The hotel industry demands a great deal of its professionals. All employees must have extensive knowledge of all areas of the facility, and they must understand the overall function of all departments. This understanding must be reflected in professional business plans. Employees must also have good communication skills and good interpersonal skills. The industry requires great flexibility in scheduling work responsibilities and personal life. It demands that the professional understand the entrepreneurial role of corporate owners while operating within budgeted resources.

Students who enter the lodging industry will find that each area in which they work contributes to a good background for the ultimate position of general manager. When trying to decide where to begin, consider reviewing the job responsibilities of department managers to learn what tasks are required to complete each job and who executes them.

Try to work in as many areas as you can before taking the leap into a general manager position. The job will be a lot easier, and you will go a long way toward meeting the establishment's goals, if you are well prepared. You will make mistakes, no matter how much experience you have had; however, your success rate will be much higher if you have a varied background in many departments.

Researching Growth Areas in the Hospitality Industry

Areas that offer the greatest potential for growth should be explored. Because such areas change frequently, it is not possible to list them in a textbook. However, factors that support continued growth and strong business activity are regularly reported in such publications as *Trends*, by PKF Hospitality Research. Hospitality industry futures projections publications usually cover such issues as new hotel developments; hotels under consideration; activities of convention and visitors' bureaus; strength of local economies; development of business, recreation, and arts activities; the need for office space; and area hotel occupancy percentages and average room rates. This information is listed for selected cities both within the United States and at international sites.

The Internet is increasingly used as a method for researching career opportunities in hospitality management. Search engines will produce multiple listings of hospitality recruiters with key words such as *hotel manager*, *front office manager*, and *hotel careers*. Also, professional hospitality organizations usually offer a job-posting service on their websites.

The Internet provides many opportunities for a new graduate to examine trends that are driving the industry and new technologies that will shape a career in hotel management. This information can assist job applicants in exploring the employment possibilities and prospects in different geographic areas.

Your survey of career possibilities should include a review of a potential employer's economic performance on a balance sheet and other features of its profit-and-loss statement. This information is available on computerized business databases. Take the time to research the economic potential of the company you are considering. Your interview

INTERNATIONAL HIGHLIGHTS

 Students of hotel management should consider international employment opportunities. Current trade journals allow you to review the many job opportunities for hospitality professionals who have prepared themselves through education and work experience. International employment requires managers to know operations *and* to desire to learn and work in another culture. This option can be very exciting and a great addition to your career.

FRONT-LINE REALITIES

 Esther, front office manager of The Times Extended-Stay Hotel, received a phone call from the home office of The Times Hotel Management Company asking her to participate in a meeting to discuss the new trend in long-term visitors. The home office is thinking of renovating some of the rooms to attract guests who want to stay for 5 to 15 days. How would Esther prepare for this meeting?

preparations should include reviewing the regional economic prospects and the company's economic performance. This preparation could set the stage for an investment that lasts many years, perhaps a lifetime.

Solution to Opening Dilemma

The effort you put into preparing for a visit to a career fair is essential to making this a learning and networking opportunity for you. Questions you could ask a representative of a select-service hotel include, "What are the typical management responsibilities of an assistant general manager in your organization? What types of visitors frequent your hotels during the week and on the weekend? What is the typical size of your hotels?" Questions you may want to consider asking a representative of a full-service hotel include, "What size staff is employed in your hotel? Do you have any convention hotels in your portfolio? What services do you typically offer in a hotel in your organization?" These types of questions open lines of communication and help you present yourself as a future professional.

Chapter Recap

This chapter introduced the future professional to the hotel industry. It began with a historical review, including founders of the hotel industry—Statler, Hilton, Ritz, Astor, Waldorf, Wilson, the Marriotts, Henderson and Moore, and Schultz. It also discussed historical developments that have shaped the products and services offered to guests, management trends, and economic factors. A new concept of social media and networking was included. It covered the atrium concept, marketing and operational emphasis, geographic relocation, the emergence of select-service hotels, the major reorganization of 1987–1988, the adoption of total quality management, technological advances, the continued effects of 9/11, wireless technology in the hotel industry, and the economic downturn of the late 2000s. It provided an overview of the industry in terms of types of hotels; market orientation/location (residential, commercial, airport, and highway); sales indicators of occupancy, average daily rate, and RevPAR; levels of service (full-service, all-suites, select-service, and extended-stay); and type of affiliation or nonaffiliation (franchise, referral, company-owned, management contract, and independent ownership). Branding was discussed as an approach to understanding the industry configuration. Trends fostering growth in the hotel industry were reviewed (leisure time, me/pleasure concept, discretionary income, family size, household size, business travel, female business traveler, and travel as an experience). Factors affecting a student's career development choice were discussed, including educational preparation, work experience, professional memberships, ports of entry in a hotel, and researching growth areas in the hospitality industry.

End-of-Chapter Questions

1. Name some of the hotels you have visited. What exciting things did you notice while you were a guest there?

2. With which departments of the hotel did you come into contact before, during, and after your visit to the property you named in question 1?

3. Investigate some of the properties in your area. In what year were they built? What kind of competition do they have? What services or facilities did they introduce to your community?

4. How do residential and commercial properties differ?

5. What are the four most common locations for hotel properties? What determines the end destination of the guest?

6. Define sales indicators. Give working examples.

7. How would you use social media to promote hotel reservations?

8. Define four levels of service. Relate them to room rates and guest expectations.

9. Name some of the types of properties developed by major chains to meet demands by market segments.

10. Differentiate between franchises and company-owned properties in a chain. What is the difference between franchises and referral groups?

11. What are the major differences between chain and independent properties?

12. Name a few hotel brands you are familiar with and look them up on the Internet. What similarities and differences did you find?

13. Review a recent article in the *Wall Street Journal* that reports on growth in leisure time of the American worker, the me/pleasure concept, discretionary income, or travel habits of the business traveler.

14. List attractions in your area that may entice visitors. Do these attractions provide education, culture, or personal development? What makes them attractions?

15. Compare your career plans with the concepts presented in this chapter. Do you feel the steps presented here will be useful to you in your first job? in subsequent jobs?

16. Go to a current hospitality-related website such as hotel-online.com and research a trend in the hotel industry such as real estate investment trusts (REITs), extended-stay hotels, or RevPAR. How does that concept affect your future career plans?

17. Go to the website of the American Hotel & Lodging Association (ahla.com) and determine how this professional trade association (formerly known as the American Hotel & Motel Association) will be helpful to you in your career.

CASE STUDY 101

Professor Catherine Vicente has allotted time in the HRI-201 Introduction to Front Office Management course for a field trip this semester. After the first few lectures, she wants to take her class to the hotel establishments in the vicinity of City College. The area is well known for its tourist attractions and is the headquarters of several major U.S. businesses.

She appoints a group of students to assist her in setting up tours.

One of the students, Maria, is a resident of the area and suggests they visit the grand old St. Thomas Hotel in the downtown area. She would also like to see a hotel located at the Wide World Airport. Ryan, another student, has worked at a select-service prop-

erty in his hometown. He understands another hotel in that chain is located on the outskirts of the city. David, who is applying for a job at a local hotel, wants to get information on all-suites hotels. Linda has heard of a new extended-stay hotel in town and wants to know what makes it different from a select-service hotel.

The group has sifted through all the requests and decided to form five teams to visit these places. Each team will appoint one spokesperson for a panel discussion. The spokesperson will present a five-minute summary of what was learned from the visit.

What items do you think each spokesperson will include in his or her summary?

CASE STUDY 102

A recent survey in a suburban community projects an influx of new citizens into the area. Several computer industries will be relocating to the area, and they are expected to employ 25,000 persons at all levels of the organizations. Also, one of these computer companies will locate its corporate headquarters here, with an additional 500 executives arriving soon.

The local hotel association has contacted Professor Catherine Vicente of the HRI program at City

College for assistance in determining the impact these new residents will have on their hotels with regard to occupancy and use of facilities.

If you were Professor Vicente, what actions would you undertake? Justify your responses with regard to hotel operations and development. If you lived in this community, how would these developments affect your career in the hotel industry?

CASE STUDY 103

The director of tourism in your local community has recently spoken with your hospitality management professor and requested some volunteers to develop a few package plans for visiting tourists from international destinations. The director indicated one group of 25 tourists will originate from Germany and stay 7 days and 6 nights in your area. The second group of 100 from England will holiday with

your community for 4 nights and 3 days. The third group of 80 from a nearby metropolitan area will stay only overnight. The director wants the packages to include a list of lodging properties, restaurants, and tourist attractions to accommodate these guests. The director promised a worthwhile internship to group of students that developed the best package.

Notes

1. Madelin Schneider, "20th Anniversary," *Hotels & Restaurants International* 20, no. 8 (August 1986): 35–36.
2. 1993, Grolier Electronic Publishing, Inc.
3. Paul R. Dittmer and Gerald G. Griffin, *The Dimensions of the Hospitality Industry: An Introduction* (New York: Van Nostrand Reinhold, 1993), 87.
4. 1993, Grolier Electronic Publishing, Inc.
5. Ibid.
6. Dittmer and Griffin, *Dimensions,* 52–53.
7. John Meyjes, Lou Hammond & Associates, 39 E. 51st Street, New York, NY 10022. Public relations flier.
8. Ray Sawyer, "Pivotal Era Was Exciting," *Hotel & Motel Management* 210, no. 14 (August 14, 1995): 28.
9. Marriott Corporate Relations, Marriott Drive, Dept. 977.01, Washington, DC 20058.
10. ITT Sheraton Corporation, Public Relations Department, 60 State Street, Boston, MA 02109.
11. Cathy Planchard, "Limited Service Pioneer Hampton Inns Now Has 800 Properties," www.hotel-online.com/News/PressReleases1998_4th/Oct98_HamptonPromus.html.
12. Saul F. Leonard, "Laws of Supply, Demand Control Industry," *Hotel & Motel Management* 210, no. 14 (August 14, 1995): 74.
13. Carol Peacher, "Joe M. Hindsley Named General Manager at Hyatt Regency Atlanta on Peachtree Street and Scott B. VandenBerg Named General Manager at Grand Hyatt Atlanta in Buckhead," www.hotel-online.com/News/PR2004_2nd/Apr04_AtlantaHyatts.html. April 20, 2004.
14. Planchard, "Limited Service Pioneer Hampton Inns."
15. Leonard, 74, 80.
16. Max Starkov and Marina Mechoso, "Local Internet Market Strategies for Franchised Hotels," September 2008, www.hotel-online.com/News/PR2008_3rd/Sept08_InternetStrategies.html.
17. Leonard, 80.
18. P. Anthony Brown, "Hotel REITs—Legislation Heralds a New Era," *Virginia Hospitality and Leisure Executive Report* (Spring 2000), as reported for Arthur Andersen in Hotel-Online.com, www.hotel-online.com:80/Neo/Trends/Andersen/2000_HotelReits.html.
19. R. Mark Woodworth, "More Insights into the Realities of the Post 9/11 Period," as reported in Hotel-Online.com, PKF Consulting, www.hotelonline.com/News/PR2003_3rd/Sep03_MoreInsights.html. Sept. 2003.

20. Rick Swig, "Recent Occupancy, ADR Growth Still Do Not Spell Post-9/11 Relief," RSBA & Associates, San Francisco, CA 94105, as reported in Hotel-Online.com, www.hotel-online.com/News/PR2004_4th/Nov04_Inflation.html. Nov. 2004.

21. Tom Belden, "Business Cut Back on Travel Budgets, Shop for Better Airfares," *Philadelphia Inquirer*, Knight Ridder/Tribune Business News, as reported in Hotel-Online.com, www.hotelonline.com/News/2004_Oct_26/k.PHB.1098815827.html. Oct. 2004.

22. Andrew MacGeoch, "Terrorism: Who's Liable? The Legal Status of Hotel Owners and Management Companies," *Hotel Asia Pacific Legal Correspondent* (October 2003), as reported in Hotel-Online.com, www.hotelonline.com/News/PR2003_4th/Oct03_TerrorismLiability.html.

23. Mark Woodworth, "U.S. Lodging Turning Point Arrives But Growth Remains on Distant Horizon," June11, 2009, as reported in Hotel On-line.com, www.hotelonline.com/News/PR2009_2nd/Jun09_LodgingTurningPoint.html.

24. Carol Verret, "Selling Into a Bad Economy: Overcoming Fear and Stealing Share," October 4, 2008, as reported in Hotel On-line.com, www.hotel-online.com/News/PR2008_4th/Oct08_VerretSelling.html.

25. Julie-Keyser Squires, "ALIS:2009 Industry Looks to the Long-term, Leaders, and Innovation," February 1, 2009, as reported in Hotel On-line.com, www.hotel-online.com/News/PR2009_1st/Feb09_ALIS2009.htm.

26. Leon Stafford, "Extended-Stay Hotels Driven by Customers with Long-Term Assignments and an Interest in Frugality; About × Extended-Stay Properties Built for Every Traditional Hotel Between 2001 and 2004," *Atlanta Journal-Constitution*, Knight Ridder/Tribune Business News, November 14, 2004, as reported in Hotel-Online.com.

27. Younes & Kett, GOPPAR, a Derivative of RevPAR! March 7, 2003.

28. Cline, Roger S. "Hospitality 2000: A View to the Next Millennium Global Study Yield Insights about the Future," Summer 2000. Arthur Andersen, New York.

29. Woodworth, "U.S. Lodging Turning Point Arrives."

30. Joan MacKeith and Angela Bliss, "aloft Brand Expected to Reinvent the Select Service Market," July 7, 2008, as reported in Hotel On-line.com, www.hotel-online.com/News/PR2008_3rd/Jul08_aloftdesign.html.

31. Tony Lima, "Chains vs. Independents," Lodging Hospitality 43, no. 8 (July 1987): 82.

32. Bryan E. Young, "The Role of Hotel Brands in the War of Survival," April 2, 2009, as reported in Hotel, On-line.com, www.hotel online.com/News/PR2009_2nd/Apr09_BrandBattle.html.

33. Andrea Newell, "Do Female Business Travelers Have Different Needs? Survey Says: Yes," June 5, 2009, as reported in Hotel On-line.com, www.theglasshammer.com/news/2009/06/05/do-female-travelers-have-different-needs-survey-says-yes/.

Key Words

all-suites

American Hotel & Lodging Association

atrium concept

average daily rate (ADR)

business affiliations

chain

chain affiliations

commercial hotels

company-owned property

conference call

demographic data

discretionary income

distance learning

ecotourists

extended stay

front office

full service

independent hotel

inservice education

limited service

management contract property

market segments

mass marketing

occupancy percentage

PictureTel

potential gross income

psychographic data

quality assurance

real estate investment trust (REIT)

referral property

residential hotels

revenue per available room (RevPAR)

room revenues

sales indicators

select service

service quality

social networking

total quality management (TQM)

yield percentage

CHAPTER 2

Hotel Organization and the Front Office Manager

OPENING DILEMMA

At a recent staff meeting, the general manager of The Times Hotel asked if anyone wanted to address the group. The director of housekeeping indicated he was at a loss in trying to work with the front desk clerks. He had repeatedly called the desk clerks last Tuesday to let them know that general housecleaning would be performed on the seventh and eighth floors on Wednesday morning and that they should not assign rooms on those floors to guests on Tuesday night. When the cleaning crew came to work on Wednesday morning, they were faced with 14 occupied rooms on the seventh floor and 12 occupied rooms on the eighth floor. This cost the hotel several hundred dollars because the cleaning crew was from an outsourced contract company, which charged the hotel a basic fee for failure to comply with the contract. The front office manager retorted that a bus group had called two weeks earlier and asked if any rooms were available because there was a mixup in room rates at

the group's original hotel. The front office manager indicated that something must

have gone awry in the computer system. After all, this was a good opportunity to

bring in 26 additional room-nights.

Organization of Lodging Properties

The objective of most hospitality establishments is to produce a profit. To meet this goal, factors such as current economic conditions, marketing plans, competition, and staff size and ability are constantly reviewed.

The *general manager*, the person in charge of directing and leading the hotel staff in carrying out its financial, environmental, and community responsibilities, develops organization charts that fit his or her plan to meet the goals of the company. The *organization charts*—schematic drawings that list management positions in an organization—included in this chapter are offered as instructional examples only. An organization chart represents the span of control for the general manager. Not all hotels have every position listed in these organization charts. Persons pursuing a career in the hotel industry will be called on many times to develop or restructure an organization. The people who are part of these operational plans will have a direct influence on the type of structure developed or reorganized. The goals of the organization must be paramount in the decision-making process. However, flexibility is necessary to make the plan work. This section points out the major organizational features of a lodging property and typical managerial duties of the people within the organization.

It is not uncommon for the general manager of a property to move people from department to department of the hotel. This is done for many reasons. The *front office manager*, the person responsible for leading the front office staff in delivering hospitality, may express interest in the position of *controller*, the internal accountant for the hotel, or in a position in the marketing and sales department. The general manager realizes a candidate must possess certain skills before being placed in any new position. To prepare someone for an opening in the controller's office, the general manager may assign him or her some of the controller's busywork. The front office manager might also spend slack periods with the *director of marketing and sales*, the person who analyzes available markets and sells products and services at a profit, to become familiar with that department.

The general manager may also use the weekly staff meeting to explain the financial condition and marketing plans of the property. This tactic reinforces the management team concept. By exposing interested employees to the responsibilities of other departments and by keeping the staff informed of the current situation of the property, the general manager enables staff members to meet their career goals within the organization.

Flexibility is the key to hospitality organization. At the operations level, familiarity with the staff's strengths and weaknesses is essential to meeting the demands of the situation. When the property experiences an expected slow period, regrouping may be necessary to maintain full-time positions. The front office manager may have to assist the marketing and sales office in advertising or hosting tour directors for a specific weekend. The food and beverage director may have to spend time in the controller's office completing reports and developing budgets. This interdepartmental cooperation provides the backdrop for a smooth-running organization. In addition, such flexibility prevents departmental jealousies and territoriality from becoming roadblocks to communication.

The general manager receives additional operational support from the director of security, the person who takes a proactive role in establishing and maintaining a safe environment for guests and employees. Because of the precautions necessary in delivering hospitality, the director of security is vital to the operation of the lodging property.

Organization Charts

The major positions found in a large full-service hotel or resort are presented in Figure 2-1. This lodging property features:

- 500+ rooms in a commercial property
- Center-city or suburban location
- $142 *average daily rate (ADR)*—total room revenue divided by the number of rooms sold
- 60 *percent occupancy*—number of rooms sold divided by the number of rooms available
- 36 *percent yield*—number of rooms sold at average daily rate divided by the number of rooms available at *rack rate*, the highest room rate category offered by a hotel
- $84.93 RevPAR (Revenue per Available Room)—room revenue divided by the number of rooms available *or* hotel occupancy times average daily rate
- Rack rate of $235.91
- $15.5 million in revenues
- Full service
- Chain—company ownership
- *Corporate guests*—frequent guests who are employed by a company and receive a special room rate
- *Convention guests*—guests who attend a large convention and receive a special room rate
- Meeting and banquet rooms
- Dining rooms
- Lounge with entertainment

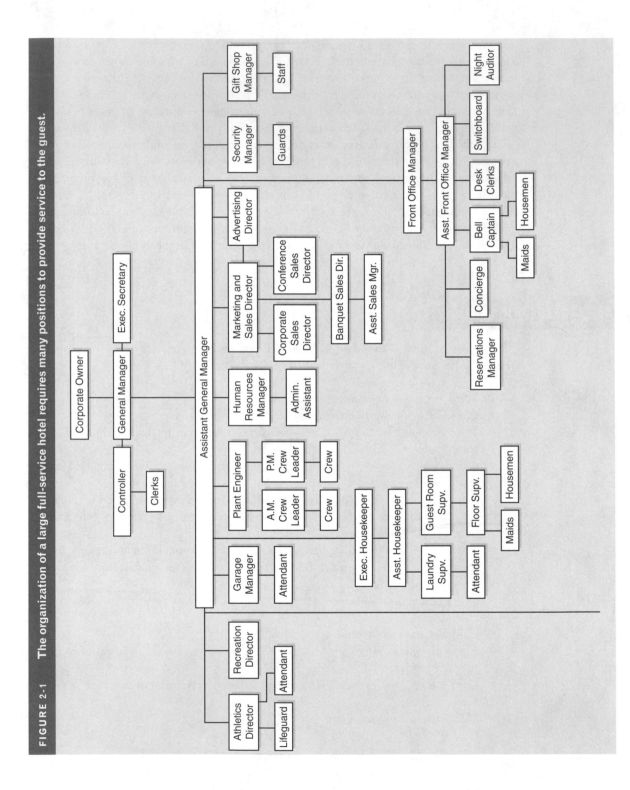

FIGURE 2-1 The organization of a large full-service hotel requires many positions to provide service to the guest.

FIGURE 2-1 (Continued)

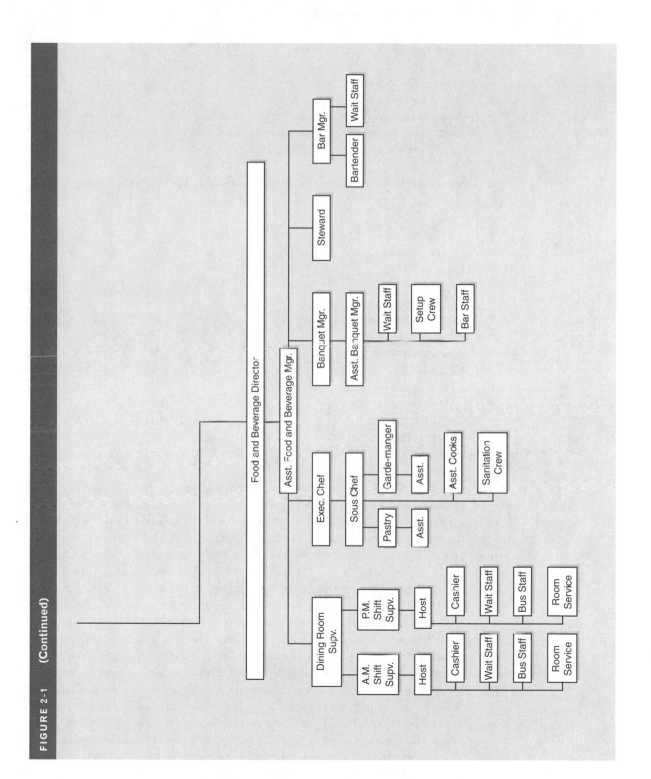

- Exercise facilities with indoor pool
- Gift shop
- Business office and retail rentals
- Attached parking garage
- *In-house laundry*—a hotel-operated department that launders guest linens
- *Referral reservation service*—a service offered by the management company of a chain of hotels to franchisee members

To function as a well-run lodging facility, this property requires the following department heads:

- General manager
- Assistant general manager
- Controller
- Plant engineer
- Executive housekeeper
- Human resources manager
- Director of security
- Recreation director
- Athletics director
- Marketing and sales director
- Gift shop manager
- Front office manager
- Food and beverage director
- Garage manager

The corporate owners have entrusted the financial success of this organization to the general manager, who must organize departments to provide optimum service to the guest. Each department is organized and staffed to allow the supervisor time to plan and develop the major revenue-producing areas. The marketing and sales director, gift shop manager, front office manager, food and beverage director, and garage manager develop programs that increase sales and profits and improve cost-control methods. Those supervisors who do not head income-generating departments—controller, plant engineer, executive housekeeper, director of security, human resources manager, recreation director, and athletics director—provide services to the guest, principally behind the scenes.

For example, the controller develops clear and concise performance reports that reflect budget targets. The *plant engineer*, the person responsible for the operation and maintenance of the physical plant, establishes an effective preventive maintenance program. The *executive housekeeper*, the person responsible for the upkeep of the guest rooms and public areas of the lodging property as well as control of guest room inventory items, stays on top of trends in controlling costs and effective use of personnel. The director of security trains the staff in meeting the front-line safety needs of guests. The *human resources manager*, the person who assists department managers in organizing

FIGURE 2-2   Notice that several of the positions listed in the full-service hotel organization chart are eliminated from this one for a medium-size lodging property.

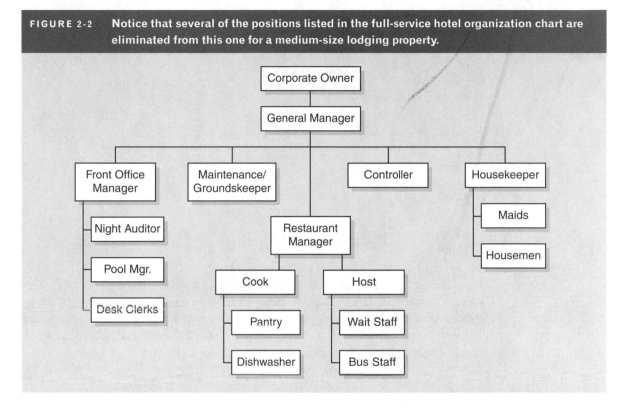

personnel functions and developing employees, provides leadership in attracting new hires and maintaining a stable yet progressive approach to utilization of personnel. The *recreation director*, the person in charge of developing and organizing recreational activities for guests, and the *athletics director*, who is responsible for supervising physical exercise facilities for guests, provide direct hospitality services for the guest, helping ensure their safe and interesting stay.

Figure 2-2 outlines the organization of a somewhat smaller lodging property. This hotel features:

- 200 rooms in a commercial property
- Suburban location
- 58 percent occupancy
- 40 percent yield
- $4 million in revenues
- $94 average daily rate
- $54 RevPAR
- Rack rate of $135
- Full service
- Chain-franchise

- Corporate guests
- Local community guests
- Dining room
- Lounge
- Outdoor pool
- Referral reservation service

The department heads required includes:

- General manager
- Maintenance/groundskeeper
- Front office manager
- Controller
- Restaurant manager
- Housekeeper

This managerial staff seems skeletal compared to that of a large hotel or resort. This type of organization chart is possible because the level of service provided to guests is reduced. At this property, the guest's stay is one or two nights, and a dining room and lounge are provided for convenience. Many of the department heads are *working supervisors*, which means they participate in the actual work performed while supervising. Laundry and other services are contracted out. The controller provides accounting services as well as human resources management. The maintenance/groundskeeper oversees indoor and outdoor facilities. The front office manager and the clerks take care of reservations as well as registrations, posting, checkout, and the like. The restaurant manager works closely with the cook and hostess in maintaining quality and cost control and guest services. The executive housekeeper inspects and cleans rooms and maintains linen and cleaning supply inventories as well as leading the housekeeping staff. Security services are provided by the general manager and outsourced as needed.

Figure 2-3 shows the organization chart of a typical select-service property, much scaled down from that of a large hotel. The features of the property are:

- 150 rooms in a commercial property
- Highway location
- 55 percent occupancy
- 44 percent yield
- $40.18 RevPAR
- $2.2 million in revenues
- $73 average daily rate
- $90 rack rate
- 2.2 million in room revenues
- Selected services
- Chain-franchise

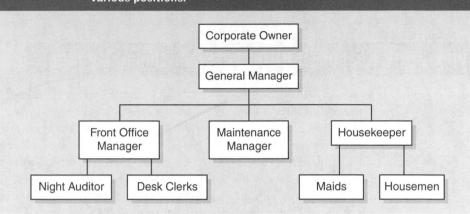

FIGURE 2-3   **The organization chart for a small select-service lodging property features minimal staffing only. Several duties are combined under various positions.**

- In-house laundry
- Vacation travelers
- Business travelers
- Complimentary *continental breakfast*—juice, fruit, sweet roll, cereal
- Referral reservation service
- *Business services and communications center*—guest services including copying, computers, and fax

The department heads include:

- General manager
- Front office manager
- Housekeeper
- Maintenance manager

The general manager is a working supervisor in that he or she participates in the actual work performed while supervising at the front desk. The general manager at this type of property assists with marketing plans, reservations, maintenance, and grounds-keeping; maintains financial records; and implements cost-control measures. The front office manager works regular shifts to provide coverage along with the night auditor and desk clerks. The housekeeper, also a working supervisor, assists the *room attendants*, employees who clean and maintain guest rooms and public areas.

The organization charts shown here were developed by evaluating the needs of guests. The organization of departments and the subsequent staffing are influenced by the available labor pool, the economic conditions of the region, and the financial goals of the organization. Each organization chart varies depending on the factors influencing a particular lodging establishment. Flexibility is essential in providing service to the guest and leadership to the staff.

Typical Job Responsibilities of Department Managers

As you begin your career in the lodging industry, you will undoubtedly come in contact with hotel department managers. Some of the positions seem to be shrouded in mystery, while others are clear. The controller, for example, works behind the scenes, and little about his or her role is obvious. The security director seems to be everywhere in the hotel, but what does this person do, and for what is he or she responsible? The food and beverage director holds a visible position that seems to encompass much. The general manager must be aware of both the forest and the trees, overseeing all operations while staying on top of the small details. How can all of these positions be coordinated to provide hospitality to the guest and profit to the investors?

General Manager

Several years ago I invited a guest speaker to my class. This person was the general manager of an inn in our community. He was well prepared for the lecture and described the organization chart and staff he had developed. After he explained the work of the various departments and the responsibilities of the respective supervisors, a student asked, "What do you do as the general manager if all the work is being done by your staff?" This honest question made me terribly aware that the role of the general manager is not easy to understand. Indeed, detailing this managerial role could fill volumes and encompass decades of experience. However, the legitimacy of the question compels me to be specific in describing this essential job in the organization chart.

The leadership provided by the general manager is undoubtedly the most important quality he or she brings to this position. The general manager orchestrates the department directors in their efforts to meet the financial goals of the organization through their employees. The general manager is required to use the full range of managerial skills—planning, decision making, organizing, staffing, controlling, directing, and communicating—to develop a competent staff. Performance is judged according to how effectively supervisors are directed to meet the goals of the organization. Efficiency depends not on how well tasks are performed but on how well employees are motivated and instructed to meet the goals and objectives of the plans the general manager and staff have formulated. Figure 2-4 presents a group of managers, supervisors, and front-line employees who carry out the goals of the general manager.

The plans developed by the general manager along with the department supervisors provide the vision the business needs to compete for the hospitality markets. The evaluation of candidates for positions based on a well-structured division of labor begins the

FIGURE 2-4

The general manager of a hotel is responsible for orchestrating the efforts of managers and employees to produce a financially successful establishment. Photo courtesy of Red Lion Hotels.

process of meeting the goals and objectives of the planning stage. Who should be chosen to lead operations? What skills and strengths are necessary to get the job done? What degree of business acumen must this person have? What vision should be brought to the job? How will the new hire fit into the existing staff? These are just a few of the questions a general manager must consider and act on.

The *operational reports*—operational data on critical financial aspects of hotel operations—a general manager must review can be overwhelming in both quantity and complexity. However, the efficient general manager knows which key operating statistics reflect the profitability and efficiency of operations. Do the food cost percentage, labor cost percentage, alcohol beverage cost percentage, and sales item analysis provide enough information to indicate the success of the food and beverage department? Are the daily occupancy percentage, average daily room rate, and total sales for the day adequate to indicate the hotel's profitability? Each general manager develops key indicators that measure the financial success and operational success of the department directors. These concepts are flexible and dependent on the goals the corporate ownership established.

Communicating ideas and goals and providing feedback on performance are skills the general manager must develop. The general manager is a pivotal link in the communication process. Each department director works from communications received (or not received) from the general manager. Weekly staff meetings serve as a major vehicle for sharing information. Individual meetings with department directors additionally support the communication process. At one-on-one meetings, the general manager helps department directors transform organizational goals into operational functions.

The general manager offers practical supervisory training to his or her staff. For example, the director of marketing and sales may have set a goal of increasing guest room sales by 10 percent in the next quarter. At an individual meeting with the general manager, the director of marketing and sales agrees to meet that goal over the next three months.

What does a general manager do? He or she provides leadership to meet organizational goals of profitability and service. Leadership skills are acquired by studying theories of management and the behavior of other managers as well as practicing leadership and receiving constructive criticism from superiors on efforts expended. The job of general manager is a professional position. It is a career goal the achievement of which is based on operations experience and education.

The role of the general manager, whether in a full-service or select-service property, must encompass the concepts previously discussed. The general manager in a select-service property may have additional hands-on responsibilities, but he or she is required to provide leadership to the other members of the management team. The use of *total quality management (TQM)*, or the application of managerial concepts to understanding operational processes and developing methods to improve those processes (described in chapter 11), allows managers in full-service and select-service properties to extend leadership to front-line supervisors and employees. In full-service and select-service properties, where profit margins are based on lean departmental budgets, total quality management is encouraged.

Assistant General Manager

The *assistant general manager* of a lodging property has a major responsibility for developing and executing plans developed by the corporate owners, the general manager, and other members of the management staff. The relationship between the general manager and the assistant general manager must be founded on trust, skill, and excellent communication. The assistant general manager works with department directors to meet their respective goals and objectives through efficient operations. Often, he or she is the liaison between management and operations. The more thoroughly the assistant general manager understands the reasons for management decisions, the better able he or she is to communicate plans to the operations supervisors. The assistant general manager is sometimes referred to as the *rooms division manager*. He or she is responsible for the entire front office operation, which includes front desk, housekeeping, bell staff, concierge, and parking garage. The assistant general manager may also be called the *operations manager*.

The assistant general manager often must oversee the beginning of a task and ensure that others complete it. He or she must also complete, review, and summarize statistical reports and share them with the general manager. The assistant general manager is everywhere on the property, checking on operations, providing feedback, and offering assistance as needed. This job requires a wide variety of established operational skills, such as front office, food and beverage, marketing and sales, and accounting skills. A large property may divide the responsibilities of the assistant general manager between a rooms division manager and an operations division manager.

Select-service hotels usually do not have an assistant general manager position in their organization chart. The department managers report directly to the general manager to streamline guest services and operational budgets. Again, the general manager of a select-service property may perform some hands-on tasks, but he or she is required to provide direct leadership to the other members of the management team.

Food and Beverage Director

The *food and beverage director* is responsible for the efficient operation of the kitchen, dining rooms, banquet service, room service, and lounge. This includes managing a multitude of details with the supervisors of these outlets. Such details include food quality, sanitation, inventory, cost control, training, room setup, cash control, and guest service, to name a few. The food and beverage director keeps a keen eye on trends in food and beverage merchandising, cost-control factors in food and beverage preparation, and kitchen utilities. The food and beverage director works closely with the assistant food and beverage director, a highly skilled executive chef, a dining room supervisor, a banquet manager, and a bar manager. This team's goal is to provide high-quality products and services around the clock, every day of the year. Constant supervision of products, employees, and services is essential to ensure a fair return on investment.

Although food and beverages are served at a continental breakfast or cocktail hour at a select-service property, there is no food and beverage director position; here, the responsibility for serving food and beverages is an extension of the front office manager's duties. However, the same principles of sanitation, food purchasing and storage, marketing, standards of service, and so forth must be followed to provide good service to the guest.

Physical Plant Engineer

The plant engineer is important in the overall delivery of service to the guest. This person oversees a team of electricians, plumbers, heating, ventilating, and air-conditioning contractors, and general repair personnel to provide behind-the-scenes services to the guests and employees of the lodging property. With today's emphasis on preventive maintenance and energy savings, the plant engineer must develop a plan that will keep the lodging property well maintained within budget targets. Knowledge of advances in equipment and machinery is essential. This position requires a range of experience in general maintenance and a positive attitude about updating skills and management concepts through continuing education.

The plant engineer interacts with all the departments of the hotel. This person is part of the management team and can be relied on to provide sound advice about structural stability, equipment maintenance, and environmental control. He or she can be one of the most treasured assistants in a lodging business.

A role similar to that of the plant engineer in a select-service property is that of *maintenance manager*, a staff member who maintains the heating and air-conditioning plant, produces guest room keys, helps housekeeping attendants as required, and assists with safety and security. The select-service property emphasizes quality in guest service, which is delivered by an efficient staff.

Executive Housekeeper

The executive housekeeper is responsible for the upkeep of the guest rooms and public areas of the lodging property. This person must work through other people to get the job done. Each room attendant must be thoroughly trained in cleaning techniques. Each *floor inspector*, a person who supervises the housekeeping function on a floor of a hotel, and each housekeeping employee must be trained in standard inspection techniques. (Many hotels are moving away from the use of floor inspectors and instead are implementing self-inspection systems.) Speed and efficiency are paramount in performing the vital service of maintaining guest rooms and public areas.

Skill in supervising unskilled labor is essential. Survival fluency in foreign languages is important to the executive housekeeper, who must communicate effectively with employees. Accurate scheduling of employees is also necessary to maintain control over labor costs. The executive housekeeper is further responsible for maintaining and controlling an endless inventory of linens, soap, guest amenities, furniture, in-house marketing materials, live and artificial plants, and more. The executive housekeeper, like the plant engineer, must stay abreast of new ideas and techniques through trade journals and continuing education courses.

The executive housekeeper supervises the in-house laundry, if one is present. The equipment, cleaning materials, cost controls, and scheduling are handled in cooperation with the laundry supervisor.

The select-service property depends on this member of the management team to supervise the staff that provides clean rooms and operates an in-house laundry. This hands-on supervisor works with the staff to provide many behind-the-scenes guest services. The housekeeper travels the elevators of high-rise select-services properties, stopping at each floor to provide employees with constant supervision and motivation.

Interdepartmental cooperation and communication with the front desk and maintenance department are vital for the executive housekeeper in both full-service and select-service hotels. The release of cleaned rooms for occupancy and the scheduling of periodic maintenance are only two functions demonstrating why interdepartmental cooperation is critical. In addition, the marketing and sales efforts in hotels depend on the housekeeper to enforce cleanliness and appearance standards in the public areas so that guests are attracted to and impressed by the property. More information about the executive housekeeper and that department is detailed in chapter 15.

INTERNATIONAL HIGHLIGHTS

Managers in a hotel have a particular responsibility to prepare their employees to communicate with their guests. This is very important for international guests. Front-line employees can assist an international guest by adopting an attitude of "hospitality without question." This simple concept encompasses a front-line employee maintaining a watchful eye for guests who appear confused, express difficulty in communicating in the local language, or seem hesitant about responding to inquiries. Training programs with role-playing exercises that focus on visitors who can't communicate in the local language and employees who must respond to their inquiries allow front-line employees to practice hospitality without question. This concept can be further advanced when a front office manager maintains an inventory of employees who speak several languages.

Human Resources Manager

In a full-service lodging property, the luxury of employing a human resources manager is beneficial for everyone. This person is responsible for administering federal, state, and local employment laws as well as advertising for and screening job candidates and interviewing, selecting, orienting, training, and evaluating employees. Each department director can rely on the human resources manager to provide leadership in the administration of complex personnel programs such as implementation of wage and salary laws.

Staffing a hotel involves many time-consuming tasks:

- Writing and placing classified ads
- Screening, interviewing, testing, and selecting candidates
- Orienting, training, and evaluating new employees

The preparation of job descriptions, while perceived by many in the hotel industry as a luxury, is mandatory if the employees are represented by a *collective bargaining unit*—that is, a labor union. The human resources manager can assist in preparing the job analysis and subsequent job description. This process helps him or her develop realistic job specifications.

The development of employees by providing a plan for the growth of each takes a great deal of planning and evaluating. Each department director works under pressure to meet budget guidelines, quality control levels, sales quotas, and other goals. The human resources manager can assist each director in making plans to motivate employees, to develop career projections for them, to provide realistic pay increases, and to establish employment policies that reflect positively on the employer.

Select-service properties do not employ a human resources manager but rather divide the responsibilities among department heads. Although the emphasis remains on well-planned and competently delivered human resources activities, the streamlined select-service property relies on interdepartmental cooperation to accomplish its objectives.

Marketing and Sales Director

In this job title, the marketing function is emphasized. The person in this position plays an essential role in all departments of the hotel. An effective director of marketing and sales not only attracts external sales such as conventions, small business conferences, wedding receptions, and dining room and lounge business but also provides direction for promoting in-house sales to guests.

This is an exciting position that requires endless creativity. The director of marketing and sales is constantly evaluating new markets, reviewing the needs of existing markets, watching new promotions by the competition, organizing sales blitzes, working with community and professional groups to maintain public relations, working with other department directors to establish product and service specifications and in-house promotional efforts, and following up on details, details, and more details. This is a high-energy position that not only provides financial vitality but also fosters the attainment of financial goals by all departments.

Some select-service properties employ a full-time or half-time marketing and sales director. The duties of this position may also be shared by the general manager and front office manager; these duties (with the exception of soliciting food and beverage business) are the same as those of the marketing and sales director. Competition for room sales to the corporate, group, and pleasure travel markets is enormous, and each hotel must address this planning need.

Front Office Manager

The role of the front office manager is detailed more completely later in this chapter. In short, however, the major responsibilities of the front office manager include reviewing the final draft of the *night audit*, a daily review of the financial accounting procedures at the front desk and other guest service areas during the previous 24-hour period and an analysis of operating results; operating and monitoring the reservation system; developing and operating an effective communication system with front office staff and other department directors; supervising daily registrations and checkouts; overseeing and developing employees; establishing in-house sales programs at the front desk; preparing budgets and cost-control systems; forecasting room sales; and maintaining business relationships with regular corporate and community leaders. The front office manager works with an assistant front office manager, a night auditor, a reservations manager, and a bell captain to tend to the details of running an efficient department.

These are just a few of the responsibilities of the front office manager. The front office is a pivotal point in communication among in-house sales, delivery of service to the guest, and financial operations. The position requires an individual who can manage the many details of guest needs, employee supervision, interdepartmental communication, and transmittal of financial information. The person who holds this exciting position can develop an overview of the lodging property with regard to finances and communication.

FRONT-LINE REALITIES

A future guest has called the hotel and wants to arrange a small dinner party for his guests on the first day of his visit. The marketing and sales office is closed for the day, and the banquet manager has left the property for a few hours. What would you suggest the front desk clerk do to assist this future guest?

Controller

The controller is the internal accountant of a hotel. He or she is responsible for the actual and effective administration of financial data produced daily in the hotel. In the lodging property, appropriate daily financial information must be available to corporate owners, management, and guests. This requires a well-organized staff, not only to prepare operating statistics but also to assist the general manager in determining the effectiveness of each department manager. Often the general manager relies on the controller for financial insight into the operations of the property, including cash flow, discounts, evaluation of insurance costs, fringe-benefit cost analysis, investment opportunities, computer technology applications, banking procedures, and more.

The controller's department processes *accounts payable* (amounts of money the hotel owes to vendors), *accounts receivable* (amounts of money owed to the hotel by guests), the *general ledger* (a collection of accounts the controller uses to organize the financial activities of the hotel), *statement of cash flows* (a projection of income from income-generating areas of the hotel), the *profit-and-loss statement* (a listing of revenues and expenses for a certain period), and the *balance sheet* (a listing of the financial position of the hotel at a particular point in time). This busy department provides financial information to all department directors.

The general manager of a select-service property acts as the controller with the assistance of the night auditor. (In some properties, the night audit is performed during the day and the night auditor is replaced with a lower-salaried front desk clerk for late-night coverage.) The ownership of a select-service hotel may be a part of the larger financial portfolio of a business, which helps the general manager perform the controller's responsibilities by processing accounts payable, accounts receivable, and payroll.

Director of Security

The *director of security* works with department directors to develop cost-control procedures that help ensure employee honesty and guest safety. This person supervises an ongoing training program in cooperation with department directors to instruct employees in fire, job, and environmental safety procedures. Fictional stories often depict the security director as someone who investigates crimes after the fact. On the contrary, this person's primary responsibility is to implement programs that make employees security-minded, helping prevent crime from occurring.

Unfortunately, the lodging industry has always been involved in lawsuits, which have multiplied in both number and cost in recent years. A substantial body of law provides regulations under which properties must operate. Preventive security precautions are the central theme of the security department today. The director of security's background is usually in police or detective work or in security or intelligence in the armed services. He or she usually has an understanding of the criminal mind and the practices of criminals. This person is constantly on the lookout for suspicious people and circumstances.

The responsibilities of this necessary position in a select-service property are shared by the front office manager and the general manager. Security services for on-site and parking lot patrol are often outsourced, but this practice does not relieve the general manager of the need to develop and provide ongoing procedures to train employees to become security-minded. More information about the director of security is explained in chapter 14.

Parking Garage Manager

The responsibility for ensuring a safe environment for guests' vehicles falls to the *parking garage manager*. This person supervises the work of garage attendants and maintains the security of guests and cars in the parking garage. Garage maintenance, in cooperation

HOSPITALITY PROFILE

Eric O. Long, general manager of the Waldorf=Astoria in New York City, has been employed by Hilton Corporation for 30 years. He has served in various management positions at the Hilton Short Hills, Chicago Hilton and Towers, Hilton Walt Disney Village, Fontainebleau Hilton Resort, and Palmer House.

His well-thought-out career with Hilton allowed him to develop a strong network of relationships and vital experience to prepare him for the position he holds today. Mr. Long indicates there are four major areas of responsibility in his job: finance, marketing, customer service, and human resources management. Although other employees carry out the day-to-day administration of those departments, he feels he is ultimately responsible for their success. For example, he wants to ensure that a marketing and sales plan is current and operating, and he attends an 8:00 A.M. customer feedback meeting each day to review feedback on the previous day's efforts to provide high-quality service. He adds that he wants to ensure that the level of talent in the organization is nurtured through motivation, training, development, and so forth.

Early in Mr. Long's career, his mentor encouraged him to gain expertise in any three areas of the hotel and a solid working knowledge of all the others. He feels that achieving this has been an overriding factor in his career progression. He encourages future hoteliers "to take complete ownership and responsibility for your own career. Don't take promotions just for the sake of the promotion; be selective of the moves that you make. Each move should be weighed against the potential that it will have in growing your career."

with the engineering and housekeeping departments, is another responsibility of this position. Often a hotel rents parking spaces to local businesses and professional people, and the associated accounting process involves accurate billing and recording of funds and subsequent deposits. The parking garage manager also must develop budgets and recruit and train employees. He or she often provides driver assistance to guests when their cars break down and directional information to departing guests. Even though these jobs may seem small in the overall operation of a lodging property, they build a strong foundation in providing service to the guest.

Organization of the Front Office Department

Typical Front Office Organization

The organization chart in Figure 2-5 depicts a typical organization of staff for a front office manager. The staff includes desk clerk, cashier, reservations manager, concierge, night auditor, telephone operator, bell staff, and elevator operator. Not all of these positions are found in every lodging establishment. In some operations, the front desk clerk acts as desk clerk, cashier, telephone operator, and reservations clerk, as required by the volume of business. Many large full-service hotels, in contrast, employ the complete staff as listed.

FIGURE 2-5 **This organization chart lists positions found in a front office.**

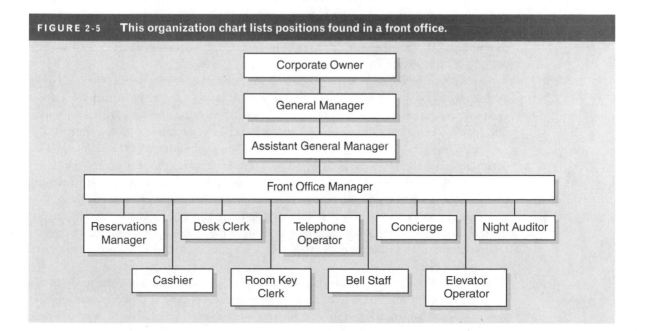

Staffing the front desk positions incurs a cost. The front office manager, in consultation with the general manager, usually prepares a personnel budget related to salary levels throughout the lodging establishment.

The responsibilities of the front office staff are quite varied. The position of the *desk clerk* can encompass many duties, which typically include verifying guest reservations, registering guests, assigning rooms, distributing keys, communicating with the housekeeping staff, answering telephones, providing information about and directions to local attractions, accepting cash and giving change, and acting as liaison between the lodging establishment and the guest as well as the community.

The responsibilities of a *cashier* include processing guest checkouts and guest legal tender and providing change for guests. This position is found in a number of lodging establishments, and it helps make the front desk workload manageable when a *full house*—a hotel that has *all* of its entire guest rooms occupied (sometimes referred to as *100 percent occupancy*)—is checking out. Given the possibility that every attendee of a 400-guest convention could check out within a few hours, this division of labor is a well-planned concept. Even with the best-planned systems—such as *express checkout*, whereby the guest uses computer technology in a guest room or a computer in the hotel lobby to check out; *prior approved credit*, the use of a credit card to establish creditworthiness; or *bill-to-account*, an internal billing process—the lines at the cashier station can be long and seem longer when a guest is in a hurry.

The *reservations manager* can be found in many of the larger lodging establishments. This person is responsible for taking incoming requests for rooms and noting special requests for service. The particulars of this position are endless, aimed at providing the guest with requested information and services as well as accurate confirmation of these items. The reservations manager is responsible for keeping an accurate room inventory by using the reservation module of a property management system. This person must communicate effectively with the marketing and sales department. Peak as well as slow periods of sales must be addressed with adequate planning.

The *night auditor* balances the daily financial transactions. This person may also serve as desk clerk for the night shift (11:00 P.M. to 7:00 A.M.). He or she must have a good grasp of accounting principles and the ability to resolve financial discrepancies. This position requires experience as a desk clerk and good communications with the controller.

The *telephone operator* has a very important job in the lodging establishment. This person must be able to locate both registered guests and management staff at a moment's notice. He or she also must be able to deal with crises up to and including life-threatening emergencies. With the introduction of *call accounting*, a computer technology application that tracks guest phone calls and posts billing charges to lodging establishments, the telephone operator's job has been simplified, as the tracking of telephone charges to registered guests can now be done with ease. This person may also assist the desk clerk and cashier when necessary.

The *bell captain*, with a staff of bellhops and door attendants, is a mainstay in the lodging establishment. The *bell staff* starts where the computerized property management system stops. They are the people who lift and tote baggage, familiarize guests with their

FIGURE 2-6

The concierge
provides
information
on tourist
attractions and
entertainment
in the area to
hotel guests.
Photo courtesy
of Wyndham
Reading Hotel,
Reading,
Pennsylvania.

new surroundings, run errands, deliver supplies, and provide guests with information on in-house marketing efforts and local attractions. These people also act as the hospitality link between the lodging establishment and guests. They are an asset to a well-run lodging establishment.

The *elevator operator*, a person who manually operates the mechanical controls of the elevator, is almost extinct in the lodging establishment, replaced by self-operated elevators and escalators. Some elevator operators now serve as *traffic managers*, who direct hotel guests to available elevators in the lobby. In large full-service hotels, the traffic manager can be a welcome sight; the confusion of check-ins and checkouts can be lessened when he or she is on duty.

The *concierge* (Figure 2-6) provides guests with extensive information on entertainment, sports, amusements, transportation, tours, church services, and babysitting in the area. He or she must know the area intimately and be able to meet the individual needs of each guest. This person also obtains theater tickets and makes reservations in restaurants. In most cases, the concierge is stationed at a desk in the lobby of the lodging property.

Select-service Hotel Front Office Organization

The organization chart in Figure 2-7 portrays a simpler workforce than that seen with a full-service property. The desk clerks perform multiple duties such as reservations and registrations, and they act as cashiers, telephone operators, and so forth. Whatever guest need is presented, the front desk clerk is called on to meet it with efficiency and

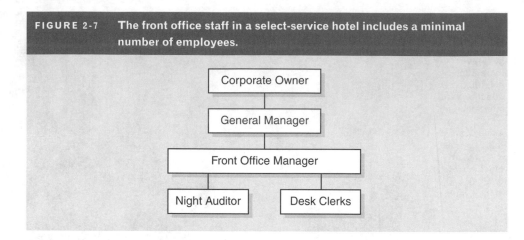

FIGURE 2-7   The front office staff in a select-service hotel includes a minimal number of employees.

professionalism. In select-service properties, the general manager may also assist, when needed, to process reservation requests, check guests in upon arrival, and check guests out upon departure.

The night auditor's role in a select-service property is unlike that of his or her counterpart in a full-service hotel. Because there are usually no departmental transactions from restaurants, banquets, lounges, gift shops, or spas, the night auditor is mainly concerned with posting room and tax charges and preparing statistics for the hotel. With the utilization of computer technology, the completion of the night audit has been reduced to a minimum of time. As previously mentioned, this task may be performed early in the morning prior to guest checkouts.

Function of the Front Office Manager

A successful front office manager conveys the spirit of a particular lodging property to the customer. By applying management principles, he or she works through the front office staff to communicate feelings of warmth, caring, safety, and efficiency to each guest. The front office manager must train personnel in the technical aspects of the *property management system (PMS)*, a hotel computer system that networks the software and hardware used in reservation and registration databases, point-of-sale systems, accounting systems, and other office software. He or she also must maintain the delicate balance between delivery of hospitality and service and promotion of the profit centers, and maintain the details of the communication system.

The front office manager has at his or her disposal the basic elements of effective management practice: employees, equipment, inventory (rooms to be sold), a budget, and sales opportunities. This manager is responsible for coordinating these basic elements to achieve the profit goals of the lodging property.

Front office employees must be trained properly to function within the guidelines and policies of the lodging establishment. The front office manager cannot assume that an employee knows how to do certain tasks. Every employee needs instruction and guidance in how to provide hospitality; front office employees' attitudes are of utmost importance to the industry. To ensure the proper attitude prevails, employers must cultivate an atmosphere in which employees are motivated to excel and that nurtures their morale and teamwork.

The property management system gives the front office manager an unlimited opportunity for managerial control. He or she can easily track information such as ZIP codes of visitors, frequency of visits by corporate guests, and amount of revenue a particular conference generated, and pass this information on to the marketing and sales department.

An unsold guest room is a sales opportunity lost forever. This is one of the major challenges of the front office manager. Cooperation between the marketing and sales department and the front office is necessary to develop profitable advertising and point-of-sale strategies. The subsequent training of front office personnel to seize every opportunity to sell vacant rooms helps ensure the financial goals of the lodging property are met.

Budgetary guidelines must be developed by the front office manager and the general manager, as the front office manager does have a large dollar volume under his or her control. The budgeting of money for payroll and supplies, the opportunity for improving daily sales, and accurate recording of guest charges require the front office manager to apply managerial skills.

The foremost concept that characterizes a front office manager is *team player*. The front office manager does not labor alone to meet the profit goals of the lodging property. The general manager sets the goals, objectives, and standards for all departments to follow. The assistant manager offers the department heads additional insight into meeting the operational needs of the establishment. The controller supplies valuable accounting information to the front office manager as feedback on current performance and meeting budgetary goals. The food and beverage manager, housekeeper, and plant engineer provide essential services to the guest. Without cooperation and communication among these departments and the front office, hospitality cannot be delivered. The director of marketing and sales develops programs to attract guests to the lodging property. These programs help the front office manager sell rooms. The human resources manager completes the team by providing the front office with competent personnel to accomplish the goals, objectives, and standards set by the general manager.

Job Analysis and Job Description

A *job analysis*, a detailed listing of the tasks of a job, provides the basis for a sound job description. A *job description* is a listing of required duties to be performed by an employee in a particular position. Although almost nothing is typical in the lodging industry, certain daily tasks must be performed. A job analysis is useful in that it allows the person preparing the job description to determine certain daily procedures. These procedures, along with typical responsibilities and interdepartmental relationships involved in a job, form the basis for the job description. The future professional will find this management tool helpful in preparing orientation and training programs for employees. It also helps the human resources department ensure each new hire is given every opportunity to succeed.

The following is the job analysis of a typical front office manager:

7:00 A.M.	Meets with the night auditor to discuss the activities of the previous night. Notes any discrepancies in balancing the night audit.
7:30	Meets with the reservation clerk to note the incoming reservations for the day.
8:00	Greets the first-shift desk clerks and passes along any information from the night auditor and reservation office. Assists desk clerks in guest checkout.
8:30	Meets with the housekeeper to identify potential problem areas of which the front office staff should be aware. Meets with the plant engineer to identify potential problem areas of which the front office staff should be aware.
9:00	Meets with the director of marketing and sales to discuss ideas for potential programs to increase sales. Discusses with the banquet manager details of groups that will be in-house for banquets and city ledger accounts that have left requests for billing disputes.
9:30	Checks with the chef to learn daily specials for the various restaurants. This information will be typed and distributed to the telephone operators.
9:45	Meets with the front office staff to discuss pertinent operational information for the day. Handles guest billing disputes.
11:00	Meets with the general manager to discuss the development of the next fiscal budget.
12:30 P.M.	Works on forecasting sheet for the coming week. Prepares preliminary schedule and anticipated payroll.
1:30	Has a lunch appointment with a corporate business client.
2:15	Works on *room blocking*—reserving rooms for guests who are holding reservations—for group reservations with the reservations clerk.
2:30	Works with the controller on budgetary targets for the next month. Receives feedback on budget targets from last month. Checks with the housekeeper on progress of room inspection and release.
2:45	Checks with the plant engineer on progress of plumbing repair for the eighteenth floor.
3:00	Greets the second-shift desk clerks and relays operational information on reservations, room assignments, room inventory, and the like.

3:15	Assists the front desk clerks in checking in a tour group.
4:00	Interviews two people for front desk clerk positions.
4:45	Assists the front desk clerks in checking in guests.
5:15	Reviews trade journal article on empowerment of employees.
5:45	Telephones the night auditor and communicates current information pertinent to tonight's audit.
6:00	Checks with the director of security for information concerning security coverage for the art exhibit in the ballroom.
6:30	Completes work order request forms for preventive maintenance on the front office posting machine.
6:45	Prepares "things to do" schedule for tomorrow.

This job analysis reveals that the front office manager has a busy schedule involving hands-on participation with the front office staff and communication with department heads throughout the lodging establishment. The front office manager must be able to project incomes and related expenses, to interview, and to interact with potential business clients.

Based on this job analysis, a job description for a front office manager is easily prepared, as shown in Figure 2-8. The job description is an effective management tool because it details the tasks and responsibilities required of the job holder. These guidelines allow the individual to apply management principles in the development of an effective front office department. They also challenge the person in the job to use prior experience and theoretical knowledge to accomplish the tasks at hand.

The Art of Supervising

The art of supervising employees encompasses volumes of text and years of experience. Management experts have analyzed the complexities of supervising employees. Some of your other management courses explain this vital management responsibility in detail. This chapter covers a few concepts that will assist you in developing your own supervisory style.

The first step in developing a supervisory style is to examine the manager's position in the context of the management team. As the front office manager, you are assigned certain responsibilities and granted certain areas of authority. These are areas for participation, growth, and limitation on and in the management team. Although this is a simplified overview of the management team, it does help clarify intended managerial performance.

Early in his or her new job, a manager should review personal career goals with this organization. The ports of entry to the position of general manager (described in chapter 1) will help an aspiring general manager clarify goals and understand which areas of the hotel will provide good exposure and experience. Once you have clarified your arena of participation and plan for growth, you can decide how best to lead a team to financial success and personal growth.

FIGURE 2-8   The job description is based on the job analysis of a front office manager.

JOB DESCRIPTION

Title: *Front Office Manager*
Reports to: *General Manager*

Typical duties:

1. Reviews final draft of night audit.

2. Operates and monitors reservation system for guest room rentals.

3. Develops and operates an effective communication system with front office staff.

4. Supervises daily operation of front office staff—reservations, registrations, and checkouts.

5. Participates with all department heads in an effective communications system facilitating the provision of guest services.

6. Plans and participates in the delivery of marketing programs for the sale of rooms and other hotel products and services.

7. Interfaces with various department heads and controller regarding billing disputes involving guests.

8. Develops final draft of budget for front office staff.

9. Prepares forecast of room sales for upcoming week, month, or other period as required.

10. Maintains business relationships with corporate community leaders.

11. Oversees the personnel management for the front office department.

12. Performs these and other duties as required.

Review cycle:

1 month   _____
                         (date)

3 months   _____
                         (date)

6 months   _____
                         (date)

1 year   _____
                         (date)

The first concept a new supervisor should address is employee motivation. What helps each employee perform at his or her best? The emphasis is on *each* employee; different incentives motivate different people. The better shift scheduling that motivates the second-shift desk clerk may have no effect on the part-time night auditor who is a *moonlighter*, a person who has a full-time job at another organization and a part-time job at a hotel, two days a week on your property. The young person who prefers the second shift (3:00–11:00 P.M.) because it better fits his or her lifestyle will not be inspired by the possibility of working the first shift. Tuition reimbursement may motivate the recent graduate of an associate degree program who wants to continue toward a four-year degree; this same benefit will mean little to someone uninterested in higher education. The possibility of promotion to reservations clerk may not have the same motivating effect on a telephone operator who is a recently displaced worker concerned about a schedule that meets the needs of a young family as it does on a front desk clerk who has no dependents. Sometimes a supervisor cannot figure out what motivates a person. It is a manager's ultimate challenge to discover how to motivate each member of his or her staff. By using this knowledge, a manager can promote not just the best interests of the employee but also the best interests of the hotel.

Another supervisory responsibility is to achieve a balance among varying personalities in a group work setting. This is a constant and evolving situation. Very often, a new supervisor does not have time to assess each employee's relationship with others on the team, yet these dynamics are key to establishing a positive and effective team setting. The front office staff may jockey for position with the new boss; this common situation must be addressed as part of the job. Once the new supervisor shows himself or herself capable and competent, he or she can move on to the day-to-day tasks. The staff needs this time to learn their new manager's reactions under stress. They also want to make sure their supervisor will be their advocate with top management. All new supervisors are tested in this way. You should not be discouraged by this challenge but rather embrace it as the first of many to come.

After working out whatever personality clashes exist among the employees, the manager must be objective about their strengths and weaknesses. Who is the unofficial leader of the group? Who is the agitator? Who is the complainer? Objective views of staff are probably shared by the rest of the team. Often staff members are quite aware of the shortcomings of their coworkers. They also know on whom they can rely to check out the full house and check in the convention three hours later. The unofficial leader of the group can assist the supervisor in conveying important ideas.

Some supervisors respond negatively to such accommodation of the staff. Their response is based on the assumption that the supervisor has the first and last word in all that goes on in the front office. Of course, authority is important, but any supervisor who wants to maintain authority and have objectives met by the staff must constantly rework his or her strategy.

Adequate personnel training (discussed in chapter 12) makes the job of a supervisor much easier. When training is planned, executed, and reinforced, the little annoyances of human error are minimized. As previously discussed, each job description lists the major duties of the employees, but the gray areas—handling complaints, delivering a positive image of the lodging property, selling other departments in the hotel, and covering for a new trainee—cannot be communicated in a job description. *On-the-job training*, employee training that takes place while producing a product or service, and videotape training are excellent methods for clarifying such tasks. These methods serve not only to demonstrate skills but also to communicate the financial goals, the objectives of hospitality and service, and the idiosyncrasies of the lodging property and the people who work in it.

Employees always have special scheduling needs as well as other job-related requests, and supervisors should try to accommodate them. The new hire who made commitments four to six months prior to accepting a position at the front desk will appreciate and return a supervisor's consideration. The individual who wants to change shifts because of difficulties with another person on the job may just need advice on how to handle that person. These individuals may make a good team, but they wear on each other's patience. A longtime employee might ask you how he or she can advance in the organization. You may not have an immediate response, but you can indicate you will act on the request in the near future. Sometimes employees know that a good thing takes time to develop. Listen to their needs; their requests may answer your problems by fitting into the demands of the job. For example, a desk clerk who needs additional income may request overtime hours. An opportunity may arise for this employee to fill a vacancy caused by another employee's illness or vacation.

The responsibility of communications within the hotel usually rests with the front office. From the guests' perspective, this department is the most visible part of the lodging establishment. The various departments in the hotel realize the transfer of information to guests is best done through the front office. When such communications fail to reach guests, it is often the front office that bears the brunt of their unhappiness at checkout time.

The more systematic the communication process, the better for all concerned. For example, messages that will affect the next shift of desk clerks can be recorded in the *message book*, a loose-leaf binder in which the front desk staff of any shift can record important messages. This communication tool is vital to keeping all front office personnel informed of additions, changes, and deletions of information and activities that affect the operation of a front office. Additionally, *daily function sheets*, which list the planned events in the hotel and their updates, must be delivered routinely to the front office. The daily function board or electronic bulletin board in guest rooms, available on in-room television or in public areas, is usually maintained by the front office. The guest who complains about the maintenance of a room must have the complaint passed to the right person. The complaint is then reviewed by a member of the staff, front office manager, member of the housekeeping staff, housekeeper, member of the maintenance staff, or maintenance director to ensure it is resolved.

Inquiries about hotel services, reservations, *city ledger accounts* (a collection of accounts receivable of nonregistered guests who use the services of the hotel), accounts payable, scheduled events, and messages for registered guests constitute only some of the many requests for information. Desk clerks and telephone operators are expected to know the answers to these questions or to whom they should be referred.

Some of this advice is based on my own experience. One of the jobs I was responsible for as a front desk clerk included operating the switchboard. This job was truly stressful, involving accuracy at every contact. Finding the right department head to meet the request of an incoming caller and ensuring messages are passed to guests are only two among the many tasks required every minute a person is on the job. If a message is conveyed inaccurately or if an employee fails to complete the communication process, hospitality is not projected to the guest.

Ways of applying employee empowerment concepts are explored in chapter 12. The contemporary front office manager needs extensive training and experience in this vital area to manage a workforce that delivers hospitality every day. Ensuring an employee can conduct business without constant approval from a supervisor is the goal of empowerment. The mastery of empowerment requires a supervisor to train employees and to practice much patience. Employees accustomed to direct supervision on all matters may not readily adapt to a work environment that requires independent thinking to address challenges.

Staffing the Front Office

The schedule for the front office staff is based on both budgetary targets and anticipation of guest check-ins and checkouts. An increase in the frequency of guest requests for information and front office services may affect the schedule. The front office manager must also determine labor costs by reviewing salaries and hourly wages and respective rates. The resulting figures show if the front office manager has adhered to the projected budget. Table 2-1 (page 70) shows how the costs for staffing are determined. Table 2-2 (page 72) compares these projected costs with the projected revenue generated by room rentals, which allows for a preevaluation of income and labor expenses.

The preparation of the front office schedule is broken into four steps. The first step requires the front office manager to estimate or forecast the needs of his or her department for a certain period. The front office manager must review the sales history of previous events, current functions, current reservations, anticipated walk-ins, stayovers, and checkouts for that period to determine their impact on the labor requirements for the workweek. As you can see from the listing of personnel in Step 1 (Table 2-1), all job categories are included so the front office manager can determine how each job will be affected.

Step 2 (Table 2-1), developing the schedule, is a twofold process that requires meeting both the needs of the lodging establishment and the needs of employees. The lodging establishment must deliver hospitality to the guest by remaining open 24 hours per day, seven days per week. Also, employees have personal requests for time off as well as the needs to work around family responsibilities and to put in more or less time depending on financial motivation.

Step 3 (Table 2-1), calculating the anticipated payroll, requires the front office manager to price out each category of employee. This allows the manager to determine how much money he or she has spent against the predicted income sales.

TABLE 2-1   Front Office Scheduling Process

Step 1. Estimate Needs (Review Front Office Forecast First)

	10/1	10/2	10/3	10/4	10/5	10/6	10/7
Desk Clerks							
Night Auditors							
Cashiers							
Concierges							
Telephone Operators							
Bell Captain							
Bellhops							

Step 2. Develop Schedule

	10/1	10/2	10/3	10/4	10/5	10/6	10/7
Desk 1	7–3	7–3	7–3	7–3	X	X	7–3
Desk 2	9–5	X	9–2	10–6	X	7–3	9–Noon
Desk 3	3–11	3–11	3–11	3–11	3–11	X	X
Desk 4	X	X	X	3–7	7–3	3–11	3–11
Aud. 1	11–7	11–7	11–7	X	X	11–7	11–7
Aud. 2	X	X	X	11–7	11–7	X	X
Cash.	8–Noon	X	9–2	9–Noon	X	X	11–3
Concierge 1	Noon–8	Noon–8	Noon–8	Noon–5	Noon–5	X	X
Concierge 2	X	X	X	X	X	Noon–5	Noon–8
Tel. 1	7–3	X	X	7–3	7–3	7–3	7–3
Tel. 2	3–11	3–11	3–11	X	X	3–11	3–11
Tel. 3	X	7–3	7–3	3–11	3–11	X	X
Bell Capt.	7–3	7–3	7–3	7–3	X	7–3	X
Hop 1	9–5	X	X	10–6	7–3	3–11	7–3
Hop 2	3–11	X	3–11	3–11	3–11	X	3–11
Hop 3	X	3–11	8–2	X	X	X	11–5

Step 3. Calculate Anticipated Payroll

Category: Desk Clerk = $1,300.00

	10/1	10/2	10/3	10/4	10/5	10/6	10/7
	8 hrs. @ $ 9.50 = $ 76.00 8 hrs. @ $11.00 = $ 88.00 8 hrs. @ $ 8.00 = $ 64.00 $228.00	8 hrs. @ $ 9.50 = $ 76.00 8 hrs. @ $11.00 = $ 88.00 $164.00	8 hrs. @ $ 9.50 = $ 76.00 8 hrs. @ $11.00 = $ 88.00 5 hrs. @ $ 8.00 = $ 40.00 $204.00	8 hrs. @ $ 9.50 = $ 76.00 8 hrs. @ $11.00 = $ 88.00 8 hrs. @ $ 8.00 = $ 64.00 4 hrs. @ $ 8.00 = $ 32.00 $260.00	8 hrs. @ $ 8.00 = $ 64.00 8 hrs. @ $11.00 = $ 88.00 $152.00	8 hrs. @ $ 8.00 = $ 64.00 8 hrs. @ $ 8.00 = $ 64.00 $128.00	8 hrs. @ $ 9.50 = $ 76.00 8 hrs. @ $ 8.00 = $ 64.00 3 hrs. @ $ 8.00 = $ 24.00 $164.00

Category: Night Auditor = $704.00

	10/1	10/2	10/3	10/4	10/5	10/6	10/7
	8 hrs. @ $13.00 = $104.00 $104.00	8 hrs. @ $13.00 = $104.00 $104.00	8 hrs. @ $13.00 = $104.00 $104.00	8 hrs. @ $11.50 = $ 92.00 $ 92.00	8 hrs. @ $11.50 = $ 92.00 $ 92.00	8 hrs. @ $13.00 = $104.00 $104.00	8 hrs. @ $13.00 = $104.00 $104.00

Category: Cashier = $128.00

	10/1	10/2	10/3	10/4	10/5	10/6	10/7
	4 hrs. @ $ 8.00 = $ 32.00 $ 32.00	0 hrs. @ $ 0.00 = $ 0.00 $ 0.00	5 hrs. @ $ 8.00 = $ 40.00 $ 40.00	3 hrs. @ $ 8.00 = $ 24.00 $ 24.00	0 hrs. @ $ 0.00 = $ 0.00 $ 0.00	0 hrs. @ $ 0.00 = $ 0.00 $ 0.00	4 hrs. @ $ 8.00 = $ 32.00 $ 32.00

Category: Concierge = $501.00

	10/1	10/2	10/3	10/4	10/5	10/6	10/7
	8 hrs. @ $11.00 = $ 88.00 $ 88.00	8 hrs. @ $11.00 = $ 88.00 $ 88.00	8 hrs. @ $11.00 = $ 88.00 $ 88.00	5 hrs. @ $11.00 = $ 55.00 $ 55.00	5 hrs. @ $11.00 = $ 55.00 $ 55.00	5 hrs. @ $11.00 = $ 55.00 $ 55.00	8 hrs. @ $ 9.00 = $ 72.00 $ 72.00

Category: Telephone Operator = $920.00

	10/1	10/2	10/3	10/4	10/5	10/6	10/7
	8 hrs. @ $ 8.00 = $ 64.00 8 hrs. @ $ 9.00 = $ 72.00 $136.00	8 hrs. @ $ 8.00 = $ 64.00 8 hrs. @ $ 7.50 = $ 60.00 $124.00	8 hrs. @ $ 7.50 = $ 60.00 8 hrs. @ $ 9.00 = $ 72.00 $132.00	8 hrs. @ $ 8.00 = $ 64.00 8 hrs. @ $ 7.50 = $ 60.00 $124.00	8 hrs. @ $ 8.00 = $ 64.00 8 hrs. @ $ 7.50 = $ 60.00 $124.00	8 hrs. @ $ 8.00 = $ 64.00 8 hrs. @ $ 9.00 = $ 72.00 $136.00	8 hrs. @ $ 8.00 = $ 64.00 8 hrs. @ $ 9.00 = $ 72.00 $136.00

Category: Bell Staff = $720.00

	10/1	10/2	10/3	10/4	10/5	10/6	10/7
	8 hrs. @ $ 7.00 = $ 56.00 8 hrs. @ $ 7.50 = $ 60.00 $116.00	8 hrs. @ $ 7.00 = $ 56.00 8 hrs. @ $ 7.50 = $ 60.00 $116.00	6 hrs. @ $ 7.00 = $ 42.00 8 hrs. @ $ 7.50 = $ 60.00 $102.00	8 hrs. @ $ 7.00 = $ 56.00 8 hrs. @ $ 7.50 = $ 60.00 $116.00	8 hrs. @ $ 7.00 = $ 56.00 8 hrs. @ $ 7.50 = $ 60.00 $116.00	8 hrs. @ $ 7.00 = $ 56.00 $ 56.00	8 hrs. @ $ 7.00 = $ 56.00 8 hrs. @ $ 7.50 = $ 60.00 6 hrs. @ $ 7.00 = $ 42.00 $158.00

Category: Salaries—Front Office = $1,757.00

Front Office Manager: $807/wk. Reservations Manager: $575/wk. Bell Captain: $375/wk.

Step 4. Summary

Desk Clerks	$1300.00
Night Auditors	704.00
Cashiers	128.00
Concierges	501.00
Telephone Operators	920.00
Bell Staff	720.00
Salaries	1757.00
Subtotal	$6030.00
Taxes/Fringe Benefits	× .27
	= $1628.10
	+ 6030.00
Total Projected Payroll for Week	$7658.10

TABLE 2-2 **Comparison of Projected Income from Weekly Room Sales and Projected Weekly Payroll**

	10/1	10/2	10/3	10/4	10/5	10/6	10/7
Yesterday's sales	135	97	144	147	197	210	213
Departures	−125	−10	−72	−75	−5	−15	−125
Stayovers	10	87	72	72	192	195	88
Arrivals	+72	+40	+50	+125	+10	+15	35+
Walk-ins	+20	+20	+30	+10	+10	+5	+50
No-shows	−5	−3	−5	−10	−2	−2	−3
Number Sold	97	144	147	197	210	213	170

Total rooms sold (sum of number sold each day)   1178

Income from rooms sold (at average daily rate of $75.00) $88,350.00

Projected payroll budget (from weekly estimate, Table 2-1) $ 7658.10

Percentage of income required for payroll ([payroll × 100] ÷ income) 8.66%

Step 4 (Table 2-1), summarizing costs by category, involves grouping costs by category for each subdepartment in the front office. This total payroll figure is needed to compare projected income for weekly room sales and weekly payroll. Table 2-2, Comparison of Projected Income from Weekly Room Sales and Projected Weekly Payroll, allows the front office manager, general manager, and controller to anticipate financial performance in a hotel for a certain time frame. As you can see, room sales are tracked from Yesterday, Departures, and Stayovers, while Arrivals, Walk-ins, and No-shows are projected.

The information in Table 2-2 allows the front office manager to be more effective. He or she has the opportunity to review and adjust data for departures, stayovers, arrivals, and walk-ins, which affects the number of rooms sold each night. For example, if the front office manager realizes that on a certain day at 6:30 P.M. there are 25 vacant rooms and no more confirmed or guaranteed reservations are being held, desk clerks can be empowered to negotiate a reasonable room rate with guests to obtain their business (in order to secure a full house). If there were three vacant rooms and eight guaranteed reservations being held, desk clerks would not be so empowered.

Solution to Opening Dilemma

Communication in a hotel is essential to efficiency, delivery of high-quality service, and making a profit. In this case, the front office staff failed to place a room block in the computer system for the additional 26 rooms. Does this happen frequently in the hotel business? Unfortunately, it does. However, the delivery of high-quality service is dependent on the upkeep of a hotel's physical property, and this is an important operational procedure. The front office manager and the director of housekeeping must cooperate in setting up times for taking guest rooms out of available inventory. The front office manager must be made aware of the costs involved in contracted services and work in partnership with the director of housekeeping.

Chapter Recap

This chapter outlined the organizational structure of lodging properties and typical job responsibilities of department managers. Specific analysis of the role of the front office manager revealed many related concepts. Success in providing effective supervision begins with a review of the resources available to the front office manager, such as employees, equipment, room inventory, finances, and sales opportunities. After analyzing these resources, the front office manager can direct the department more effectively; the objectives of making a profit and delivering hospitality to the guest can be achieved more easily.

The functional role of the front office manager can be understood by preparing a job analysis and job description. This process allows the future professional to see the major responsibilities of the job and the departmental relationships involved. The many positions found in a front office staff have the common goal of providing hospitality to the guest. Training, empowerment, and flexibility are necessary to make the team work.

Forecasting, scheduling, developing a supervisory style, motivating personnel, balancing staff personalities, delegating tasks, training, and effectively communicating are only a few of the skills a good supervisor must master. This lifelong effort is developed through continuing education and trial and error.

End-of-Chapter Questions

1. If you are employed in the hotel industry, sketch the organization chart of the property where you work. Have you seen this hierarchy change since you have been employed there? If so, what do you think caused this change? For those students who are not employed in the hotel industry, interview one of your classmates who is employed in the lodging industry about their departmental hierarchy, and briefly sketch their organization chart of their department.

2. Compare the organization of a full-service hotel and a select-service hotel. How can a select-service property operate with such a seemingly minimal staff?

3. If you are employed in the hotel industry, describe the tasks your general manager performs daily. Describe the tasks your department director performs daily. What relationship do these positions have to the overall success of the hotel? For those students who are not employed in the hotel industry, interview one of your classmates who is employed in the lodging industry about what they think their general manager does on a daily basis, and prepare a 50-word summary of the interview.

4. How are the positions in a front office organized? Describe the positions found at the front office in a full-service hotel. Which positions are most crucial to providing guest service?

5. If you have ever worked in the front office in a lodging property, summarize what you think the front office manager does. If you have not worked in a front office of a hotel, you might want to visit with a front office manager and ask for insight into this position.

6. What resources are available to the front office manager? Rank the importance of these resources in providing service to guests and supervising employees.

7. How does the front office manager relate to other members of the hotel management staff? Give examples.

8. Why should a job analysis be performed prior to preparing a job description? Do you think this procedure is necessary? Why or why not?

9. What are the four steps required in preparing a schedule?

10. How do you think your supervisor developed his or her supervisory style? What dó you think will be the basis in developing your supervisory style?

11. What does the expression *the art of supervision* mean to you? Reflect on your answer and highlight which concepts are important to your future supervisory style.

12. Why does trying to understand individual motivation help in supervising?

13. What are some personality clashes you have noticed where you work? How did your supervisor handle them? Would you have handled them differently if you were the supervisor?

14. Generally speaking, what benefits can a well-trained front office person offer the front office manager?

15. Give examples of how the front office is responsible for communication with other departments, with hotel guests, and with the public.

CASE STUDY 201

Ana Chavarria, front office manager, has been with The Times Hotel for several years. She recalls her first few months as a time of great stress. Milo Diaz, the personnel manager, was always calling her to post her schedules on time and authorize payroll forms. Thomas Brown, the executive housekeeper, seemed a great friend off the premises of the hotel, but at work, he continually badgered the front desk clerks on guest check-in and checkout problems. Yoon-Whan Li, executive engineer, also had communication problems with Ana, such as the time a desk clerk called Yoon-Whan at home to say an elevator was stuck on the fourth floor when it was only manually stopped by a group of children. Eric Jones, the food and beverage manager, blamed Ana's desk clerks because hotel guests were not frequenting the dining room and lounge, asking her, "When will the desk clerks ever learn to talk about those free coupons for the dining room and lounge that they so stoically hand out?" Then there was Lorraine DeSantes, director of marketing and sales, who had just about all she could take from desk clerks who misplaced phone messages, directed hotel guests to restaurants across the street, and offered information on "a good restaurant right around the corner."

Ana has taken those comments to heart and feels she can justify her shortcomings and those of her staff. She knows the schedules are to be posted by Tuesday morning of each week, but several of her employees give her last-minute requests for days off. Her payroll forms are usually delayed because she wants to spend time with guests who are registering or checking out. The front desk clerks have made major errors in checking guests into rooms that are not ready, but she offers, "It must be that the computer system gives them the wrong information." The elevator issue wasn't the front desk clerk's fault; it was his third night on the job, and no one had thought to explain what constitutes an emergency call to the executive engineer. She wants her front desk clerks to distribute those food and beverage coupons, but they just don't get excited about it. And Lorraine DeSantes's messages are always given to her; "She just makes no attempt to look in her mailbox."

She also remembered when Margaret Chu, general manager of The Times Hotel, asked her to visit in her office. She let Ana know that her six-month probationary period would be over in one month and it was time to discuss Ana's progress before a permanent offer was made. Ana was uneasy, knowing her colleagues had reported major errors on her behalf. However, Margaret Chu took an approach that was different from that of other general managers with whom Ana had worked. Ms. Chu asked her to prepare a list of strategies to use in working toward improvement in the following areas:

- Employee motivation
- Personnel training
- Effective scheduling of employees
- Communication
- Empowerment

Ms. Chu has asked you to assist Ana in developing strategies to use for improving her ability in the art of supervising employees. What would you suggest?

CASE STUDY 202

A local hotel developer has called you to assist her corporation in designing job descriptions for a new hotel. This is the corporation's first venture into the hotel business, so the developer wants you to be explicit in writing the job descriptions. The hotel is similar to the 500+-room full-service hotel depicted

(*continues*)

CASE STUDY 202 *(CONTINUED)*

in Figure 2-1. Prepare job descriptions for the following management positions:

- General manager
- Front office manager

- Executive housekeeper
- Food and beverage director
- Assistant general manager
- Facilities manager

CASE STUDY 203

Ana Chavarria, front office manager, Milo Diaz, the personnel manager, and Thomas Brown, executive housekeeper, want to design a simple but effective training program titled "The Art of Supervising" for their new front-line supervisors. Use information provided in this chapter to suggest an outline they might use. Remember to keep it simple.

Key Words

accounts payable	corporate guests
accounts receivable	daily function sheet
assistant general manager	desk clerk
athletics director	director of marketing and sales
average daily rate (ADR)	director of security
balance sheet	elevator operator
bell captain	executive housekeeper
bell staff	express checkout
bill-to-account	floor inspector
business services and communications center	food and beverage director
call accounting	front office manager
cashier	full house
city ledger accounts	general ledger
collective bargaining unit	general manager
concierge	human resources manager
continental breakfast	in-house laundry
controller	job analysis
convention guests	job description
	maintenance manager

message book

moonlighter

night audit

night auditor

on-the-job training

operational reports

organization chart

parking garage manager

percent occupancy

percent yield

plant engineer

prior approved credit

profit-and-loss statement

property management system (PMS)

rack rate

recreation director

referral reservation service

reservations manager

room attendants

room blocking

statement of cash flows

team player

telephone operator

total quality management (TQM)

traffic managers

working supervisors

CHAPTER 3

Effective Interdepartmental Communications

- Role of the front office in establishing and maintaining effective communications with other departments

- Discussion and application of total quality management techniques used in improving interdepartmental communication

OPENING DILEMMA

The leader of a workshop in one of the conference rooms is uneasy about his program today. After noticing the connection for the teleconference is not working, he stops by the front desk and asks if the convention representative can come to the conference room. The desk clerk on duty offers to locate the convention representative and send her to the room. After the workshop leader leaves the front desk area, the desk clerk remarks, "You would think we have to be all things to all people at all times!"

Role of the Front Office in Interdepartmental Communications

The front office plays a pivotal role in delivering hospitality to guests. It sets the stage for a pleasant or an unpleasant visit. Guests, often in an unfamiliar setting and wanting to proceed with their business or vacation plans, are eager to learn the who, what, when, where, and how of their new environment. Requests for information often begin with the bellhop, switchboard operator, front desk clerk, cashier, or concierge, because these employees are the most visible to the guest and are perceived to be the most knowledgeable. These employees are believed to have their finger on the pulse of the organization and the community. Their responses to guests' requests for information on public transportation, location of hotel facilities, special events in the community, and the like indicate how well the hotel has prepared them for this important role. Front office managers must take an active part in gathering information of interest to guests. They must also be active in developing procedures for the front office to disburse this information.

The relationships the front office manager develops with the other department directors and their employees are vital to gathering information for guests. Developing positive personal relationships is part of the communication process, but it cannot be relied on to ensure accurate and current information is relayed. How does the front office manager encourage effective *interdepartmental communication* (communication between departments)? This chapter provides relevant background for you as you begin your professional career. It is important to note that this discussion is applicable to *intradepartmental communication* (communication inside a department) as well.

Figure 3-1 shows the departments in a hotel that interact with the front office. The front office is at the center of the diagram to illustrate the many interdepartmental lines of communication. These lines are based on the direction each department is given to provide hospitality in the form of clean rooms, properly operating equipment, safe environment, well-prepared food and beverages, efficient table service, and professional organization and delivery of service for a scheduled function as well as accurate accounting of guest charges and the like. These general objectives help department directors organize their operations and meet the overall goal of delivering professional hospitality. However, in reality, constant effort is required to manage the details of employees, materials, procedures, and communication skills to produce acceptable products and services.

Front Office Interaction with Other Departments in the Hotel

The front office staff interacts with all departments of the hotel, including marketing and sales, housekeeping, food and beverage, banquet, controller, maintenance, security, and human resources. These departments view the front office as a communication liaison in providing guest services. Each of the departments has a unique communication link with the front office staff. The front office in any type of lodging property provides the face and voice of hospitality for the organization around the clock. Guests are most likely

FIGURE 3-1 The front office serves as a clearinghouse for communication activities.

to approach the front office staff for connections to staff in other departments. As you review the following lodging facility departments, try to grasp the role of the front office in communication with each. As shown in Figure 3-1, the front office is a clearinghouse for communication activities. The members of the front office team must know to whom they can direct guest inquiries for assistance. They learn this by means of a thorough training program in in-house policy and procedures and a constant concern for providing hospitality to the guest.

Marketing and Sales Department

The marketing and sales department relies on the front office to provide data on *guest histories*, or details concerning each guest's visit. Some of the information gathered is based on ZIP code, frequency of visits, corporate affiliation, special needs, reservations for sleeping rooms, and social media such as postings on Facebook, messages from Twitter, and visits to websites or YouTube. It is also the front office's job to make a good first impression on the public, to relay messages, and to meet the requests of guests who are using the hotel for meetings, seminars, and banquets.

The guest history is a valuable resource for marketing and sales, which uses guest registration information to target marketing campaigns, develop promotions, prepare mailing labels, and select appropriate advertising media. The front office staff must make every effort to keep this database current and accurate.

The process of completing the booking of a special function (such as a wedding reception, convention, or seminar) depends on the availability of sleeping rooms for guests.

The marketing and sales executives may have to check the lists of available rooms three or six months or even a year in the future to be sure the hotel can accommodate the expected number of guests. A database of available rooms is maintained in the property management system by the front office.

The first guest contact with the marketing and sales department is usually through the hotel's switchboard. A competent switchboard operator who is friendly and knowledgeable about hotel operations and personnel makes a good first impression, conveying to the prospective client that the hotel is competent. When the guest finally arrives for the function, the first actual contact with the hotel is usually through the front office staff. The front office manager who makes the effort to determine which banquet supervisor is in charge and communicates that information to the desk clerk on duty demonstrates to the public that this hotel is dedicated to providing hospitality.

Messages for the marketing and sales department must be relayed completely, accurately, and quickly. The switchboard operator is a vital link in the communication between the prospective client and a salesperson in the marketing and sales department. The front office manager should instruct all new front office personnel about the staff in the marketing and sales department and what each person's job entails. (This applies to all departments in the hotel, not just marketing and sales, as explained in chapter 12.) Front office employees should know how to pronounce the names of all marketing and sales employees. To help front office staff become familiar with all these people, managers should show new employees pictures of the department directors and supervisors.

Requests for service at meetings, seminars, banquets, and the like are often made at the front office. The *banquet manager*, the person responsible for fulfilling the details of service for a banquet or special event, or a *sales associate*, who books the guest's requirements for banquets and other special events, might be busy with another function. If a guest needs an extension cord or if an electrical outlet malfunctions, the front desk staff must be ready to meet the guest's needs. The front office manager should establish standard operating procedures for front office employees to contact maintenance, housekeeping, marketing and sales, or the food and beverage department to meet other common requests. Knowing how to find a small toolkit, adapters, adhesive materials, extra table covers, or window cleaner will help the guest and save the time involved in tracking down the salesperson in charge.

Housekeeping Department

Housekeeping and the front office communicate about *housekeeping room status*, the report on the availability of the rooms for immediate guest occupancy. Housekeeping room status can be described in the following communication terms:

- Available Clean or Ready—room is ready to be occupied
- Occupied—guest or guests are already occupying a room
- Stayover—guest will not be checking out of a room on the current day

- Dirty or On Change—guest has checked out of the room, but the housekeeping staff has not released the room for occupancy
- Out of Order—room is not available for occupancy because of a mechanical malfunction

Housekeeping and the front office also communicate on the details of potential *house count* (a report of the number of guests registered in the hotel), security concerns, and requests for *amenities* (personal toiletry items such as shampoo, toothpaste, and mouth-wash; electrical equipment). These issues are of immediate concern to the guest as well as to supervisors in the hotel.

Reporting of room status is handled on a face-to-face basis in a hotel that does not use a property management system (PMS). The bi-hourly or hourly visits of the housekeeper to the front desk clerk are a familiar scene in such a hotel. The official reporting of room status at the end of the day is accomplished with a *housekeeper's room report*—a report prepared by the housekeeper that lists the guest room occupancy status as vacant, occupied, or out of order. Sometimes even regular reporting of room status is not adequate, as guests may be anxiously awaiting the opportunity to occupy a room. On these occasions, the front desk clerk must telephone the floor supervisor to determine when the servicing of a room will be completed.

The housekeeper relies on the *room sales projections*—a weekly report prepared and distributed by the front office manager that indicates the expected number of departures, arrivals, walk-ins, stayovers, and no-shows—to schedule employees. Timely distribution of the room sales projections assists the executive housekeeper in planning employee personal leaves and vacation days.

The front desk also relies on housekeeping personnel to report unusual circumstances that may indicate a violation of security for the guests. For example, if a maid or house-man notices obviously unregistered guests on a floor, a fire exit that has been propped open, or sounds of a domestic disturbance in a guest room, he or she must report these potential security violations to the front office. The front office staff, in turn, relays the information to the proper in-house or civil authority. The front office manager may direct front desk clerks and switchboard operators to call floor supervisors periodically to check activity on the guest floors.

Guest requests for additional or special amenities and guest room supplies may be initiated at the front desk. The prompt relay of requests for extra blankets, towels, soap, and shampoo to housekeeping is essential. This is hospitality at its best. More examples of communication between the housekeeping and front office departments are presented in chapter 15.

Food and Beverage Department

Communication between the food and beverage department and the front office is essential. *Transfers*, which are forms for communicating charges to a guest's account, are used to relay messages and provide accurate information. Communication activities also include reporting *predicted house counts*, an estimate of the number of guests expected

Michael DeCaire was the food and beverage manager at the Houston Hilton, Houston, Texas. His previous experience included positions as executive chef at the Park Hotel in Charlotte, North Carolina; executive and executive sous chef at the Pacific Star Hotel on the island of Guam; and executive sous chef at the Greenleaf Resort in Haines City, Florida.

Mr. DeCaire relied on the front desk for accurate forecasting of arrivals, notification of VIPs and Hilton Honors Club members, communication of complaints and positive comments concerning food and service, and processing of guest bills. He also worked with the front desk to obtain a thorough knowledge of the needs and location of banquet and meeting guests through a ten-day forecast of banquet and meeting events.

The communication emphasis at the Houston Hilton extended into a nine-week cross-training program in which all departments (food and beverage, front desk, housekeeping, sales, etc.) participated in learning the basics of each department. This training effort allowed the salesperson to appreciate the duties of a cook, the waiter or waitress to understand the duties of a front desk clerk, and the front desk clerk to value the duties of a housekeeper. Another area of cooperative training efforts was fire command post training.

Mr. DeCaire offered the following advice for students wanting to make a career in the hotel industry: Take an entry-level job in the hospitality industry so you can understand the work requirements of weekends, holidays, and nights prior to investing in a college education. This effort will pay big dividends for your career growth.

to register based on previous occupancy activities, and processing requests for *paid-outs*, forms used to indicate amounts of money paid out of the cashier's drawer on behalf of a guest or an employee of the hotel. These vital services help an overworked food and beverage manager, restaurant manager, or banquet captain meet the demands of the public.

Incoming messages for the food and beverage manager and executive chef from vendors and other industry representatives are important to the business operation of the food and beverage department. If the switchboard operator is given instructions on screening callers (such as times when the executive chef cannot be disturbed because of a busy workload or staff meetings, or vendors in whom the chef is not interested), the important messages can receive top priority.

In a hotel that has *point-of-sale terminals*, computerized cash registers that interface with a property management system, information on guest charges is automatically posted to a guest's *folio*—his or her record of charges and payments. When a hotel does not have such terminals, the desk clerk is responsible for posting accurate charges on the guest folio and relies on transfer slips. The night auditor's job is made easier if the transfer slip is accurately prepared and posted. The front office manager should work with the food and beverage director in developing standard operating procedures and methods to complete the transfer of charges.

The supervisors in the food and beverage department rely on the predicted house count prepared by the front office manager to schedule employees and predict sales. For example, the restaurant supervisor working the breakfast shift needs to know how many guests will be in the hotel so he or she can determine how many servers to schedule for breakfast service. Timely and accurate preparation of this communication tool assists in staffing control and sales predictions.

Authorized members of the food and beverage department occasionally ask the front office for cash, in the form of a pay-out to purchase last-minute items for a banquet, the lounge, or the restaurant or to take advantage of unplanned opportunities to promote hospitality. Specific guidelines concerning cash limits, turnaround time, prior approval, authorized signatures, and purchase receipts are developed by the general manager and front office manager. These guidelines help maintain control of pay-outs.

Banquet Department

The banquet department, which often combines the functions of a marketing and sales department and a food and beverage department, requires the front office to relay information to guests about scheduled events and bill payment.

The front desk staff may also provide labor to prepare the *daily announcement board*, an inside listing of the daily activities of the hotel (time, group, and room assignment), and *marquee*, the curbside message board, which includes the logo of the hotel and space for a message. Because the majority of banquet guests may not be registered guests in the hotel, the front office is a logical communications center.

A daily posting on a felt board or an electronic bulletin board provides all guests and employees with information on scheduled group events. The preparation of the marquee may include congratulatory, welcome, sales promotion, or other important messages. In some hotels, an employee in the front office contacts the marketing and sales department for the message.

The banquet guest who is unfamiliar with the hotel property will ask at the front office for directions. This service might seem minor in the overall delivery of service, but it is essential to the lost or confused guest. The front office staff must know both how to direct guests to particular meeting rooms or reception areas and which functions are being held in which rooms. Front desk clerks, as shown in Figure 3-2, must be ready to provide information for all departmental activities in the hotel.

The person responsible for paying the bills for a special event will also find his or her way to the front office to settle the city ledger accounts. If the banquet captain is not available to personally present the bill for the function, the front desk clerk should be informed about the specifics of food and beverage charges, gratuities, rental charges, method of payment, and the like.

Controller

The controller relies on the front office staff to provide a daily summary of financial transactions through a well-prepared night audit. This information is also used to measure management ability to meet budget targets. Because the front office provides the controller with financial data for billing and maintenance of credit card ledgers, these

FIGURE 3-2

Front desk clerks must be able to provide immediate responses to guests' requests for information. Photo courtesy of Radisson Hospitality Worldwide.

two departments must relay payments and charges through the posting machine or property management system.

The information produced by the front office is a necessary first step in the process of the factual guest accounting process and the financial assembly of data for the controller. Without accurate daily entry by desk clerks and without the night audit, the controller does not have the figures to produce reports for the owners, general manager, and supervisors. One might expect this communication to be in the form of reports. However, the front office and controller departments often communicate orally. They share a common concern for guest hospitality, and when finances are concerned, oral discussion is inevitable.

Maintenance or Engineering Department

The maintenance or engineering department and front office communicate on room status and requests for maintenance service. Maintenance employees must know the occupancy status of a room before attending to plumbing, heating, or air-conditioning problems. If the room is reserved, the two departments work out a time frame so the guest can enter the room on arrival or be assigned to another room. Cooperative efforts produce the best

James Heale is the corporate controller for Meyer Jabara Hotels and formerly the controller at the Sheraton Reading Hotel in Wyomissing, Pennsylvania. As the controller at the hotel, he was responsible for the money that comes in and expenses and taxes that are paid out. He prepares daily audits, is responsible for payroll preparation, and produces monthly, quarterly, and annual financial statements. He also prepares financial forecasts and subsequent budgets.

Mr. Heale says his relationships with guest service agents, cashiers, and night auditors are important; however, his relationships with their respective managers are more important. He audits the work of the guest service agents, cashiers, and night auditors but does not directly supervise them. If they make mistakes, Mr. Heale tries to show them why. He makes sure they receive proper training,

which includes letting them know the results of audits and making them aware of their individual performance.

Mr. Heale has a good relationship with the front office manager. They work together to forecast room sales and to audit cash banks. The front office manager monitors the front office payroll and may ask for Mr. Heale's assistance. The front office manager is also involved in cash management problems; he and Mr. Heale alert each other to problems and work together to solve them. The front office manager monitors accounts receivable and is required to let Mr. Heale know when a guest has exceeded his or her credit limit.

Mr. Heale points out that every hotel employee is a salesperson. Selling through fostering good relationships with local vendors is a big part of his job. His efforts encourage vendors to become customers of the hotel.

solutions to difficult situations. Figure 3-3 depicts the essential communication and planning by departmental managers to provide guest services at a time that does not interfere with delivering hospitality.

Likewise, requests from guests for the repair of heating, ventilating, and air-conditioning units, plumbing, televisions, and other room furnishings are directed to the front desk, which relays them to the maintenance department. The front desk clerk must keep track of the repair schedule, as guests want to know when the repair will be made.

Security Department

Communications between the security department and the front office are important in providing hospitality to the guest. These departments work together closely in maintaining guest security. Fire safety measures and emergency communication systems as well as procedures for routine investigation of guest security concerns require the cooperation of these departments. Because of the events of September 11, 2001, the nature of the security hotels offer their guests has changed. All members of the front office team must be alert for people who don't belong in the lobby and must report inconsistencies to the security department. This professional view of security allows the front office to support the security department.

FIGURE 3-3

Coordination of maintenance service requires cooperation between the maintenance and front office departments. Photo courtesy of Host/Racine Industries, Inc.

Human Resources Management Department

The human resources management department may rely on the front office staff as an initial point of contact for potential employees in all departments. It may even ask the front office to screen job candidates. If this occurs, guidelines for and training in screening methods must be provided.

Some directors of human resources depend on the front office to distribute application forms and other personnel-related information to job applicants. The potential employee may ask for directions to the personnel office at the front desk. The human resources management department may also develop guidelines for the front desk clerk to use in screening candidates. These guidelines may cover concerns about personal hygiene, completion of an application, education requirements, experience, and citizenship status. This information helps executives in the human resources management department interview potential job candidates.

Analyzing the Lines of Communications

This section describes situations in which communication between the front office and other departments plays a role. Each situation involves communication problems between departments, traces the source of miscommunication, analyzes the communication system, and presents methods of improving communications. The purpose of this method of presentation is to help future professionals develop a systematic way of continually improving communications.

Situation 1: Marketing and Sales Knows It All—But Didn't Tell Us

Mr. and Mrs. Oil Magnate are hosting a private party for 200 people in the Chandelier Room of City Hotel. On arriving at the hotel, they approach the front desk and ask if Mr. Benton, the director of marketing and sales, is available. The desk clerk checks the duty board and sees that Mr. Benton has left for the day. He responds, "Sorry, he's left for the day. What are you here for anyway?" The Magnates immediately feel neglected and ask to see the manager on duty.

Mr. Gerard, the assistant general manager, arrives on the scene and asks what he can do for the Magnates. Mr. Magnate has a number of concerns: Who will be in charge of their party? Will their two favorite servers be serving the cocktails, appetizers, and dinner? Have the flowers that were flown in from Holland arrived? Mr. Gerard says, "Gee, you'll have to speak with André, our banquet captain. He knows everything."

When André arrives, he tells the Magnates that Mr. Benton left no instructions about who will be serving the party, and he has not seen any tulips in the walk-in. Mrs. Magnate declares her party will be a disaster. Mr. Magnate decides to proceed with the party and take up the lack of professional service later.

Later has arrived: Mr. Magnate has complained to the general manager and I. M. Owner—the owner of City Hotel—and both are upset about the situation. Mr. Magnate and I. M. Owner are co-investors in a construction project. Even if the two men were not business associates, the treatment of any guest in such a shabby way spells disaster for future convention and banquet sales.

Analysis

The communications breakdown in this case was the fault of all the employees involved. Communication is a two-way process, and both senders and receivers must take active roles. As the sender, Mr. Benton, the director of marketing and sales, did not do his homework. Assuming he was aware of I. M. Owner's relationship with Mr. and Mrs. Magnate, he should have adjusted his work schedule so he could be there for the party. He also should have informed the front office manager of the Magnates' scheduled event, explained who they were, and asked that he be summoned immediately on their arrival. Mr. Benton should also have worked more closely with André, the banquet manager, in scheduling employees and receiving and storing the flowers. Although Mr. Gerard, the assistant general manager, would not normally be involved in the details of a party, in this case, the VIP status of the guests would be a reason for him to be aware of the presence of the Magnates in the hotel.

The receivers in the communication process are also at fault. These include the front office staff, the banquet manager, and the assistant general manager. At times, a member of the management team fails to communicate the particulars of an upcoming event. However, the front office staff, the banquet manager, and the assistant general manager are responsible for reviewing the daily function board as well as the weekly function sheet. They are also responsible for learning about the backgrounds of the people who stay at the hotel and of the associations and corporations that conduct business with it.

Several things can be done to avoid this type of situation. First, the front office manager can ensure the initial guest contact will be professional by reviewing the function board with each front desk employee on each shift. The manager can then help the front office staff focus on the day's upcoming events. Weekly staff meetings may also provide an opportunity for the director of marketing and sales to give brief synopses of who will be in the hotel in the coming week. At that point, special requests for VIP treatment can be noted.

Situation 2: Peace and Harmony in 507

Veronica is busy at the front desk checking in a busload of guests. Several of the guests ask her for directions to the nearest dining facility because they are hungry. Two of the guests seem restless and want to get into their room right away. One of them is an elderly traveler who needs assistance with his luggage and the other one, his young grandson, had experienced motion sickness on the bus. Although it seemed normal that a couple of guests would be restless and require special attention, something about these two disturbs Veronica. The blank look on the elderly man's face and his uneasy restlessness make her wonder what is on his mind. She checks them into room 507, calls the bell staff and asks for assistance with the elderly guest's luggage, suggests the elderly guest take a nap so he can rest from the bus trip, and directs the younger guest to do likewise.

The day continues, and several more routine check-ins and checkouts occur. Veronica takes a mid-afternoon break and happens to notice the elderly traveler crossing the lobby of the hotel on her way to the hotel's restaurant. She remarks to herself, "He seems to be walking much straighter and taller than he did when he checked in. It's only been two hours since he got off the bus; that nap must have done him some good!" Likewise, on her return from her break, she sees the younger guest laughing and talking with friends while they listened to their boom box in the lobby. That nap must have helped cure his motion sickness.

Veronica greets her replacement afternoon coworkers, John and Delaney, and checks out. She has to hurry because she had an appointment in the city. Two hours into their shift, John receives a phone call from room 505 complaining of loud, strange noises in the hallway. John alerts Ishmael, the security guard on duty, and Ishmael investigates the situation. When Ishmael approaches room 507, he can't believe his eyes. The two guests are hosting a nondenominational religious party complete with live animals, musical instruments, and oh, yes—a bright 1,000-watt lamp. Ishmael said later, "There must have been at least 45 people in the room, and they invited me in to share peace and harmony." They are taken aback when Ishmael tells them the party will have to break up because state law prohibits more than two people in that particular room. However, they cooperate and abide by the law.

Analysis

In this situation, we can see three communication opportunities were overlooked. First, when Veronica had misgivings about the elderly traveler and his grandson who had experienced motion sickness, she should have discussed them with a coworker or supervisor. It may have been nothing, but then again, it may have been a situation warranting further investigation. Then, when these misgivings were supported by the quick cures two hours later, this should have alerted her to something questionable—and precipitated a discussion with her supervisor or a call to the director of security. Again, it could have led to nothing, but a polite courtesy call to room 507 could have saved time later on. The third missed opportunity was Veronica's failure to relate her concerns about these two guests to John and Delaney. This shift-change communication is vital for keeping guests safe. All the communication training employees receive does not override the human instinct that should underlie the communication process.

Situation 3: I Know What You Said, and I Think I Know What You Mean

The director of maintenance, Sam Jones, has assigned his crew to start painting the Tower rooms at the hotel. Prior to making this assignment, he checked with the reservations manager, Keith Thomas, for approval to place the Tower rooms out of order for four days. Keith consented because a prior reservation for 150 rooms for Photo Bugs International had been confirmed for only 100.

At 1:00 P.M., Sam receives a call from Keith asking if it is possible to reassign the painting crew to some other duty. The Photo Bugs have arrived—all 150 rooms' worth! The lobby is filled with guests for whom no rooms are available. Sam tells Keith to give his crew one hour to clean up the mess and air out the south wing. He says the north wing has not been prepared for painting, so those guest rooms are ready for occupancy.

Analysis

What went right? What went wrong? This case demonstrates that cooperation between two staff members can resolve even the most unfortunate of situations. Sam was aware of the need for prior approval to take guest rooms out of service. Keith's decision to grant the request had a legitimate basis. Sam was also able to head off a nasty situation for the guests by being flexible. But what *caused* the situation to go awry?

The words people use in communicating with hotel staff members must be clarified. In this case, the person who booked the convention said there were confirmations for 100. Was this 100 guests for 50 rooms or 100 guests for 100 rooms? This lack of clarity was at the root of the problem. In some hotels, the reservations manager may require a change in reservations to be written (in the form of a letter); these written instructions are then attached to the convention contract.

These examples of day-to-day problems in a hotel underscore the importance of good communication between the front office and other departments. Similar problems will occur again and again throughout your career in the hospitality industry. You will grow as a professional if you adopt an analytical view of the communication system. Front office managers who actively participate in systematic communications are more effective managers. Training employees in proper procedures for dealing with other employees as well as their own departments helps improve the delivery of professional hospitality.

The Role of Total Quality Management in Effective Communication

Total quality management (TQM) is a management technique that encourages managers to look with a critical eye at processes used to deliver products and services. Managers must ask front-line employees and supervisors to question each step in the methods they use to provide hospitality for guests. Examples: "Why do guests complain about waiting in line to check out?" "Why do guests say our table service is rushed?" "Why do guests get upset when their rooms aren't ready on check-in?" Managers and their employees must then look for answers to these questions.

Total quality management was developed by W. Edwards Deming, a management theorist, in the early 1950s. His intent was to offer a new way for American manufacturers to improve the quality of their products by reducing defects through worker participation in the planning process. American manufacturers were reluctant at first to embrace total quality management, but Japanese manufacturers were quick to adopt Deming's principles of streamlining methods to manufacture products such as automobiles. He gave managers tools such as flowcharts to analyze production by dividing the manufacturing process into components and then focusing on the segments of processes that produce the end product.

INTERNATIONAL HIGHLIGHTS

Justin, the front desk clerk on duty, cannot speak Spanish fluently but knows how to communicate phonetically with the Spanish-speaking housekeeping staff. When Victorio, the houseman, approaches the front desk to inform Justin which rooms are clean, they use the phonetic pronunciation of numerals and housekeeping status. For example:

English	Phonetic Spanish
Room 2180	(doughs, ooe no, oh cho, sarh o)
Is	(es tah)
Clean	(limp e oh)

The most important aspect of total quality management in the context of the hotel industry is the interaction between front-line employees and their supervisors. The interaction of employees in a group setting or on a one-on-one basis to determine the root of the problem and how the desired end result can be achieved thrusts them into an atmosphere of cooperation that may not have previously existed. First-shift and second-shift employees, who usually do not understand each other's activities, find they do have common concerns about serving the guest. Housekeeping and front desk employees come to realize that a guest's request for a late checkout plays havoc with the delivery of hospitality. Total quality management practices ensure the front office checks with housekeeping to determine room availability in such a situation. The bottom line is that interdepartmental communication is enhanced each time a team of members of various departments meet to analyze a challenge to the delivery of hospitality. Figure 3-4 provides a view of the interaction necessary to make total quality management a success.

An Example of Total Quality Management in a Hotel

Total quality management in a hotel may be applied as follows: The general manager has received numerous complaints about the messy appearance of the lobby—furniture and pillows are out of place, ashtrays are overflowing, flowers are wilted, and trash receptacles are overflowing. The front office manager recruits a total quality management team, consisting of a front desk clerk, a maid, a waiter, a cashier, and the director of marketing and sales. The team discusses how the lobby area could be better maintained. The maid says her colleagues are overworked and are allotted only 15 minutes to clean up the public areas on the day shift. The front desk clerk says he would often like to take a few minutes to go out to the lobby to straighten the furniture and pillows, but he is not allowed to leave the front desk unattended. The director of marketing and sales say she is embarrassed when a prospective client comes into the hotel and is greeted with such a mess. She has called housekeeping several times to have the lobby cleaned but is told, "It's not in the budget to have the lobby cleaned six times a day." All of the team members realize the untidy lobby creates a poor impression of the hotel and the situation must be remedied.

FRONT-LINE REALITIES

 While a guest in room 421 is checking out, she indicates a dripping faucet in that room. After the guest departs, the desk clerk brushes off her remark, saying to a fellow desk clerk, "There are so many dripping faucets in this hotel that one more won't mean anything." If you were the front office manager and you heard this exchange, what would you do? How would you encourage better communication between the front office and maintenance?

FIGURE 3-4

FIGURE 3-4

Group analysis of jobs is an essential element in total quality management. Photo courtesy iStockphoto.com.

The team decides to look at the elements in the situation. The furniture is on wheels for ease of moving when the housekeeping staff cleans. The pillows add a decorative touch to the environment, but they are usually scattered about. The waiter jokingly says, "Let's sew them to the back and arms of the sofa!" Might the ashtrays be removed and receptacles added for guests to use in extinguishing a cigarette? Could a larger waste receptacle with a swinging lid be used to avoid misplaced litter? "The fresh flowers are nice," adds one of the team members, "but many hotels use silk flowers and plants. This must save money over the long run."

The team discussion encourages each person to understand why the maid can't straighten the lobby every two or three hours and why the desk clerk can't leave his post to take care of the problem. The employees' comments concerning furniture and appointments foster an atmosphere of understanding. Team members start looking at one another with more empathy and are slower to criticize on other matters. Was the issue of the messy lobby resolved? Yes, but more important, the team members developed a way to look at a challenge in a more constructive manner.

Solution to Opening Dilemma

Upon initial review, the problem seems to be that all employees should be encouraged to assist guests in an emergency. However, in this case, the desk clerk has a perception problem about his job. This shortsightedness probably results from poor training, a lack of opportunities for employees from various departments to exchange ideas and socialize, and an atmosphere for employee motivation. The front office manager should discuss the situation with the convention representative and emphasize the benefits of total quality management. Supervisors must concentrate on guests' needs and foster employee growth and development so their employees will likewise concentrate on guests' needs. These concepts are at the heart of effective interdepartmental communications.

Chapter Recap

This chapter analyzed the interdepartmental communications that must be maintained in a hotel. In particular, it focused on how the front office relates to employees in all departments—marketing and sales, housekeeping, food and beverage, banquets, controller, maintenance, security, and human resources. Guest needs are met when employees cooperate and communicate to provide hotel services. However, when these lines of communication break down, so does quality of service. The front office manager must take an objective view of these communications, considering the needs of the guest, the actions of the employees, and the policies and procedures in effect. There are times when segments of the communication system will seem overwhelming, but the professional hotelier improves with each new challenge.

Situations illustrating communication lapses and their subsequent analysis provided insights into the complex process of communicating. Each employee must develop an appreciation for the work of other departments and an understanding of how each employee's activities affect the delivery of hospitality. Well-developed operational policies and training programs assist employees in communicating within a department and between departments.

Total quality management was introduced as a management tool that encourages interdepartmental cooperation and communication. This management technique focuses on ways all employees can work together to discuss issues and problems and resolve them as a team. This method produces the best products and services for the guest.

End-of-Chapter Questions

1. How do the communication efforts of front office employees help set the tone for a guest's visit? Give examples.

2. Give examples of how the marketing and sales department and the front office communicate.

3. Communications between the front office and the housekeeping department revolve around room status. How can each department director ensure these communications are effective?

4. How does the banquet department interact with the front office? Do you think any of these duties should be shifted to the banquet captain's staff? Why or why not?

5. What does the controller expect of the front office every day? Why is this communication tool so important?

6. What role does the front office play in communications between the guest and the maintenance department?

7. How can the human resources department include the front office in the operations and communications process?

8. What does *tracing and analyzing the lines of communication* mean to you? Do you think this concept will assist you in your career in the hospitality industry?

9. What is your reaction to the use of total quality management as a means of developing better communications between departments?

10. Identify a problem area in your place of employment and develop a plan to use total quality management to resolve the issue. Whom would you place on the total quality management team? What results would you expect?

CASE STUDY 301

It is Thursday morning at The Times Hotel. The reservations manager has printed the list of reservations for the day. The front office staff has prepared 252 packets for guests who have preregistered for the Pet Owners of the Americas Conference. The Times Hotel has been designated the headquarters for the cat owners, while The Sebastian Hotel, two blocks away, has been designated the headquarters for the dog owners. The participants in the Pet Owners of the Americas Conference are supposed to start arriving at noon.

The Times Hotel had a full house on Wednesday night. A planning group (179 rooms) for the Biology Researchers Conference was in the hotel. They held a meeting that ran into the early hours of Thursday morning. Several of the guests posted DO NOT DISTURB signs on their doors.

Yoon-Whan Li, the executive engineer, has noticed the air conditioning going on and off on the fifth and sixth floors. Yoon-Whan investigates the problem and estimates it will require about 12 hours of repair time. Yoon-Whan calls the front office to report the problem, but the desk clerks are busy and fail to answer the phone. Meanwhile, another repair call comes in, and Yoon-Whan is off again. The air conditioning situation is never reported to the front office.

(continues)

CASE STUDY 301 (CONTINUED)

The chef is busy preparing vendor orders for the day. He is also planning the food production worksheets for the Pet Owners of the Americas. The chef has left word with one of his suppliers to return his call early in the afternoon to clarify an order for the banquet that night. The organizer for the Pet Owners of the Americas wants a special Swiss chocolate ice cream cake roll. The sales office has also included an order for two ice sculptures—one cat and one dog. The banquet manager and several of his crew are scheduled to arrive about three hours prior to the banquet to begin setting up furniture and tabletops. The servers will arrive about one hour before the banquet begins.

It is now 11:00 A.M., and a group of conferees has arrived to register. They have brought along their cats and want to know where they can house them. The front desk clerk does not know where the cats are to be housed. He calls the sales department and asks for directions. The sales department says the person who organized this conference specifically told the participants they were to leave their pets at home. This was not to be a pet show, only a business/seminar conference.

The housekeeping staff is unable to get into the rooms (checkout time is noon). The Biology Researchers Conference attendees have not risen because of the late planning meeting. Also, two of the room attendants did not report to work this morning.

It is now 1:30 P.M., and the majority of the Pet Owners are in the lobby, with their pets, waiting to get into the rooms. With the air conditioning out of order, the lobby is bedlam. The odor and noise are beyond description. Housekeeping calls down and says it will need about two more hours before the first 75 rooms can be released.

The switchboard has been bombarded with telephone calls for the Pet Owners. The chef is anticipating his call from the vendor for the Swiss chocolate ice cream cake roll. He finally calls the supplier and finds out she has been trying to call him to say she is out of this product, but no one answered the phone at the front desk. The chef is beside himself and runs out of the kitchen into the lobby area. He finds the switchboard operator and verbally rips him apart. The front office manager is up to her ears in kitty litter and responds likewise to the chef. It is not the best of situations.

Just when it seems nothing else can go wrong, a new group of ten Pet Owners of the Americas arrives in the lobby with guaranteed reservations. The hotel is completely booked, and these additional reservations represent an overbooked situation. The reservationist forgot to ask if these guests were cat or dog owners. You guessed it—they all brought along Fido. The clamor in the lobby is now unbearable—dogs are barking at cats, cats are hissing at dogs, and guests are complaining loudly.

The banquet manager and his crew have finished setting up the room for the banquet. One of the crew turns on the air conditioning; there is a dull roar, and blue smoke pours from the vents. Thinking this is only a temporary condition, he does not report it to the banquet manager. Later on, the banquet manager instructs the setup crew to take the ice sculptures from the freezer and set them in front of the podium and head table. The banquet servers will be arriving within an hour to start the preparations for the banquet.

If you were the front office manager, what would you do to solve the immediate problems? After the commotion had settled down, how would you analyze the situation? List the opportunities for improving communications between the front office and other departments.

CASE STUDY 302

The following script fictionalizes a hotel general manager's weekly staff meeting. Several students should act the roles of staff members, while other students observe and analyze the communications.

Margaret Chu (*general manager*): Good morning, everyone! It's great to gather once again to discuss our challenges and plan for the future. Let's see, Ana, you asked for time today to discuss the issue of too few parking spaces in the hotel garage.

Ana Chavarria (*front office manager*): Yes, and this problem is causing all kinds of difficulties for my staff. At least ten guests a day threaten to cancel their next reservation if I don't find them a parking space. How am I supposed to achieve 100 percent occupancy with such a little thing as parking causing such a big problem?

Andy Roth (*parking garage manager*): Hold on there, Ana. Running a parking garage isn't an easy job. We have a lot of new monthly business customers who are helping us make plenty of money. Did you forget those new monthly business customers paid for the property management system you just bought? You were pretty happy about that new business six months ago.

Margaret Chu: Look, folks, we have to focus on the customer right now; I think both of you have lost sight of who the customer is.

Eric Jones (*food and beverage manager*): It seems to me we have too few customers. I would like to see some of those new parking customers stop in to one of my restaurants to have lunch. We have been tracking our lunch guests with business card drawings, and so far only three of them came in for lunch. Let's get rid of those new parking customers and stick to the regular hotel guests.

Frank Goss (*director of maintenance*): I agree. Those new parking customers are littering all over the garage. They dump their cigarette butts and fast-food trash all over the place.

Andy Roth: I'll tell you just like I told Ana, those new parking customers bought you that fancy machine to change light bulbs in your department. Where were all of you people when I asked Margaret if we could start to market the sales of new parking garage permits? This hotel should be called Hotel Second Guess!

Eric Jones: I think we are getting carried away with this concern; the real problem we have here is the lack of cooperation with security. Ana, didn't you have two guest rooms broken into this month? It's too bad the director of security isn't here to tell us more about it. We never seem to get any follow-up reports on what's going on or what we can do to prevent it from happening again.

Margaret Chu: Eric, that is a good point you bring up, but we have to resolve Ana's problem first. What do all of you suggest we do about the parking problem? Should we abandon a profitable profit center or keep the hotel guests happy?

Andy Roth: Ms. Chu, if I may be so bold as to say so, the solution we need is neither of those two options but a third one. Let's lease some off-premises parking from the Reston Hotel across the street for our hotel guests during the business week. My friend Margo runs that garage, and she says it is only about 75 percent full most weekdays.

Margaret Chu: Well, Andy, I will have to check this out with the general manager of the Reston. He and I have a meeting with the City Visitors Association tomorrow.

Frank Goss: Ms. Chu, before we get to that security problem, let's discuss my need to cover

(continues)

CASE STUDY 302 (CONTINUED)

the second shift over the weekend. That is an impossible request, because I am so understaffed. Do any of you have any extra employees who are handy in fixing things and would like to earn a few extra bucks?

Margaret Chu: Frank, it's not that easy. We are on a tight budget, and there are no extra dollars to pay overtime. Let's think about it and put a hold on scheduling a person for the second shift until we can resolve the issue.

Frank Goss: Sounds good to me.

Margaret Chu: OK, Frank, we can meet right after this meeting and talk about it. Many of you do have challenges running your departments, and most of the time you do a great job. However, from what I am hearing today,

we need to start anticipating problems before they happen. Recently I ran across a management technique called total quality management. It will help us understand one another's challenges and make us a little more patient. I will schedule a few workshops for you and your employees in the next few weeks.

As observers of this staff meeting, how do you feel the staff members interact with one another? What role is Margaret Chu playing? If you were the general manager, what role would you play? What effect do you feel the total quality management workshops will have on this group? What effect will they have on communication between the front office and other departments?

CASE STUDY 303

The following script fictionalizes a conversation between a front desk clerk, a guest, and a housekeeper. Several students should act the roles; the remaining students should observe and analyze the communications.

Betty Kaye: Good morning, Mr. Jenkins, did you have a restful night at The Times Hotel?

Mr. Jenkins: Well, thanks for asking, but your place has problems.

Betty Kaye: You don't say! Not many people tell us that. Like what?

Mr. Jenkins: Like what! Have you ever had a window that wouldn't close and keep the rain out? Or a faucet in the sink that wouldn't stop dripping? And those towels were grimy!

Betty Kaye: Look who's here—Bertha Mae, the housekeeper from your floor. Bertha Mae, tell

this man how professional we are. Like last quarter we won an award or something from the home office.

Bertha Mae: Sir, good day to you. Did you have some problems last night? We at The Times Hotel pride ourselves in providing clean rooms. Wasn't your room clean?

Mr. Jenkins: Yes, my room was clean, other than the grimy-looking towels. But it didn't work right!

Betty Kaye: We have to get the maintenance people here to get things straightened out for your next visit. Hope you will be back the next time.

Mr. Jenkins: Next time I will stay at your competitor's property where their advertising says "We hear our guests."

Key Words

amenities

banquet manager

daily announcement board

folio

guest histories

house count

housekeeper's room report

housekeeping room status

interdepartmental communication

intradepartmental communication

marquee

paid-outs

point-of-sale terminals

predicted house count

room sales projections

sales associate

total quality management (TQM)

transfers

CHAPTER 4

Property Management Systems

OPENING DILEMMA

At a recent hotel trade show, you noticed a new property management system that seems to produce all the types of reports your current system cannot produce. The vendor at the show said she will set up a meeting with you in a week or two to talk more about this system. How will you prepare for her visit?

The first three chapters of this text provided an overview of the hotel industry, organization of the hotel, organization and management of the front office, and interdepartmental communication, which laid the groundwork for understanding how the front office fits into a network for providing service to the guest. In this chapter, we focus on the operational aspects of the front desk department, including the physical structure and positioning of the front desk, selecting a property management system (PMS), and using PMS applications.

Computer applications are central to front office operations in today's modern hotels and are being adopted by most other lodging facilities. For new properties, computers are standard equipment; for existing hotels, computers are being integrated into everyday operations to assist in providing hospitality to guests. Computer applications include routinely processing reservations as well as registrations, guest charges, guest checkout, and the night audit. *Interfacing*—the electronic sharing of data, of hotel departments such as food and beverage and the gift shop through *point-of-sale*, an outlet in the hotel that generates income (restaurant, gift shop, spa, garage)—maintenance through monitoring of energy and heating and cooling systems, and security through control of guest keys are just a few of the applications that are explored in this chapter.

As you begin your career in the lodging industry, you will want to develop a thorough understanding of front office computer applications. This text does not refer to one particular computer hardware or software system; your training at any lodging property will include specific operating procedures to produce reports or review information from the database. Instead, this chapter provides general information on which you can base your understanding of computer applications at the front desk. These applications are encompassed by the term *property management system (PMS)*, a generic term for applications of computer hardware and software used to manage a hotel.

You will notice that the PMS is not confined to the front office; it interfaces with housekeeping, food and beverage, marketing and sales, gift shop, controller, engineering, safety and security, and other departments, all of which are service departments of the hotel. Each department plays a role, along with the front office, in serving the needs of the guest—before, during, and after the guest's stay. The front office staff coordinates the communications, accounting, security, and safety requirements of the guest. As the nerve

HOSPITALITY PROFILE

 Kevin Corprew, director of rooms operation at the Marriott in Overland Park, Kansas, is a graduate of the University of Houston in hotel and restaurant management. Mr. Corprew has worked with Marriott Hotels in several places and positions, including the Marriott Medical Center in Houston, Texas, as a desk clerk, rooms controller, and supervisor; the Airport Marriott in Houston, Texas, as a banquet manager; and the Marriott Courtyard in Legacy Park, Dallas, Texas, in rooms care (housekeeping and engineering), front office, and restaurant and bar areas. He also worked at the Hilton Washington and Towers in Washington, DC, in sales.

Mr. Corprew says the ambiance of the front desk requires a simple, elegant appearance. Preliminary discussions of new trends in front desk structure include a walk-through for associates that allows them to pass in front of and behind the desk to accommodate guests. Also, the front desk and lobby should be considered together in design and function.

The organization of the front desk, with its computers and vast amounts of detail, revolves around an uncomplicated guideline: Keep it simple. Mr. Corprew provides plenty of key machines (electronic devices to make electronic guest room keys); ensures all staff follow standard operating procedures, such as keeping faxes and mail in one location; and requires associates to be considerate of guests' needs. His organizational principle is continued at the time of check-in, when a 100 percent automated property management system requires the associate only to swipe a credit card and to prepare and present the room key to the guest.

Mr. Corprew urges young professionals who want to make a career in the hospitality industry to lead by example with high morals and standards. He encourages students to start in entry-level jobs so they have a basis for dealing with employees.

center of the hotel, the front office handles most of the recordkeeping and so benefits most from a computerized system.

The first part of this chapter sets the stage for adopting a PMS. Software and hardware are discussed,[1] as are other considerations in choosing a PMS. The final section of the chapter discusses the modules of the PMS as they apply to the lodging industry.[2]

Physical Structure and Positioning of the Front Desk

Figure 4-1 shows the layout of a computerized front office. While manual equipment is still used in some independent properties, the computer system has become the system of choice, primarily because it serves the needs of guests, management, and owners.

Guest First Impression

The front desk has always held a pivotal position of importance in the lodging operation. It is one of the first points of contact with the guest, and, as such, its ambiance sets the tone for the hotel. Neatness, orderliness, attractiveness, quality, and professionalism are just a few of the impressions the front desk should convey to a guest. The guest wants to feel important, safe, and in the hands of professionals. The impression conveyed by the physical layout of the desk assists the front office in creating a positive image for the operation. Providing hospitality to the guest and promoting in-house sales (covered in more detail in chapters 11 and 13) are of great importance to the continued financial success of the operation. To provide an environment in which these objectives can be met, a well-planned physical arrangement of the front desk is important.

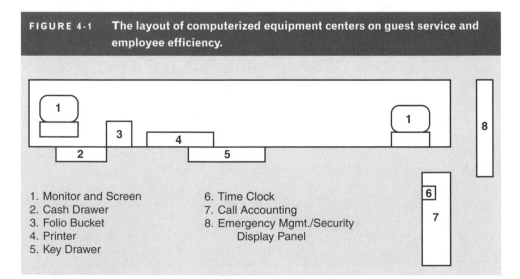

FIGURE 4-1   The layout of computerized equipment centers on guest service and employee efficiency.

1. Monitor and Screen
2. Cash Drawer
3. Folio Bucket
4. Printer
5. Key Drawer
6. Time Clock
7. Call Accounting
8. Emergency Mgmt./Security Display Panel

Creating a Balance Between Guest Flow and Employee Work

Equipment

The front desk should be positioned to accommodate guests while enabling employees to work efficiently. Guests who wait in line for five minutes only to be told they are in the wrong line will have a negative first impression. Likewise, a desk clerk who must wait to use a printer or share a computer terminal will not be as efficient as possible. As you become familiar with the practice of processing guests at the front desk, you will see how easy it is to plan the workable layout of the physical equipment needed.

Guest Safety

The position of the front desk is usually determined by the main entrance of the building and the location of the elevator. The front desk clerk and the night auditor must be able to see everyone who enters the hotel; this helps ensure a safe environment for the guest. Positioning the front desk on the same side as the main entrance and the elevator is not recommended. Figure 4-2 shows a few arrangements that allow entrances to be monitored. In all three settings, the front desk clerk has a view of who is coming into the hotel from the street entrance and who is coming off the elevator. This view is essential to the night auditor, who assists security in monitoring the activities in the hotel lobby.

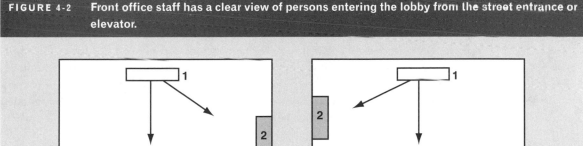

FIGURE 4-2   Front office staff has a clear view of persons entering the lobby from the street entrance or elevator.

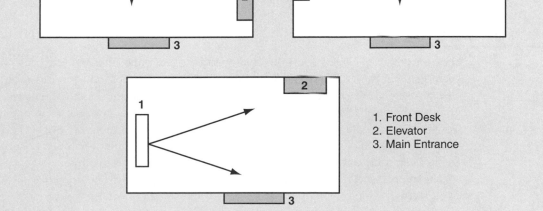

1. Front Desk
2. Elevator
3. Main Entrance

In light of security issues that emerged after 9/11, the positioning of the front desk is even more important in allowing the front desk staff to be the front-line sentinels of the hotel. Although they may not leave their post, they must be trained to be observant and efficient in summoning the right people to investigate a situation. Positioning a hotel front desk facing the main entry and exit allows the desk clerk to more easily monitor who is entering and leaving the building—an important advantage when considering hotel security.

Selecting a Property Management System

This section focuses on the components that should be included when deciding to adopt a PMS. The decision-making process begins with understanding the importance of a needs analysis performed by a team of front-line staff members. The needs analysis should focus on the flow of guests through the hotel and on interdepartmental communications. A review of administrative paperwork produced by management in all areas of the hotel is also a consideration. After management has gathered relevant data concerning operational needs, it must objectively determine whether a computer will help improve guest service. Other important concepts covered here include software selection considerations and computer hardware terminology. A review of how people interact with computers and how a hotel must make provisions while hardware is being installed is also offered. The importance of computer training and planning a backup power source for continued computer operation is reviewed. The often overlooked maintenance agreement and the important financial payback complete the discussion of selecting a PMS.

Importance of a Needs Analysis

Selecting new equipment for a hotel property is best done after a needs analysis is performed.[3] A *needs analysis* indicates the flow of information and services of a specific property to determine whether the new equipment—in this case, computers—can improve the flow. The bottlenecks that occur at registration or the lack of information from the housekeeping department on the occupancy status of a room can be alleviated by the use of computers at the front desk. Only after the completion of an operational flow analysis can computer applications be developed to improve the situation.

The importance of needs analysis can be most clearly seen when you consider what can go wrong if such an analysis is not made. The first area of concern for property owners and managers is cost, both initially and over the long term. As the technology has evolved and the equipment become more common, the cost of computerizing a hotel has decreased and the payback period has shortened. However, even with these lower costs, installing and operating a PMS is not inexpensive, and the cost of installing and operating a system that does not meet the specific needs of a particular property is exorbitant.

A system that works well for one downtown hotel may not meet the needs of a downtown hotel in another city or of a motel in the same area. All the technological gadgetry in the world will not impress a guest if the equipment fails to deliver service. The system must work for the staff as well as the guests. An inappropriate PMS will produce control reports that are not useful to management; the functions of such software, therefore, are limited, and the cost of the system exceeds its value. For example, a hotel owner who believes a PMS will speed registrations and decides to purchase a system that does not allow housekeeping staff to input room status from the guest room phone will be disappointed.

Procedure for Performing a Needs Analysis

The following list shows the procedure for performing a needs analysis.

1. Select a team to analyze needs.

2. Analyze the flow of guests through the lodging property.

   - Reservations
   - Registration
   - Guest accounting
   - Checkout
   - Night audit
   - Guest history

3. Analyze the flow of information from other departments to the front office.

4. Analyze the administrative paperwork produced in other departments.

5. Review the information gathered in Steps 2, 3, and 4.

6. Evaluate the identified needs—such as control reports, communication, and administrative paperwork produced in other departments—in terms of importance.

7. Combine needs to determine desired applications.

Selecting a Team

The first and most important step in performing a needs analysis for adopting a PMS in a hotel is to select a team to identify the reports and information being generated. The analysis team should include employees at both management and staff levels. Such a team is better able to see all aspects of the operation; management can provide input on the overall objectives, while staff is more aware of day-to-day needs. The front office manager who feels the reservation system is inefficient may find the desk clerk not only agrees but can offer suggestions for improving the situation. This desk clerk may not know the first thing about *flow analysis processes*—preparing a schematic drawing of the operations included in a particular function—but the hands-on information he or she can provide will assist the front office manager in evaluating the reservation system. In another instance, the general manager may request that certain additional room sales analysis reports be produced by the marketing and sales department only to find the front office manager already produces that information. Current information from social networking applications that is garnered by many employees may offer a great opportunity for marketing ideas and their inclusion on the team.

Analyzing the Flow of Guests through the Hotel

The second step in the needs analysis is to analyze the flow of guests through the visit to the property, which provides a structure for this detailed analysis process. The guest stay does not start at registration but at the time a reservation is made. (In reality, the guest stay starts even before this, because guests often select a property as a result of marketing efforts.)

Issues that can be analyzed are quite diverse. They include the social networking applications utilized, the ease with which the telephone system can be used, the availability of room occupancy status for guests on any specific date, the length of time it takes to complete a reservation request, the method used to confirm a reservation, the procedure used to block rooms, and the means of finding a single reservation. Also subject to analysis are the methods for gathering guest information upon check-in and the processes for ensuring the correct posting of guest charges, the time required for a guest to check out, the procedure used to resolve a guest's dispute of charges, and the process for posting meal and phone charges just before checkout. How are the daily room charges and taxes posted to the rooms? How long does it take to do this? Are any vital statistics not being produced by completion of the night audit report? How is the information assembled in the night audit? How long does it take to produce this information? Also determine if guest information already on hand from reservation, registration, and guest accounting is being applied for additional visits. Guest concerns for the hotel's responsible management of environmental resources may also be an issue.

Communicating Information

The third step in the needs analysis process is to look at the information flowing from other departments to the front office. How is information concerning occupancy status received from the housekeeping department? How can a guest report an emergency or fire on the property? How do the food and beverage department and gift shop report guest charges? How does the marketing and sales department determine if blocks of rooms are available on certain dates? How does the engineering department monitor energy use in guest rooms? How does the security department ensure the integrity of guest keys? How is email used? A good PMS can embrace all these lines of communication.

Reviewing Administrative Paperwork

The fourth step is to review the administrative paperwork produced in the hotel that is necessary to assist management. How does the human resources department maintain personnel files and former employee records? How is direct mail advertising generated in the marketing and sales department? How are function books and individual function sheets maintained? How are *tickler files* (files used to prompt notice of when certain events will be occurring) maintained? How are work orders processed? What method is used to devise daily menu specials?

Management Review of Information

In the fifth step of this analysis, management must take charge of reviewing the information compiled to determine if needs are being met. Is the marketing and sales department making mistakes because incorrect information concerning the inventory of available rooms is provided by the front office staff? For example, is incorrect room data inventory provided to a third-party website such as Orbitz.com? Are desk clerks unable to check the occupancy status of a guest room because the housekeeping department is not providing immediate information? Have misquotes on room rates caused lost revenue for the hotel? Is the night auditor unable to retrieve room status information to confirm or guarantee reservations?

The significance of each need and the consequences, if the need is not met, are then established. Customer satisfaction and quality of service, as well as financial implications, are considered. How often have conventions not been booked because accurate information on room availability was not at hand? How much revenue was lost as a result? How frequently does a general manager receive complaints because a guest was sent to a room that was under repair or not cleaned? How often must the front office manager adjust a guest's room rate because of a misquote? How does the number of guaranteed reservations compare with the number of confirmed reservations? Why are guaranteed reservations not requested by the night auditor?

Evaluate Needs That Have Been Identified

This step requires discussion among department managers about the significance of the reports produced as they relate to producing customer service and financial success of the operation. Each module in the PMS has a related cost, and the justification for that cost can be simplified if all discussions focus on the goals of the operation.

Assessing Needs Based on Findings

The final step in the analysis is to combine operational and administrative needs to determine which computer applications are appropriate for the property. Often the shared use of a room inventory database is well worth the financial investment. A word processing program to produce direct mail letters, regular correspondence, and daily menus may also justify a particular module of a PMS. The needs analysis enables you to know what you need and what you do not need and will help you choose from the many systems available.

Choosing Software

Selecting *software*, the computer programs or applications that process data, such as guest information, and aid in financial transactions and report generation, is more important than selecting *hardware*, or actual computer equipment such as central processing units, keyboards, monitors, and printers. The effectiveness of a PMS depends on selecting software that allows management to increase guest satisfaction and to access financial and informational data for control purposes. The information obtained from the needs analysis provides a framework for evaluating the numerous software packages on the market today.

Each software package offers numerous features; it is important to choose one package that is most appropriate for your needs. Software on the market today includes guest service, accounting, and information options that are standard in the hotel industry. Investigate the guest service features, accounting options, and information applications to determine which PMS is best for your property. Software vendor personnel will discuss with you the options that fit the size of your hotel and the needs of its guests. Hoteliers should also look ahead and think of the expansion and growth of their property, or perhaps consider possible changes in the mix of their market. For example, one hotel may plan to add 200 rooms to the same market, while another hotel may not add any rooms but have a shift in guest type from 20 percent family and 80 percent business to 80 percent family and 20 percent business. Now the family market is doing much more dining in the restaurant (indicating a need for a point-of-sale system that interfaces with the PMS), purchasing more in the gift shop (another need), and indicating more gift purchases for day-trip packages (yet another need).

If you feel the applications of a particular software package will not help you manage your property, that adding a particular guest service will not increase guest satisfaction, that no significant savings will result from producing more sophisticated accounting reports, or that the arrangement of historical information about guests will not be beneficial, then you should not adopt that PMS. You control the software selection; its function is to help you do a better job. Only you can decide which applications are most useful in your facility. Some of the more common options for various departments are listed in Figure 4-3.

Here are a few examples of how PMS modules can be applied. The marketing and sales department in any size hotel will clearly find that computerization of client files, meeting room information, and guest history is useful. Preparation of direct mail for a smaller property perhaps would best be outsourced, while a larger property may make better use of a PMS module. The travel agent mode for maintaining a database of travel agents and processing their fees is useful to properties of any size. The social networking applications feed into guest history data. The night audit is almost a universal necessity for properties of all sizes. The former eight hours of labor over balancing the guest ledger and city ledger are replaced by a few keystrokes, in some cases. The front desk module, with its applications for check-in, checkout, room status, postings to guest accounts,

FIGURE 4-3   Common software options in a PMS.

Marketing and Sales

- Client file
- Direct mail
- Guest history
- Meeting room information
- Travel agent
- Facebook
- Twitter
- LinkedIn

Night Audit

- Room and tax posting
- Operational reports

Accounting

- Accounts payable
- Accounts receivable
- General ledger
- Payroll
- Profit-and-loss statement
- Balance sheet

Human Resources Management

- Personnel files
- Time and attendance

Electronic Mail

Security

Reservations

- Room availability
- Yield management

Front Desk

- Check-in
- Room status
- Postings to guest accounts
- Guest credit audit
- Advance deposits
- Cashier

Call Accounting

- Guest information
- Phone call posting

Housekeeping

- Room status
- Environmental issues

Maintenance

- Work orders
- Environmental issues

Food and Beverage

- Point of sale
- Menu profitability
- Inventory
- Recipes

FIGURE 4-4	Examples of Property Management Systems vendors.
1. Remco Software, Inc.	www.remcosoftware.com/Pages/default.aspx
2. MICROS Systems—Opera PMS	www.micros.com/Products/OPERA/property-management.htm
3. Room Key PMS	www.welcometorsi.com/
4. ICSS—Atrium	www.inn-client.com/index.php
5. MindSpring Software—HotelSMART Suite	www.mindspringsoftware.com

advance deposits, and cashier options, are also useful at both small and large properties. The call accounting system is an option that found its way to the hotel's front desk (even at smaller hotels because of the deregulation of telecommunication systems in the United States) before some of the other modules, such as the point-of-sale in the restaurant. A maintenance module is more appropriate for a large hotel, whereas a small hotel can rely on an in-house email system, telephone, or paper mail system. These examples, as any other technologies that are developed, should always be evaluated against the goals of the hotel, the needs of its guests, and the budget.

Future hoteliers should maintain a library of current PMS vendors. The Internet provides a useful and immediate resource for most hoteliers. This first step is accomplished by going to your favorite Web browser and typing in such key phrases as "property management system," "hotel pms" "hotel computer," or "HITEC" (Hospitality Industry Technology Exposition and Conference, which features all the latest computer software for the hospitality industry sponsored by the Hospitality Financial and Technology Professionals). Another method of keeping your PMS file up to date is to attend local and regional trade shows. Stopping by a booth at the hotel show and discussing your current needs with a software vendor will assist you in maintaining awareness on the developments in the industry and matching them with the needs analysis of your guests. Examples of Property Management System vendors are included in Figure 4-4.

Choosing Hardware

Choosing hardware for a PMS is not as difficult as choosing software. Today, most available hardware is compatible with standard computer operating systems (such as Northwind's Maestro™ Property Management Suite, which connects with Windows Server 2003 or Windows XP Pro). This consideration is essential because most software programs are written to run on standard operating systems. In short, you must choose your hardware based on its ability to handle the software; review this with your hardware vendor.

Other technology factors to consider include the following working concepts:

Processor speed: how fast a central processing unit (CPU) makes calculations per second; expressed in gigahertz (GHz)

Disk drive: a place in the computer where data is stored or read; CD or DVD drive or key drive

Megabyte: 1024 kilobytes of formatted capacity

Gigabyte: 1024 megabytes of formatted capacity

Access time: the amount of time required for a processor to retrieve information from the hard drive; recorded in milliseconds

Internet: a network of computer systems that share information over high-speed electronic connections

Intranet: a computer network over which in-house users share timely operational information to conduct business

I/O ports (input/output devices): keyboard, monitor, modem, mouse, joystick, light pen, printer, and trackball

Monitor: a television screen with color or monochrome capacity to view input and output data, control column width and line length of display, adjust height of character display, and allow visual control

Keypad: a collection of numeric typewriter keys and function keys that allow the operator to enter numbers or perform math functions in a computer

Keyboard: a standard or Dvorak-type typewriter-style keypad that allows the operator to enter or retrieve data

Printer: computer hardware that produces images on paper

Inkjet: a printer that produces small dots printed with liquid ink on paper

Laser: a printer that produces photo images on paper

Letter-quality: a better type of dot-matrix print

Single-sheet: a type of printer that uses single-sheet paper

Modem: computer hardware that allows for transfer of data through telephone lines; expressed in baud (information transfer) rates

CPS (characters per second): measure of the speed with which individual characters are printed

Computer supplies: paper, forms, and ink cartridges, needed to operate the system

Megahertz (MHz): one million cycles per second; indicates computer speed

PPM (pages per minute): printer speed capability

The front office manager must be aware of the operational capabilities of the PMS. Computer texts and trade journals can help you understand the hardware options available; *PC (Personal Computer)* magazine, in particular, is helpful for keeping up to date with hardware configurations and software applications. Visits to hospitality industry trade shows also help keep you informed on state-of-the-art systems. The standard hardware used to operate a PMS is shown in Figure 4-5. The basic hardware requirements are organized around the point-of-sale and customer service areas. Keyboards, monitors, disk drives, and printers constitute the basic user setup. The data manipulation and storage area is part of the mainframe, minicomputer, or personal computer.

FIGURE 4-5

Computer
hardware, such
as keyboards
and monitors,
typically have a
standard setup.
Photo courtesy of
PhotoDisc, Inc.

The interfacing of computer databases (sharing or networking of information) is vital. This ability must be designed into the PMS for it to contribute to the effective delivery of hospitality to the guest and to generate a return on the investment in it. As computer applications become more sophisticated, sharing databases is increasingly important. For example, the information secured at the time a reservation is made can be used by the marketing and sales department to generate more business. The point-of-sale data captured in the restaurants can be reviewed by front office staff to check how they can sharpen their hospitality delivery skills for guests on arrival. For example, if the staff knows a guest likes to order a certain Italian pastry as part of his meal, then they can perhaps use that as part of the welcoming chat upon arrival. Or if a review of a guest folio reveals that she played a particular sport during her previous stay, the staff could mention the opportunity to set a start time for that sport. All of these ideas help make the guest feel important and help make a positive return on the investment for the PMS.

The positioning of the hardware at workstations should be based on the same work-flow analysis used for any new process or equipment. Consider the needs of the guest (who will be the end user), the employee who will operate the equipment, and the other staff who will want access to information. The information you gain from the needs analysis will assist you in explaining your particular needs to the computer consultants who will install your PMS.

The installation of the electronic cables that connect all of the hardware must also be analyzed. Installation and replacement of cables that run through walls and floors can be costly. Proper computer functioning requires an air-conditioned environment; in guest service areas, this may not present a problem, but in other areas, it may pose difficulties.

Ergonomics, the study of how people relate physiologically to machines, is also a consideration for the front office manager. Glare and flicker from the *cursor*, a flashing point on a monitor that indicates where data can be entered, and movement on screens can cause eyestrain. In fact, it is fairly common for computer operators to require lenses to correct eyestrain. Another common complaint is neck pain due to improper positioning of the monitor. The swivel base provided on most hardware helps eliminate these problems. Pain in the wrist may also occur if the keyboard is positioned above the waist of the operator. Carpal tunnel syndrome, or compression of a nerve in the wrist and fingers, is another unfortunate result of overuse of computer keyboards. Because carpal tunnel syndrome causes extreme pain for a computer operator, the keyboard should be positioned at or below waist level. Also, pain in fingers and hands can occur with extensive entry of data on a keyboard.

Other PMS Selection Considerations

Other factors to consider in choosing a PMS are vendor claims, installation plans, training, backup power sources, and maintenance.

Vendor Claims

The prospective PMS purchaser should contact current users of the system being considered and ask relevant questions: How easy is it to operate this system? How useful are the reports you obtain? Has the vendor been available to help train staff and provide emergency service? Answers such as "I don't know how the property could manage without it" or "It is difficult to operate, and the reports are awkward" may alert you to potential advantages or problems. (Remember, however, that different properties have different needs and priorities; a rave review because the system provides an option you consider unimportant is meaningless for your purposes.) Consider the amount of time these properties spent on a needs analysis. A visit to the hotel property is worth the effort. Learning how different features of the system work, how various departments interact with the PMS, and what kinds of forms are used will help you with part of your decision. You will also develop a feeling for how guest services are affected.

Hardware Installation Plans

A careful plan for hardware installation will help the management maintain both guest service and employee morale. First, it is key to determine who will install wiring or cables. Next to be determined is which hardware will be installed and at what times, followed by which departments will receive hardware first and what methods will be required to get all departments of the property *online*, a term used to indicate that a computer is operational and connected with a central computer. This information should be used to develop a flowchart, which will help departments adapt and interact using online operations.

Computer Training Programs

The training offered by a computer company ranges from classes held at the corporate headquarters to on-the-job training sessions and informal consultant hot lines. The staff members who will use the computers must be thoroughly trained if the equipment is to be put to its best use. Training at the terminals should be preceded by an explanation of how the system will help staff members in their work. Some computer companies lend a dummy computer setup to a lodging property so the staff can experiment with the training modules (Figure 4-6). This allows them to make mistakes in private and to become familiar with the keyboard configuration. Documentation of procedures will also assist

FIGURE 4-6

Employees need time to practice using computer hardware and software. Photo courtesy of the author.

the staff in developing an awareness of the system's capabilities, as will individual hotel-developed step-by-step computer application cue cards.

It is also important to note that employee resistance to change can be overcome with early buy-in to a new concept and a user-friendly training program. The team concept will help employees overcome resistance to change because they are included on the team. Members of the needs analysis team will see an idea develop from concept to fruition. Many employees resist change because they fear they will be unable to perform a new task; a training program that allows adequate time and practice will help introduce the technology and decrease this fear.

Backup Power Sources

What happens if the power goes out? This concern about *blackouts*, or total loss of electricity, as well as the possibility of *brownouts*, or partial loss of electricity, is addressed by computer dealers. Battery-powered temporary energy units are used when power is lost or cut to ensure operational data are not lost. Hotel managers who have experienced power losses are well versed in maintaining communication among the departments and posting charges as required. Once the power returns in full, the staff can catch up on posting to the electronic folio.

Maintenance Agreement

One final consideration in adopting a PMS is the maintenance agreement, which should spell out the related costs of repair and replacement of hardware and software. Allowance for emergency service and times available for general service should also be listed. Loaner or backup equipment availability enhances the attractiveness of the agreement.

Financial Considerations

Purchasing or leasing a PMS for hotel use is a major financial decision. Such an investment can tie up cash flow. If the costs and benefits are not realistically projected, profits may be in jeopardy. The first part of this chapter stressed the importance of performing a needs analysis. Hotel properties that match computer applications with needs by going through this process will achieve the most realistic assessment of costs versus benefits when adopting computer systems.

The controller of a lodging property usually prepares a budget in consultation with the general manager. Sales of room-nights, food and beverages, and other products and services are projected. Considered with these projections are the related costs of producing those goods and services. The controller is usually aware of the specific costs in each department—the amount of overtime pay required at the end of the month to produce the monthly inventory in the food and beverage department, the extra part-time help required to staff the front desk for a busy checkout or check-in, the cost to produce a direct mail piece for the marketing and sales office, and the fee charged by the outside accountant to produce a monthly profit-and-loss statement. This knowledge is helpful in determining how much money could be saved if a PMS were to be introduced. The amount of money that can be saved (along with tax depreciation advantages) must be equal to or greater than the amount spent on the computer system. Sometimes management may feel less tangible benefits, such as greater service to guests or improved morale among employees, justify the cost even when dollar savings are not quite equal.

The decision to purchase, lease, or connect to the Internet must also be made. The outright cost of purchase, related finance charges (if applicable), discount for cash, and depreciation are only a few of the points to review if the hotel decides to purchase. These considerations must be weighed against continuance of cash flow, application of lease payments to the purchase price, and tax advantages of leasing.

Determining the *payback period*—the time required for the hotel to recoup purchase price, installation charges, financing fees, and so forth through cost savings and increased guest satisfaction—will also assist management in deciding whether or not to install or adopt a new computer system.

If the controller reports a series of financial problems such as the following, the payback period becomes clearer:

- 2 percent of all check-ins have to have their rates adjusted down because of lack of communication between front office and housekeeping
- 2 percent of sales are lost every month because guest checks are inaccurately totaled in the food and beverage department
- 10 hours of overtime could be saved through internal preparation of paychecks for each pay period

As the department directors review their respective profit-and-loss statements with the controller, additional areas for cost recovery can be noted. The time invested in preparing an accurate needs analysis will pay off in the long run.

The above concerns of the controller include areas in addition to the front desk. Remember that the adoption of a PMS involves the management of *all* guest services and accounting functions. While the needs of the front desk alone—for a call accounting system or the rental of a reservations system—may not justify the expense of a PMS, the needs of all departments can make such a system cost-effective and provide more efficient guest services.

PMS Applications

The property management system is organized around the functions needed to deliver service to the guest. The software options listed earlier in this chapter are only a few of the many available to hoteliers. For purposes of this review, assume the lodging property is equipped with a state-of-the art PMS and the system is up and running. The software

FIGURE 4-7	Main menu of a property management system.
1. Reservations	10. Back Office
2. Revenue Management	11. Housekeeping
3. Registration	12. Food and Beverage
4. Room Status	13. Maintenance
5. Posting	14. Security
6. Call Accounting	15. Marketing and Sales
7. Checkout	16. Personnel
8. Night Audit	17. Electronic Mail
9. Inquiries/Reports	18. Time Clock

program *main menu* lists on the screen all the available individual programs (modules) included in the system. Refer to Figure 4-7. These modules lie at the heart of the ability of the front office manager and his or her staff's ability to deliver excellent service to the guest because of the front office's role in communication between departments and the sharing of financial information. The PMS has become so much an essential part of lodging operations that to operate a hotel without one would be very difficult. The front office manager relies on the reservation module almost hourly to check changes that may affect the day's service and financial operations. The night audit, if completed as it was in previous years—tallying columns or using a mechanical audit machine—would take much training and many labor hours. The posting module is another timesaver that produces a much more accurate and efficient-looking guest ledger.

The options shown in Figure 4-7 are similar to those previously listed in this chapter. The front desk clerk can access any of these individual programs by typing the designated keystrokes or by following directions on a *touchscreen*, a type of computer monitor that allows the operator to input data with the touch of a finger. Documentation, consisting of either printed or on-screen (monitor) instructions, explains how to operate the hardware or software that accompanies a specific PMS. It comprises written step-by-step instructions as well as a flowchart of individual programs and subprograms, all of which are valuable in training staff. The flowcharts are comparable to the blueprints of a building. The following discussion of individual modules and subprograms highlights the applications of these software options in a property management system.

Reservations

The reservations module (refer to Figure 4-8) consists of subsystems that can receive individual guest or group data, check a guest's request against a data bank of available rooms, and store this information. The guest data are received through a personal phone call, through another computer in the referral system, or via the Internet. All of the

FIGURE 4-8	Reservations module.
1. Guest Data	8. VIP
2. Room Inventory	9. Projected Occupancy
3. Deposits	10. Travel Agents
4. Special Requests	11. Guest Messages
5. Blocking	12. Social Networking
6. Arrivals	13. Reports
7. Departures	

possible room types and locations, room rates, and special requests can be matched with the existing room inventories. This information can be stored for 52 weeks (or longer) in most systems. *Social networking* applications such as Facebook, Twitter, LinkedIn, You-Tube, message boards, websites, and blogs also have their application in this module.

Information concerning guarantees with credit cards or confirmed reservations is captured at this time. Details on deposits, blocking, times of arrival and departure, VIP guest lists, projected occupancies, and reports on these reservation functions assist the front office manager.

The guest who is checking out of the Select-Service Inn in Dallas, Texas, and wants to make a reservation at the Select-Service Inn in Chicago for that evening, can have the reservation confirmed within seconds. The guest information is already available in the data bank, and through electronic transmissions, the request is verified (via a check of the existing room inventories held in the data bank for the Select-Service Inn in Chicago) by a central computer. Other referral agencies follow similar procedures. (Further examples of computerized reservations options are provided in chapter 5.)

Revenue Management

Revenue management, a process of planning to achieve maximum room rates and the most profitable guests (those guests who will spend money at the hotel's food and beverage outlets, gift shops, etc.), encourages front office managers, general managers, and marketing and sales directors to target sales periods and develop sales programs that will maximize profit for the hotel. This module (Figure 4-9) shares similar databases

FRONT-LINE REALITIES

 As the reservations manager of a hotel, you receive the following tweet on your Twitter account: "2 ovr ngt rms ned desprly 3/12." How would you begin to deal with this?

FIGURE 4-9   Revenue management module.

1. Master Rate Table
2. Per-Person Increments
3. Guest Type Increments
4. Revenue Management

with the reservations module—room inventory, room rates, reservation status, and guest information. If a hotel is entering a maximum demand sales period, the revenue management module allows the reservations manager to block out that period to prevent guest requests for room reservations for less than the minimum time. Also, the computer prompts the reservations clerk on which room rate category to apply. Daily reports on how well the front office achieved maximum yield of *rack rates*, the highest room rates charged in a hotel, provide feedback to the general manager and owners. A history of guest sales in food and beverage also assists sales and marketing managers in determining if a group reservation has potential for profitability.

Registration

Guest registration modules have greatly improved the check-in process. Because information has already been captured at the time of reservation, less time is required for registration. The front desk clerk need only verify the guest's request for room type, location, and rate with room inventory and room status. Provisions for walk-in guests without reservations are similarly handled. Method of payment is also established. The hard plastic key can be issued after the security module has changed the entrance code for the room. The guest registration procedure can also be completed by the *self-check-in process*, a procedure that requires the guest to insert a credit card having a magnetic stripe containing personal and financial data into a self-check-in terminal and answer a few simple questions concerning the guest stay (Figure 4-10). (Self-check-in is discussed in more detail in chapter 7.) Also note the inclusion of an intranet in this module; it greatly supports the communication required by the front office staff for delivering hospitality at the time of check-in.

FIGURE 4-10   Registration module.

1. Reservations	5. Security
2. Guest Data/Registration	6. Reports
3. Room Inventory	7. Self-Check-In
4. Room Status	8. Intranet

FIGURE 4-11	Room status module.

1. Room Inventory
2. Availability
3. Reports
4. Intranet

As an example of how this module works, consider the guest who flies to Chicago from Dallas, signs a guest registration form, waits while the desk clerk checks the status of the room, and receives a key—check-in is complete. All guest information was captured when the initial reservation was made at the Dallas Select-Service Inn. The data bank of room occupancy information provided by the housekeeper at the Chicago hotel is available to the front desk via the computer. The front desk clerk chooses the room the guest will occupy and issues a key. The total time required for registration is less than five minutes.

Room Status

The *room status* module provides information on availability of entry to a guest room. There are two types of room status: reservation and housekeeping. Reservation status can be open, confirmed, guaranteed, or repair. Housekeeping status can be ready, on change, or out of order. Reservation status is maintained by the reservation department or reservation system, while housekeeping status is provided by the housekeeping department.

Room status is one of the most valuable features of the PMS (Figure 4-11). It streamlines the operation problems of check-in and assists other departments as well. This module, which may share the same room data bank with reservations, provides reports used by the housekeeper, front office manager and staff, maintenance engineer, night auditor, reservations clerk, and marketing and sales department. The housekeeper must know which guest rooms have been occupied and need cleaning, desk clerks must know if the guest room is reserved or open for sale, the maintenance engineer must plan for routine painting and refurbishing, the night auditor must verify which rooms have been sold to complete the night audit, the reservations clerk needs information on the availability of guest rooms, and the marketing and sales department must have current information on room availability for conventions.

FRONT-LINE REALITIES

 The general manager of the hotel asks you to help determine the payback period for a $20,000 PMS. How would you begin?

FIGURE 4-12	Posting module.	
1. Point-of-Sale		6. Paid-Out
2. Room		7. Miscellaneous Charges
3. Tax		8. Phone
4. Transfer		9. Display Folio
5. Adjustment		10. Reports

This is another module that might utilize the intranet; however, room status information is immediate in nature, and the posting of a message with a delayed response time may not be appropriate. On the other hand, if a series of rooms will be taken out of use for an extended period, the intranet could be the appropriate place to post an advance notice for the marketing and sales department and the front office. Such a notice would prevent taking reservations for unavailable rooms.

Posting

The *posting* module of a PMS often supplies one of the first benefits realized by the front office manager: immediate posting of charges incurred by the guests (Figure 4-12). Not only is the posting operation streamlined but also accuracy is ensured. A PMS allows the posting to occur at the point of sale in the restaurant, lounge, or gift shop. Similarly, room and tax charges or telephone calls can be posted to the electronic folio in a very short time. Transfers and adjustments of guest charges (because empowerment policies allow front desk staff to deal with guest concerns or with approval by management of those concerns that go beyond stated policies) to folios are easily made. Charges incurred on behalf of the guest can be posted to the electronic folio by entering room number, amount of charge, department, and transaction type. These data are stored in memory and retrieved after an inquiry, during report generation, or at checkout. The accuracy of these charges still depends on the employee operating the point-of-sale terminal in the restaurant. Entering an inaccurate room number (room 412 entered as 712) or a reversed amount ($32.23 entered as $23.32) will still result in an incorrect posting.

Our guest at the hotel in Chicago wants to charge his valet expense of $20.95 to his room account. After the desk clerk has processed the paid-out to the delivery person, this charge is posted to the electronic folio by entering the room number, amount of charge, department, and type of transaction. The night auditor verifies the integrity of all department totals.

Call Accounting

The *call accounting* module of a PMS automatically posts telephone charges and a predetermined markup to a guest's folio (Figure 4-13). The individual subscriber to the telephone system (the lodging property) can charge a service fee for any local or

FIGURE 4-13 Call accounting module.	
1. Guest Information	4. Messages
2. Employee Information	5. Wake-up Calls
3. Post Charges	6. Reports

long-distance call. The hotel can now use the telephone system to generate profit rather than to simply supply service to the guest. The ability to make a profit through adding service charges, combined with the increased frequency and accuracy of electronic posting, has made the call-accounting option a desirable one. However, with the increased use of cell phones and personal digital assistants (PDAs), telephone revenue has declined. The PMS call-accounting feature retrieves data for time, charges, and service fees and then posts these charges to the electronic folio. The accuracy of processing telephone charges is greatly increased through the use of a PMS call-accounting feature.

Checkout

The inconvenience of guest checkout (long lines, disputes over charges) is greatly reduced with the PMS checkout feature, which prints out an accurate, neat, and complete guest folio in seconds (Figure 4-14).

Disputes over guest charges still occur at checkout, but not as often. The posting of a long-distance telephone call to room 295 instead of room 296 is less likely to occur with a PMS because the PMS interfaces with the call-accounting system and the phone charge is automatically posted to the guest's electronic folio.

Efficiency at time of checkout is also improved when the desk clerk retrieves a hard copy of the folio and presents it for review to the guest. The guest has already indicated method of payment at check-in. An imprint of the credit card has been made, or prepayment has occurred. The *floor limit*, a dollar amount of credit allowed by the credit card agency, and *house limit*, a dollar amount of credit allowed by the hotel, have been monitored by the PMS. These controls help avoid high *debit balances*, the amount of money the guest owes the hotel. Last-minute purchases of products or services are automatically posted at the point-of-sale terminals.

FIGURE 4-14 Checkout module.	
1. Folio	4. Back Office Transfer
2. Adjustments	5. Reports
3. Cashier	6. Guest History

The guest completes the checkout process by confirming the method of payment. The desk clerk may suggest making future reservations at this property or other properties in the chain or referral group. Transfers to the city ledger are made electronically at this time. Cashier activity reports are monitored, as is other information about the day's checkouts (such as number of guest departures and time of departures). A PMS can generate a *paid in advance* (PIA) listing, which monitors guests who paid cash at check-in. The PIA prevents guests from charging products or services to their guest folio.

Guests can avoid checkout lines by using *in-room guest checkout*, a feature of the property management system that allows the guest to use a guest room television to check out of the hotel. For this process, the night desk staff slips a copy of an updated guest folio under the door the night before checkout. The guest enters a few digits on the television control panel to start the process. After he or she answers questions about multiple guest accounts in the same room, accuracy of charges, and method of payment, for example, the process is complete. The guest can pick up a copy of the folio at the front desk if desired. In many hotels this process is automatic, and it is assumed the guest will check out without dropping by the front desk; all guest charges are accounted for by the credit card captured at the time of registration.

Night Audit

The night audit has always been labor-intensive. In addition to acting as a desk clerk and posting the room and tax charges, the night auditor must balance the guest transactions of the day. To extend credit to guests, debits and credits must be balanced daily. The debits originating from the various departments must be checked against the totals posted to the guest folios. The credits, the amount of money the hotel owes the guests (collected in the form of guest payments), must be accounted for by reviewing the guests' outstanding balances. Although this sounds like a simple process, the procedure can be very involved (Figure 4-15).

The PMS simplifies the night audit by producing totals from departments and guest folios. These data are assembled into standard report forms. Financial information is presented in the daily report, used by the management of the lodging property to determine the financial success of a particular day. Note that the intranet can also be included in this module because the night auditor can post emails to departmental employees concerning the final night audit or other operational details from the previous evening.

FIGURE 4-15	Night audit module.
1. Guest Charges	5. Financial Reports
2. Department Totals	6. Housekeeping
3. City Ledger	7. Intranet
4. Cashier	

FIGURE 4-16   Inquiries/reports module.

1. Reservations
2. Registrations
3. Checkouts
4. Housekeeping
5. Credit Balances

Inquiries/Reports

The *inquiries/reports* feature of the PMS allows management to retrieve operating or financial information at any time. The front office manager may want to check the number of available rooms in the room inventory for a particular night, the number of guests expected to be checked in, the number of guests to be checked out for the day, the current room status from the housekeeping department, or the *outstanding balance report*, a listing of guests' folio balances. These reports can be produced easily by a PMS (Figure 4-16). The inquiries/reports feature of the PMS enables management to maintain a current view of operations and finances.

Back Office

The hotel's accounting office, known as the *back office*, uses the accounting module of a PMS for support in the overall financial management of the hotel (Figure 4-17). The PMS simplifies the accounting processes, which include the labor-intensive posting procedure of *accounts payable*, which is the amount of money the hotel owes vendors; the transfer of *accounts receivable*, which is the amount of money owed to the hotel, based on the guest ledger and city ledger; compilation and production of the payroll; budget preparation; the production of the *profit-and-loss statement*, which is an official financial listing of income and expenses; and the *balance sheet*, which is an official financial listing of assets, liabilities, and owner's equity at a certain point.

For example, financial information concerning a certain vendor is entered once on a terminal located in the back office (also referred to as *controller's office*). This information

FIGURE 4-17   Back office module.

1. Accounts Payable	5. General Ledger
2. Accounts Receivable	6. Reports
3. Payroll	7. Intranet
4. Budgets	

is then reflected throughout the accounting process. Likewise, the financial information produced through the night audit can be accessed for various reports. These and other features assist in streamlining the accounting process. The intranet is another feature on this module that is most useful in communicating to front desk staff about situations where a guest's charges may need clarification after checkout or about cost centers that have incurred charges requiring clarification.

Housekeeping

Obtaining current information about guest room status has always been a challenge for the front desk staff. Guests become impatient when delayed at check-in. Desk clerks who have not received a room release from housekeeping have no choice but to remain calm and try to appease the guests. The process of obtaining ready status is quickly achieved with a PMS (Figure 4-18). The maid or houseman enters the ready status immediately through a computer terminal on the guest floor instead of waiting to report a block of rooms to the floor supervisor. The housekeeper no longer needs to make several trips per day to the desk clerk to release blocks of rooms. The efficiency of this module depends on the continued efforts of the housekeeping staff to report room status.

Assigning room attendants to clean rooms can be done easily. Labor analysis of number of guest rooms cleaned by room attendants and number of labor hours required to clean guest rooms is performed faster, and the daily housekeeper's report is quickly generated. Likewise, a quick notation entered into the PMS concerning the number of guests opting to reuse their linens for a second or third day provides the hotel with feedback/control statistics. Inventory of equipment and guest room supplies is also readily available.

Maintenance requests for guest rooms can be communicated instantly through the PMS. The maintenance department staff can also check room status information to determine if the housekeeping staff noted repairs to be made. If the maintenance department wants to take a room out of service for a few days to perform repairs, this information can be relayed to housekeeping and front desk staff through the housekeeping module on the intranet. Also, with the concern for a green environment, tracking of light bulb replacement can be a cooperative venture with housekeeping and maintenance via this module.

FIGURE 4-18	Housekeeping module.
1. Room Availability	5. Equipment/Supplies Inventory
2. Personnel Assignment	6. Maintenance Requests
3. Analysis	7. Intranet
4. Housekeeper's Report	

FIGURE 4-19	Food and beverage module.
1. Point-of-Sale	5. Recipes
2. Posting	6. Sales Control
3. Cashier Reports	7. Sales Production Analysis
4. Food/Beverage Inventory	8. Labor Analysis

Food and Beverage

The food and beverage module reduces paper flow (vouchers) as well as telephone calls from the restaurants and lounges to the front desk (Figure 4-19). It also facilitates the accounting process, verifying the integrity of the point-of-sale system. Cashier reports (cash, credit, room service) are easily produced. Other features include inventory control and calculation, recipe development, pricing, item profit evaluation, and sales projections. Sales production analysis and labor analysis are also possible with this module.

Maintenance

Using a PMS streamlines the processing of work orders. Repair orders are entered by various department members throughout the hotel as repairs are needed. Incomplete jobs can be prioritized, and completed jobs can be analyzed for cost. Inventories of equipment and parts can be maintained. The maintenance module is also used to track energy costs and areas of use. In fact, heating and air conditioning in guest rooms can be activated at the front desk. This module enables the management of a hotel to analyze operational information of this vital department (Figure 4-20).

Security

Electronic key production has enhanced key control. Each guest receives an electronic key with a unique electronic code because the PMS changes the key configuration or combination for each new guest room. Blank key cards, usually plastic, can be coded at the front desk for each new guest.

FIGURE 4-20	Maintenance module.
1. Review Work Order	5. Repair Cost Analysis
2. Room Status	6. Energy Usage Analysis
3. Cost/Labor Analysis	7. Guest Room Power Start
4. Inventory	

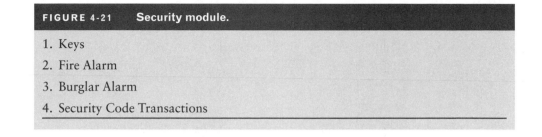

FIGURE 4-21   Security module.

1. Keys
2. Fire Alarm
3. Burglar Alarm
4. Security Code Transactions

Continual monitoring is a feature of the security module of the PMS. Fire alarm systems, including sprinklers and smoke detectors in guest rooms, public areas, and operational areas, are under constant surveillance via a *fire safety display terminal*. An alarm system or a voice telephone monitoring system alerts guests to a fire anywhere on the property. Elevators return automatically to the main lobby or other designated floor. Burglar alarms are also monitored through this module. The security feature of a PMS monitors security codes in other modules as well (Figure 4-21).

Marketing and Sales

The marketing and sales department makes extensive use of the PMS (Figure 4-22). This department can retrieve *guest histories*—information from guests' previous stays that reveals geographic origin, telephone information, organizational affiliation, credit card usage, room accommodation preferences, and the like—from reservation and registration files. The source of the reservation (secretary, group, travel agent), type of accommodation requested, and ZIP code of business office or personal domicile are only some of the data that can be obtained from the reservation files. Additional marketing data (newspapers read, radio stations listened to, source of recommendation) can be collected at the time of registration to give the marketing and sales department information on advertising media for target markets.

Another PMS application the marketing and sales department can use is the ability to produce *direct mail letters*, which are letters sent directly to individuals in a targeted

FIGURE 4-22   Marketing and sales module.

1. Guest History
2. Word Processing
3. Client Files
4. Banquet Files
5. Desktop Publishing
6. Reports
7. Travel Agencies
8. Room Status—Meeting Rooms
9. Social Networking

FIGURE 4-23　　Personnel module.
1. Employee File
2. Job Control List
3. Word Processing
4. Analysis
5. Reports

market group. Individual letters advertising certain products and services, together with mailing labels, can be prepared. Weekly *function sheets*, which list daily events such as meetings, banquets, and receptions, can be produced by assessing individual *banquet sheets*, which list the details of an individual event at which food and beverages are served. Information on clients can be stored and updated as required. Contracts can also be produced. Tickler files on upcoming events are a great asset in keeping an edge on the competition.

In addition, monthly newsletters can be produced through the word processing and desktop publishing applications. Further, this module maintains reserved occupancy status of meeting and banquet rooms—a valuable organizational feature. Tracking social networking applications used by the guest to contact the hotel, such as Facebook, Twitter, LinkedIn, YouTube, message boards, websites, and blogs for reservations or other information, assists in creating personal files on individual guests.

Personnel

The maintenance of personnel files is greatly enhanced by using a PMS (Figure 4-23). Information concerning job category, date of hire, record of orientation and training, rate of pay, last evaluation date, promotions, pay increases, payroll deductions, and the like assist management in developing a well-operated human resources department. The amount of paper involved in employee recordkeeping can be kept to a minimum. The word processing application is used to generate form letters, job descriptions, reports, employee procedures, and policy manuals. The PMS also permits labor analysis to be performed with ease.

Electronic Mail

The electronic mail feature, commonly referred to as *email*, is a communication system that uses an electronic network to send messages via computers. It is helpful in distributing current information on policies and procedures to a large staff as well as communicating with current and former hotel guests. Social networking applications

FIGURE 4-24   Electronic mail module.

1. Security Codes
2. Mail
3. Social Networking
4. Hard Copy
5. Intranet

such as Facebook, Twitter, LinkedIn, message boards, and blogs have expanded the concept of electronic mail for employees and guests alike. When email is used, security codes are issued to maintain privacy. Staff members are able to check their email at the computer terminal, while guests can develop an individual relationship with the lodging property. Copies of email messages can be printed if needed for future reference (Figure 4-24).

In a large corporation with many company-owned properties or franchises, email supports communication among establishments. In a hotel with many operating departments and thus many department heads, this feature is a great asset to the communication process. Regardless of the size of the lodging property, the email function in an intranet configuration is a useful communication tool. Throughout this section, applications highlight its value to the front office manager and his or her staff as well as to other department managers and their staffs.

Time Clock

Individual employees are issued a security code and an individual personal identification number. Upon entering their work area, they need only enter that number to record their start time. As they leave the work area for breaks or at a shift's end, they again need only enter that number. This information is stored and used by the controller's department when compiling the payroll. This feature saves a great deal of time in calculating the number of hours an employee worked on any given day (Figure 4-25).

FIGURE 4-25   Time clock module.

1. Security Codes	4. Time Out
2. Personal Identification Number	5. Analysis
3. Time In	6. Reports

Solution to Opening Dilemma

Prior to the PMS vendor's visit, it is advisable to perform a needs analysis. Although such an analysis may have been performed five years ago, the needs of hotel guests, management, and operations change over time. Forming a team of front-line employees and supervisors allows for a good decision. This team should analyze the flow of guests throughout their stay to establish a list of guest needs that could be enhanced through PMS technology. Because the team is composed of employees from different departments, other departmental requirements, including administrative paperwork, must also be discussed. These discussions enable the team to prepare a list of ways to enhance the guest's stay, assist departments in preparing reports, and improve communications among departments. The final step is to prioritize the identified needs and measure them against the budget.

Other considerations include verifying vendor claims, developing installation plans, discussing training programs provided by the computer company, investigating the availability of backup power sources, and securing a reasonable maintenance agreement. Financial considerations include cost-benefit analysis, the decision to purchase or lease, and working out a realistic payback period.

Chapter Recap

This chapter reviewed the importance of positioning the front desk to allow front office personnel a view of guests entering the lobby from both street entrances and elevators to underscore the hotel's responsibility for guest security. The guest's first impression is enhanced by the ambiance, physical appearance, and orderliness of the equipment and personnel. The front office manager must establish a balance between guest service and work processing to allow for efficiency.

This chapter also examined the use of computers by a hotel property, particularly in the front office. Deciding to purchase a computer system and choosing that system begins with a thorough needs analysis, a detailed procedure that allows the front office manager (and other department managers) to assess the value of automating particular functions. Evaluating software is a prime prerequisite in determining which computer applications best meet the needs of a particular property. The front office manager should also evaluate the hardware needed to operate the selected software package.

The decision to adopt a system is further clarified by examining vendor claims concerning operation, installation, training, backup power sources, and the maintenance agreement. The financial considerations of purchasing or leasing complete the computer decision. Front office managers should be aware of the computer applications—reservations, registration, room status, posting, call accounting, checkout, night audit, inquiries/reports, back office, housekeeping, food and beverage, maintenance, security, marketing and sales, personnel, electronic mail, and time clock—of a property management system as they relate to the successful operation of a front office.

End-of-Chapter Questions

1. When arranging equipment at the front desk, what factors should be considered?

2. Why is the position of the front desk in a hotel lobby important?

3. Describe the evolving role of computers in the hotel industry.

4. Explain in your own words what a property management system is. How does a property management system help provide hospitality to guests?

5. Why should a needs analysis be performed before computers and software are purchased? What are the components of a needs analysis?

6. Why are computer software considerations more important than computer hardware considerations?

7. If you are employed at a hotel that uses a property management system, which of the software options described in the text do you use? Explain the advantages of these modules.

8. If you are employed in a hotel with a property management system, discuss computer hardware descriptions with your front office manager. What equipment does your manager find most valuable? Why?

9. Why is interfacing important in a property management system? What are some examples of interfacing?

10. What is ergonomics? How does the ergonomics of computer terminals affect the front office staff?

11. How would you go about verifying vendor claims when considering the purchase of a property management system?

12. How does a well-developed installation plan for a property management system assist hotel management?

13. Why should management be sure employees are properly trained to use a property management system?

14. If the power goes out in a 200-room lodging property for four hours, how would you preserve the data in the property management system?

15. If you are employed in a hotel, ask your front office manager if there is a maintenance agreement for the property management system. What items are covered? How well has the vendor stood behind the agreement?

16. Discuss the purchase-versus-lease consideration in terms of financial profitability.

17. What does the main menu of a PMS tell an operator? How is it organized?

18. Review the computer applications described in this chapter. Explain how they are used to provide better service to the guest and to improve financial control in the hotel.

19. What is an intranet? How might an intranet be used in a lodging property?

20. Provide examples of how social networking applications such as Facebook, Twitter, LinkedIn, YouTube, message boards, websites, or blogs could be used to increase guest reservations, improve guest communications, or create a guest history.

CASE STUDY 401

Ana Chavarria, front office manager, and Lorraine DeSantes, director of marketing and sales, have just returned from a computer conference at which they were able to look at the latest property management systems for hotels. Ana is enthusiastic about updating and adopting front office applications for reservations, registration, room status, posting, call accounting, checkout, and night audit. Lorraine is sure the marketing and sales applications will help her department be more efficient.

Both realize the cost involved in obtaining modules for a property management system. What would you suggest they do prior to discussing this issue with Margaret Chu, general manager of The Times Hotel?

Assuming Ms. Chu is willing to consider the purchase of a PMS, how should Ana and Lorraine proceed? Whom should they include in developing a PMS adoption plan, and why? What areas should they investigate?

CASE STUDY 402

The computer team of The Times Hotel is in the process of updating a computer needs analysis. The team is ready to decide which new modules should be adopted. Ana Chavarria, front office manager and chair of the committee, is seeking consensus on whether the team should recommend the purchase of a point-of-sale module for the restaurant operation or a guest history module for the marketing and sales department. Eric Jones, food and beverage

manager, says the point-of-sale module will pay for itself in six months because guests are walking out of the hotel before their breakfast charges are posted to their folios. Lorraine DeSantes, director of marketing and sales, says the purchase of the guest history module will increase business by 25 percent in the first year. The budget allows for only one purchase. What concepts would you recommend the team do or consider to break the stalemate?

CASE STUDY 403

The owner of an independent full-service lodging property has reviewed your proposal for the installation of a property management system. The proposal is thorough; it includes all the necessary steps outlined in this chapter. However, the owner says that due to economic conditions at this time, "we have to cut back and purchase only five of the eleven modules" in the proposal. Which of the five modules would you maintain? Justify your decision.

1. Reservations
2. Revenue Management
3. Registration
4. Room Status
5. Posting
6. Call Accounting
7. Back Office
8. Housekeeping
9. Food and Beverage
10. Marketing and Sales
11. Night Audit

Notes

1. CARA Information Systems, Inc.; Computerized Lodging Systems, Inc.; ECI/EECO Computer, Inc.; Hotel Information Systems; and Lodgistix, Inc.

2. Ibid.

3. Reprinted from *Hospitals* 56, no. 9 (May 1, 1982), by permission. Copyright 1982 by American Hospital Publishing, Inc.

Key Words

access time
accounts payable
accounts receivable
back office
balance sheet
banquet sheet
blackouts
brownouts
call accounting
computer supplies
characters per second (CPS)

cursor
debit balance
direct mail letters
disk drive
email
ergonomics
fire safety display terminal
floor limit
flow analysis processes
function sheets
gigabyte

guest histories

hardware

house limit

inkjet

inquiries/reports

in-room guest checkout

interfacing

Internet

intranet

I/O ports (input/output devices)

keyboard

keypad

laser

letter-quality

main menu

megabyte

megahertz

modem

monitor

needs analysis

online

outstanding balance report

paid in advance (PIA)

payback period

point-of-sale

posting

ppm (pages per minute)

printer

processor speed

profit-and-loss statement

property management system (PMS)

rack rate

revenue management

room status

self-check-in process

single-sheet

social networking

software

tickler files

touchscreen

CHAPTER 5

Systemwide Reservations

OPENING DILEMMA

Two days remain before the first guest checks in for the Forest Conservation Conference. A quick review of the reservation module report indicates several of the new desk clerks took guaranteed reservations (35 rooms) for the convention that account for 10 percent more rooms than are available.

Reservations are a necessity for travelers and an important marketing tool for lodging establishments. Travelers in various market segments depend on a well-organized reservation system that is easily accessible via toll-free telephone numbers or the Internet, or at a few moments' notice through social networking opportunities such as Facebook, Twitter, and LinkedIn. Lodging establishments want to provide a continuous flow of guests, which will bring profits. A reservation system must ensure efficient means of accessing, processing, and confirming information (Figure 5-1). Without an efficient reservation system, all aspects of managing a hotel are negatively affected. For example, while overbooking reservations may guarantee a full house for the hotel, it also leaves the guest who is turned away with a negative impression. This not only decreases the hope of repeat business but also ensures the dissatisfied customer will tell others of the negative experience. This chapter examines the reservation system as an integral part of progressive front office management and discusses the operation of a well-run system.

CHAPTER FOCUS POINTS

- Importance of guest reservations to travelers and lodging establishments
- Overview of reservation system
- Sources of reservations
- Forecasting reservations
- Overbooking (occupancy management)
- Processing guest reservations

FIGURE 5-1

A reservation clerk is ready to process a guest's request for a room reservation. Photo courtesy of the author.

Importance of a Reservation System

Profitable business ventures rely on effective marketing, which includes reviewing people who require hotel products and services, determining their specific needs, developing products and services that meet those needs, and making a profit on the sale of those products and services.

A well-organized reservation system allows hotels to ensure a steady flow of guests into their properties. Hotel chains, through their central reservation system, enable member establishments to fill 30 percent or more of available rooms nightly. Independent hoteliers, in contrast, must create exciting marketing programs to capture room business. Easy access to a chain hotel's data bank of rooms helps hotels meet customers' needs as well as reach a targeted daily occupancy rate, average daily rate, yield percentage, and RevPAR. A reservation system is the primary means of producing positive cash flow and a favorable income statement. Social media applications are a recent emphasis:

There appears to be little doubt that the social media networking tidal wave has hit the hotel industry. To varying degrees, many hotels and hotel companies are attempting to implement some active level of social media marketing. Whether it is Facebook,

Twitter, corporate blogs, LinkedIn, or a myriad of other platforms, social media is rapidly changing the networking landscape. In addition to SEO [search engine optimization], now social media optimization (SMO) and, online reputation management (ORM), are emerging as viable factors in managing effective online visibility.[1]

Overview of the Reservation System

The hotel industry is powered by sales derived from the use of computerized reservations systems. The systems used to fill rooms consist of the hotel's primary efforts (via marketing and sales and use of their own brand reservation system), their toll-free number, global distribution systems (GDS), travel agents, and third-party sources such as wholesalers who buy rooms from the hotel and resell them on the Internet. The following information shows how hotels rely on a combination of these well-organized systems to produce a profit.

Choice Hotels International

The following information on Choice Hotels International, (formerly Bass Hotels & Resorts), Carlson Hospitality Worldwide, and Pegasus Solutions provides a concise view of the importance of computerized reservation systems to the hospitality industry.

Choice Hotels International, with 5900 franchisees in 30 countries and territories, and with more than 479,000 rooms, operates under the Comfort Inn, Quality, Clarion, Sleep Inn, Econo Lodge, MainStay Suites, Rodeway Inn, Comfort Suites, Cambria Suites, Suburban Extended Stay Hotel, and Ascend Collection brands. Choice's implementation of a new training program for reservations in 2004 assisted in the success of their reservation system.

By fall 2007, [the] central reservation system had handled six $10 million days and two $11 million days of gross revenue. The training improvements also resulted in a conversion increase from 36 percent to 43.8 percent in the last four years. This conversion brought an incremental $5.6 million in revenue through [the] reservations centers in 2007.[2]

Hilton Hotels

Hilton Hotel Corporation has taken a new approach to managing its reservations services by developing a home-based reservation service.

Hilton currently has more than 3000 hotels and 500,000 rooms in 74 countries and territories. Keeping those rooms booked is Hilton's top priority. The challenge for managers at Hilton Reservations & Customer Care is to provide high-quality customer service as efficiently as possible. The company decided that a work-at-home program for its call center staff could both increase its quality of customer service and decrease its call center costs. Hilton Reservations also saw in work-at-home programs an opportunity to reduce its number of call center locations, potentially resulting in savings on real estate, power, natural resources, and other physical support costs. The group has since reduced call center staff numbers enough to close one full call center and shift the work out to 200 home-based agents. In this way Hilton Reservations avoids costs associated with rent, utilities, and maintenance.

To outfit an agent completely, Hilton Reservations supplies a Wyse client, Netgear firewall, Citrix license, and a Microsoft Terminal Server license. This costs approximately $1200, which compares favorably with the $1300 it costs to outfit an agent station at a call center. "Saving $100 on equipment costs per employee may not sound like much," says Rick Sloane, IT support manager for Hilton Reservations and Customer Care, "but we are rolling this out to 2500 individuals throughout time, representing close to $250,000." Hilton also saves resources by adjusting the hours available to its work-at-home staff to match changing levels of demand. This enables Hilton to respond to seasonal variance and to deliver excellent customer service, with minimal wait times for incoming callers, without having to pay staff when it doesn't need that extra capacity.

Although the amount the company pays per hour worked has gone down significantly, overall the performance and quality of services agents deliver to Hilton customers has dramatically increased. "With the convenience and flexibility of working at home, we attract more applicants and can afford to be more selective," says Sloane. "Many applicants already have full-time jobs, but [they] can work extra hours if they don't have to drive to a workplace and if they can choose their own hours. Agents use an online program to build their schedule each week, signing up for specific hourly slots to meet expected levels of demand."[3]

Marriott International

Marriott International has more than 3200 lodging properties in the United States and 66 other countries and territories. Executives have sought additional marketing expertise in booking sources, rates, and length-of-stay patterns from TravelCLICK, Inc. The following information provides insight about managing a reservation system, reviewing guest-stay data, forecasting, and evaluating the competition.

> Marriott International recently signed an agreement with TravelCLICK Hotelligence® in 150 of its select service and extended stay properties including Courtyard, Residence Inn, Fairfield Inn, TownePlace Suites, and SpringHill Suites. Hotelligence reports will provide Marriott properties with insight on booking sources, rates, and length-of-stay patterns for their individual hotels and for hotels they define as their competitors. By 2012, 65% of the largest companies—like Marriott—will leverage information, processes, and business intelligence tools to make informed, responsive decisions on significant changes in their business and markets."[4]

Global Distribution Systems (GDS) in Securing Reservations

A global distribution system (GDS) is a distributor of hotel rooms to corporations such as travel agents that buy rooms in large volume. GDSs that play a prominent role in securing guest reservations include Amadeus, Galileo, SABRE, and Worldspan. The following details the concept of their operations.

TravelCLICK, is a Global Distribution Systems (GDS) that also has capability for measuring advertising, reach to a travel agent audience. A new feature that has been added is the best available rate (BAR) display in their ads. These features increase transparency and functionality. The constant update of BAR data increases the likelihood of a booking. Also, next-generation methodology pinpoints participating travel agents.[5]

How important is electronic distribution as a means of gaining reservations and boosting revenue? Representing almost 30 percent of hotelier bookings, in 2008 GDSs delivered over 115 million room-nights with a revenue value of almost $20 billion.[6]

Role of the Internet in Securing Reservations

The business and pleasure traveler have entered the marketplace with a great degree of sophistication. Armed with information from advertising television promotions, direct mail promotions from credit cards, airline frequent flyer incentive plans, Facebook, LinkedIn, Twitter, and other promotional sources, they want to secure the best rates and value for their accommodations. They search the Internet for the best price and make sure they are satisfied with their hit. How did this free marketplace come about? How did it seem to become a buyer's marketplace? Why do hoteliers grimace at the thought of the Internet rate? The following discussions on the background of room rates offered via the Internet, the effect of the Internet on pricing rooms, and consumers' use of the Internet in making reservations show how technology has changed the way hoteliers do business. Jerome Wise, vice president of eCommerce for TravelCLICK International, reports, "According to Google™, networking is going to be the second-most-popular online activity by 2012, overtaking shopping and surpassing both communication—such as email—and entertainment." He adds, "Hoteliers who explore social networking early on in its development will have a clear competitive advantage as it matures."[7]

Background on Room Rates Offered via the Internet

Sharon H. McAuliffe outlines thoughts for you to consider on room rates offered via the Internet. Prior to the Internet's entrance into the marketing of rooms, the only public rates available for consumers were those published in brochures or obtained by telephoning the hotel property or a travel agent. Any discounts were offered to wholesalers and corporate clients based on their volume of business or length of stay. When the dot-com mania hit consumers, wholesalers decided to advertise free offers to entice consumers to use the Internet. This left a lasting impression on the consumer's purchasing manner. An initial wholesaler offered to take empty hotel rooms into inventory on the Internet, and hoteliers were grateful to sell the rooms at low sale prices. Internet volume was light, and everything seemed fine. Then other Internet sites began to offer similar models with discounts and a guaranteed lowest price. The result is a transparency of rates. Guests can explore room rates before check-in to see if their guaranteed room rate has been offered at a lower price online.[8]

However, a new concept—customer relationship management (CRM), or management of guest services with technology—has entered the hoteliers' workaday world via electronic media. Max Starkov provides insight into the electronic application of CRM.

The truth is that CRM in travel is much more than technology or database management. CRM and its online application, e-CRM, are business strategies aiming to engage the customer in a mutually beneficial relationship. Electronic customer relationship management (e-CRM allows travel companies (travel suppliers and online travel agencies—OTAs) to engage customers in strong, personalized and mutually beneficial interactive relationships, increase conversions and sell more efficiently. The main components of an e-CRM strategy in travel and hospitality include the following:

- Know Your Customer
- Customer Service
- Personalization
- More Efficient Marketing
- Build Customer Loyalty[9]

Effect of Internet on Pricing Rooms

Visitors to a hotel's website must be turned into guaranteed reservations. An article from SynXis shows how this marketing challenge of room pricing is managed:

Hoteliers using Guest Connect Booking Engine are already reporting significant increases in both the volume of bookings and conversion rates from visitors to their websites. Guest Connect was developed by SynXis, the Sabre Holdings.

Guest Connect templates guide the flow of the booking process and enable the hotelier to incorporate the specific product elements that will best merchandise their property or chain, from expanded property descriptions and rich images to dynamic packaging, promotional pricing (with "slash-through" pricing), room preference selection, upgrades or links to a virtual concierge for additional services. In addition, hotel managers have access to integrated, comprehensive tracking tools that give a complete view of their return on investment (ROI) for online marketing efforts.

At Remington Hotels at its Inn at Key West by comparing before and after statistics, they found that the Guest Connect booking engine produced over 250% more bookings than the old booking engine when compared on a weekly basis. This increase resulted in more than $45,000 in incremental revenue each week for the 100-room property.[10]

Consumers Response to Use of the Internet—Third-Party Websites

Third-party websites, such as Expedia and Travelocity, provide the consumer an opportunity to view hotel room availability and rates with a few keystrokes on the computer. Consumer response to the opportunity to book room reservations online has been overwhelming. TravelCLICK, a Chicago-based electronic provider of reservations for consumers, serves over 14,000 customers in more than 140 countries. It indicated consumers' reliance on the Internet to process reservations.

TravelCLICK, Inc., the leading provider of ecommerce solutions for the global hotel industry, announced that as global markets realized a decline in demand through the first part of the year, TravelCLICK's independent client properties are performing strongly across more than 100 markets worldwide, delivering 39% more revenue and 29% more room nights for year-to-date May 2008 than in previous years. TravelCLICK hotels' direct web performance led the way, increasing 42% in web direct reservations and 46% in web revenues.[11]

This overwhelming response to the Internet continues. Starkov emphasizes the importance of e-CRM, evidenced by high consumer use of computer generated travel bookings:

Even with [an] expected decline in travel demand, online travel bookings in North America in 2009 are projected to grow by 10.5% and reach $116.1 billion and grow by 11% in 2010 (eMarketer). This growth is primarily the result of the dramatic shift from the offline to online channel. Similar is the situation in Europe and APAC. In 2009, more than 55% of all travel bookings and up to 40% of all hotel bookings in North America will be generated from the Internet (eMarketer, HeBS), which represents a double-digit growth over 2008. At least another third of hotel bookings will be directly influenced by online research, but booked offline. Over 65% of online hotel bookings will come from the direct online channel, i.e., via the hotel's own website (76% for the major hotel brands). The hotel website has become the first, main, only and in many cases last point of contact with past, current and potential guests.[12]

Social Media

The new methods of reaching consumers via *social media* technologies such as Facebook, Twitter, YouTube, LinkedIn, and blogs requires hoteliers to consider these options in developing their marketing plans. John Davies provides several concepts to consider in deciding how to develop such a plan.

1. **Define your strategy and long-term objective.** Is your goal to communicate to or with your prospective guests? Are you seeking fleeting fans or building long-term, lasting relationships with your customers? Is the goal to enhance the credibility and reputation of your brand or promotion of the week?

2. **Make sure there is a commitment to Social Media Marketing (SMM).** Social media marketing is a process that involves participation, interaction, resources, commitment, follow-through, and time. Someone has to be there to monitor and be the resource for the guest.

3. **Social media should not be the anchor to your marketing plan.**

4. **Make it a team effort with the unique applications of social media.** Get your property GM and company leadership on the SMM bandwagon.

5. **Seek out the experts and observe those having success with SMM.** Be on the lookout for educational webinars and SMM "boot camps."[13]

Financial Effects of Third-Party Reservations

The financial effects of this consumer response should be evaluated. The chapter on revenue management considers the job of the revenue manager, which includes evaluating channels of room reservations. For example, a reservation completed via a travel agent may incur a 10 percent commission, while a third-party reservation may incur a commission as high as 18 percent. If you do the math on a room that sells for $100, the commission equals $10 for the 10 percent and $18 for the 18 percent. If you extend that $8 difference to just 10 rooms per night for 365 nights per year, the result is $29,200 ($8 × 10 × 365 = $29,200). However, there is another side to that argument. What if you didn't place those extra rooms for sale on the *third-party reservation website*? Would they have remained unsold? Would you have lost all income, let alone the differential of $29,200? It is indeed a struggle of wits and experience to compete in the revenue management venue.

Types of Reservation Systems

Franchisee

A *franchisee* is a hotel owner who has access to a national reservation system and receives the benefits of the corporation's management expertise, financial backing, national advertising, and group purchasing. A franchise member of a reservation system or a member of a referral system gains significant advantages from *interhotel property referrals*, a system in which one member-property recommends another member-property to a guest, and national advertising.

Referral Member

A *referral member of a reservation referral system*, a worldwide organization that processes requests for room reservations at a particular member hotel, is a hotel developer/owner who has access to the national reservation system. Hotels that are members of the reservation system are more than able to justify the associated costs; for example, a chain property may obtain 15 to 30 percent of its daily room rentals from the national reservation system, depending on local economic and market conditions. Compared to the costs incurred by an independent property that must generate every single room sale with individual marketing and sales efforts, franchise referral costs seem minimal.

Use of the reservation system by franchises and referral properties incurs fees such as those for royalty, marketing, and reservations. For example, in 2009, Hilton requires an initial fee of $85,000 for the first 275 guest rooms or suites plus $300 for each additional guest room or suite, with a minimum fee of $85,000. Five percent of monthly gross rooms revenue is considered the royalty fee. The monthly program fee is 4 percent of monthly gross rooms revenue. Hilton requires installation of their OnQ proprietary business software and hardware system; the up-front costs for these systems range from $40,000 to $150,000. Additionally, a monthly fee of 0.75 percent of hotel gross revenue is charged for use of OnQ.[14]

Marriott charges similar franchise fees for an investor seeking a Fairfield Inn franchise. An application fee of $50,000 or $400/room (whichever is greater) is charged. The royalty fee is based on 4.5 percent of the gross room revenues. Marriott assesses 2.5 percent of gross room revenues fee for marketing. Reservation fees include 0.80 percent of gross room revenues, $2.60 per non-property reservation, and a communication support fee of $212.00 per accounting period.[15]

If you do the math on the cost of operating a hotel under the auspices of either of these franchises, you can determine that a franchise is a very expensive business option. However, the benefits (reservation system, advertising, management development, etc.) of operating a hotel with a franchise are numerous and far outweigh the costs.

Sources of Reservations

Guest reservations come from a variety of market segments. Some of the more common groups are corporate clients, social/military/educational/religious/fraternal (SMERF) organizations, group travelers, leisure travelers, and current guests who want to return to the same hotel. This is only one way of classifying guest reservations. The purpose of analyzing these segments is to understand the needs of each group and to provide reservation systems that meet their needs. Keep in mind that reviewing these needs will assist you in gaining insight into guests' methods of communication. The more you learn about those methods, the better you will be able to monitor and improve current reservation communication systems.

Corporate Clients

The *corporate client* is a hotel guest employed by a business or a guest of that business. Corporate clients provide a hotel with an opportunity to establish a regular flow of business during sales periods that would otherwise be flat. For example, a hotel located in an area popular with weekend tourists would operate at a loss if an aggressive marketing effort were not made to secure corporate clients from Sunday through Thursday nights. Corporate clients are usually in town to visit corporate headquarters or to attend business meetings or conventions. Visits are usually structured in advance, with detailed agendas and itineraries. Such structured schedules suggest the corporate guest requires reservations to ensure a productive business visit.

The reservation for the corporate guest may be initiated by a secretary or an administrative assistant. These office personnel are vital to hotel marketing efforts. Many hotels offer a secretaries club, which is a powerful marketing and public relations effort aimed at this group. The program encourages the secretary or administrative assistant to make room reservations with the hotel for visiting business clients by providing incentives such as gift certificates for the person who books the most reservations, free meals, and free special-interest seminars. This system forms the basis for a loyal contingent of secretaries and administrative assistants who think of the club's hotel first. This marketing program helps the front office manager and the reservationist get to know the leaders in the business community in an indirect way. If such people need a quick reservation on a busy night, they feel they will receive special consideration from the hotel's management.

A toll-free phone number assists the cost-conscious corporate client by allowing corporate guests calling from outside the property's area code to save on phone bills. The independent lodging property that has installed a toll-free phone number gives itself a marketing advantage. If the person making the reservation wants to check out rates, location, amenities, related hotel services, and the like, he or she can do so without incurring expense. Even with today's common use of cell phones, the toll-free number is appreciated. The corporate client can then match travel needs with available lodging properties.

The corporate client can also place the reservation through the reservation/referral system of the chain organization. The large chains, which advertise by radio, television, billboard, and print, allow the corporate client to make reservations easily through a toll-free number. The number connects the caller to a reservationist who has access to a data bank of available rooms at lodging properties that are members of the chain or referral system. The reservation can be completed in minutes. The use of a single phone number to access all properties offers the corporate client an easy, standard way to make reservations for stays in several cities with one call. In the lodging industry, this opportunity to gain repeat business is important.

Travel agents also make reservations for corporate clients. The travel agent who is booking air or other transportation for clients usually books room reservations as well.

The corporate client can also visit a hotel's website to obtain information and make a room reservation.

A more recent means of communicating reservations to lodging properties is LinkedIn. Carol Verret describes how LinkedIn can assist the sales representative in a lodging property.

Meeting and travel planning departments have been downsized in many cases—they really don't have time for lunch or to travel for a site inspection. Social networks are a great place for building those relationships. Maximize the page and have a company profile on LinkedIn. Recommendations from other meeting and travel planners on your page serve as a "third party" referral and are more likely to inspire confidence in you and the hotel.[16]

Social/Military/Educational/Religious/Fraternal (SMERF)

The SMERF market provides a good opportunity to fill vacancies in odd times of the business of the cycle because this market will travel at off-peak times to save money. For example, educators may hold meetings during the Christmas vacation or summer recess so they can secure a lower room rate. SMERF groups may number just 50 to 100, but there are many such groups to be courted. They can be mined through the combined efforts of a local travel and tourism board, Internet searches to determine when groups schedule their annual, semiannual, or quarterly meetings, and a review of local newspapers to identify the leaders of local chapters.

Meetings/Incentive/Conference/Event (MICE)

The lucrative MICE market requires a devoted hotel marketing and sales team or agency to locate large groups of conference attendees who want to schedule their meeting at a conference hotel. Many details are involved in encouraging a group to book an event, including airfares, supply of hotel rooms, room rates, and area cultural activities. The support of a local tourism and travel association is a major asset.

Group Travelers

Group travelers are persons traveling as a group either on business or for leisure. Convention guests and seminar attendees are examples of groups that travel on business. Participants in organized tours who pursue recreation, education, hobbies, and special interests constitute some of the leisure segment. The key to marketing reservations to this group is providing an efficient access method for planning details of a tour. The *group planner* is the person responsible for securing guest room accommodations, food and beverage programs, transportation reservations, meeting facilities, registration procedures, tours, and information on sightseeing as well as maintaining a budget for group travelers. The group planner must satisfy the needs of the group in an efficient, orderly, and professional manner. The details involved in organizing a three-day convention in a large city for 700 attendees or a seven-day tour of points of interest for 44 people are quite extensive. How does the group planner begin?

Options available for the tour or meeting planner include tapping into the *bus association network*, an organization of bus owners and tour operators who offer transportation and travel information to groups, using directories listing lodging properties, communicating with hotel representatives of lodging properties, and contacting hotel brokers. Hoteliers provide information concerning lodging facilities and tourism through these sources.

Bus associations are professional organizations on the national and state levels that provide their members with organized destination information needed for planning tours and conventions. Usually these associations organize conventions of their own by working with hotels, tourist attractions, and travel and promotion associations in the public sector that supply facilities and points of interest to the group traveler. Through the monthly publications of these associations, members can remain current on the travel industry. The lodging operation that advertises in these publications will reach a market that is looking to add variety to group tours.

Travel directories, organized listings of hotel reservation access methods and hotel geographic and accommodations information, also help the group travel planner match facilities with the needs of groups. The most common of these directories is Hotel and Travel Index.com. Other directories include Travel Books &Guides from the American Automobile Association (AAA), the *Michelin Guide*, and Weissmann Travel Reports. A Nielsen survey reports 156,557,641 active Internet home users. From this data we can presuppose consumers have ease of access to information on a hotel's products and services via the Internet.[17]

Working with a *hotel representative*, a member of the hotel's marketing and sales department who actively seeks group activities planners, is another method the group planner may find useful. Armed with details about the lodging facility, points of interest in the area, and community background, the hotel representative can prepare a package deal for the planner. The active solicitation of group business can prove profitable for a hotel.

Another type of active solicitation for group travelers is done by the *hotel broker*. This is the person who sells hotel room prize packages to corporations, sweepstakes promoters, game shows, and other sponsors. By booking reservations in volume, a hotel broker obtains a discount for the organization that wants to offer a hotel visit as a prize. Chain and referral organizations usually have people in their corporate marketing and sales divisions who contact organized groups or brokers to sell the hotel rooms and facilities.

As mentioned earlier, the key to securing the business of group travelers is to develop a structured access system that assists the planner in meeting the needs of the group. The more readily available the information concerning the lodging property, tourist attractions, and the community, the easier it is for the planner to choose a property. (Please note hotel brokers also solicit room blocks from hoteliers on certain dates for resale on their third-party website.)

Leisure Travelers

Leisure travelers are people who travel alone or with others to visit points of interest or relatives, or for other personal reasons. These travelers, who are often unrestricted by deadlines or schedules, are more flexible in their travel plans than are corporate clients and group travelers. They are more willing to seek someplace to stay along the way; however, some of the people in this group may want to obtain guaranteed reservations to ensure a trip with no surprises. This fragmented group consists of many subgroups, including singles, married couples, young families, senior citizens, and students. Some of the methods the leisure traveler can use to secure room reservations are travel agencies, toll-free numbers, reservation/referral systems, the Internet, Twitter, and Facebook.

Although using travel agents to place reservations may not be as common with leisure travelers as it is with businesspeople, the ease of one-stop shopping that travel agents offer encourages hotels to develop strong business relationships with them. The fee a lodging facility pays for accepting a reservation placed by a travel agent is usually 10 percent or more of the room rate, a minimal sum compared to the increase in volume and subsequent profits an agent can generate for a property. Another reservation method used by travelers is the toll-free phone number. Calling these numbers, which are listed in travel guides and the phone book, provides travelers with up-to-the-minute room rates and reservation availability status.

The third method available for the traveler is the reservation/referral system. This option offers a quick way to contact a particular hotel via a national or international reservation/referral system. Travelers planning long trips or visits to unfamiliar areas usually prefer some assurance that accommodations will be available, clean, safe, and comfortable. The name recognition built up over time by a chain provides that assurance and convinces the traveler to place room reservations through its reservation/referral system.

A fourth approach used by the leisure travel market to make reservations is the Internet. Travelers can visit the website of participating hotels to investigate accommodations and pricing as well as to make reservations. The leisure market has embraced this method via home computers and widespread Internet connection.

The last methods of social media—Twitter and YouTube—are being incorporated into the marketing efforts of this segment. Some examples include those offered by Marriott.

Marriott Resorts Hawaii is celebrating Hawaii's 50th anniversary of statehood with a "Tweet Yourself to Hawaii" online campaign. The campaign will award free trips to Hawaii aboard Hawaiian Airlines with stays at Marriott hotels in Hawaii. In January 2010, a select number of the best fan videos will be posted for public judging, with the highest vote-getter winning the free Hawaiian tweetup for them and 11 friends/ family members. The campaign is the result of a collaborative effort between Marriott, Hawai'i Visitors and Convention Bureau (HVCB), Hawaiian Airlines and Hertz. "With social networks building at incredible speeds, this campaign has the potential to spread very quickly," said John Monahan, president and CEO of the Hawaii Visitors and Convention Bureau (HVCB). "It's an exciting program and we're pleased to be part of it," said Glenn Taniguchi, senior vice president of sales and marketing for Hawaiian Airlines. "The free trips are a fun incentive that will bring new visitors to our website and increase brand awareness."[18]

Current Guests

An often overlooked way to attract room reservations is through *current guests*, guests who are registered in the hotel. (Although this topic is covered in more detail in chapter 13, it is important to mention it here as a source of reservations.) This potential market is a promising source of repeat business. The people in this group have already experienced the services and facilities of a lodging property and may be willing to make an immediate commitment to more hospitality from the same hotel or another hotel in the same chain or referral group.

The opportunity to book additional reservations occurs during the check-in and checkout phases of the guest's stay. After registering the guest, the front desk clerk may ask if he or she will be continuing to travel after leaving the hotel. If the guest mentions plans to travel to another city, the desk clerk may inquire if a reservation is needed. Likewise, the desk clerk may ask the guest on checkout if additional reservations are needed for continuation of this trip or for future trips. The hotel that promotes its facilities to current guests in this way will be rewarded with an increase in room occupancy.

Forecasting Reservations

Forecasting, or the *rooms forecast*, which involves projecting room sales for a specific period, is a natural next step after collecting the data from the reservation process. This step includes previewing the effects of reservations on the income statement, scheduling labor, and planning for the use of facilities. In addition to presenting a practical method for preparing a rooms forecast (sometimes referred to as a *projection of room sales*), this section also explains how such a forecast can be used as a means of communication with other departments (Figure 5-2).

One of the purposes of a rooms forecast is to preview the income statement. The forecast enables hotel managers to determine projected income and related expenses for a certain period. The front office manager who has estimated total room occupancy to be 100 rooms with an average room rate of $90 for a seven-day period can project a revenue of $63,000 (100 × $90 × 7) from room sales. Budgeted cost-control policies allow the front office manager to allocate a certain amount of that income for front office staff. This process of projecting sales and related expenses is important to the successful management of the front office (Figure 5-3).

The front office is not the only department that depends on a well-constructed rooms forecast. The food and beverage department, housekeeping department, and maintenance department rely on the *house count*, or the number of persons registered in a hotel on a specific night. This is important for scheduling labor, using facilities, planning improvements or renovating facilities, ordering supplies, and the like. For example, if a *full house*, or 100 percent hotel occupancy, is predicted and there are no

FIGURE 5-2   A rooms forecast assists in planning for delivery of service.

ROOMS FORECAST   FROM: __ SUN DEC 1 __ TO: __ SAT DEC 7 __

	1	2	3	4	5	6	7			
GUAR RES	25	50	55	40	45	10	10			
CONF RES	20	25	20	20	25	10	15			
WALK-INS	80	80	80	5	5	5	5			
GROUPS	20	0	0	30	30	30	0			
TTL ROOMS	145	155	155	95	105	55	30			
TTL GUESTS	180	195	190	110	125	75	45			

COMMENTS: DEC 1/2/3 WALK-INS FROM DDS CONVENTION AT STONE HILL MANOR
DEC 4/5/6 JOHNSON TOURS FROM CANADA—ALL MEALS IN DINING
ROOM A LA CARTE

CC: HOUSEKEEPER   GENERAL MGR

FRONT OFFICE MGR   DIR MKTG AND SALES

SWITCHBOARD   FOOD AND BEV MGR

MAINT ENGR   EXEC CHEF

GARAGE MGR   BANQ MGR

RESTAURANT MGR   HOSTESS A.M./P.M.
LOUNGE MGR

scheduled banquet-breakfasts, extra waitstaff must be scheduled in the dining room. Employees in the housekeeping department may be refused vacation when a full house is expected. Other contingencies include a maintenance department's need to schedule major repairs and preventive maintenance, annual cleaning, and remodeling of guest rooms when occupancy is low; a controller's need to prepare a cash flow estimate; an executive housekeeper's need to schedule adequate staff based on guest room occupancy; a security department's requirement to be aware of activity projected for the hotel; and a parking garage manager's need to know if the garage can meet the auto/van space requirements for the anticipated guests. These are just a few of the uses of the rooms forecast.

The front office manager determines the revenues projected by this rooms forecast. To do this, the average room rate or the specific room rate for a group may be applied. This information is important to the controller, general manager, and owner of the hotel, who use it in managing the hotel's finances. This system can also be used to prepare quarterly or yearly forecasts.

Figure 5-3   The front office forecast is issued to all department heads.

TIMES HOTEL
Weekly Room Sale Forecast

	10/1	10/2	10/3	10/4	10/5	10/6	10/7
Departures	0	10	72	75	5	15	125
Arrivals:							
Confirmed	40	20	30	25	5	8	22
Guaranteed	30	18	17	90	4	2	10
Total	70	38	47	115	9	10	32
Walk-ins	20	20	30	10	10	5	50
Stayovers*	10	85	68	65	175	177	65
No-shows	5	3	5	10	2	2	3
TOTAL**	95	140	140	180	192	190	144

*Yesterday's total—departures
**Yesterday's total—departures + arrivals + walk-ins – no-shows

Notes:

10/1   Dental Commitee (125 rooms), checkout 9:00 A.M.–10:30 A.M.
Lion's Convention (72 rooms), check-in 1:00 P.M.–4:00 P.M.

10/3   Lion's Convention, checkout after 10:00 A.M. group brunch; checkout extended until 1:00 P.M.
Antique Car Show in town. Most are staying at Hearford Hotel (only 50 reservations so far); expect overflow from Hearford, about 30 walk-ins.

10/4   Antique Car Show over today.
Advanced Gymnastics Convention. Mostly ages 10–16.
Check-in 4:00 P.M.–6:00 P.M.

10/7   Advanced Gymnastics checks out at 12:00 noon.
Painters Convention in town. Headquarters is the Anderson Hotel.
Expect overflow, 50 walk-ins.

Overbooking (Occupancy Management)

The practice of *overbooking*—accepting reservations for more rooms than are available by forecasting the number of no-show reservations, stayovers, understays, and walk-ins, with the goal of attaining 100 percent occupancy—is viewed by the general public with skepticism. As a future hotelier, you should prepare for the onerous task of developing a policy on overbooking. The front office manager is responsible for administering this policy.

American courts seem to agree that "in many instances, overbooking to overcome the problem of no-shows and late cancellations may produce advantages by way of operating efficiencies that far outweigh the occasional inconveniences to guests and travelers." They have held hotel overbooking to be customary and justifiable practice for offsetting the losses from no-shows. Writing in February 1980, Gould et al. could find no direct statutory or administrative law governing hotel overbooking with the exception of one Florida regulation.[19] Hoteliers and front office managers who practice overbooking do so to meet an organization's financial objectives. They do not intentionally overbook to cause problems for the traveler. Rex S. Toh reports "the no-show rate is anywhere between 5 and 15% in most markets."[20]

Most hotels do not accept confirmed reservations. However, the financial loss due to no-shows may be substantial. In a hotel that typically has confirmed reservations (not guaranteed with a credit card) and experiences a 5 percent no-show rate, one room per night would remain unsold. With an average room rate of $85, this one room would cost the hotel $85 in revenue. Over a year, this amounts to $31,025. Lost revenues of this volume force the hotelier to develop an aggressive occupancy management policy. This policy is based on management of the occupancy categories into which guests are placed: those with confirmed reservations, those with guaranteed reservations, stayovers, understays, and walk-ins. However, most hoteliers require guests to guarantee their stay with a credit card number to ensure their intent of arrival and thus guarantee payment.

Confirmed reservations, prospective guests who have a reservation for accommodations that is honored until a specified time, represent the critical element in no-shows. After that time (usually 4:00 P.M. or 6:00 P.M.), the hotel is under no obligation to hold the reservation. The front office manager must keep accurate records of no-shows in this group. Various types of travelers with confirmed reservations—corporate, group, leisure—have different no-show rates. For example, corporate confirmed reservations may have a 1 percent overall no-show rate. Group travelers may have a 0.5 percent no-show rate, with no-shows all coming from one or two particular bus companies. Leisure travelers may have a 10 percent no-show rate. A detailed investigation of each of these categories will suggest methods for minimizing no-show rates. Please note this category is used in only a small segment of the lodging industry due to the demand for securing a reservation.

Guaranteed reservations, prospective guests who have made a contract with the hotel for a guest room, represent a less volatile group because the guest provides a credit card number to hold a room reservation. Toh reports the no-show rate for guaranteed reservations is 2 percent, compared to 10 percent for confirmed reservations.[21] The front office manager should investigate these no-shows to determine their sources and plan accordingly.

Stayovers are currently registered guests who wish to extend their stay beyond the time for which they made reservations. Accurate records by traveler category (corporate, group, leisure) reveal the stayover rate of each. For example, employees of a corporation who travel with spouses may extend a Thursday and Friday business trip to include Saturday. Similarly, a group conference scheduled from Monday through Thursday may encourage the attendees to stay longer to sightsee.

Understays are guests who arrive on time but decide to leave before their predicted date of departure. Leisure travelers may find their tourist attraction less interesting than anticipated. Urgent business may require the corporate client to return to the office sooner than expected. Maintaining accurate records helps the front office manager predict understays.

A welcome sector of the hotel market, *walk-in guests*, can enhance daily occupancy percentages when effectively managed. The front office manager must be aware of activity in the local area. Heavy tourist seasons, special tourist events, conventions, and the like will increase the number of potential guests. Awareness of such possibilities helps the front office manager plan. Walk-in numbers are often higher if the front office manager maintains good relations with the front office managers of nearby hotels, who may refer guests to the property when their own are fully booked. Sending guests who cannot be accommodated to nearby hotels is a win-win situation for guests and hotels.

When these occupancy categories are tracked, the front office manager can more accurately predict occupancy. The front office manager can obtain the data for this formula by reviewing the property management system (PMS) reservation module, which lists the groups, corporate clients, and individual guests who have made reservations for a specific period. Also, the front office manager should check tourist activity in the area, business events planned in other hotels, and other local special events.

The following *occupancy management formula* considers confirmed reservations, guaranteed reservations, no-show factors for these two types of reservations, predicted stayovers, predicted understays, and predicted walk-ins to determine the number of additional room reservations needed to achieve 100 percent occupancy. *No-show factors* are based on prior experience with people with confirmed or guaranteed reservations who did not show up.

	total number of rooms available
-	**confirmed reservations; × no-show factor based on historical data**
-	**guaranteed reservations; × no-show factor based on historical data**
-	**predicted stayovers**
+	**predicted understays**
-	**predicted walk-ins**
=	**number of additional room reservations needed to achieve 100 percent occupancy**

Here is an example of how to use this formula:

1. If a 200-room lodging property has 75 confirmed reservations with a 5 percent no-show factor in a particular category, 71 rooms can be predicted to be occupied by guests with confirmed reservations. The no-show factor is based on historical records of this category for this property maintained and reviewed by the front office manager.

2. The hotel also has 100 guaranteed reservations with a historical no-show rate of 2 percent. This means 2 rooms have probably been reserved by no-show guests

and may be available for sale. The policy of the hotel may or may not allow the sale of these 2 rooms. If the hotel knows of other hotels in the immediate area that have available rooms for that particular night, the front office manager might be willing to walk a guest with a guaranteed reservation to another hotel if all the guests with guaranteed reservations arrive. It is important to be extremely cautious in this category. An unpleasant scene can occur if an exhausted guest arrives at 3:00 A.M. with a guaranteed reservation and finds no vacancies.

3. The hotel's predicted number of stayovers at this time—based on historical records, with considerations for the season of the year, tourist attractions, nature of the current guests (convention, tourist, or business travelers)—is 4 rooms. This number of rooms must be subtracted from the number of rooms available for sale.

4. The hotel's predicted number of understays at this time, considering factors similar to those applied to stayovers, is 5. This number of rooms is added to the number of rooms available for sale.

5. The hotel's predicted number of walk-ins for this period—using historical records and available information concerning tourist events, activity at other hotels, attractions in nearby communities, and the like—is 8.

The arithmetic for this example works out as follows:

200 rooms available
- **71 confirmed reservations (75 − [75 × 0 05])**
- **98 guaranteed reservations (100 − [100 × 0 02])**
- **4 stayovers + 5 understays**
- **8 walk-ins**

= **24 number of additional room reservations needed to achieve 100 percent occupancy**

The occupancy management formula indicates to the front office manager that 24 additional rooms must be rented to achieve 100 percent occupancy. In predicting this number, the front office manager can reasonably accept 24 additional reservations for the evening.

Revenue Management

Revenue management is the technique of planning to achieve maximum room rates and the most profitable guests. This practice encourages front office managers, general managers, and marketing and sales directors to target sales periods and to develop sales programs that will maximize profit for the hotel. This topic is fully explored in chapter 6. Revenue management is part of the successful administration of a reservation system because it forces the front office manager to realistically attempt to produce a favorable income statement. Applying rate categories to specific periods with minimum length of reservations and reviewing potential markets and their spending habits assist the front office manager not only in meeting the goal of 100 percent occupancy but also in achieving maximum profitability.

Processing Guest Reservations

Means of communication with the client; room inventory data banks; systems for reservation, confirmation, deposits, and cancellations; and *blocking procedures*, a process of reserving a room on a specific day, are the major components of a well-organized guest reservation processing system.

The guest who wants to secure overnight lodging accommodations must have an efficient means of communicating the room reservation to the hotel, such as a toll-free phone number, fax number, social media, or personal computer. In turn, the hotel must have a way to check reservation requests against a data bank of available rooms. To ensure the reliability of the room reservation, the hotel establishes a deposit or guarantee system that commits the guest to the purchase of the accommodation. A cancellation process allows the guest and the hotel the flexibility necessary to function in a complex society. A blocking procedure that balances future commitments with present room requirements also helps the front office manager provide an effective room reservation processing system.

Systemwide Reservation Systems

The lodging property associated with a systemwide reservation service is connected to the system via a nationwide toll-free telephone number. The telephone number is widely distributed by the marketing and sales departments of the corporation. The potential guest who dials this toll-free number is greeted by an operator at the central reservation headquarters. This operator has access to the computerized data bank of available rooms at each participating lodging property—so, for example, a request for a certain type of room for three consecutive nights (February 15, 16, and 17) at a property in Boston can be matched through the data bank. If the participating property has rooms available for those nights, the request can be processed. If it does not have space available, the operator can suggest properties in the reservation/referral system that do have rooms available.

After the operator determines the guest's room request can be satisfied, he or she asks for the guest's needs for the accommodations as well as the credit card number to secure the arrival.

Outsourcing Reservations

In addition to central reservation systems (CRSs) operated by hotels, *outsourcing* providers of central reservation systems are available for hotel managers.

This new breed of CRS and service provider processes voice, Internet, and Global Distribution System–based reservations on behalf of hotels. This hybrid group provides reservation systems to clients that want to manage closely their reservation processing while offering all the services of a traditional representation company. In addition, these companies offer their services through web-enabled application-service provider (ASP) models. Doug Kennedy describes how "to establish a proactive, positive relationship that perpetually views CenRes [Outsourced-Central Reservation] as being an invaluable partner."

Use Descriptions That Allure and Entice. Use visually descriptive language that agents can use to paint pictures in the minds of callers.

Update Your Property Information: Update your property's information fields at least every six months. Talk about the wonderful hospitality and service guests will enjoy. Remember also that your location/destination is a key component of your hotel's overall "product." Add major attractions and entertainment venues. Consider adding information regarding local events and festivals, such as marathons, air shows, sporting events.

Keep Room Inventories Loaded and Updated. Make as many rates as possible open to your CenRes provider. Do not offer non-exclusive rates on third-party channels—which charge significant commissions—and not have those same rates available in the CenRes system.

Keep the Lines of Communication Open. Make a list of discussion points and schedule regular conference calls to review in an organized manner. If possible, visit your CenRes office and meet the agents who represent your hotel.[22]

One provider of reservations outsourcing is Pegasus Solutions. The company's representation services, including Utell® Hotels and Resorts and Unirez by Pegasus™, are used by nearly 11,000 member hotels in more than 130 countries, making Pegasus the hotel industry's largest third-party marketing and reservations provider. Pegasus has 18 offices in 11 countries, including regional hubs in London, Singapore, and Scottsdale, Arizona.[23]

Types of Reservations

Confirmed Reservations

As previously mentioned in the discussion with occupancy management, this category has been discontinued in most lodging properties. However, for those properties that continue to use it, the confirmed reservation is comparable to a contract that becomes void at a certain hour of a certain day. The confirmed reservation allows the hotel to project the number of guests that will check in by the deadline hour. After that deadline, the hotel is free to sell unclaimed rooms to walk-in guests or to accept overflow guests from another property. The hotel usually keeps track of the number of no-shows and compares them to the total number of confirmed reservations that were made; these historical records help in predicting occupancy—and revenue—accurately. (They are also used in overbooking, discussed earlier in this chapter.)

Guaranteed Reservations

Guaranteed reservations, as previously discussed with occupancy management, enable lodging establishments to predict revenue even more accurately. They commit the guest to paying for a room-night and the hotel to providing accommodations regardless of arrival time. If the guest does not show up (without prior cancellation), the hotel may process a credit card voucher for payment. Likewise, no matter when the guest arrives on the reserved night, the hotel must have the reserved accommodation available. The guaranteed reservation requires the hotel to determine the method of guest payment. The guest may secure the method of payment with a valid credit card, an advance payment, or a preauthorized line of credit. (Each of these methods is described in detail in chapter 9.)

Reservation Codes

Reservation codes are a sequential series of alphanumeric combinations that provide the guest with a reference for a confirmed or guaranteed reservation. (Reservation codes are also referred to as *confirmation numbers*.) Such a code indicates accommodations have been secured for a specific date with a commitment to pay for at least the first room-night. The code, which usually consists of several letters and digits that do not necessarily have any meaning to the guest, may identify the hotel in the chain/referral group, the person who processed the reservation, the date of arrival, the date of departure, the type of credit card, the credit card number, the room rate, the type of room, and/or the sequential number of the reservation. The organization that develops the code includes in it information appropriate for the efficient management of a particular reservation system. A guaranteed reservation code may look like this:

122-JB-0309-0311-MC-75-K-98765R

- *122*: the identification number of the property in the chain
- *JB*: the initials of the reservationist or desk clerk who accepted the reservation
- *0309*: the date of arrival
- *0311*: the date of departure
- *MC*: the type of credit card (MasterCard)
- *75*: the nightly room rate of $75
- *K*: indication that the reserved room has a king-size bed
- *98765R*: the sequential reservation number

A few points should be kept in mind when establishing a reservation code system. The amount of memory available to store the code information in a computer data bank may be limited. Therefore, a short code that provides less information may be necessary. The reservation code should be designed to give adequate information to the hotel property that must provide accommodations for the guest. The purpose of the code is to communicate the details of a guaranteed accommodation to the host property. The guest data are already entered into the central computer and usually can be easily retrieved. However, there are times when these data may not be available, or they may be misplaced. When this happens, a reservation code allows the host property to provide appropriate accommodations.

The method of paying for a guaranteed reservation is established when the reservation is made. Credit cards or previously approved direct billing are the most common methods. Sometimes the guest sends a bank check or delivers cash to secure a reservation. A bank check is acceptable, as long as adequate time is available to process it. The cash advance payment and bank check, however, should alert the front office manager that this guest has not established a line of credit with a credit card organization or with the hotel. Determining how the guest will pay the final bill is essential. The folios of guests who pay cash in advance must be monitored.

Cancellation Codes

A *cancellation code* is a sequential series of alphanumeric combinations that provides the guest with a reference for a cancellation of a guaranteed reservation. (Cancellation codes are also referred to as *cancellation numbers*.) Such a code verifies the cancellation has been communicated to the hotel property and assures the guest that he or she is not liable for the canceled reservation. For example, if the front office staff mistakenly processes a charge for a guaranteed reservation that had been canceled, the guest can refute the credit card billing with the cancellation code.

A cancellation code is composed like a reservation code and consists of letters and digits that may identify the hotel property, the person who processed the cancellation, the date of arrival, the date of departure, and/or the sequential number of the cancellation. This and other information is included to ensure efficient management of room cancellations. If the guest had applied a cash deposit to the room, a credit balance on the guest folio would have to be processed. A cancellation code may look like this:

122-RB-0309-1001X

- ■ *122*: the identification number of the property in the chain
- ■ *RB*: the initials of the reservationist or desk clerk who accepted the cancellation
- ■ *0309*: the date of arrival
- ■ *1001X*: the sequential number of the cancellation

Blocking Procedure

After a reservation is received, the reserved room is blocked in the room inventory. In a computerized reservation system, the room is automatically removed from the available-room data bank for the dates involved. For example, if each of the participating 75 hotels in the reservation/referral system has 200 rooms available, the room bank has 15,000 rooms available to be sold on any one night. As a reservation request is processed, the room or rooms involved are blocked out of the available-room inventory. Reservation requests for 4,000 rooms on a particular night at the participating properties require the computer to block (or reserve) those rooms at the appropriate hotels. If additional reservation requests are received for that night at a particular property and that hotel is already filled to capacity, the computer will not process the requests. It may, however, tell the computer terminal operator that a hotel in the same geographic area has vacancies. This is undoubtedly one of the major advantages of participating in a reservation/referral system. This type of blocking is usually referred to as *blocking on the horizon*—that is, in the distant future. Another type of blocking, referred to as *daily blocking*, involves assigning guests to their particular rooms on a daily basis.

Process of Completing Reservations through a PMS

The previous discussion focused on processing guest reservations through a central reservation headquarters. However, the individual PMS at a member hotel of a reservation/referral system is also able to process a reservation request. Chapter 4 discusses the reservation module and includes the list of applications available to the reservationist or desk clerk (shown in Figure 4-7). If the reservationist selects option 1, Guest Data, the screen of the video display terminal will look like that in Figure 5-4. The clerk enters the data into the PMS as requested. The data are then cleared through the rooms reservations bank to confirm the availability of the room requested.

HOSPITALITY PROFILE

Gary Budge is the general manager of the Algonquin Hotel in New York City. He graduated from Penn State University in Food Service and Housing Administration and began his work experience with Stouffer Hotels in Atlanta, Georgia, in food and beverage management. These positions included catering director and food and beverage director. He continued grooming his food and beverage management expertise at the Sheraton Washington Hotel, Washington, DC; the Sheraton Bal Harbour Hotel, Bal Harbour, Florida; and Hyatt Hotels Corporation in Chicago. Later he became partner and vice president of food and beverage for Medallion Hotels in Washington, DC. He also served as corporate director of food & beverage for Princess Hotels, headquartered in New York City. Mr. Budge's hotel career has also included management positions as hotel manager of The Sheraton New York and Sheraton Manhattan and as general manager of Sheraton Russell, New York City, and Sheraton Parsippany Hotel in Morris County, New Jersey. Budge holds a master's degree in Hospitality Industries Studies from New York University.

The 174-room, 5000-square-foot flexible meeting space Algonquin Hotel, in New York City attracts both the corporate and leisure markets. Its landmarked 1902 design allows it to be entrenched in the fabric of the local community as New York's longest-operating hotel. The Algonquin is synonymous with New York.

Mr. Budge indicates there are many options for potential guests to make reservations at the hotel. The central reservation system (CRS) is the main source of reservations. The operations of the CRS include a toll-free number, a direct call to the hotel, or a visit to the website, http://www. algonquinhotel.com. He notes that when a prospective guest calls the hotel reservation number, he

or she is connected to a regional call center where the personnel are well versed in the Algonquin's rates, amenities, services, availability, etc. Other opportunities to sell guest rooms include sales through global distribution systems (GDS) such as Amadeus, Galileo, SABRE, and Worldspan. This provides opportunities for the corporate market to purchase a volume of rooms at a discount by entering their code into the computer and selecting the number of rooms at the price they have negotiated. Travel agents continue to offer guests opportunities to make reservations through their agencies. More recent reservation services, referred to as *third-party reservation services*, include Expedia, Hotels.com, and Travelocity to name a few. Those third-party online reservation services offer a "shopping opportunity to consumers." While this provides new sales to the hotel, initially it may not be a source for brand-loyal customers to target for booking reservations.

Each of these reservation methods has an effect on management's ability to produce a positive financial picture for a hotel. For example, the commission rate charged by the third-party online reservation service other reservation sources may be higher. Mr. Budge recommends each general manager, in consultation with his or her revenue manager, monitor the sources of reservation activity, number of rooms available for sale, and rates in each category. This process can be performed with computer software such as IDEAS, a yield management–based program that reviews the history of occupancy by category, rate, date, etc. He reminds students the goal of revenue management is to achieve occupancy and average daily rate greater than those goals which have been set in the budget and to trump the competitive set of hotels in your market. This is achieved by the "daily" monitoring of room inventory and room rate. The RevPAR (revenue per available room), which

(*continues*)

contrasts room revenue (number of rooms sold at various rates) and against available rooms in the hotel. He recommends students become familiar with RevPAR by creating "what-if" scenarios of various numbers of rooms sold at one rate versus numbers of rooms sold at another rate to accomplish the maximum yield.

Mr. Budge advises students to view revenue management as a hot concept in hotel management. It requires sound, analytical thinking skills

that can be supported by the previously mentioned "what-if" rate and rooms-sold scenario. He says today's students will also find revenue management entering into other areas of the hotel, such as the catering department. It will furnish the guide that filters all pricing and availability factors for several departments into a management tool for generating a greater profit for the hotel and a more efficient and effective use of dates, space, and manpower.

FIGURE 5-4   The Guest Data screen prompts the reservationist to obtain information about the guest and his or her stay.

RESERVATIONS—ENTER GUEST DATA

NAME:		
COMPANY:		
BILLING ADDRESS:		ZIP:
PHONE NUMBER:		
DATE OF ARRIVAL:	TIME OF ARRIVAL:	DATE OF DEP.:
AIRLINE:	FLIGHT #:	TIME OF ARRIVAL:
ROOM:	# GUESTS:	RATE:
COMMENTS:		
CONFIRMATION:		
CREDIT CARD:	NUMBER:	
TRAVEL AGENCY:	AGENT:	ID #:
ADDRESS:		ZIP:

Other options in the menu are accessed as needed. For example, option 2, Room Inventory, lists the *reservation status*, or the availability of a guest room to be rented on a particular night—that is, *open* (room is available for renting), *confirmed* (room is reserved until 4:00 P.M. or 6:00 P.M.), *guaranteed* (room is reserved until guest arrives), and *repair* (room is not available for guest rental) (Figure 5-5). Option 3, Deposits, is accessed when the clerk must determine whether the guest had a deposit

FIGURE 5-5   The room inventory screen keeps track of guest room reservation status.

ROOM INVENTORY 11.06

ROOM	TYPE	RATE	STATUS	GUEST
101	K	65	OPEN	
102	K	65	CONF	SMITH, V.
103	K	65	CONF	GREY, R.
104	DB	55	GUAR	LITTLE, N.
105	DB	55	GUAR	THOMAS, P.
106	K	75	OPEN	
107	K	75	OPEN	
108	KSUITE	95	GUAR	DENTON, K.
109	DB	55	OPEN	
110	DB	55	GUAR	SLAYTON, J.
115	K	75	REPAIR	
116	K	75	REPAIR	
117	KSUITE	95	REPAIR	
120	SUITE	150	GUAR	STONE CO. CONV.
121	K	95	GUAR	STONE CO. CONV.
122	K	95	GUAR	STONE CO. CONV.
123	K	70	GUAR	STONE CO. CONV.
124	K	70	GUAR	STONE CO. CONV.
125	K	70	GUAR	STONE CO. CONV.

on file (Figure 5-6). The information for this option is compiled from the Guest Data option, where the clerk indicates the guest wanted to guarantee a reservation with a credit card or send a cash (bank check) deposit. Option 4, Special Requests, assists the reservationist or desk clerk in determining if rooms are available to meet the specific needs of a guest (Figure 5-7). Facilities for guests with physical handicaps, smoking/no smoking options, particular views, and locations near other hotel facilities are some of the features listed here. This option helps the desk clerk provide hospitality to guests.

Option 5, Blocking, provides reports to the front office manager on which rooms are to be reserved for incoming guests on a particular day or on the horizon (Figure 5-8). This option assigns a guest or guests to a specific room. Option 6, Arrivals, lists the individuals or groups expected to arrive on a specific date (Figure 5-9). Option 7, Departures, indicates which guests are expected to check out on a particular date. This option is used by the front office manager or desk clerk to determine room availability for guests who wish to overstay their reserved time as well as to sell future visits (Figure 5-10). Option 8,

FIGURE 5-6   The **Guest Deposits** data screen displays a guest's deposit for a particular visit.

DEPOSITS—RETRIEVE DATA

NAME: GROSSMAN, S.

MANDRAKE INSURANCE CO.

ADDRESS: 47 LANKIN DRIVE

PHILADELPHIA, PA 00000

ARRIV: 0917   CASH 75.00   FOLIO: 55598R

NAME: LINCOLN, D.

KLINE SHOE SALES

ADDRESS: 7989 VICTORY PLAZA

NY, NY 00000

ARRIV: 0917   CASH 100.00   FOLIO: 56789R

FIGURE 5-7   The **Special Requests** screen assists reservationists in meeting a guest's request for specific room accommodations.

SPECIAL REQUESTS—ROOM AVAILABILITY 06 05

ROOM	TYPE	RATE	STATUS
101	DB/RAMP NEARBY	65	OPEN
108	K/RAMP NEARBY HDKP BATH	75	OPEN
109	DB/RAMP NEARBY HDKP SHOWER	75	REPAIR
115	K/HEARING & VISUAL IMP/HDKP SHOWER	75	OPEN
130	K/OCEAN VIEW	85	OPEN
133	K/OCEAN VIEW	85	OPEN
136	K/HEARING & VISUAL IMP/HDKP SHOWER	75	OPEN
201	K/HDKP TUB	75	OPEN
208	K/HDKP TUB	75	OPEN
209	DB/HDKP SHOWER	55	OPEN
211	K/POOLSIDE	75	OPEN
301	K/HDKP TUB	75	OPEN
333	K/OCEAN VIEW	85	OPEN
428	DB/MEETING ROOM	95	OPEN
435	DB/MEETING ROOM	95	REPAIR

FIGURE 5-8   The Blocking Report screen provides front office staff with room reservation status on the horizon.

BLOCKING REPORT 02 MONTH

ROOM	STATUS	COMMENTS
101	GUAR	PENN CONFR
102	GUAR	PENN CONFR
103	GUAR	PENN CONFR
104	GUAR	PENN CONFR
105	GUAR	PENN CONFR
106	OPEN	
107	OPEN	
108	OPEN	
109	GUAR	0205114501
110	OPEN	
201	GUAR	PENN CONFR
202	GUAR	PENN CONFR
203	GUAR	PENN CONFR
204	GUAR	PENN CONFR
205	GUAR	PENN CONFR
206	GUAR	PENN CONFR
207	OPEN	
208	OPEN	
209	GUAR	0219BR4567
210	GUAR	0418BR4512
301	OPEN	
302	GUAR	PENN CONFR
303	GUAR	PENN CONFR

VIP, provides the desk clerk with information on guests with VIP status (Figure 5-11). Even though all guests are very important persons, VIP status is granted to persons who may be regular guests and expect special treatment and to celebrities or officials who need to spend minimal time checking in. If this information is obtained with the reservation request, it will assist the desk clerk at registration.

FIGURE 5-9	The Arrival Report screen lists incoming guests with reservations.		
RESERVATIONS INCOMING 01 15			
NAME	**ROOM**	**RATE**	**DEP**
ABERNATHY, R.	400	75	0216
BROWNING, J.	201	75	0217
CANTER, D.	104	65	0216
COSMOE, G.	105	65	0219
DEXTER, A.	125	70	0217
DRAINING, L.	405	95	0216
GENTRY, A.	202	70	0216
KENT, R.	409	70	0218
MURRY, C.	338	80	0218
PLENTER, S.	339	80	0217
SMITH, F.	301	75	0218
SMITH, S.	103	65	0216
WHITE, G.	115	75	0216

Option 9, Projected Occupancy, provides various departments with information concerning the number of guests who will be in the hotel on a certain day (Figure 5-12). Option 10, Travel Agents, allows the reservationist to maintain data on the travel agent or travel agency that initiated a reservation (Figure 5-13). This option allows speedy processing of the agent's or agency's fee for placing a reservation with the hotel. The option also interfaces with the accounts payable module. Option 11, Guest Messages, allows the front desk clerk to relay important information to the guests on registration (Figure 5-14). This feature is another way the hotel can convey hospitality to the guest by demonstrating attention to details. Reports concerning reservations can be obtained by the front office manager by selecting option 12, Reports.

These examples are only a brief overview of the capabilities of the reservation module of a PMS. Your hands-on experience will provide you with real-life applications of a valuable management tool. Managing reservation data allows the front office manager to organize hundreds of details into usable information—information that helps provide hospitality to guests and brings financial success to the lodging property.

Database Interfaces

To plan their work, department managers rely on information captured at the time a reservation is made. *Database interfaces*, which transfer shared information among

FIGURE 5-10 The Departures screen lists names of guests and groups for a particular day.

DEPARTURES 03 09

ROOM	NAME	COMMENTS
207	SMITH, V.	GREATER COMPANY
208	ANAHOE, L.	GREATER COMPANY
209		
211	LISTER, B.	MERCY HOSPITAL
215		
233	CRAMER, N.	KRATER INSURANCE CO.
235		
301	SAMSON, N.	MERCY HOSPITAL
304		
319	DONTON, M.	JOHNSON TOURS
321		JOHNSON TOURS
322	ZIGLER, R.	JOHNSON TOURS
323		JOHNSON TOURS
324	ASTON, M.	JOHNSON TOURS
325	BAKER, K.	JOHNSON TOURS
	BAKER, P.	JOHNSON TOURS

FIGURE 5-11 The VIP Information screen lists details of special needs of guests.

VIP INFORMATION

BLAKELY, FRANK M/M
GRANITE DEVELOPMENT COMPANY
2234 WEST RIVER DRIVE
GRANITE, IN 00000
000-000-0000

LIKES SUITE 129/30 OR SUITE 145/46. PERSONAL SECURITY GUARD NEEDS ROOM 131 OR 147. ALERT HOTEL SECURITY OF THEIR ARRIVAL.

CEO/GRANITE DEVELOPMENT COMPANY WILL WANT BABYSITTER (CHILDREN AGES 5 AND 7). CALL CHEF TO SEND WINE AND CHEESE AND CHOCOLATE CHIP OR OATMEAL COOKIES AND MILK. CALL GIFT SHOP FOR YELLOW ROSES FOR MRS. BLAKELY.

DIRECT BILL (TIMES HOTEL ACCT. NO. 420G) TO GRANITE DEVELOPMENT COMPANY, 301 THOMPSON DRIVE, GRANITE, IN 00000

FIGURE 5-12   The Projected Occupancy screen assists front office managers in meeting projected income.

PROJECTED OCCUPANCY 12 18

CONF RES	42 ROOMS	50 GUESTS
GUAR RES*	89 ROOMS	93 GUESTS
STAYOVERS**	50 ROOMS	85 GUESTS
WALK-INS***	35 ROOMS	50 GUESTS
TOTALS	216 ROOMS	278 GUESTS

OCCUPANCY 86%   ROOM INCOME $15,120

* JOHNSON AEROSPACE ARRIVAL AFTER 10 P.M.
** SMITHMILL CORP. BUFFET BREAKFAST AND BANQUET DINNER.
*** LANCER STAMP SHOW AT ST. THOMAS HOTEL.

FIGURE 5-13   The Travel Agent screen assists hotels in keeping track of commissions paid to travel agents.

TRAVEL AGENT INFO

DATE	AGENCY	AGENT	ACTIVITY	COMM STATUS
09 23	MENTING #4591 32 KAVE SIMINTON, NJ 00000 000-000-0000	BLANT, E. #4512 B	GUAR 5 @70	PD 09 30
09 30	MENTING #4591	CROSS, L. #4501 B	GUAR 10 @65	PD 10 05
02 01	MENTING #4591	CROSS, L. #4501 B	GUAR 20 @75	PD 02 10
02 05	MENTING #4591	BROWN, A. #4522 B	GUAR 10 @70	PD 02 15

computers, allow managers to retrieve this information at will. Marketing directors need current data to monitor projected sales, while sales representatives in the marketing department need immediate information on room availability for specific periods. Housekeeping staff members plan routine care and maintenance activities with projected

> **FIGURE 5-14 The Guest Message screen is available for front office staff at a moment's notice.**
>
> **MESSAGE—GUESTS**
>
> BRINKE, L. W. 01 02 12:57 P.M.
>
> TOM WASKIN OF GN MERCH IS NOT ABLE TO KEEP APPT ON 01 02 AT 4:00 P.M.
>
> CALL HIM TO RESCHEDULE 000-000-0000 BEFORE 7:00 P.M. 01 02. SWE
>
> BRINKE, L. W. 10 12 1:38 P.M.
>
> JENNIFER HOW OF STERN ELEC WILL MEET YOU AT 5:00 P.M. IN TIMES HOTEL LOBBY AS PLANNED. BRING ALONG DATA ON RESEARCH PROJECT 21-Z. SWE

occupancy in mind. Maintenance crews plan refurbishing and repairs when projected occupancy is low. Food and beverage directors can promote a positive cash flow by increasing food and beverage marketing programs during slow room sales periods. The controller also needs to access the reservation database when planning fiscal budgets.

True Integration

The term *true integration* denotes a hotel's central reservations system and property management sharing a database. Rebecca Oliva describes how the CRS and PMS use the same database for processing reservations.[24] This allows for real-time reservations, a perceived benefit for consumers, as well as a lower technology investment for data storage, a benefit for hotel investors. Hotels can access reservation data via the Internet.

Solution to Opening Dilemma

The override feature of the reservation module in a property management system allows individual employees to book reservations beyond the number of rooms available and beyond the occupancy management limit. This feature must be controlled by the reservations manager, front office manager, or manager on duty. The front office staff must investigate room availability in nearby hotels and notify guests that their room reservations will be handled at another hotel. In some cases, guests can't be notified prior to their arrival, and the front desk staff must be prepared to deliver customer service with utmost composure.

Chapter Recap

This chapter addressed hotel reservation systems. As the popularity of computerized reservation systems has increased, chains and referral properties have adopted them to meet the needs of the traveling public. The consumer's increasing reliance on the Internet and social media to make room reservations has affected the profitability of hotels.

Reservations ensure that corporate, group, and leisure travelers have accommodations at their destination and provide the hotel with a steady flow of business. Determining the sources of these reservations assists the front office manager in developing procedures to satisfy the needs of guests. The traveler can use various means to make reservations, such as toll-free telephone numbers, fax numbers, the Internet, and social media. The concept of customer relationship management links hospitality and technology. The management of social media applications helps develop this concept.

The rooms forecast is used to communicate occupancy status to other departments in the hotel. Overbooking, used to balance no-shows and understays, can be carefully structured using the occupancy management formula. Computerized reservation systems also help front office managers manage guest information databases, dates of arrival, lengths of stay, and so forth. Confirmed and guaranteed reservations assure the guest of accommodations on arrival, with various degrees of assurance based on time of arrival and willingness to prepay. These levels of assurance also affect the financial success of the hotel. All elements discussed in this chapter combine to provide means of access for the guest and a technique for marketing rooms for the hotel. The front office manager is responsible for providing this service to the guest.

End-of-Chapter Questions

1. How does a well-organized reservation system meet the needs of travelers?

2. How does the lodging industry meet the need of travelers for assured reservations?

3. What advantages does a hotel belonging to a reservation/referral system enjoy?

4. What are the major sources of guest reservations? What information does this analysis reveal?

5. How can a lodging property use social media to communicate reservation offers?

6. Discuss which social media are appropriate for corporate clients, leisure traveler, and SMERF.

7. Discuss the nature of a typical corporate client's travel plans, and explain how these plans are supported by a well-organized reservation system. What reservation access methods are available to corporate clients?

8. Why are tour or meeting planners important to the hotel with regard to group reservations? What reservation access methods are available to group tour planners?

9. How do leisure travelers differ from corporate clients and group travelers? What reservation access methods are available to them?

10. If you have been or are currently employed at a front desk in a hotel, what do you think of the potential for repeat business from current guests? Does your hotel have a procedure to secure reservations on check-in or checkout?

11. Why is it necessary to prepare a rooms forecast? What are the components of this management tool? Besides the front office manager, who uses the room forecast?

12. What does *overbooking* mean? Discuss the legal and financial implications of this practice.

13. What are the components of an aggressive occupancy management procedure? How are they applied to the occupancy management formula?

14. What are the major steps involved in processing a guest reservation?

15. Briefly describe the method used to process a reservation with a computerized system.

16. Discuss the differences between confirmed reservations and guaranteed reservations. What financial implications does each entail?

17. Design a reservation code for a computerized reservation system. Why did you choose the control features in your code?

18. Develop a cancellation code for a computerized reservation system. Why did you choose the control features in your code?

19. What does room blocking involve? Give examples.

20. How do you think true integration of the central reservation system and a hotel's property management system affect guest satisfaction and the hotel's financial success?

CASE STUDY 501

Margaret Chu, general manager of The Times Hotel, and Ana Chavarria, front office manager, are in the process of developing a policy on overbooking. The current policy prohibits the reservations manager from booking more than 100 percent of the available rooms. Reservations are composed of 60 percent confirmed and 40 percent guaranteed.

In the past six months, about 5 percent of confirmed reservations have been no-shows, resulting in a financial loss of about 500 room-nights. This situation has not been analyzed because Ms. Chavarria has not had time to organize such a study. The loss of $42,500 (500 rooms × $85 average room rate) has forced management to consider developing an aggressive occupancy management program.

Offer some suggestions to Ms. Chu and Ms. Chavarria concerning the following related concepts: the legality of overbooking, the need to maintain an accurate accounting of the financial impact of no-shows, and the management of the reservation/occupancy categories that make up the hotel's room sales (confirmed reservations, guaranteed reservations, stayovers, understays, and walk-ins).

CASE STUDY 502

Use the following data to prepare a rooms forecast for the first week of May for The Times Hotel:

Number of rooms available = 600
Number of rooms occupied on April 30 = 300

May 1:
Departures = 200 rooms
Arrivals = 200 rooms (70 percent confirmed, 30 percent guaranteed)
Walk-ins = 40 rooms
No-shows = 0.02 percent of expected arrivals

May 2:
Departures = 50 rooms
Arrivals = 100 rooms (60 percent confirmed, 40 percent guaranteed)
Walk-ins = 10 rooms
No-shows = 0.02 percent of expected arrivals

May 3:
Departures = 200 rooms
Arrivals = 100 rooms (50 percent confirmed, 50 percent guaranteed)
Walk-ins = 20 rooms
No-shows = 0.02 percent of expected arrivals

May 4:
Departures = 50 rooms

Arrivals = 100 rooms (20 percent confirmed, 80 percent guaranteed)
Walk-ins = 10 rooms
No-shows = 0.01 percent of expected arrivals

May 5:
Departures = 300 rooms
Arrivals = 70 rooms (30 percent confirmed, 70 percent guaranteed)
Walk-ins = 25 rooms
No-shows = 0.0143 percent of expected arrivals

May 6:
Departures = 50 rooms
Arrivals = 175 rooms (92 percent confirmed, 8 percent guaranteed)
Walk-ins = 10 rooms
No-shows = 0.04 percent of expected arrivals

May 7:
Departures = 200 rooms
Arrivals = 180 rooms (10 percent confirmed, 90 percent guaranteed)
Walk-ins = 25 rooms
No-shows = 0.0223 percent of expected arrivals

CASE STUDY 503

Margaret Chu, general manager of The Times Hotel, Lorraine DeSantes, director of marketing and sales, and Ben DiCanta, revenue manager, are interested in developing social media options for attracting guests. Margaret is a member of LinkedIn and feels that media would be a good marketing option. Tom says Facebook is the way to go. Lorraine says Twitter is the in thing and will generate more customers than they can handle.

They are aware that they should start slowly and have a plan. What tips could you provide to start them on the right path?

Notes

1. J. Davies, "Social Media: Marketing Magic or Madness" *The Knowland Group*. Retrieved from Hotel Online: www.hotel-online .com/News/PR2009_3rd/Jul09_ SocialMediaMagic.html, July 3, 2009.

2. S. Boehle, *Managesmarter*. Retrieved from www.managesmarter.com: www.managesmarter.com/msg/content_display/training/ e3iab4a1c734bf748910f209ef8808acaa, March 8, 2008.

3. Hilton Corportation 2009, http://www.hiltonfranchise.com/Marketing/Disclosures/ PDFs/2009FranchiseDisclosureDocument_Hilton.pdf.

4. Katrina Pruitt-Andrews, "Hotels Are Using Business Intelligence To Do More Than Survive the Recession" April 30, 2009, http://www.hotel-online.com/News/ PR2009_2nd/Apr09_TravelCLICKMAR.html.

5. Katrina Pruitt-Andrews "New Technology Enhances Advertising to Travel Agents Who Book $8 Billion in Hotel Revenue" July 3, 2009, http://www.hotel-online. com/News/PR2009_3rd/Jul09_TravelCLICKTAs.html.

6. Katrina Pruitt-Andrews "Hotels That Withhold Commissions Are Losing Travel Agent Business" March 1, 2009, http://www.hotel-online.com/News/PR2009_ 1st/Mar09_TravelCLICKWPS.html.

7. Katrina Pruitt-Andrews "Hotels Build Connections Through 'Friends' and 'Fans' on Social Networks," http://www.hotel-online.com/News/PR2009_1st/Mar09_ TravelCLICKITB.html.

8. Sharon H. McAuliffe, "Wresting Back Control from the Online Wholesalers," January, 2003.

9. Max Starkov, "Speak To Me . . . In My 'Language' Building Customer Loyalty via CRM Strategies on the Hotel Website" Travel Daily News, July 22, 2009, http://www.traveldailynews.com/pages/show_page/32115-Optimising-Internet-Booking-By-Max-Starkov—Courtesy-of-Cleverdis 2009.

10. Carol Levitt, "SynXis Guest Connect Improves Look-to-Book Conversion and Increases Bookings for Hotel Groups" June 2, 2008, http://www.hotel-online. com/News/PR2008_2nd/Jun08_SynXisConnect.html.

11. Katrina Pruitt-Andrews "TravelCLICK Properties Perform as Clients Increase Revenue 39%, Room Nights 29% Despite Slowing Market," http://www. hotelonline.com/News/PR2008_2nd/Jun08_TravelClickProperties.html. Hotel Online, June 2, 2008.

12. Ibid. Max Starkov 2009, Travel Daily News, 2009.

13. John Davies, "Social Media: Marketing Magic or Madness" July 3, 2009, http:// www.hotel-online.com/News/PR2009_3rd/Jul09_SocialMediaMagic.html.

14. Hilton Corporation, 2009, http://www.hiltonfranchise.com/Marketing/Disclosures/ PDFs/2009FranchiseDisclosureDocument_Hilton.pdf.

15. Marriott, 2009, http://www.marriottdevelopment.com/pdfs/CFRSTFeeStructure.pdf.

16. Carol Verret, "The New 'Tipping Points' in the Planners Decision Process-You May be Surprised!" June 2, 2009, http://www.hotel-online.com/News/PR2009_ 2nd/Jun09_TippingPoints.html.

17. Enid Burns, "Active Home Internet Users by Country, May 2009," June 29, 2009. http://www.clickz.com/3634181.

18. The Honolulu Advertiser News, "Marriott Resorts Launch Twitter, Facebook and YouTube Campaign for 25 Free Trips to Hawaii," August 3, 2009, http://www.hotel-online.com/News/PR2009_3rd/Aug09_HawaiiMarriott.html.

19. Rex S. Toh, "Coping with No-Shows, Late Cancellations, and Oversales: American Hotels Out-do the Airlines," *International Journal of Hospitality Management* 5, no. 3 (1986): 122.

20. Ibid., 121.

21. Ibid., 122.

22. Doug Kennedy, "To Get More Bookings – Work With – Not Against Your Central Reservations Providers" May 2, 2009, http://www.hotel-online.com/News/PR2009_2nd/May09_CentralRes.html.

23. Ariel Herr, "Pegasus Solutions Appoints Industry Veterans to Key Management Positions" October 8, 2008, http://www.hotel-online.com/News/PR2008_4th/Oct08_PegasusVeterans.html.

24. Rebecca Oliva, "Singular Solution," *Hotels* 35, no. 7 (July 2001): 99.

Key Words

blocking on the horizon	leisure traveler
blocking procedures	no-show factor
bus association network	occupancy management formula
cancellation code	outsourcing
confirmed reservations	overbooking
corporate client	referral member
current guests	reservation code
daily blocking	reservation referral system
database interfaces	reservation status
forecasting	revenue management
franchisee	rooms forecasts
full house	social media
group planner	stayovers
group travelers	third-party reservation service
guaranteed reservations	third-party reservation website
hotel broker	travel directories
hotel representative	true integration
house count	understays
interhotel property referrals	walk-in guests

CHAPTER 6

Revenue Management

OPENING DILEMMA

The sales manager has left a message for the front office manager,

the food and beverage manager, and the revenue manager requesting

clearance to book a conference of 400 accountants for the first three

days of April. The front office manager needs to check out some things

before returning the call to the sales manager.

CHAPTER FOCUS POINTS

- Occupancy percentage
- Average daily rate
- RevPAR
- History of revenue management
- Use of yield management
- Components of revenue management
- Applications of revenue management

As mentioned in earlier chapters, *revenue management* is the technique of planning to achieve maximum room rates and the most profitable guests. This concept originated with the use of *yield management*, a similar concept, in hotel management circles in the late 1980s; in fact, yield management was borrowed from the airline industry to assist hoteliers in becoming better decision makers and marketers. It forced hotel managers to develop reservation policies that would build a profitable bottom line. Although the adoption of yield management was slow in the hotel industry, it offers far-reaching opportunities for hoteliers in the twenty-first century in the form of revenue management. This chapter applies concepts of yield management to the demands of aggressive applications of revenue management. For example, we see in the following description by Dr. Robert McMullin, professor of hotel, restaurant, and tourism management at East Stroudsburg University, how aggressive applications of yield management are employed in revenue management.

As with other businesses, pricing for the lodging industry is based on supply and demand. A good illustration of this is room rates at hotels near the Pocono Raceway in Pennsylvania, where there are two big races (the NASCAR Pocono 500 and the Pennsylvania 500) every year. Hotels in the area are full for the races, which define the peak season. During peak season, hotels collect rack rates. However, during the valleys, or off seasons, hotels must offer discounts and accept group travel discounts. The period between the peaks and valleys is called shoulder time, during which hotels build business and offer a variety of rates.[1]

Occupancy Percentage

To explain revenue management, we first review traditional measures of success in a hotel. *Occupancy percentage* historically revealed the success of a hotel's staff in attracting guests to a particular property. This traditional approach to measuring the effectiveness of the general manager, marketing staff, and front office staff was used to answer questions like these: How many rooms were sold due to the director of sales' efforts in creating attractive and enticing direct mail, radio and television ads, billboard displays, or newspaper and magazine display ads? How effective were reservation agents in meeting the room and amenity needs of the guests? Did travel agents book reservations? How competent were front office staff members in making sales? Today's questions include: Did the director of sales choose the right website to advertise the hotel's excess room inventory? Did the revenue manager price the rooms at the correct rate for the correct period? Are we hitting the right market segment? While interpretations of occupancy percentage are still indicators of the staff's efforts, in this chapter we focus on revenue management because it provides a more comprehensive review of factors such as room rate potential, revenue potential, and the nature of groups.

The occupancy percentage for a hotel property is computed daily. The method used to determine it is as follows:

$$\frac{\text{Number of Rooms Sold}}{\text{Number of Rooms Available}} \times 100 = \text{Single Occupancy \%}$$

To see how this formula works, consider a hotel that sold 75 rooms with a room inventory of 100 rooms, resulting in 75 percent occupancy:

$$\frac{75}{100} \times 100 = 75\%$$

Investors also use occupancy percentage to determine the potential gross income of a lodging establishment. For example, a 100-room property with a daily average 65 percent occupancy and an $89 average daily rate generates about $2.1 million in sales annually: 100 rooms × 0.65 occupancy = 65 rooms occupied daily; 65 × $89 room rate = $5785

FIGURE 6-1

A front office manager discusses the elements of yield management as it applies to revenue management in a training session. Photo courtesy of Hotel Information Systems.

revenue per day; 5785×365 days in a year = $2,111,525 gross income from room sales annually.

However, it is important not to assume that occupancy is standard each night. Variations are reflected in the following example:

A 65 percent occupancy is usually achieved on Monday, Tuesday, and Wednesday evenings. However, Thursday, Friday, and Saturday night statistics reveal a 40 percent occupancy, with Sunday night occupancy at 50 percent. Therefore:

Monday–Wednesday:	$100 \times 0.65 \times \$89 \times 156$ (52 $\times$ 3) =	**$902,460**
Thursday–Saturday:	$100 \times 0\ 40 \times \$\ 89 \times 156$ (52 $\times$ 3) =	**$555,360**
Sunday:	$100 \times 50 \times \$89 \times 156 \times 52$ =	**$231,400**
		Total: $1,689,220

Double occupancy is a measure of a hotel staff's ability to attract more than one guest to a room. Usually a room with more than one guest requires a higher room rate and thus brings additional income to the hotel. This method is also traditional in determining the success of building a profitable bottom line. The method to determine *double occupancy percentage* is as follows:

$$\frac{\text{Number of Guests} - \text{Number of Rooms Sold}}{\text{Number of Rooms Sold} \times 100} = \text{Double Occupancy \%}$$

If a hotel sold 100 rooms to 150 guests, then the double occupancy percentage is 50 percent, computed as follows:

$$\frac{150 - 100}{100} \times 100 = 50\%$$

Average Daily Rate

Average daily rate (ADR) is a measure of the hotel staff's success in selling available room rates. Such questions as why more $85 rooms than $99 rooms were sold, or whether the marketing office developed attractive weekend packages to sell the $80 rooms instead of relying on the desk clerk on duty to take any reasonable offer from walk-in guests, are typically answered when the ADR is reviewed.

The method to compute the ADR is as follows:

$$\frac{\textbf{Total Room Sales}}{\textbf{Number of Rooms Sold}}$$

If a hotel has daily room sales of $4800 with 60 rooms sold, the ADR is $80, computed as follows:

$$\frac{\$4800}{60} = \$80$$

The ADR is used in projecting room revenues for a hotel, as described above in the discussion of occupancy percentage. Occupancy percentage and ADR computations are essential parts of revenue management because they challenge hoteliers to maximize occupancy and room rates.

RevPAR

RevPAR (revenue per available room) was introduced in chapter 1 to allow you to recognize it as one of the financial determinants that hoteliers use in discussing revenue management. RevPAR is determined by dividing room revenue received for a specific day by the number of rooms available in the hotel for that day. The formulas for determining RevPAR are as follows:

$$\frac{\textbf{Room Revenue}}{\textbf{Number of Available Rooms}}$$

or

$$\textbf{Hotel Occupancy} \times \textbf{Average Daily Rate}$$

This type of financial insight into a hotel's ability to produce income allows owners, general managers, and front office managers to question standard indicators of hotel success. RevPAR answers the question, "How many dollars is each room producing?" If certain rooms are always occupied because of a lower rate, attractive amenities, or other reasons, then the hotel's administration may want to replicate those sales in similar markets. This questioning opens the door for revenue management, which turns the passive efforts of hoteliers into aggressive financial strategies.

History of Yield Management

Yield management is the source of the concepts that underlie revenue management. The history of yield management provides a framework for developing a background knowledge of revenue management. The airline industry instituted yield management after deregulation in the late 1970s.[2] The airlines blocked out time periods when seats on flights were priced at certain levels; the potential passenger either booked the flight at the price quoted or found other means of transportation. This bold marketing policy met with some problems such as consumer uproar concerning airfare strategies over holidays and weekends, but established the economic structure of airfares.

Hotels and airlines share similar operational features. Each has a fixed number of products (hotel rooms and airline seats) that, if not sold on a given day or flight, cannot be resold. Airlines and hotels sell to market segments that have distinct needs in product and service level. Each has demand periods (holidays, weekdays, and weekends in hotels; holidays, weekdays, and time of day for airlines) that place the provider in a favorable position. Airlines and hotels offer a range of rates from which guests can choose. Reservations allow managers to use yield management.[3] By using computers to track a database of products (hotel rooms and airline seats) and to process reservations, managers have the ability to look at a sales horizon of 45 to 90 days and to set price and reservation policies that will allow a prediction of profitability.

One of the major differences in how yield management is used in airlines and hotels is that at the hotel, the guest may also spend money for products and services besides the room itself. The airline passenger usually does not have an opportunity to spend large amounts of money during a flight. Because of this difference, hoteliers must consider the financial potential of one prospective guest over another in determining reservation policies. For example, one group may want to book a block of 500 rooms with a $50,000 value plus banquets and other food and beverage service events that total $25,000, while another group may want to book a block of 600 rooms with a value of $60,000 but no additional food and beverage income.

Use of Yield Management

Yield management has now caught on in the hotel industry. It is imperative that hoteliers understand the importance of the basic factors of yield management—room rate categories, room inventory, and group buying power—to navigate their way through revenue management. The goal of revenue management is twofold: to maximize profit for guest room sales and to maximize profit for hotel services. These goals are important for future hoteliers to understand, because if they set out to maximize room sales only, the most profitable guest may not stay in the guest room. This is the difference between airline yield management and hotel revenue management.

The following discussion shows how revenue management is used in the hotel industry. As you read, note how the management staff is using technology to make informed decisions that will reflect favorably on the bottom line. (The terms *yield management* and *revenue management* are now interchangeable. Yield management was the earlier concept from which revenue management developed.) The real challenge of developing any computer application is to support the goals of the management staff. The following quote from the International Hotel Association summarizes the importance of using yield management as a business tool: "Yield Management is the must-have business planning tool for hoteliers. The computerized functioning [mathematical model] of yield management is complex, but the concept is simple: By using a combination of pricing and inventory control, a hotelier can maximize profits from the sale of rooms and services."[4] This statement continues to be relevant in today's hotel marketplace.

A common misperception about hotel revenue management (RM) is that its value diminishes when room occupancy falls. With a healthy economy, an RM system can often appear to be a well-running car engine, doing its job to manage the mix of bookings to maximize revenues. During low-occupancy periods, some hotel management teams mistakenly view RM as a low-priority activity. However, it is precisely during these challenging times that hotel professionals should be looking under the hood and asking questions regarding the methods and the data used to manage hotel pricing and customer mix. Hotel teams should rely on RM processes to enable responsive sales, marketing, cost containment and pricing decisions that work in today's economy.[5]

So how are hotel general managers, revenue managers, directors of marketing, and front office managers applying this technology to produce more profit? Here is an example:

Warren Dehan, president of NORTHWIND-Maestro PMS says, "But no matter how tightly you manage your operation, revenue is the engine that drives property performance. And to maximize revenue it is essential to utilize an effective revenue management system. Manual rate setting is no longer an option."

Industry analysts agree that current market dynamics indicate that Internet channels will be much more important to property revenue as the meeting and corporate segment cools in 2009. "With payrolls being trimmed, hotel staffs do not have time to manage Online Travel Agency (OTA) allotments and prices throughout the day," says Dehan. "Hotel operators must learn to rely on solid revenue management technology to monitor all sales channels, particularly Internet booking channels."[6]

Revenue Manager

Because revenue management has become such an active part of hotel management, a new operational position has emerged: the revenue manager. The *revenue manager* reports to the general manager, works closely with the marketing and sales department, and consults with the front office manager. The job of the revenue manager is to oversee the room inventory and room rates offered throughout the year to groups and individuals and through the various channels: central reservation systems, global distribution systems, third-party reservation systems, toll-free reservation numbers, and so on. The revenue manager also identifies trends and methods to match those trends. The person in this job communicates regularly with members of a revenue management team. The following is a management job listing for a revenue manager.

1. Monitor, analyze, and report on demand patterns, sales, and losses.

2. Develop, implement daily, and improve sales strategies as needed.

3. Work with Sales, Catering, and Conference Planning to balance transient and group business. Provide feedback about potential new customers.

4. Analyze no-shows, cancellations, early departures, and unexpected stayover patterns.

5. Direct weekly revenue meetings.

6. Assist with product development and marketing of transient packaging.

7. Adjust all rates and restrictions on property and through all transient channels.

8. Provide weekly reports about business pace and changes in consumer behavior that affect revenue.[7]

Jeffrey Beck, in a study focusing on professional issues of revenue managers, asked survey questions about concepts such as software, career path, commitment to organization, allocation of time, and activities for success. A majority of respondents (55 percent) expected to be in their current positions within the next two years. The survey delved deep into time spent on specific revenue management activities, from managing inventory, developing offers, and forecasting the property's room revenues to evaluating revenue management activities, managing customer relationships, and interacting with other managers regarding revenue management activities.[8]

HOSPITALITY PROFILE

Debra Kelly is the revenue manager for the Sheraton Parsippany Hotel in Parsippany, New Jersey. She began her career as a travel agent and then worked at Loews Hotel as a guest service agent and in catering sales, group sales, and reservations. She moved on to the Sheraton Parsippany Hotel, where she was "director of rooms pricing" prior to her current position.

(continues)

HOSPITALITY PROFILE (*CONTINUED*)

Ms. Kelly's role as revenue manager focuses upon several objectives in the hotel. The main objective is producing a profit for the hotel which is supported through knowing the various markets, competition, and trends. The various Markets such as corporate, group, and or leisure each have various needs with regard to rooms, room rates, and accommodations. The competition has to be observed for new hotels entering those that are departing, or ones that are sold out on a particular night. Trends and shifts in the meeting patterns of groups, corporate travel, and leisure travel has to be closely watched also. Another part of her job is the creation and interpretation of reports. She uses Top Line Profit Enterprise revenue management software to assist her in her role as revenue manager. She inputs historical data of room numbers at certain rates, and at specific dates. It then produces an invaluable piece of advice on trends for upcoming dates. For example, she may consider taking a group of 200 rooms for May 10, May 11, and May 12, Top Line Profit Enterprise, could cite that the hotel already has 35 rooms booked on May 10 and May 11 with a busy leisure business, that weekend expected. It says that the hotel will probably be sold out and should not take that piece of business for those dates.

Ms. Kelly adds that you have to regularly feed the computer program with current data such as past weather conditions, the closing of nearby hotels, and other business situations that would affect the business climate. This information assists the computer software in making accurate decisions.

The revenue manager doesn't work alone in a hotel. Ms. Kelly said that she works with the general manager and the director of sales and marketing. She said the front office manager has to be kept informed of the position that the revenue team is taking on room inventory and room pricing. This information is then shared with the front office staff and feedback is solicited from guests to share with the revenue team. Also, the front office staff is involved in selling rooms, so they have to know this information on room inventory and room pricing.

Expedia and Travelocity, referred to as third-party reservation services, provide a wealth of information to prospective guests. Hoteliers have come to the recognition that we are partners with them. Ms. Kelly indicates that it is costlier to be involved with them (as opposed to selling rooms directly through the Sheraton.com website or through the toll-free number), but it is a cost that is justified in order to attract a certain amount of additional business. She uses the Extranet to place their hotel's inventory of rooms on the third-party reservation services. She also receives a channel report from Sheraton that lists all the sources of reservations that have been used. This allows the revenue management team to determine which reservation sources—central reservation systems, global distribution systems, travel agents, toll-free numbers, direct calls to the hotel, visits to the Starwood website, or third-party reservation services—are most profitable.

Debra Kelly highly recommends a career in the hotel business if you want a job where something new pops up each day. If you like to work with numbers, then try the revenue management area of the hotel; if you like advertising, work your way into the marketing department. The marketing department is trying many new concepts on their web-sites. She also advises a career in the hotel business because there are so many different types of hotels to continue your profession.

Components of Revenue Management

To understand revenue management, you first must understand its components and their relationships. Each part of revenue management feeds into a network that supports the goal of maximizing profit for a hotel.

Definition of Yield

Traditionally, a hotel's goal was 100 percent occupancy. Using this concept, a certain percentage of the rooms may have been sold, but how profitable was the venture? For example, Table 6-1 shows Hotel ABC, which has 500 rooms. It sells 200 rooms at $80 and 200 rooms at $95 (rack rate), earning $35,000 in room sales and achieving an 80 percent occupancy. Hotel XYZ also has 500 rooms and sells 100 rooms at $80 and 300 rooms at $95 (rack rate), earning $36,500 and achieving the same 80 percent occupancy. This additional daily income ($1500) would lead to a better profit-and-loss statement. The process of creating additional income leads us to the definition of yield. *Yield* is the percentage of income that could be secured if 100 percent of available rooms were sold at their full rack rate. *Revenue realized* is the actual amount of room revenue earned (number of rooms sold × actual rate). *Revenue potential* is the room revenue that could be received if all the rooms were sold at the rack rate. The formula for determining yield is as follows:[9]

$$\text{Yield} = \frac{\text{Revenue Realized}}{\text{Revenue Potential}}$$

Table 6-2 demonstrates the effects of revenue management strategies. Both hotels achieve an 80 percent occupancy, but Hotel XYZ achieves a higher yield while selling the same percentage of rooms.

TABLE 6-1   Occupancy Percentage Comparison

Hotel	No. Rooms Available	No. Rooms Sold	Rate	Income	Occupancy %
ABC	500	200	$80	$16,000	
					80
		200	$95	19,000	
		400		$35,000	
XYZ	500	100	$80	$8,000	
					80
		300	$95	28,500	
		400		$36,500	

TABLE 6-2	Yield Comparison		
Hotel	Revenue Realized	Revenue Potential	Yield %
ABC	$35,000	$47,500*	73.68
XYZ	$36,500	$47,500*	76.84

*500 rooms × $95 (rack rate) = $47,500

Another example of determining yield is as follows: If The Times Hotel has 300 rooms available for sale and sells 200 rooms at $85 with a rack rate of $110, the yield is 51.51 percent.

$$\frac{200 \times \$85 = \$17,000}{300 \times \$110 = \$33,000} \times 100 = 51.51\%$$

The determination of yield provides a better measure of a hotel staff's effort to achieve maximum occupancy than the traditional occupancy percentage. The 51 percent yield means the staff's effort in achieving maximum occupancy could have been improved by using effective strategies to sell more $110 rooms. Thus, one of the goals of revenue management is to sell all available rooms at the highest rate (rack rate). A later subsection of this chapter deals with the development of effective strategies to ensure maximum yield.

Optimal Occupancy and Optimal Rate

Achieving the best yield involves redefining occupancy percentage and average daily rate. Although these concepts are important to the long-range potential financial picture, they take on a new meaning with revenue management. *Optimal occupancy*, achieving 100 percent occupancy with room sales, which will yield the highest room rate, and *optimal room rate*, a room rate that approaches the rack rate, work together to produce the yield. The following scenario illustrates the harmony that must be achieved to maximize yield:

A 300-room hotel has sold 100 rooms at $76, 150 rooms at $84, and 35 rooms at $95 (rack rate). The yield for this combination is 83 percent. If revenue management were in use and the daily report revealed 200 rooms sold at $90 and 85 rooms at $95, a 91 percent yield could have been realized. Not only could an additional 8 percentage points have been achieved but also an additional $2550 could have been earned. In both situations, 95 percent occupancy was achieved, but the average daily rate in the first case was $82.54, while the optimal room rate in the second case was $91.49. The $91.49 optimal room rate more closely approaches the $95.00 rack rate.

Strategies

E. Orkin offers a simple policy for developing strategies to implement yield management: When demand is high, maximize rates; when demand is low, maximize room sales.[10]

TABLE 6-3	Revenue Management Strategies
Demand	**Strategy**
High	Maximize rates, require minimum stays
Low	Maximize room sales, open all rate categories

[Author's note: Orkin's term *yield management* can be interchanged with the term *revenue management*.] This idea is expressed in Table 6-3. Orkin also offers specifics on developing strategies. He says when demand is high, "restrict or close availability of low-rate categories and packages to transients [guests], require minimum length of stays, and commit rooms only to groups willing to pay higher rates. When demand is low, provide reservation agents with special promotional rates to offer transients who balk at standard rates, solicit group business from organizations and segments that are characteristically rate sensitive, and promote limited-availability low-cost packages to local market."[11] Restricting or closing availability was initially a challenge because most front office managers were familiar with the sell-out-the-house operating procedure and were unsure this aggressive marketing tactic would work. Some hoteliers were setting reservation policies that required minimum length of stay during heavy demand periods. The procedure recommended for low demand (special promotional rates and soliciting group and local business) was the strategy used during any demand period. As revenue management continues to be tried and tested in hotels, various combinations of maximizing room rates and room sales continue to challenge hoteliers, revenue managers, and front desk managers.

For example, Carol Verret discusses the importance of developing a revenue management strategy:

A revenue management strategy establishes "target" numbers to be achieved through a variety of ways: sales, manipulating the GDS, controlling the allocation and rate in the electronic distribution channels, etc. In other words, it is a proactive rather than reactive function that simply turns the faucets on and off.[12]

She also describes the components of revenue management.

Revenue drivers are defined as all areas of revenue generation within the organization. This includes central reservations, property-level reservations, the sales department, the electronic distribution channels and the web site.[13]

Another example is provided by Neil Salerno, who suggests aggressive revenue management tactics based on the history of reservation performance.

Too many hoteliers set rates blindly for the future and then panic when reservations are disappointing just a week or two in advance. Most hotels should take a picture of reservations at least six months in advance; many hotels should look out a year or more into the future. Advance reservations represent occupancy demand for each night in the future. Use special rates, packages, and group discounts to build future demand; then adjust rates upwards to match that demand.

When reviewing future reservations, remember to check past history for those dates, movable holiday dates, current and past booking pace.[14]

Forecasting

An important feature of yield management is forecasting room sales. Orkin suggests using a daily decision orientation rather than a seasonal decision-making scheme in developing a particular strategy.[15] (Revenue managers continue to apply these concepts of yield management daily.) Accurate forecasting of transient demand assists hoteliers in developing strategies to maximize sales to this group. For example, if a hotel has group business reservations for 95 percent of available rooms, seeking transient business with special promotional packages during that period would not be advisable. If the period following the group business is low, then advance knowledge of this situation allows time for marketing and sales to develop special promotional packages aimed at the transient and local markets.

Star Report

One of the most important applications of revenue management is reviewing your hotel's performance as well as that of your competitors'. The international system that is available for hoteliers is the STAR Report that is made possible by STR and, since 2008, STR Global. Some of the highlights of that option is as follows.

In 2008 STR combined its non-North American operations with the two international leaders in the benchmarking arena, Deloitte's HotelBenchmark™ and The Bench, to form STR Global. STR continues serving the North-American market which they have been supporting since its foundation in 1985 and STR Global brings the benefits of the well-known STAR reports to a truly global audience. STR and STR Global track supply and demand data for the hotel industry and provide valuable market share analysis for all major international hotel chains and brands. With tens of thousands of hotels participating in our hotel performance surveys, we are the world's foremost source of historical hotel performance trends on daily and monthly basis and we will offer the definitive global hotel database and development pipeline.

Randy Smith began studying and analyzing the lodging industry more than 25 years ago. With a strong background in research and a keen interest in technology, Smith had

---

FRONT-LINE REALITIES

 The controller of the hotel has asked the front office manager to project room sales for the next 45 days. This is necessary for the controller to estimate cash flow for a loan payment due in 30 days. How will the use of revenue management help the front office manager make an accurate projection?

an idea: create a service that provides the best information on overall performance trends in the lodging industry to the lodging industry and its observers.

STR's initial concept was to create a complete list of all properties in the United States and provide that list to suppliers in order to create districts and territories for their sales staff. And the company has remained dedicated to that concept for more than a quarter of a century.

The promise? Absolute confidentiality. After legitimizing his goal, Smith created a database that tracked the performance of individual properties and compared them with the competition. With the support of a few key chains, STR launched the STAR program in January 1988. The STAR program has become THE source of information for chains and management companies. Smith has always maintained that the data would only be used in generating aggregate reports. Along the way, lenders, appraisers, consultants and developers began using STR's aggregate data to assist in the performance of their jobs.[16]

STR and STR Global offers an excellent web site with tutorials and Questions & Answers to assist clients in reading their reports. This web site can be accessed at www.strglobal.com/Resources/Resources.aspx.

Block-out Periods

The strategies just discussed for high-demand periods require revenue managers, hotel managers, and front office managers to block out certain days when potential guests who seek reservations must commit to a minimum length of stay. If a guest requests a reservation for October 25 but that date falls in the block-out period of October 24, 25, and 26, the reservation agent must refuse the request. If the guest is willing to commit to all three days, then the reservation can be processed. Establishing block-out periods allows a hotel to develop standardized reservation operating procedures for a 24-hour-a-day reservation system. Forecasting these periods is an essential feature of yield management.

Systems and Procedures

Orkin suggests that a front office manager who implements yield management use an automated system that processes reservations, tracks demand, and blocks out room availability during certain periods.[17] The details of operating a reservation system for a year-round 500-room hotel that uses yield management would be overwhelming if left to manual calculation. Orkin also advises initiating specific rate-setting policies that will ensure profitability. Establishing block out periods requires an ongoing marketing effort by the hotel to ensure sales in projected low demand periods. Orkin urges front office managers to develop a well-trained staff who understand and use yield management procedures. Training is a key element in making a complicated system workable (Figure 6-2).

Those of you with experience in the hotel industry will appreciate Orkin's last caution: Be adaptable to changes in demand. If a four-day convention booked 90 percent of the rooms for arrival on April 5 but 25 percent of those reservations cancel by March 30, the front office manager should drop the restrictions for a four-day stay and encourage reservation agents to offer promotional packages to transient guests.

FIGURE 6-2

In a training session, a front office manager encourages discussions of the application of yield management as the basis of revenue management. Photo courtesy iStockphoto.com.

Channel Management

As noted in chapter 5, guest room sales can be completed via a central reservation system, GDS, third-party reservation systems, toll-free phone numbers, travel agents, social networking/media, and other means. Revenue management requires the objective review of those sales channels to determine which approach would have afforded the hotel with maximum opportunity for financial gain.

Kim Stephenson of EZ Yield, in an article on channel management software, describes how this technology can assist revenue managers in this important task:

> EZ Yield is a channel management solution that lets users effectively monitor and manage inventory for third-party websites at the touch of a button. But what makes EZ Yield particularly unique is that it's the only proven system in the world where users can view and alter rates and inventory as well as update advanced bookings, minimum night stay and availability simultaneously on third-party websites.
>
> Websites can be amended in real time from any PC, saving users both time and money. And because it's fully automated, it's extremely fast, accurate and instant. Other features include multi-lingual and multi-currency capability that empower the user.[18]

Feedback

Feedback on decisions employed in revenue management is essential to any new venture in management. A record of the date and amount of turnaway business is vital for hoteliers to assess the viability of revenue management and to update revenue management

TABLE 6-4	Turnaway Business Report		
Date	Yield %	No. Rooms Turned Away	Dollars Lost [@ $95 Rack Rate]
May 1	98	35	3325
May 2	96	20	1900
May 3	93	60	5700
May 4	50	90	8500
May 5	50	88	8360

and marketing strategies for the future.[19] A general manager who reviews the report of a recent five-day block-out period, as depicted in Table 6-4, would find the period restricted for a five-day minimum length of stay worked well for May 1–3, but 178 room reservations were lost for May 4–5. The director of marketing and sales must research the contracts the hotel had with the groups involved. Also, the front office manager should ask if the front desk clerks, bell staff, or cashiers heard any guest comments on why they checked out earlier than scheduled. The turnaway business on May 3–5 might also indicate the convention events scheduled on these days were more interesting or the members of this group did not want to commit to a five-day stay and wanted reservations for only the last three days of the convention.

Management Challenges in Using Revenue Management

An enormous problem facing hotels that employ revenue management is alienation of customers.[20] Potential guests who have a reservation refused because they do not want to comply with minimum-stay requirements or who feel they are victims of price gouging may not choose that hotel or any hotel in that chain the next time they need lodging. It is important that employees be well trained in presenting reservation policies to the public.

Considerations for Food and Beverage Sales

The previous discussion of revenue management focused on rates, room availability, minimum stay, and the like. However, another issue that assists hoteliers in setting revenue management policies cannot be overlooked: potential food and beverage sales.[21] Certain market segments tend to purchase more food and beverages than other segments. This factor must be taken into consideration to determine the most profitable customer to whom to offer the reservation.

Review Table 6-5 to determine which potential group would bring in the most income to the hotel. Group B, with projected income of $92,500 due to projected food and beverage costs (perhaps guests with larger expense accounts or scheduled banquet meals), will bring more projected income to the hotel, even though the room rate for group B is lower than for group A.

Some hoteliers debate the food and beverage issue because the profit from food and beverage sales is not as great as that from room sales. Other debates in applying revenue

TABLE 6-5	Considerations of Food and Beverage Income in Setting Revenue Management Strategies				
Group	No. Rooms	Rate	Room Income	Food and Beverage Income	Projected Income
A	350	$110	$38,500	$18,750	$57,250
B	300	$100	$30,000	$62,500	$92,500

management center on the type of guests who request reservations and the subsequent effects on room furnishings and use of hotel facilities. For example, group B may be a conference group of high school students who may damage hotel facilities, while group A may be senior citizens attending a conference. Developing effective revenue management policies that identify groups who may yield additional income (or expense) is necessary to make revenue management work. This is indeed a challenge to you as you begin your career as a hotelier.

Applications of Revenue Management

The best way to understand revenue management is to apply it to various situations. Try your hand at the following scenarios to become familiar with the basics of revenue management.

Scenario 1

A front office manager has reviewed the daily report, which reveals that 240 rooms were sold last night. The hotel has 300 rooms and a rack rate of $98. Using the following breakdown of room sales, determine the yield for last night:

> 85 rooms at $98
>
> 65 rooms at $90
>
> 90 rooms at $75

Scenario 2

The general manager has asked you to develop a block-out period for the October Annual Weekend Homecoming event at The Times Hotel. There is a definite possibility of 100 percent occupancy, but the general manager is concerned that several of the alumni will dine off-premises. He would like a package rate that includes a kickoff breakfast and a dinner after the game. How will you proceed?

Scenario 3

A representative from the Governor's Conference has requested a block of 200 rooms for three days at a $75 rate. This conference is attended by people who know how to entertain, and the projected food and beverage expenditure per person is significant. During that same three-day period, a jazz concert is scheduled in the city. In the past, reservations from this group plus walk-ins have allowed you to achieve 100 percent occupancy (200 rooms) at a $135 rate (rack rate is $95). However, the jazz enthusiasts do not have a positive history of large food and beverage purchases. What would you do, and on what would you base your decision?

Solution to Opening Dilemma

The front office manager must check the room availability for this period in the reservation module. She must determine if any block-out periods already exist and, if so, what minimum room-night restrictions are in force. She must also check with the food and beverage manager to determine the availability of banquet facilities and food services and the financial implications that may influence the decision. The revenue manager must provide information on rates and minimum reservation periods appropriate for the dates requested. If the decision leans toward rejection of the offer, the sales manager should consider public relations implications.

Chapter Recap

This chapter discussed the traditional concepts of occupancy percentage and average daily rate in determining the effectiveness of management's efforts to achieve a positive income statement. RevPAR was used to answer the question "How many dollars is each room producing?" Yield management was introduced as a tool hoteliers can use in developing guest room sales strategies and evaluating potential food and beverage purchases to ensure a higher profit. The concept of yield management was borrowed from the airline industry, which shares a common operational design with the hotel industry. Components of yield management include revenue realized, revenue potential, optimal occupancy and optimal rates, strategies, block-out periods, forecasting, systems and procedures, feedback, and challenges front office managers face in implementing and using yield management. These concepts have been adopted into a daily revenue management operations practice and require the services of a revenue manager to monitor all opportunities to sell room inventory at various room rates and evaluate the potential financial impact of groups.

End-of-Chapter Questions

1. Explain in your own words the concept of revenue management.

2. What does a revenue manager do as a member of the hotel management team?

3. How are yield management and revenue management related?

4. What does occupancy percentage tell the owner of a hotel? Discuss the shortcomings of this concept in measuring the effectiveness of a general manager.

5. Similarly, discuss the use of occupancy percentage versus the average daily rate (ADR) in determining the effectiveness of a general manager. What impression does quoting the ADR only give the owner of a hotel?

6. How can RevPAR assist hotel managers in measuring the effectiveness of front desk staff and marketing managers?

7. What similarities in operational design do the airline industry and the hotel industry share?

8. What are the goals of revenue management? If you are employed at a front desk in a hotel, do you see these goals being achieved?

9. Determine the yield for a hotel that has 200 rooms available for sale with a rack rate of $80, all of which are sold at $75.

10. Determine the yield for a hotel that has 275 rooms available for sale with a rack rate of $60, of which150 are sold at $75.

11. Determine the yield for a hotel that has 1000 rooms available for sale with a rack rate of $135, of which 850 are sold at $100.

12. Determine the yield for a hotel that has 100 rooms available for sale with a rack rate of $95, of which 85 are sold at $75.

13. Determine the yield for a hotel that has 190 rooms available for sale with a rack rate of $125, of which 100 are sold at $93.

14. Determine the yield for a hotel that has 525 rooms available for sale with a rack rate of $140, of which 367 are sold at $119.

15. Discuss the concepts of yield and occupancy percentage as illustrated in questions 10 through 14.

16. Discuss strategies to use when demand is high.

17. Discuss strategies to use when demand is low.

18. Why should a revenue manager set daily rate strategies as opposed to general period rate strategies?

19. In your own words, explain the term *block-out period*.

20. Why is sharing revenue management strategies with the front office staff so important to the success of the revenue management program?

21. What role does the transient guest play in the success of achieving yield?

22. What information can be obtained by reviewing the breakdown of rooms sold by rate category in the daily report? What should a hotel staff do with this information?

23. How can review of the various sales channels assist the revenue manager in his or her job?

24. Why should turnaway business be reviewed daily? What should the hotel staff do with this information?

25. What role do potential food and beverage sales play in revenue management? What are your thoughts on rejecting the role of this concept in achieving yield?

CASE STUDY 601

Ana Chavarria, front office manager at The Times Hotel, has completed a revenue management seminar at Keystone University and is preparing an argument in favor of adopting this concept at The Times Hotel to present to Margaret Chu, the general manager. Ana begins by compiling a history of room occupancy and ADRs, which she hopes will reveal areas in which revenue management could help. She prepares an electronic spreadsheet that lists rooms sold with corresponding room rates and correlates the data to tourism activities in the area. Ana sends an analysis of revenue realized and revenue potential to Ms. Chu for review prior to their discussion.

After reviewing the analysis, Ms. Chu concludes, "This is just another scam; the industry is slow to adopt this," and disregards the entire report. She knows that occupancy percentage, ADR, and RevPAR are all you need to be efficient today, so why change?

Ana passes Ms. Chu in the lobby. Ms. Chu indicates her distrust of the revenue management concept but says she will listen to Ana's presentation tomorrow.

What tips could you give Ana to help her present a sound case for the adoption of revenue management?

CASE STUDY 602

Suggest revenue management strategies to use under the following circumstances at The Times Hotel:

Situation 1: The Train Collectors will be in town from November 10 through November 15 and will draw 50,000 people. Every room in town is expected to be taken for that period. What policy should the hotel develop for guests who want to reserve a room for the following periods?

- November 10 only
- November 10 and 11 only
- November 10, 11, and 12 only
- November 11, 12, and 13 only

- November 12, 13, and 14 only
- November 13, 14, and 15 only
- November 13 and 14 only
- November 14 and 15 only
- November 15 only

Situation 2: The last two weeks of December are usually slow for room sales, but a local Snow and Ice Festival will attract visitors who may request reservations for single overnight accommodations. What policy should the hotel develop for accepting such room reservations?

CASE STUDY 603

Suggest revenue management strategies to use under the following circumstances at The Times Hotel:

Situation 1: The Bee Keepers will be in town from January 19 through January 25 and will draw 8,000 people. No other conferences are scheduled for the nights of January 19–21 in the area; two other conferences are opening in town on the night of the 22nd that will last through the night of the 25th. These last two conferences will take up all the existing rooms in town. What policy should the hotel develop for guests who want to reserve a room for the following periods?

- January 19 only
- January 19 and 20 only
- January 19, 20, and 21 only
- January 19 through 24 only
- January 19 through 25 only
- January 20 through 24 only
- January 21 through 24 only
- January 22 through 24 only
- January 23 and 24 only
- January 24 and 25 only

Situation 2: The Times Hotel wants to rethink its policy on food and beverage sales with regard to its impact on revenue management. What concepts would you suggest they review as they develop their policy?

Notes

1. Robert McMullin, "Why Do Hotel/Resort Room Rates Fluctuate Throughout the Year?" *Pocono Record*, August 29, 2002.
2. S. E. Kimes, "Basics of Yield Management," *Cornell Hotel and Restaurant Administration Quarterly* 30, no. 3 (November 1989): 15.
3. Ibid., 15–17.
4. "The ABCs of Yield Management," *Hotels* 27, no. 4 (April 1993): 55. Copyright *Hotels* magazine, a division of Reed USA.
5. Manizer, 2009. "Revenue Management Doesn't Take a Back Seat During a Downturn," http://www.hotel-online.com/News/PR2009_1st/Jan09_RMSystem.html
6. Julie Squires, 2009. "Build Profitability in 2009: Maestro PMS Proactive Yield Management Enables Operators to Thrive in Challenging and Competitive Marketplace," http://www.hotel-online.com/News/PR2009_2nd/Apr09_MaestroPMS.html.
7. Benchmark Hospitality International at Leesburg, VA (Benchmark Hospitality managed by The Woodlands—Houston, TX). Management job listing, benchmark, hospitalityonline.comjobs/6300/.
8. HSMAI, 2007. "Study Delves into the Revenue Management Profession," http://www.hotel-online.com/News/PR2007_2nd/Jun07_RevMgrIssues.html.
9. E. Orkin, "Boosting Your Bottom Line with Yield Management," *Cornell Hotel and Restaurant Administration Quarterly* 28, no. 4 (February 1988): 52.
10. Ibid., 53.

11. Ibid., 54.

12. Carol Verret, "The Revenue Management Strategy," July 2004, www.hotel-online. com/News/PR2004_2004_3rd/Jul04_PrePlanMarketing.html.

13. Carol Verret, "Revenue Management: The Integration of Revenue Drivers," March 2004, www.hotel-online.com/NewsPR2004_1st/_RevenueDrivers.html.

14. Salerno, 2008. http://www.hotel-online.com/News/PR2008_1st/Feb08_RevMgmt. html, "What the Heck is Hotel Revenue Management, Anyway? A Hotel Marketer's Guide to Revenue Management."

15. Ibid., 53. [This is an Orkin reference.]

16. Smith Travel Research, Inc., 2008–2009. "STR Global Hompage," http://www. strglobal.com/About/About_Us.aspx.

17. Ibid.

18. Stephenson, 2008. "'We just couldn't say no to EZYield,'" http://www.hotelonline. com/News/PR2008_1st/Feb08_EZYieldHotelProphets.html.

19. Rebecca Oliver, 2004 "Multiple Forecasts," 2004, Hotels, http://www.hotelsmag. com/archives/2004/02/tech-revenue-management-systems.asp.

20. Kimes, "Basics of Yield Management," 19.

21. Ibid., 18–19.

Key Words

average daily rate (ADR)	revenue manager
double occupancy percentage	revenue potential
occupancy percentage	revenue realized
optimal occupancy	yield
optimal room rate	yield management
revenue management	

CHAPTER 7

Guest Registration

The group leader of a busload of tourists approaches the front desk for

check-in. The front desk clerk acknowledges the group leader and begins

the check-in procedure, only to realize no clean rooms are available. The

desk clerk mutters, "It's 4:00 P.M., and you would think someone in

housekeeping would have released those rooms by now." The group leader

asks, "What's holding up the process?"

CHAPTER FOCUS POINTS

- Importance of the first guest contact
- Capturing guest data
- Guest registration procedures
- Registration with a property management system

One of the first opportunities for face-to-face contact in a hotel occurs when the guest registers. At this point, all the marketing efforts and computerized reservation systems should come together. Will the guest receive what has been advertised and promised? The front desk clerk who is well trained in the registration process is able to portray the hotel in a positive manner. This good first impression helps ensure an enjoyable visit.

The first step in the guest registration process is to capture guest data such as name, address, email address, ZIP code, length of stay, and company affiliation, needed by various departments during the stay and after departure to provide service to the guest. The registration process continues with the extension of credit, room selection, room rate application, the opportunity to sell hotel services, room key assignment, and folio processing. Continually efficient performance of the registration process is essential to ensuring hospitality for all guests and profitability for the hotel.

Importance of the First Guest Contact

The first impression a guest receives of a lodging facility during registration is extremely important in setting the tone for hospitality and establishing a continuing business relationship. The guest who is warmly welcomed with a sincere greeting will respond positively to the hotel and will expect similar hospitality from other hotel employees. If the guest receives a halfhearted welcome, he or she will not be enthusiastic about the lodging facility and will be more likely to find fault with the hotel during the visit. Today's guest expects to be treated with respect and concern, and many hotels make the effort to meet those expectations. Those that do not should not expect the guest to return.

What constitutes a warm welcome? This varies. It begins with the front desk employee's empathizing with the feelings of the traveler, someone who has been away from familiar surroundings for many hours or many days. He or she may be stressed by the frustrations of commercial travel, delayed schedules, lost luggage, jetlag, missed meals, unfamiliar surroundings, unclear directions, or unfamiliar public transportation. The hotel employee who is considerate of the traveler under these circumstances is more likely to recognize anxiety, restlessness, and hostility and respond to them in a positive, understanding manner.

A typical scenario is as follows: Mr. Traveler arrives at 9:15 A.M. at the registration desk of a hotel. He is visibly upset because he is late for an important presentation to a group of investors. He wants to get into his room, drop off his luggage, and get public transportation to the corporate center. The desk clerk knows no clean rooms are available at this time. The desk clerk rings for a bellhop to escort Mr. Traveler to the luggage storage area. When the bellhop arrives, the desk clerk describes Mr. Traveler's situation. The bellhop calls the doorman to obtain a taxi, gives Mr. Traveler a receipt for his luggage, and escorts him to the main entrance of the hotel. Then he takes Mr. Traveler's luggage to the storage area. These timesaving practices allow Mr. Traveler to arrive at the presentation in a reasonable amount of time. When Mr. Traveler returns to the hotel later that day, he expresses his appreciation to the desk clerk on duty. The stage has been set for an enjoyable, hospitable stay.

However, the situation could have gone like this: When Mr. Traveler arrives, the desk clerk tells him, "Checkout time is not until 12 noon, and we don't have any rooms available yet. Check back with us after 4:00 P.M." Mr. Traveler searches for the luggage room, drops off his luggage (losing minutes because of a long line), manages to find his way back out to the main entrance, and asks the doorman to hail a cab (losing another ten minutes because it is rush hour). Mr. Traveler arrives late for the presentation because of the delay at the hotel and heavy traffic. Because Mr. Traveler is unaware of the availability of other room accommodations in the area, he returns after the presentation and waits in the hotel's lobby or lounge until 4:00 P.M. This time, the stage is set for an unpleasant visit. Mr. Traveler will probably choose another hotel the next time he has business in the area.

These two scenarios are repeated frequently in the hospitality industry. The latter, too often the norm, gives rise to discussions of overpriced accommodations and unfriendly, unhelpful hotel staff. A system must be in place to ensure that all travelers are extended hospitality as a standard operating procedure. The first guest contact is too vital to the delivery of a well-managed guest stay to leave it to the personal discretion of an individual.

Components of the Registration Process

The registration process is one of the many points of interaction with the guest and, ultimately, the cornerstone of delivering service before, during, and after the guest stay. Early in this section, we discuss the importance of capturing guest data that is confirmed from the previous reservation process or initiated with a walk-in guest. While guests are in our care, we can communicate with them, maintain an accurate accounting record, respond to inquiries about financial concerns, and follow up on service.

The registration process follows a succinct procedure of offering the guest hospitality, retrieving a reservation, reviewing the registration card for completeness, extending credit, selecting a room to meet the needs of the guest, checking room status, confirming room rates, promoting additional room sales, assigning room keys, and processing the guest folio. All these steps occur within the space of several minutes, but the organization behind the scenes is essential. Let's look at how the hotel's operational policies and procedures are developed to support a smooth registration process.

Capturing Guest Data

It is important to note at the outset the value of capturing guest data at registration. This information is used by many employees in the hotel to provide service and hospitality to the guest. It is used to transfer messages to the guest, inform the staff of the guest's needs, check credit background, and process charges.

Guests receive phone calls, phone messages, mail, packages, and fax transmissions the hotel must deliver. Recording the proper spelling of a guest's name, including the middle initial, during registration will assist the telephone operator and bellhop in locating the correct guest. A person with a common last name should not miss an important message just because more than one Tina S. Rodriguez, T. S. Rodriguez, or T. Samuel Rodriguez are registered at the hotel. In addition, hotel employees need to know who each guest is so standard operating procedures can be carried out. For example, the director of security wants the housekeeping staff to be alert for indications that more people are staying in a room than are registered for it. Not only does this information assist in providing security to registered guests but also it provides the hotel with additional income.

Guests' individual needs—such as certain room furnishings (cribs or rollaway beds), facilities for people who are physically challenged, separate folios for guests splitting costs, wake-up calls, or requests for rooms on lower floors that were not indicated when the reservation was made—should be noted and communicated to the appropriate hotel staff. Guests who are members of a group must have their registrations handled in a special manner to expedite the process. However, it is still important that the tour leader of the group provide individual guest information and room assignments. This information is necessary so the hotel staff can locate a specific guest or deliver messages as they are received.

The front desk clerk who accepts a guest's credit card as a means of payment must check the validity of the card and the available credit balance. Obtaining credit information from walk-ins or guests with confirmed reservations aids in the process of extending credit, billing, and collecting charges on checkout.

Guest Registration Procedure

The guest registration procedure involves several steps that, if followed accurately, allow management to ensure a pleasant, efficient, and safe visit. The process is discussed generally as these steps relate to effective front office management. Later in this chapter, use of a PMS (property management system) method of registration is discussed.

1. Guest requests to check into the hotel.

2. Front desk clerk projects hospitality toward the guest.

3. Front desk clerk inquires about guest reservation.

4. Guest completes registration card.

5. Front desk clerk reviews completeness of registration card.

6. Front desk clerk verifies credit.

7. Front desk clerk makes room selection.

8. Front desk clerk makes room assignment.

9. Front desk clerk assigns room rate.

10. Front desk clerk discusses sales opportunities for hotel products and services with guest.

11. Front desk clerk provides room key.

Guest Hospitality

The registration process begins when a guest asks to check into the hotel. The guest may arrive alone or with a group. The front desk clerk begins the check-in process with a display of hospitality toward the guest; important elements include eye contact, a warm smile, an inquiry regarding travel experience, an offer to assist the guest with a problem, and the like. As mentioned earlier, the importance of a warm welcome to a guest's positive impression of the hotel and its staff cannot be overemphasized. Most travelers expect common courtesy along with a high-quality product and a well-developed delivery system. Listen to what Doug Kennedy has to offer about the importance of the guest's front desk experience.*

Guests who have a positive experience at check-in are certain to be more understanding later, if/when they have objections or complaints later during their stay. In other words, if they have a good experience at the front desk, they will be much more forgiving later when a room service tray is delivered late, when the air conditioning breaks, or when a housekeeping request is overlooked.

Contrarily, guests who have a negative first impression can become hyper-critical; they will spend the rest of their stay almost looking for things to add to their "list," which they will [be] giving to their attorney first thing on Monday![1]

Inquiry about Reservation

After the front desk clerk welcomes the guest, he or she asks if a reservation was placed. If the guest responds affirmatively, the reservation is retrieved (called up on the computer). If the guest is a walk-in, the front desk clerk must check the availability of accommodations. If accommodations are available, the next step is to complete the registration card.

Completion of Registration Card

The *registration card* provides the hotel with the guest's billing information and provides the guest with information on checkout time and room rates (Figure 7-1). Even if the guest has a reservation, the completion of the registration card is important, as it verifies the spelling of names, addresses, phone numbers, anticipated date of departure, number of people in the party, room rate, and method of payment.

The top portion of the registration card supplies information about the guest, so the hotel has an accurate listing. With this information, phone calls, messages, and the like can be relayed as they are received. This record is also used for billing purposes. If the hotel has parking facilities, the garage manager needs information on the guest's car for security and control purposes. Obtaining complete and accurate information is important in hotels that use a PMS; this electronic folio form is preprinted. (Author's note: Some hotels do not use a registration card because the details of a reservation are recorded electronically. Therefore, the hotel's policy is to bypass this step in the registration process and have the desk clerk confirm the details of the guest's information in the following step.)

Review Completeness of Registration Card

The front desk clerk should quickly review the completeness of the registration card or electronic folio. For example, the handwriting should be legible, and the electronic form should have all appropriate boxes completed. If a revised registration card must be printed, now is the time to do it. The guest may forget to fill in a ZIP code, which is used

Source: Doug Kennedy is President of Kennedy Training Network Inc. www.KennedyTrainingNetwork.com.

FIGURE 7-1 **A registration form is used in a PMS and is often preprinted for guests who have reservations.**

Hotel Registration

NAME   GUEST
FIRM   DEPART
ADD.   ARRIVE

ROOM   AGENT   TYPE
RATE

ON CHECKING OUT, MY ACCOUNT WILL BE SETTLED BY:

☐ CASH   ☐ CARTE BLANCHE   ☐ PERSONAL CHECK
☐ AMERICAN EXPRESS   ☐ MASTERCARD / VISA   ☐ OTHER (SPECIFY)
☐ DINERS CLUB   ☐ DISCOVER   _____

          (LAST)   (FIRST)   (INITIAL)
NAME_____

                              ☐ HOME
STREET_____ ☐ BUSINESS

CITY_____ STATE_____ ZIP_____
COUNTRY_____
COMPANY_____

SIGNATURE

WHILE THE HOTEL IS NOT RESPONSIBLE FOR ANY LOSS IN YOUR GUEST ROOM OR
AUTOMOBILE, IT IS ADVISABLE THAT MONEY, JEWELS, AND OTHER VALUABLE ITEMS
BE PLACED IN THE SAFETY DEPOSIT BOXES AT THE FRONT DESK.

by the marketing and sales department to analyze market demographics as well as by the controller's office to process invoices. If a guest does not know a license plate number or other auto information, the desk clerk must explain that this information is necessary for security. If the desk clerk follows up this statement with a phone call to the garage attendant to obtain the necessary information, the effort will be appreciated by the guest, security officer, and garage manager.

Any areas on the registration card that remain blank should be called to the guest's attention. Such omissions may be oversights, or they may be an effort by the guest to commit fraud. The guest who does not supply a credit card and gives a weak excuse ("I forgot it in my car" or "It's in my suitcase, which the airline is delivering in three hours"), combined with a front desk clerk who accepts these reasons, sets the stage for fraud. A busy front desk clerk may forget to obtain this information later in the day.

Extension of Guest Credit

Front desk clerks must perform a few basic procedures to extend credit to guests. These include accepting the designated credit card from the guest, using credit card processing equipment, interpreting information from the credit card validation machine, and verifying the cardholder's identification.

Credit Cards

Credit cards are grouped according to the issuing agency. The major groupings are bank cards, commercial cards, private label cards, and intersell cards. As their name suggests, *bank cards* are issued by banks; VISA, MasterCard, and JCB are three examples. *Commercial cards* are issued by corporations; Diners Club is an example. *Private label cards* are generally issued by a retail organization, such as a department store or gasoline company; their use is usually limited to products sold by the issuing organization, but they may be acceptable for other purposes. *Intersell cards* are similar to private label cards but are issued by a major hotel chain. This type of card is acceptable at all properties of the chain and any of its subsidiaries.

The issuing agency previously verified the credit rating of the person to whom the card was issued. This enables the hotel to extend credit to the person who offers the credit card for future payment; this is an important option for hotels. Hotels extend credit to guests as a basis for doing business. Without this established certification of credit, a hotel would have to develop, operate, and maintain a system of establishing customer credit. Hotel chains that accept intersell cards do this, as do smaller hotels that are willing to bill to an account.

All credit cards are not equal from a hotel's financial point of view. The hotel may have a standing policy to request a bank credit card first or its own intersell card and then a commercial credit card. The reason for this is the *discount rate*, a percentage of the total sale charged by the credit card agency to the commercial enterprise for the convenience of accepting the credit card. The discount rate depends on the volume of sales transactions, amount of individual sales transaction, expediency with which vouchers are turned into cash, and other factors. Each general manager, in consultation with the controller and front office manager, works with each issuing agency to determine a rate that is realistic for the hotel.

The commercial credit card may require a 10 percent discount of the sale to be returned to the credit card agency, while one bank credit card requires 4 percent and another bank credit card requires 3 percent. The effect on the profit-and-loss statement is shown in the following illustration:

	Commercial	Bank Card 1	Bank Card 2
Guest bill	$200	$200	$200
Discount rate	× .10	× .04	× .03
Amount of discount	$ 20	$ 8	$ 6
Guest bill	$200	$200	$200
Amount of discount	− 20	− 8	− 6
Hotel revenue	$180	$192	$194

Even though Bank Card 2 seems most profitable, it may not be the credit card preferred by the hotel. The Bank Card 2 credit issuing agency may stipulate a seven-day turnaround time, so the hotel will not have access to the money until seven days have passed. Bank Card 1 may give the hotel instant access to the money on deposit of the vouchers. The cash flow requirements of the hotel must be thoroughly investigated and income and expenses must be projected before management can decide which credit cards it prefers.

Guests choose their credit cards for a variety of reasons, but sometimes they simply offer the first one pulled from a wallet. If the desk clerk is alert to the guest who displays several major credit cards, a request for the desired card may be accepted. This small procedure could mean more profit for the hotel over a fiscal year.

Credit Card Processing

The *credit card imprinter*, a machine that makes an imprint of the credit card the guest will use as the method of payment, and the *credit card validator*, a computer terminal linked to a credit card data bank that holds information about the customer's current balance and security status, are basic pieces of equipment at the front desk in many hotels. However, some hotels with a PMS or computerized credit card processing equipment do not require this equipment. The credit card validator can produce an electronic imprint (receipt) for the guest. The front desk clerk uses the credit card imprinter to imprint the cardholder's name, card number, and card expiration date on a preprinted voucher. The credit card validator enables the front desk clerk to establish approval for a certain amount of money to be deducted from a guest's credit line. The credit card company provides an approval code for authorization of the charge.

The data programmed into a credit card validator by the credit card issuing agencies differ from company to company. Some may indicate only that a card is current. Some indicate the credit card is valid and the amount of the sale will not cause the guest to exceed his or her credit limit; conversely, the information may indicate the amount of the sale will cause the guest to exceed the limit. For example, a guest's estimated bill of $300 for a three-day stay may not be covered by an available credit line of $173. In that case, the front desk clerk must ask for another credit card to establish credit. The information received from the credit card validator may also indicate the card was reported stolen and should be retained by the hotel. Established procedures for handling fraud indicate how hotel security should be alerted in this case.

Proof of Identification

Some hotels require proof of identification when a credit card is presented; others do not. When the hotel policy does require the guest to produce identification, a valid driver's license with a photo is usually acceptable. Alteration of non-photo identification is all too common, making it less than reliable. Hotel security departments must work with the front office in training desk clerks and cashiers to be alert to fraudulent identifications.

Bill-to-account

The credit card is the most common way to establish credit in a hotel. However, there are other means of extending credit to the guest. The *bill-to-account* requires the guest or the guest's employer to establish a line of credit and to adhere to a regular payment schedule. The guest or the employer completes a standard credit application. The controller evaluates the completed form, considering outstanding financial obligations, liquid financial assets, credit card balances, and other credit concerns. If the applicant is deemed creditworthy, then the controller establishes a line of credit. The bill-to-account client is informed of the billing and payment schedules.

When offering bill-to-account credit to the guest, the hotel takes on the responsibility of bill collection. It must anticipate the effect of the billing and payment schedule on the profit-and-loss statement and the cash flow of the hotel. The controller's office is responsible for the accounting process associated with bill-to-account clients. This can involve many hours of clerical work and computer processing time. This extra labor should be evaluated when deciding whether the 3–10 percent discount charged by the credit card issuing agency is more cost-effective than internal accounting of guest charges. Because some credit card issuing agencies offer immediate cash tender to the hotel's bank account, some hotels may prefer this method of payment, so they can meet immediate financial obligations (employee payroll, vendor accounts, tax payments, and the like).

Room Selection

Part of the registration process is the front desk clerk's selection of a guest room, which can be confusing for the front desk clerk and frustrating for the guest. This step involves blocking guest rooms prior to a guest's arrival, meeting the guest's needs, and maintaining a room inventory system. If the guest is assigned a room that does not meet his or her personal requirements, the guest then requests a different room. The front desk clerk responds with a list of available options that better satisfy the guest's request.

Blocking Procedure

The blocking procedure is important in ensuring an even flow of guests who want to check in. Blocked rooms allow the front desk clerk to immediately assign a room to a guest without searching through confirmed and guaranteed reservations as well as available room inventory. Otherwise, desk clerks must review reservations and available rooms at the guest's arrival.

The blocking procedure begins with a review of confirmed and guaranteed reservations as well as expected checkouts for a particular day. For example, if a 200-room hotel has 125 rooms occupied on the night of November 1, with 25 room checkouts scheduled for the morning of November 2, the front office manager determines that 100 rooms are available for guests to use on November 2, as follows:

> 200 rooms available in the hotel
> − 125 rooms occupied on **November 1**
> = 75 rooms available for sale on **November 1**
> + <u>25</u> room checkouts on **November 2**
> = 100 rooms available for sale on **November 2**

From this 100-room inventory, the front office manager or a designated front office staff member is able to determine which room should be assigned to which guest reservation. Continuing with this example, if there are 90 guest reservations for the evening of November 2 and 35 of them have indicated an early arrival of 10:00 A.M., then the person who is blocking the rooms for November 2 will block their rooms from the rooms unoccupied on November 1. The remaining 55 reservations can have their rooms blocked into the remaining available room inventory. In some hotels, no specific match is made between a guest reservation and guest room. Instead, the person who is blocking rooms provides a list to a front desk clerk indicating certain rooms with two double beds, a king-size bed, facilities for people with physical handicaps, and the like, are held for guests with reservations. Hence, the first-come, first-served concept of matching reservations with available rooms is followed.

Meeting Guest Requests

Guests' needs usually include bed requirements, room location, floor plan arrangements, ancillary equipment, rooms designed and equipped for special needs, immediate availability, and price. If the guest has a reservation, the room selection is blocked prior to the guest's arrival. The walk-in guest presents opportunities to the front desk clerk to optimize a sale and meet the needs of the guest. Opportunities to sell are discussed later in this section.

Special Accommodations

The first issue in room selection is meeting the guest's requests for special accommodations. The general trend in designing hotel rooms includes placing two beds, usually king-size, queen-size, or double, in one room, which can accommodate the single guest, businesspeople sharing a room, a family of two adults and three children, and various other guest parties. This design permits the front desk clerk considerable freedom in assigning a room, as so many needs can be met. Hotels with some rooms containing two twin beds or one twin bed and one double bed or one king-size bed with no room for a rollaway restrict the front desk clerk in assigning rooms and, therefore, affect the bottom-line income from each room. New hotels offer more opportunities for front desk clerks to meet guests' requests for various bed arrangements and thus maximize room income. The hotelier must provide front desk clerks with several options involving different bed sizes and rate flexibility. The front office manager who discusses guest preferences with the reservationist and the front desk clerks and reviews guest comment cards is able to determine which bed accommodations should be made available.

Location

Guests often request a certain room location—for example, on the lower levels, near the parking lot, away from the elevator shaft, in the corner of the building, or far from a convention. Also, certain views of the area may be requested—for example, ocean, bay, lake, or city square. Rooms with special views are usually priced higher, as the guest is willing to pay more, feeling the view will enhance the visit. Although these rooms are limited by the design and location of the building, they add a certain character to a lodging property. The marketing and sales department usually promotes these rooms heavily. Sometimes, guests' requests for specific locations or views can be easily met; other times, a lack of available rooms will force the guest to compromise.

Layout and Décor

The guest may request a certain floor plan or room décor. If a businessperson wants to use the room as a small meeting room as well as a sleeping area, a room with a *Murphy bed*, a bed hinged at the base of the headboard so that it can swing up into the wall for storage (such as the SICO brand wall-bed), should be assigned, if available. A guest who is on an extended business trip may request a room with a kitchenette. Several people sharing a room may appreciate one in which the sleeping and living areas are separate. The newly revived suite design meets a range of guest needs. Rooms with balconies or special themes and décors are often requested to enhance a special occasion.

Equipment

Guests may also request ancillary equipment and amenities. Although cable television and telephones are now standard room furnishings, large-screen televisions, DVD players, satellite reception, computer and Internet connections, extra telephone jacks, and more than one telephone may be requested. Some hotels provide computers, *fax machines* (equipment for facsimile reproduction via telephone lines), and convertible desks, which accommodate a businessperson's need for work space (Figure 7-2). The

FIGURE 7-2

This room is equipped with such amenities as a computer and in-room fax to facilitate the business guest's stay. Photo courtesy of the author.

availability of upscale amenities—such as terrycloth robes, fragrant soaps and shampoos, well-stocked honor bars and snack bins, complimentary local and national newspapers, popular weekly magazines, and high-speed or wireless Internet access—often plays a role in the guest's decision to stay at a hotel. If guests are not sure you offer these amenities, they may request them.

Special Needs

Guests often request rooms designed and furnished with equipment to meet special needs. Rooms equipped for the hearing-impaired and guests in wheelchairs are common. Advances in hotel marketing, building design and construction, and electronic safety features allow the guest with physical disabilities to enjoy the facilities of the hotel. Hotel owners who maintain aggressive marketing and sales departments realize the growing number of active physically challenged people in the labor force who travel for work. Legislation may also be an impetus to providing physical accommodations. Ramps, specially designed bathroom facilities, and electronic visual devices that alert the hearing-impaired to fire danger can be located on the lower floors of a hotel. Smoking and nonsmoking guest rooms are also frequently requested by guests.

Availability

Immediate availability is of great concern to most guests. Usually the traveler has spent many hours in transit and wants to unload luggage, freshen up, and move on to other activities. For other guests, registration is the last stop before collapsing from a wearying day of travel and activity. The guest is vulnerable at this time, often willing to accept a room with a higher rate that meets his or her immediate needs. Nevertheless, the front desk clerk should do all that is possible to locate a room that is ready for occupancy before trying to pitch a higher-priced room.

Long lines of people waiting to register and delayed availability of rooms can make room selection difficult for the front desk clerk. A delay by the housekeeper in releasing rooms for occupancy often causes guests to wait. Sometimes the desk clerk must ask the housekeeping department whether rooms are ready for occupancy. Guests who insist they be admitted to a room—any room—because of special circumstances make the front desk clerk's room selection decision complex (considerations of room availability, room type, room rate, etc.). When the reputation of the hotel is at risk, a quick conference with the front office manager may speed the decision-making process for the front desk clerk (if he or she is not empowered to make such decisions). In such a case, the front office manager and the general manager should assist the housekeeping department in working out rough spots and streamline communications between housekeeping and the front office.

Price Constraints

Price is often another guest concern in room selection. Guests with budget constraints may request a room for the lowest price; this is their primary concern. Room location, floor plan, room arrangements, ancillary equipment, and immediate occupancy play lesser roles in their room selection. When guests request the least expensive room available, a front desk clerk should try to accommodate them from the available inventory of rooms. Depending on the projected occupancy for the night, the front office manager may instruct the front desk staff to accommodate all such guests within reason; a sale that brings in 10–20 percent less than the designated rates is better than several rooms left unsold. Communication between front desk clerks and front office managers and the training of front desk clerks to sell rooms underlie the effectiveness of providing guests with acceptable room rates.

Room Assignment from Inventory

Maintaining a room inventory system involves constantly updating and checking a database that specifies *housekeeping status*, a term that indicates availability of a room, such as *occupied* (guest or guests are already occupying a room), *stayover* (guest will not be checking out of a room on the current day), *dirty* or *on change* (a guest has checked out of the room, but the housekeeping staff has not released the room for occupancy), *out of order* (the room is not available for occupancy because of a mechanical malfunction), and *available*, *clean*, or *ready* (the room is ready to be occupied). This facet of registration requires constant communication among front office, housekeeping, maintenance, and reservation staffs.

The following lists of reservation and housekeeping statuses are offered as a review and a means to differentiate housekeeping status from reservation status.

Reservation Status	Housekeeping Status
Open	Available, Clean, or Ready
Confirmed 4 P.M.	Occupied
Confirmed 6 P.M.	Stayover
Guaranteed	Dirty or On Change
Repair	Out of Order

Accurate, up-to-date room status reports are vital to the operation of the front desk because they allow both guest hospitality and financial viability. The desk clerk who assigns a dirty room to a guest conveys incompetence. Assigning a room that already has occupants creates hostility and embarrassment for both the new and the current guests. The opposite problem is a room thought to be occupied but in fact is vacant; such a room is called a *sleeper*. This is a lost sales opportunity that cannot be recreated the next day.

The housekeeping department must communicate the housekeeping status in an accurate, orderly, and speedy manner. The floor supervisor of the housekeeping department must inspect each room to determine if guests have indeed vacated the room, to ensure the cleanliness and servicing of the room, and to note physical repairs needed before the room is released to the front desk for rental. An orderly system whereby the housekeeping department transfers this information to the front desk—through regularly scheduled communications from the floor supervisor, maid, or houseman via the telephone, PMS, or personal visits to the front desk—is necessary to maintain the integrity of the system. Delays in transferring this information slow the process of providing hospitality.

The reservations staff must also be aware of the need to coordinate the immediate requirement of a businessperson for a small meeting room at the last minute with that of an incoming guest for a sitting room for a small gathering, the latter requiring confirmation when the reservation is made. Adequately meeting these requests is important to delivering hospitality. When the guest arrives to register and finds these essential facilities are unavailable, hostility toward the hotel—specifically directed at the front desk clerk—results. Standard operating procedures must be established to ensure the accuracy of room status.

Assigning Room Rates

The marketing plan of a hotel includes pricing programs for room rates; these are based on many intricate and market-sensitive factors. Courses in hospitality marketing and hotel operations will help you develop an understanding of their relationship to price. This introduction discusses the importance of establishing and monitoring effective room rates to ensure maximization of profit.

Establishing Room Rates

The rental charge for a room provides income to pay for hotel expenses generated in other areas, such as administrative costs, overhead, and utilities. Often students try to compare the efficiencies (control of food cost and labor costs, marketing techniques, etc.) of a freestanding restaurant with the sometimes seeming inefficiencies of a hotel restaurant. In a hotel, the general manager may plan for some of the profit from room rental to be applied to food and beverage operations. In a freestanding restaurant, the manager does not have that luxury.

When hotel real estate developers perform feasibility studies, they base the profitability of the enterprise on sales projections and related factors such as investment opportunities, investment portfolio balance, and current income tax laws. A consulting firm surveys market demand for room sales and room rates to form a basis for a room sales projection. Of course, adjustment of market demand because of the entrance of this new hotel into the market is calculated. An example of a room sales projection is shown in Figure 7-3.

The three room sales projections at various average room rates shown in Figure 7-3 give the real estate developers some idea of room income, provided management and operations are able to produce and service the sales. The investors in the Spring Time Hotel project must determine projected sales in all departments (such as food and beverage, garage, gift shop, athletic facilities, and rentals). This total income figure is the basis for total projected sales. Further consideration must be given to related expenses such as food and beverage costs, furnishings, labor, administrative costs, loan repayments, overhead, utilities, and advertising. These costs are assembled in a standard profit-and-loss statement. With computer spreadsheets, it is easy to determine whether anticipated income will be adequate to cover incurred costs and provide profit. If the projected income is inadequate, the investors manipulate the average room rate—raising it, for example, from $70 to $75 or from $90 to $95—and analyze the results. While the income

FIGURE 7-3	Room sales projections are based on room rates and market sensitivity to these rates.

SPRING TIME HOTEL PROJECT—ROOM SALES PROJECTION

	J	F	M	A	M	J	J	A	S	O	N	D
Rooms avail.	200	200	200	200	200	200	200	200	200	200	200	200
% occ.	40	40	50	70	70	80	90	100	70	70	50	40
Rooms sold/day	80	80	120	140	140	160	180	200	140	140	400	80
Days/mo.	31	28	31	30	31	30	31	31	30	31	30	31
Proj. rooms sold	2,480	2,240	3,720	4,200	4,340	4,800	5,580	6,200	4,200	4,340	3,100	2,480

TOTAL ROOMS PER YEAR = 47,680

47,680	47,680	47,680
× $70 rate	× $85 rate	× $90 rate
$3,337,600	$4,052,800	$4,291,200
	−10%	−15%
	(loss in sales because of higher rate)	(loss in sales because of higher rate)

generated may seem favorable, the price-sensitive market where the hotel will be located may not be able to produce the number of projected sales at the higher room rates.

Clearly, room rates involve many factors, including projected sales and related expenses, along with realistic considerations of market competition, marketing and sales efforts, operations, price sensitivity, and tax investment opportunities. The room rate set for one season may be adjusted up or down for another. If a competitor lowers or raises room rates, the front office manager must consult with the owners, general manager, and other department heads. The decision to lower or raise rates or offer a special package depends on the projected effect of this action on the profit-and-loss statement. In areas saturated with hotel rooms and experiencing a slowdown in tourism or business activity, price wars can spell disaster to a hotel operation. Projecting a hotel's financial success using room sales alone does not take into account the possibility of an area's future over-saturation with rooms. When room rates are adjusted to compete with those of other hotels, hotel revenues are affected. Other hotel operations that are not cost-effective then drain the profits from the total operation.

Rule-of-thumb Method

Several methods are used to establish room rates. Each provides guidelines for the hotel real estate developer. These are guidelines *only* and should be reviewed with the previous discussion in mind. The front office manager must stay in touch with the general manager and the controller to monitor room rate effectiveness. The *rule-of-thumb method for determining room rates* stipulates that the room rate should be $2 for every $1000 of construction costs. For example, if a new hotel is constructed at a cost of $45,000 per room, the room rate would initially be $90 per night. Clearly, this is a very general method of guesstimation of room rates and should not be relied on alone.

Hubbart Formula

The *Hubbart formula* considers such factors as operating expenses, desired return on investment, and income from various departments in the hotel to establish room rates. This method relies on the front office to produce income to cover operating expenses, overhead, and return on investment for the hotel operation. The following example applies these factors:

A hotel with $4,017,236 of operating expenses (departmental operating expenses and overhead), a desired return on investment of $1,500,000, and additional income of $150,000 from other sources (food and beverage, rentals, telephone), with projected room sales of 47,680 room-nights, would set its room rate at $113.

$$\frac{(\text{Operating Expenses} + \text{Desired ROI}) - \text{Other Income}}{\text{Projected Room Nights}} = \text{Room Rate}$$

$$\frac{(\$4,017,236 + \$1,500,000) - \$150,000}{47,680} = \$113$$

The Hubbart formula is also a guideline only. Room rates must be constantly monitored in light of market conditions of supply and demand. The front office manager must survey competing room rates to determine the competitiveness of his or her hotel's rates. Participation in this survey is voluntary. Figure 7-4 is an example of a weekly room rate survey.

This subsection on room rates is presented to show you the complexities of establishing a room rate. The market factors, construction costs, operating expenses, desired return on investment, efficiencies of operations, and marketing programs combine to produce a complex analysis. Front office managers must constantly monitor the effects of established room rates on the profit-and-loss statement. Other department managers in the hotel must also be aware of their importance to the overall financial success of the hotel.

Types of Room Rate

Hotels develop room rate categories to attract different markets. These rates depend on seasons, number of potential sales in a market, and other factors. Providing constant feedback on the effectiveness of room rates in attracting business and evaluating the continued need for each of these categories are the responsibilities of the front office manager and the director of marketing and sales. Commonly used room rate categories are rack rate, corporate rate, commercial rate, military/educational rate, group rate, family rate, package rate, American plan, half-day rate, and complimentary rate.

A *rack rate*, the highest room rate charged by a hotel, is the rate given to a guest who does not fall into any particular category, such as a walk-in who requests a room for the

FIGURE 7-4 **A room rate survey compares room rates of competing hotels.**

ROOM RATE SURVEY—WEEK OF 0215

	RACK		CORP.		GROUP			
Number of Persons in Room	1	2	1	2	1	2	3	4
Hotel								
SMITH LODGE	$70	$80	$68	$68	$65	$65	$65	$65
WINSTON ARMS	$72	$80	$68	$70	$60	$65	$70	$75
HARBOR HOUSE	$75	$85	$70	$75	$60	$60	$65	$65
THOMAS INN	$80	$90	$75	$80	$75	$75	$80	$80
ALLISON INN	$100	$100	$89	$95	$80	$80	$85	$90
GREY TOWERS	$85	$95	$80	$80	$75	$75	$75	$80
JACKSON HOTEL	$78	$85	$73	$78	$63	$65	$68	$70
TIMES HOTEL	$90	$100	$80	$89	$75	$75	$80	$85

night. Rack rates do not necessarily produce the most income for the hotel (see chapter 6). Charging a group $5 less than the rack rate to encourage repeat business may garner more income for the hotel in the long run.

Corporate rates are room rates offered to businesspeople staying in the hotel. This category can be broken down into businesspeople who are frequent guests (a specified number of visits per week or per month) and guests who are employees of a corporation that has contracted for a rate that reflects all business from that corporation.

Commercial rates are room rates for businesspeople that represent a company and have infrequent or sporadic patterns of travel. Collectively, this group can be a major segment of hotel guests and, thus, warrant a special rate. The hotel usually develops a frequent guest marketing program associated with a frequent guest stay program to encourage guests to accumulate points toward upgrades in rooms, free room stays, or airline miles. For example, Marriott's program is called Marriott Rewards; a card is issued and used and then validated with each visit. Hilton's is called Hilton Honors. A card is issued and then validated with each visit. After a specified number of visits, the guest is awarded a free room-night. Many variations of this concept are in use. Marketing and sales departments of large hotel corporations develop sophisticated frequent visitor marketing programs to encourage guests to stay with them.

Military and educational rates are room rates established for military personnel and educators, because they travel on restricted travel expense accounts and are price-conscious. These groups are a source of significant room sales because their frequent visits may supply a sizable amount of repeat business.

Group rates are room rates offered to large groups of people visiting the hotel for a common reason. The marketing and sales department usually negotiates this rate with a travel agency or professional organization. For example, a travel or tour agent may be granted a group rate for a bus group of 40 tourists. A meeting planner may request a group rate for 400 convention delegates. This is a lucrative source of potential business for a hotel.

Family rates, room rates offered to encourage visits by families with children, are offered during seasonal or promotional times. For example, children under a certain age are not charged if they stay in a room with an adult. Franchise organizations promote this concept vigorously through television and display advertising.

Package rates, room rates that include goods and services in addition to rental of a room, are developed by marketing and sales departments to lure guests into a hotel during low sales periods. A bridal suite package may include complimentary champagne, a cheese-and-cracker basket, flowers, and a complimentary breakfast. A Weekend in the City package may include lunch in the hotel dining room, tickets to the theater, a late-night snack, and tickets to an art gallery or a sporting event. If these packages are advertised and promoted, they become a regular source of business for low-volume weekends.

A variation of the package rate is the *American plan*, a room rate that includes meals—usually breakfast and the evening meal—as well as the room rental. The *modified American plan*, a room rate that offers one meal with the price of a room, is common in resorts, where the pace of life is more leisurely. (The system where food and beverages are kept separate from room charges is called the *European plan*.)

A frequently used rate classification is the *half-day rate*, a room rate based on length of guest stay in a room, which is applied to guests who use a room for only three or four hours of a day—not overnight—to rest after sightseeing or shopping or between flights.

Businesspeople may want to rent a room for a short business meeting. Lawyers may want to rent a room for privacy while taking a deposition from a witness. The room is then rented again that evening. If a hotel has guaranteed reservations for late arrivals, the front desk clerk can accept half-day guests for those rooms from 1 to 5 P.M. A good communication system with the housekeeping department is essential, so the room can be cleaned for the guest with a guaranteed reservation. The hotel that offers a half-day rate must establish reservations blocking procedures that indicate which rooms are available for half-day rentals. If rooms are needed by a convention group in the early afternoon following another convention group that checked out that morning, this type of sale is not recommended.

The final rate category is a *complimentary rate (comp)*, where there is no charge to the guest. The management of the hotel reserves the right to grant comp rooms for various reasons. Guests who are part of the hotel's management hierarchy or personnel group may receive a comp room as a fringe benefit. Management may offer comp rates to tour directors and bus drivers of the tour group, travel agents, tour operators, and local dignitaries who are vital to the public relations program of the hotel. This rate does cost the hotel, but the cost is usually outweighed by the goodwill generated.

These rate categories have variations in all hotels. The purpose of rate categories is to attract groups of guests who will supply repeat business and help ensure full occupancy.

Maximizing Room Rates

The front desk clerk and reservationist have the opportunity to present a range of room rates in a manner that reflects the positive features of the product. Guests assigned a room at the highest or lowest rate without any choice are not given the opportunity to participate in the sales decision. Guests who want to enjoy the best accommodations may look as though they could afford only the lowest-priced room. Guests who look as though they could afford the Governor's Suite may have budgeted only enough for the lowest-priced room. Reservations placed by telephone do not bias the reservationist according to the personal appearance of the future guest. A planned sales pitch to maximize room rates for all guests must be formulated and taught to the front office staff.

Although it is beyond the scope of this textbook, the layout and design of the computer screen for Internet reservations should capture the attention of the guest as well as provide the same information the reservationist would discuss. The prospective guest is looking for the hotel's toll-free number, address, rates, photos (3-D virtual tour, if possible), food and beverage accommodations, and so on.

Knowledge of room furnishings, special features, layout, and rate ranges is necessary to establish a room rate maximization program. In addition, these features should be described in a way that enhances them and tempts the guest. The most important part of this program is to ensure the front desk staff can carry it out; not everyone enjoys selling, and the staff must be encouraged to develop the proper attitude toward sales. Employee incentive programs are helpful in motivating front desk staff.

The desk clerk or reservationist who handles walk-in guests, guests with a reservation, or guests making a reservation must be extremely knowledgeable about the product being sold. Familiarity with room furnishings, special features, floor plans, views, and rate ranges is obtained through experience and training. The training of a new person in the front office must include visits to the various guest rooms and public areas of the hotel. These visits should be reinforced with written descriptions of room inventories that note room furnishings, special features, and floor diagrams of each category.

Room rate ranges may be printed on special brochures for the guests. However, applying room rates in special cases must be supported by clear policies and communicated to staff. The front office manager must develop case studies that illustrate exceptions to the stated rate ranges. Situational applications appropriate to periods of low projected occupancy, 100 percent occupancy, and an overbooked house can be of great assistance in training.

The staff must not only know the hotel's features but also be able to entice guests with positive descriptions. A room described as "decorated in pastels; contains two king-size beds with comforters, overstuffed chairs, and a well-stocked mini-bar and refreshment cabinet; overlooks the bay side of the Charles River; and provides complete privacy" tempts the guest to want this luxurious experience.

Coaching the Shy Employee in Sales Skills

Not everyone, of course, is a born salesperson. Indeed, most people are generally shy about selling. Desk clerks who are not comfortable selling rooms must be encouraged to develop these skills by practicing them until they become natural. How can a front office manager foster sales skills?

People are reluctant to sell because they feel they are pushing the buyer to purchase something. They can be made more comfortable in selling when they believe they are offering a service or product that will benefit the guest. Each of the room's features should be highlighted as a reason for the guest to select the room. This reason relates to guest satisfaction. For example, if the clerk promotes a guest room with an additional small meeting room (at a higher rate) as an attractive feature, the person who is registering may be grateful to learn about this valuable option because it allows him or her to conduct corporate business without renting two rooms.

Front desk clerks should be trained to recognize subtle cues to a guest's needs. Cues are usually present in both face-to-face situations and during telephone calls. Not all people recognize these cues because they are not trained to listen for them. A training procedure should be developed and presented to the front office staff. When the front desk clerk feels comfortable in being able to satisfy the guest's needs with a certain type of room, then a good sales attitude has been fostered. The idea "I have to sell" is replaced with "I want to make the guest's experience the best it can be." If a caller mentions a reservation is an anniversary gift to her parents, the reservationist may want to suggest "a bayside room that overlooks the Charles River or a room that looks out over the beautiful mountain ranges of the Poconos in Pennsylvania."

The front office manager should also devise an incentive program for the staff to maximize room rates. Incentives should be related to the needs of the employee. If money is the motivator, then a financial reward (based on the average daily rate achieved for the evening above the standard average daily rate) is presented as a bonus to the desk clerk. This bonus could also consist of preference in scheduling, additional vacation or personal days, or consideration for promotions. If employees know their individual efforts in achieving room rate maximization will be recognized, they will be more enthusiastic about selling. As with all incentive programs, the financial expenditures for the rewards must be cost-effective.

The staff with the proper knowledge, vocabulary, and attitude maximizes room rates better than the staff that is simply told to sell from the *bottom up*, a sales method whereby the least expensive rate first is presented first, or another sales method from the *top down*, where the most expensive rate is presented first. These principles are important in achieving a maximum room rate. However, if the desk clerk or reservationist is armed with facts about the product (rooms), familiar with words that accentuate its positive features, and comfortable with selling as a procedure that improves the guest's stay, then he or she is likely to generate higher room rates and encourage repeat business.

Discuss Sales Opportunities

The front desk clerk has an unparalleled opportunity to promote the services of the hotel during guest registration. The front office manager who has adopted both a marketing focus as well as a front office focus understands the benefits of developing a front office staff that is comfortable with salesmanship. The discussion here focuses on additional room reservations that can be garnered at registration and the promotion of these additional room reservations.

Future Reservations

The front office manager should consider developing procedures for front desk clerks to follow that encourage a guest to book additional reservations during the check-in process. Suggesting additional reservations during registration may remind the business-person of the need for room accommodations the following week, when he or she will visit a city with a hotel affiliated with the same chain. It may inspire the traveler who has not made reservations for the rest of his or her trip and finds your rates or frequent guest marketing program attractive to stay in a chain member property. This promotion of member properties can be a profitable marketing concept. Front office managers in independent hotels also find this concept profitable. Independent hotels have the advantage of offering unique lodging experiences. Guests who are frequent visitors to a city may want to secure reservations for their next trip. Front desk clerks must ask the guest to make additional reservations.

Developing a Plan for Promoting Future Reservations

Maximizing sales opportunities requires a program in which the front desk clerks actively participate, making it profitable for the hotel. The previous discussion of sales opportunities also applies to developing a plan for promoting future reservations.

The front office manager who wants to develop a plan to sell future rooms at the time of guest registration must consider opportunities for booking those additional rooms, salesmanship skills, incentive plans, and effects on the profit-and-loss statement. During registration, the front desk clerk should ask guests if they will need additional reservations for the remainder of their trip. Again, during checkout, the front desk clerk should inquire if the guests need additional reservations. If these inquiries are reinforced with printed materials in guest rooms and elevators that advertise the value of and offer an incentive to make additional reservations, or if repeat business is rewarded with a frequent visitor incentive program, then the possibility of securing additional reservations is realistic. If desk clerks encourage future reservations because they believe they are helping the guest with travel plans, they will be more comfortable and successful in persuading guests to make reservations.

The front office manager should develop an incentive program to assist desk clerks in achieving additional reservations at the time of registration. The effects of such a plan on the profit-and-loss statement are usually easy to determine. Additional room sales generate additional income. The controller of the hotel will notice the increase in sales. The costs of administering the incentive program should be compared to the income produced by the additional reservations; such costs may include financial bonuses and additional vacation.

Assigning Room Keys

During the guest registration process, a room key is issued to the guest. This is a fairly simple task; however, the process does involve security and maintenance of keys. Later in this chapter, computerized room key assignment is discussed.

After the front desk clerk determines the room assignment and the guest agrees to the room rate, the key or keys are obtained for the guest. The key being issued must be checked against the room number assigned on the registration card, electronic folio, or computer screen before it is handed to the guest. A key for room 969 can look like 696 if it is viewed upside down. The key for room 243 could mistakenly be picked up for room 234. These errors occur when the front desk staff is busy checking people in and out. For the guest's safety, giving him or her the room key should be handled with utmost discretion. The front desk clerk should not loudly announce, "Here is your key to room 284." It is better to say "Here is your key," or "Your room number is written on the inside of your check-in packet." It is also important to instruct a guest on the procedure for using an *electronic key*, a plastic key with electronic codes embedded on a magnetic strip. If there is a waiting period or a colored indicator light on the guest room door, the clerk should point this out.

Security of the Key System

Maintaining the security of the keys requires that they be stored in a safe place. The familiar pigeonhole key and mail rack system is still found in some hotels. Others have adopted a key drawer, located beneath the front desk. Hotels with electronic locking systems produce a new key for each new guest. The electronic combination is changed each time at the front desk. Guests who lose their key during a stay may ask for a duplicate, for which proof of identification and proof of registration should be required. This protects the guest who is registered in the room as well as other guests of the hotel. Most guests do not mind providing these proofs of identification. They are usually satisfied to know their security is a priority at the hotel.

Maintaining the Key System

The maintenance of a hard-key system requires the front office staff and housekeeping staff to return keys to their storage area, a time-consuming job when several hundred keys must be returned to their pigeonholes or slots in a *key drawer* (a drawer located underneath the counter of the front desk that holds room keys in numerically ordered slots) after a full house has checked out. If a member of the housekeeping staff [males are referred as houseman and females are referred as housekeepers] notices a key left in a room after a guest has checked out, he or she should return it to the front desk. Some hotels use a *key fob*, a decorative and descriptive plastic or metal tag attached to a *hard key* (a metal device

FIGURE 7-5

A key fob and guest room key are used in hotels with mechanical locks.

KLINE INN
422 W. Pine
Castor, MO

Please drop this
key into the
nearest
U.S. Postal Service
mailbox.
Thank you!

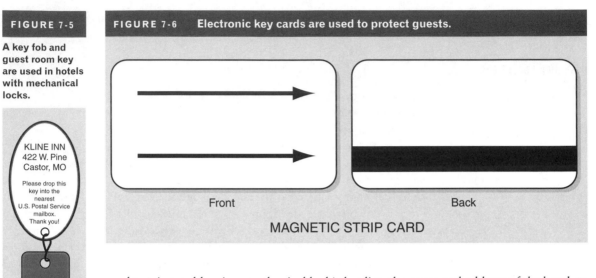

FIGURE 7-6   Electronic key cards are used to protect guests.

Front

Back

MAGNETIC STRIP CARD

used to trip tumblers in a mechanical lock) that lists the name and address of the hotel, to encourage the finder of a key to mail it back (Figure 7-5). Other hotels do not attach such a key fob because they believe that if a key is found (or actively sought) by a person with criminal intentions, guest security is at risk. Keys and locks that become worn must be replaced, a responsibility of the maintenance department. Replacement of room keys and locks can be done only with an authorized purchase order from the controller, initiated by the front office or maintenance department. The security department maintains control of key replacement activity.

Maintaining the electronic locking system is much simpler than maintaining the hard-key system. On checkout, when the guest's folio is cleared in the PMS, the plastic key is rendered invalid (Figure 7-6). When the next guest registers for that room, a new electronic combination is set and a new electronic key issued. Encoding the electronic combination on the magnetic strip of a credit card–type key is also possible.

After the guest receives the room key, the front desk clerk should ask if he or she needs help carrying luggage and other personal effects to the room. If help is needed, a bellhop is summoned to escort the guest to the room. If the guest does not require assistance, the front desk clerk should provide clear directions to the room.

Registration with a PMS

As you learned in chapter 4, property management systems have many capabilities, including registration. To review, the basic applications of the PMS registration module are as follows:

- Retrieving reservation form
- Checking room inventory option
- Checking room status option

- Verifying room rate
- Issuing room key

Retrieving Reservation Form

The registration module is put to use before the guest arrives at the hotel to register. Guests who have placed reservations with the hotel have already had their data entered into the PMS database. Figure 7-7 shows a completed version of the blank guest data screen illustrated in Figure 5-4. The guest information is now available for registration. The PMS is able to produce advance registration forms for guests, like that shown in Figure 7-8, with an interface between the registration module and the reservation module database. The PMS has the ability to preselect a room for the guest from the room inventory for the day of arrival; however, the front office staff has usually blocked the room reservations for the day. The advance registration form already is printed the night before by the second- or third-shift front desk clerks and is ready when the guest arrives. After the advance registration forms are printed, they are filed alphabetically at the front desk. Some operations choose not to preprint forms but instead have the guest complete a standard registration card. However, having preprinted registration forms available when guests arrive is invaluable in registering guests quickly, particularly when a full house is checking in or when the front desk is operating with less than its full staff.

When a guest with a reservation arrives at the front desk to register, the front desk clerk greets him or her and inquires whether the guest has a reservation. The desk clerk

---

FIGURE 7-7 **A completed reservation screen on a PMS provides information on a guest's requests for a visit.**

RESERVATIONS—ENTER GUEST DATA

NAME: BLACKWRIGHT, SAMUEL

COMPANY: HANNINGTON ACCOUNTING

BILLING ADDRESS: 467 WEST AVENUE   ARLINGTON, LA   ZIP: 00000

PHONE NUMBER: 000-000-0000

DATE OF ARRIVAL: 0309   TIME OF ARRIVAL: 6 PM   DATE OF DEP.: 0311

AIRLINE: AA   FLIGHT #: 144   TIME OF ARRIVAL: 3:45 PM

ROOM: # GUESTS: 1   RATE: 80

COMMENTS:

CONFIRMATION #: 122JB03090311MC80K98765R

CREDIT CARD: MC   NUMBER: 00000000000000000000

TRAVEL AGENCY: AGENT: ID #:

ADDRESS: ZIP:

FIGURE 7-8	**An advance registration form is prepared prior to a guest's arrival.**					

ARRIV	RESV	DEP	CONF NO		ROOM ASMT	RATE
03-09	6 PM	0311	122JB03090311MC80K97865R		722	80.00
GUEST INFO			**NO. GUEST**		**CREDIT CARD**	
Blackwright, Samuel			1		MC 000000000000000000000	
Hannington Accounting						
467 West Ave.						
Arlington, LA 00000						
000-000-0000						

Guest Signature

retrieves the preprinted advance registration form from the file. If no form is available, the desk clerk retrieves this information from the reservation module by entering the guest's last name or confirmation number. The guest information is then available for registration.

The registration module can also handle the registration of groups, allowing advance registration information for entire groups of guests to be preprinted. Figure 7-9 shows how registration details for a group can be controlled. With further processing of this information, including preassignment of rooms, group preregistration packets, like those shown in Figure 7-10, can be prepared, making the registration of groups simple for both the tour director and the front office.

Checking Room Inventory Option

What happens if a name is missing from the reservation data bank for a person or group? If the guest cannot produce a confirmation number and no reservation can be found, the front desk clerk tries to provide accommodations. The room inventory and room status options of the registration module are checked to determine if rooms are available. The room inventory option indicates the availability of rooms (Figure 7-11). It informs the desk clerk which rooms are being held for reservations (_GUAR_ for guaranteed and _CONF_ for confirmed), which have been taken out of inventory because of a needed repair (_REPAIR_), and which are available to rent for the night (_OPEN_). Additional information is provided about the features of the rooms, such as king-size bed (_K_), a room suitable for holding a conference (_CONF_), a room with two king-size beds (_2K_), a room with one double bed (_DB_), a room with a bay view (_BAY_), a room with a kitchenette (_KITCH_), a room with a studio couch (_STUDIO_), adjoining rooms (_/_), or a room with a conversation area and other amenities (_SUITE_). The rate per room for a single guest is indicated.

FIGURE 7-9 The group registration option keeps track of members of a group.

GROUP REGISTRATION

NAME OF GROUP: JOHNSON HIGH SCHOOL DEBATE TEAM

DATE IN: 0109   DATE OUT: 0112   NO. ROMS: 8

NO. GUESTS: 15   RATE: 57/S 64/D

BILLING INFO: DIRECT BILL R. SIMINGTON, 401 MADISON DR., OLIVER, DE 00000

21 DAYS. EACH PAYS INCIDENTALS AT CHECKOUT.

ROOM NO.	NAME	RATE	COMMENTS
201	VERKIN, S.	32	
201	LAKEROUTE, B.	32	
202	SIMINGTON, R.	57	ADVISER
203	CASTLE, N.	32	
203	ZEIGLER, R.	32	
204	DRAKE, J.	32	
204	DRAKE, A.	32	
205	LENKSON, C.	32	
205	SMITH, B.	32	
206	HARMON, T.	32	
206	LASTER, H.	32	
207	AROWW, C.	32	
207	THOMPSON, N.	32	
208	JONES, K.	32	
209	SAMSET, O.	32	

FIGURE 7-10 A group preregistration packet helps achieve quick registration for groups.

THE TIMES HOTEL
(GROUP REGISTRATION)

Welcome to our hotel. Your registration has been preprocessed. You have been assigned to room _____. Your tour guide has arranged to make final payment for room charges. Questions concerning other charges to your room account can be answered by dialing "3" on your room phone.

Thank you,

Front Desk Manager

FIGURE 7-11   The room inventory screen of a PMS tells front desk staff the reservation status.

ROOM INVENTORY 1225

ROOM	TYPE	COMMENTS	RATE	AVAILABILITY
109	K	BAY	68	GUAR
201	K	KITCH	75	REPAIR
202	K		65	CONF
203	K		65	CONF
204	K		65	CONF
205	K		65	OPEN
206	CONF	STUDIO	80	OPEN
207	K	/208	65	OPEN
208	K	/207	65	OPEN
209	K	BAY	68	GUAR
210	K	KITCH	75	GUAR
301	2K	SUITE	100	REPAIR
302	2K	SUITE	100	GUAR
303	DB		55	OPEN
304	K	KITCH	75	OPEN
305	K		65	OPEN
306	CONF	STUDIO	80	GUAR
307	K	/308	65	GUAR
308	K	/307	65	OPEN
309	K	BAY	68	OPEN
310	K	KITCH	75	GUAR
401	K	KITCH	75	GUAR

Checking Room Status Option

The desk clerk also needs to know which rooms are ready for occupancy; this can be determined by activating the room status option of the PMS (Figure 7-12). This option is similar to the room inventory option but does not include rates and has a column on status, telling the desk clerk which rooms are being cleaned and serviced by housekeeping (*ON CHG*), which are being repaired (*OUT OF ORDR*), which are occupied by another guest (*OCC*), and which are available for guest occupancy (*READY*). The integrity of

FIGURE 7-12	The room status screen of a PMS tells front desk staff the housekeeping status.

ROOM STATUS 0722

ROOM	TYPE	COMMENTS	AVAILABILITY	STATUS
109	K	BAY	GUAR	ON CHG
201	K	KITCH	REPAIR	OUT OF ORDR
202	K		CONF	ON CHG
203	K		CONF	ON CHG
204	K		CONF	READY
205	K		OPEN	READY
206	CONF	STUDIO	OPEN	READY
207	K	/208	OPEN	ON CHG
208	K	/207	OPEN	ON CHG
209	K	BAY	GUAR	READY
210	K	KITCH	GUAR	ON CHG
301	2K	SUITE	REPAIR	OUT OF ORDR
302	2K	SUITE	GUAR	READY
303	DB		OPEN	READY
304	K	KITCH	OPEN	READY
305	K		OPEN	ON CHG
306	CONF	STUDIO	GUAR	READY
307	K	/308	GUAR	ON CHG
308	K	/307	OPEN	ON CHG
309	K	BAY	OPEN	ON CHG
310	K	KITCH	GUAR	ON CHG
401	K	KITCH	GUAR	ON CHG

this information is maintained with constant input and updates from the housekeeping and maintenance departments. This communication is also enhanced with the use of an intranet. Staff members in housekeeping and the front office can send messages quickly informing each other of room status of rooms with a few keystrokes.

If a room is available and the front desk clerk is fairly sure the hotel will not be full that night, the guest without a confirmation number or reservation is handled as a walk-in guest. The guest data option of the registration module allows the front desk clerk to enter guest registration information (Figure 7-13). Note this option prompts the desk clerk to inquire if the guest needs additional reservations for future visits.

FIGURE 7-13   A blank registration screen in a PMS is activated to register a walk-in guest.

REGISTRATION—ENTER GUEST DATA

NAME:

COMPANY:

BILLING ADDRESS: ZIP:

PHONE NUMBER:

CREDIT CARD: TYPE: NUMBER: EXP. DATE:

AUTO MAKE: MODEL: LIC. PLATE: STATE:

TYPE OF ROOM: NO. GUESTS: RATE:

DATE IN: DATE OUT: CLERK:

FUTURE RESERVATION?   DATE: TYPE ROOM: NO. GUESTS:

HOTEL ID NO.:   CONF: YES   NO   GUAR: YES   NO

CONF NO.:

A guest may present a confirmation number when no rooms are available. When overbooking produces more guests than rooms are available for, a guest is "walked" to another hotel that can provide accommodations. Although, when *walking a guest with a reservation*, the hotel is under no obligation to provide cab fare, pay for the room at the other property, provide telephone calls to allow the guest to notify people of a change of venue, pay for a meal, or provide a complimentary future stay, some hotels try to accommodate the guest in these ways to ensure positive guest relations. While the guest is usually not satisfied with the situation, he or she may accept the alternative accommodations as better than nothing. When the front office staff realizes an overbooking situation is fast approaching, they should telephone nearby hotels to establish projected occupancy.

Verifying Room Rate

The guest may remember a quoted rate at the time of registration that is not on the confirmation form or in the PMS. It is wise to discuss any discrepancies with the guest to avoid problems at checkout. The guest who thought she was being charged $85 when in fact the rate was $125 could be embarrassed at checkout if her financial resources are inadequate. Desk clerks should have guests acknowledge the room rate by asking them to initial it on the registration form. It is also important to discuss room taxes and local municipal charges that may be added to the room rate.

Issuing Room Key

If the guest can be accommodated, the new key for the guest room is prepared with an electronic key preparation device (Figure 7-14). This device produces a new key (the size of a

credit card, made of plastic) encoded with a different electronic combination for each new guest. The combination for the door lock is controlled through the hotel's security system.

Obtaining Reports from the PMS

The PMS can also produce an alphabetical listing of the guests and their room numbers. This option, a variation of the registered guests report option shown in Figure 7-15, is available to the switchboard operator.

The front office manager can access report options of the registration module for effective front office management. The registration module options just discussed provide the basis for gathering and organizing information the front office manager needs to monitor. For example, the guest arrivals report option informs the front office manager of the guests with reservations who are expected to arrive (Figure 7-16). The group arrivals report option lists the groups with reservations that are expected to arrive (Figure 7-17).

These data can be arranged by different categories—room number, date of registration, checkout date, room rate, guest name—according to the front office manager's needs. These report options, often referred to as *data sorts*, which indicate groupings of information, vary with the type of software used for the PMS. The room inventory report option, which gives the front office manager a list of vacant rooms (Figure 7-18), is useful in achieving maximum occupancy. Variations of this option include listings of

FIGURE 7-15   Registered guests can be listed alphabetically with a PMS.

REGISTERED GUESTS 0215

ROOM	NAME	ADDRESS	DATE IN	DATE OUT	RATE	NO. GUESTS
205	ARRISON, T.	RD 1 OLANA, AZ 00000	0215	0216	75	2
312	CRUCCI, N.	414 HANOVER ST., CANTON, OH 00000	0205	0217	70	1
313	DANTOZ, M.	102 N. FRONT ST., LANGLY, MD 00000	0213	0216	70	1
315	FRANTNZ, B.	21 S BROADWAY, NY, NY 00000	0211	0216	75	2
402	HABBEL, B.	BOX 56, LITTROCK, MN 00000	0215	0217	75	2
403	IQENTEZ, G.	HOBART, NY 00000	0213	0216	70	1
409	JANNSEN, P.	87 ORCHARD LN., GREATIN, NY 00000	0215	0222	90	1
410	ROSCO, R.	98 BREWER RD., THOMPSON, DE 00000	0213	0221	70	1
411	SMITH, V.	21 ROSE AVE., BILLINGS, TN 00000	0215	0218	70	1
501	ZUKERMEN, A.	345 S HARRY BLVD., JOHNSTOWN, CA 00000	0215	0219	85	2

FIGURE 7-16   An alphabetical listing of guests who will arrive can be prepared by a PMS.

ARRIVALS—INDIVIDUAL GUESTS 0918

NAME	RESV	DATE IN	DATE OUT	CONF NO.
BLAKELY, K.	GUAR	0918	0920	09180920JCB75K9334L
BROWN, J.	CONF	0918	0919	09180919JCB75K9211L
CASTOR, V.	GUAR	0918	0922	09180922V75K8456L
CONRAD, M.	GUAR	0918	0921	09180921MC75K8475L
DRENNEL, A.	GUAR	0918	0921	09180921V80K8412L
FESTER, P.	CONF	0918	0925	09180925JCB75K8399L
HRASTE, B.	GUAR	0918	0191	09180919JCB75K8401L
LOTTER, M.	GUAR	0918	0922	09180922V80K8455L

FIGURE 7-17   A PMS can list names of groups that will arrive by date of arrival.

Arrivals—Groups 0918

NAME	DATE IN	DATE OUT	NO. ROOMS	RATE	NO. GUESTS
HARBOR TOURS	0918	0922	02/1	55/1	42
			20/2	65/2	
JOHNSON HS BAND	0918	0921	02.1	45/1	54
			13/4	60/4	
MIGHTY TOURS	0918	0919	02/1	55/1	42
			20/2	65/2	

all vacant, occupied, on-change, or on-repair rooms, sorted by type—with king-size beds, on the first floor, with a bay view, in a certain rate range. The room status report option provides a list of rooms available for occupancy (Figure 7-19). Variations of this option sort all rooms that are ready, on change, occupied, or out of order.

Self-Check-In

The PMS allows guests to check themselves in with a credit card. The guest with a reservation guaranteed by a credit card can use a designated computer terminal (Figure 7-20) that guides him or her through the registration procedure. This option assists in streamlining registration at a busy front desk. The owners, general manager, and front office manager must weigh the capital expenditures, decreased labor costs, increased speed of registration,

FIGURE 7-18   This screen on a PMS helps front office staff determine which rooms are vacant.

ROOM VACANCIES 0701

ROOM	ROOM	ROOM
103	402	701
104	411	710
109	415	800
205	506	813
206	509	817
318	515	823
327	517	824
333	605	825

FIGURE 7-19   This PMS screen shows the housekeeping status of guest rooms.

ROOM STATUS 0524

ROOM	STATUS	ROOM	STATUS
101	ON CHG	114	ON CHG
102	ON CHG	115	READY
103	ON CHG	116	ON CHG
104	ON CHG	117	ON CHG
105	READY	118	ON CHG
106	ON CHG	119	OCC
107	ON CHG	120	OCC
108	OUT OF ORDR	201	READY
109	OCC	202	READY
110	OCC	203	READY
111	OCC	204	ON CHG
112	READY	205	OUT OF ORDR
113	OUT OF ORDR	206	READY

FIGURE 7-20

A guest may choose to use the self-check-in option of a property management system. Photo courtesy of Hyatt Hotels and Resorts.

delivery of hospitality, and opportunity for selling additional hotel services within the hotel when deciding whether to provide this option. Hotels with a high occupancy percentage may choose to install this technology to keep registration lines moving. However, it is important to consider room status, such as the possibility of a room's being on change when a guest is waiting to enter it. The efficiency of the housekeeping department in cleaning and servicing rooms must also be considered. If the guest does not need to enter a room immediately, then a self-check-in system may be a cost-effective way to provide him or her an additional service.

Consider the following technology being developed by Ariane Systems Group to revamp the way check-in and checkout procedure is offered to guests:

> Ariane Systems Group (Paris, France) is pleased to announce that its mobile check-in/check-out project, nicknamed "VIKI," has been selected by the European Regional Development Fund (ERDF) to receive government financing as "one of the most innovative research and development projects for 2009." The ERDF will fund 40% of the development costs for this innovative, mobile hospitality self-service platform.
>
> "VIKI" will revolutionize the hospitality industry by enabling customers to check-in/check-out where and when they want—whether using a desktop computer, a laptop, a cell phone or another PDA. The features that will be offered with this software platform are countless, as it will integrate online mobile payment solutions and enable the user to modify their bills, addresses and guest profiles remotely.
>
> "[W]ith our new mobile check-in/check-out application, guests will be able to check-in online from their computer before arriving at their hotel, or perform their check-out from their cell phone while comfortably sitting in a taxi on their way to the airport."[3]

These technologies allow the guest to experience hospitality at its best if the lines of communications of between the front office and housekeeping are well developed. Employees' efforts to produce hospitality remain the key factor behind technology.

INTERNATIONAL HIGHLIGHTS

 Judy Colbert reports in Lodging how to deliver hospitality to international visitors: "To make foreign guests feel comfortable, the hotel [New York Hilton and Towers] has a multilingual staff that speaks 30 different languages. Each wears a lapel pin in the colors of the country flag for the language he or she speaks. Brochures, local information, and in-room materials are available in several languages. And an AT&T Language Line, which provides assistance in 140 languages, is accessible from every guestroom."[4]

Hyatt Hotels is working on an educational program to train staff in the nuances of communicating with international visitors. These materials include world culture and trends, learning a dozen or so basic phrases in foreign languages, and preparing signage and in-room pieces in multiple languages.[5]

Solution to Opening Dilemma

Good communication between the housekeeping and front office departments relies on constant effort of all participants to determine progress in releasing rooms. When the housekeeping department is short-staffed or extremely busy, its communication of the release of rooms can be delayed. In those cases, the front office staff should make an extra effort to stay in close touch with the floor supervisors to determine how soon rooms will be released for sale. In some hotels, housekeeping staff members can release rooms via the property management system.

Chapter Recap

This chapter described, in detail, the process of registering hotel guests. The process begins with emphasizing to the staff the importance of making a good first impression on guests, which sets the stage for an enjoyable stay. Accurate and complete guest information obtained during registration is the basis for a sound communication system among all the departments in the hotel that provide services to the guest. Registering the guest involves extending credit, selecting a room, constructing and applying room rates, selling hotel services, and assigning a room key.

End-of-Chapter Questions

1. How important do you think the guest's first contact with the hotel is in providing hospitality? Give examples from your experiences as a guest in a hotel.

2. Why is obtaining accurate guest data during the registration process so important? Who uses this information besides the front office? Give examples of how incorrect data can affect the guest and the hotel.

3. What are the major parts of the guest registration process? How will knowledge of this system help you as you progress in a management career in the hotel?

4. Why is the choice of credit card important to the profit-and-loss statement of the hotel? Give examples.

5. What hidden costs are involved in using a bill-to-account system? When do you think a hotel is justified in adopting a bill-to-account system?

6. Identify some of the requests guests may make with regard to room selection. How can a front desk clerk be attuned to the needs of guests?

7. Why are establishing and monitoring room rates so essential to the hotel's profit-and-loss statement?

8. What are the rule-of-thumb method and the Hubbart formula for establishing room rates? How effective do you feel each one is in ensuring profit for a hotel?

9. Describe a system of monitoring room rates. If you are employed at a front desk, do you see your supervisor or manager using such a system? How often? How effective do you feel this is in maintaining effective room rates?

10. Describe the types of room rates. If you were asked by the front office manager to determine which room rates should be eliminated and whether any new types should be initiated, how would you proceed?

11. What do you think of the room rate maximization program described in the chapter? How does it affect the profit-and-loss statement? What are the important components of this program?

12. Determine the room rates for the proposed hotels with the following information:

	Proposal A	Proposal B
Operating Expenses	$8,034,472	$5,549,021
Other Income	300,000	1,900,000
Room Nights	65,000	50,000

13. What are some opportunities for the desk clerk to sell hotel services? If you are employed at the front desk of a hotel, do you see this being done? What effect does this have on the profit-and-loss statement?

14. What pointers would you give a new desk clerk on room key assignment?

15. Explain how to use the PMS to register a guest with a reservation. Note any inefficiencies.

16. Discuss the advantages and disadvantages of registering guests with a PMS.

CASE STUDY 701

Ana Chavarria, front office manager of The Times Hotel, has been meeting with the owner and general manager for the past several weeks to discuss the upgrade of the hotel's PMS to include self-check-in and -checkout. The owner is reluctant to make the purchase; the capital investment, although reasonable, is still significant and will affect cash flow. Margaret Chu, the general manager, was previously employed by a hotel that upgraded its PMS, and she was somewhat perplexed by the advertised benefits versus the real benefits in terms of improved

customer service. Ms. Chavarria, in contrast, had an encouraging experience with a PMS upgrade. The owner asks Ana to prepare a report justifying the upgrade of the PMS at The Times Hotel.

What concepts should Ana use to justify the upgrade purchase to achieve improved customer service in registration and checkout? Consider such aspects of the registration process as registering individuals and groups, determining room status, issuing room keys, and turnover of guest rooms.

CASE STUDY 702

Margaret Chu, general manager of The Times Hotel, has finished reviewing the latest batch of comment cards from the past weekend. Several of the glitches in guest service centered on the "It took too long to get into my room" syndrome. Ms. Chu thought she had this worked out with Ana Chavarria, front office manager, and Thomas Brown, executive housekeeper. These managers had developed a plan and shared it with her just one week ago. "What could have gone wrong?" wondered Ms. Chu. She has set up a meeting with Ana and Thomas for this afternoon. Provide a brief outline of points Ms. Chu should discuss.

CASE STUDY 703

Ana Chavarria, front office manager of The Times Hotel, wants to develop a DVD to train new employees to register guests. The low-budget, self-produced DVD will be developed in-house. Prepare a brief outline of the points she should include. You might also want to write a script (something like case study 302 in this text).

Notes

1. Doug Kennedy, July 2009. "Front Desk Hotel Training Can Generate Future Business," http://www.hotel-online.com/News/PR2009_3rd/Jul09_FrontDesk-Training.html.
2. JCB International Credit Card Co., Ltd., 700 S. Flower Street, Suite 1000, Los Angeles, California, 90017, www.jcbinternational.com/htm/about/brief.html, 2009.
3. Judy Willis, August 2009. "Ariane Systems Group Awarded Government Funding to DevelopMobile Self-service Platform for Hospitality Industry, http://www.hotel-online.com/News/PR2009_3rd/Aug09_Ariane.html."
4. Judy Colbert, "The Do's and Don'ts of Attracting International Guests," *Lodging 25*, no. 8 (April 2000): 33–34.
5. Hilton Hotels, "Hilton's Customer Information System, Called OnQ, Rolling Out Across 8 Hotel Brands; Seeking Guest Loyalty and Competitive Advantage with Proprietary Technology," August 31, 2004, hotel-online.com/News/PR2004_3rd/Aug04_OnQ.html.

Key Words

American plan

bank cards

bill-to-account

bottom up

commercial cards

commercial rates

complimentary rate (comp)

corporate rates

credit card imprinter

credit card validator

data sorts

discount rate

electronic key

European plan

family rates

fax machine

group rates

half-day rate

hard key

housekeeping status

Hubbart formula

intersell cards

key drawer

key fob

military and educational rates

modified American plan

Murphy bed

package rates

private label cards

rack rate

registration card

rule-of-thumb method for determining

room rates

sleeper

top down

walking a guest with a reservation

CHAPTER 8

Managing the Financials

OPENING DILEMMA

The night auditor has been unable to track down a $35.50 shortage

in balancing the night audit. He suspects it occurred because of a

posting error on a paid-out on behalf of a guest or food service

department staff person.

The lodging industry has always prided itself on its ability to maintain up-to-date records of outstanding guest balances (Figure 8-1). The front office processes a multitude of charges and payments every day, requiring a well-organized bookkeeping system. This chapter addresses how those guest charges are processed.

- Common bookkeeping practices performed in the front office
- Forms used to process guest charges and payments
- Account ledgers
- Procedures for processing guest charges and payments
- Procedures for transferring guest and city ledgers to accounts receivable
- Importance of standard operating procedures for posting and the night audit

The electronic folio displays all the data on a guest's stay held within the PMS. Photo courtesy of the author.

Common Bookkeeping Practices

Debits and Credits

Knowledge of basic bookkeeping methods enables the front office manager to understand the reasons for following particular procedures when handling financial transactions. This ability greatly assists the front office manager in training front desk clerks and night auditors. Instead of teaching the staff which keys to press on the keyboard to process a transaction, the manager explains *why* a charge must be posted in a certain way; this facilitates bookkeeping procedures. Many of you have already taken a basic accounting course or have had experience with a bookkeeping system. However, this chapter does not assume any previous knowledge of accounting procedures.

TABLE 8-1	Effects of Debits and Credits on Assets and Liabilities	
	DEBIT	**CREDIT**
ASSETS	increases	decreases
LIABILITIES	decreases	increases

Assets are items that have monetary value. *Liabilities* are financial or other contractual obligations or debts. These two concepts provide the basics for a bookkeeping system. Examples of assets include ownership of a cell phone, a textbook, or two tickets to a concert. Examples of liabilities include a contract to pay for the cell phone on a monthly basis, a contract to pay for a car, or a promise to pay a friend for word processing a term paper. Guest charges are financial obligations owed to a hotel; these are considered an asset for the hotel. If a guest prepays an account, this is a liability to the hotel because the hotel must return the money to the guest at checkout.

Assets and liabilities are increased and decreased by an organized set of accounting practices. These are called *debits*, which refer to an increase in an asset or a decrease in a liability, and *credits*, which refer to a decrease in an asset or an increase in a liability. Debits and credits provide a basis for the hotel bookkeeping system. They provide the power (mechanical means) to increase and decrease assets and liabilities for the guest and the hotel. The effects of debits and credits on assets and liabilities are shown in Table 8-1.

While this definition may be easy to remember, it is sometimes difficult to apply. However, if you apply it with regard to the type of account, you should have no problem. The following examples demonstrate how to apply debits and credits.

If a guest charges $100 on a credit card for goods and services in the hotel on any one day, the individual charges are processed as a debit (an increase) to the guest account and an asset to the hotel's accounts receivables. A credit (an increase) of an equal value is applied to the respective departmental sales accounts (a *revenue account*, part of owner's equity).

If a guest pays $100 in advance to reserve a room, this amount is processed as a credit (an increase) to the guest account (the hotel's advance payments, a liability). A debit (an increase) of an equal amount is applied to the hotel's cash account (an asset).

Forms Used to Process Guest Charges and Payments

Folio, Transfers, and Paid-out Slips

The folio, transfers, and paid-out slips are documents that allow for the documentation and transfer of charges and payments to a guest's account (Figure 8-2). In a property management system, the electronic folio is stored in the computer memory until a hard

copy is required. The hard copy of the electronic folio is a standard folio that lists the date of transaction, item, transfer slip number for referral, debit or credit amount, and updated balance. The *transfer slip* allows the desk clerk to transfer an amount of money from one account to another while creating a paper trail. A *paid-out slip* (a numbered form that authorizes cash disbursement from the front desk clerk's bank for products on behalf of a guest or an employee of the hotel) documents the authorized payment of cash to a vendor or an employee for a quick purchase of materials for the hotel. In a hotel with a PMS that interfaces with point-of-sale departments, the transfer of charges incurred by the guest or the transfer of a portion of one guest's bill to another guest's folio is done automatically.

The front desk clerk uses these forms in *posting* charges and payments, which is the process of debiting and crediting charges and payments to a guest folio. The night auditor then tracks the procedures the front desk clerk used in posting. These forms assist in maintaining control of bookkeeping activities in the front office.

Account Ledgers

Guest Ledger and City Ledger

The guest ledger is a collection of folios (records of guests' charges and payments) of current guests of the hotel. The city ledger is a collection of folios of unregistered hotel guests who maintain accounts with the hotel. These guests may submit cash advances for

TABLE 8-2 Transactions Affecting the Guest Ledger	
State in Guest Cycle	**Type of Transaction**
Reservation	• Deposit on future reservation • Return of deposit on reservation due to cancellation
Registration	• Prepayment of account
Guest stay	• Charge for room and tax • Charge for food and beverages and gratuities • Charge for purchases in gift shop • Charge for parking • Charge for valet • Charge for phone calls • Charge for in-room movies • Charge for cash advance
Checkout	• Payment of outstanding balance • Return of credit balance to guest • Transfer of charges to another account • Correction of posting errors

a future purchase of the hotel's goods and services, such as a deposit on a banquet or on a reservation. The hotel may also offer personal billing accounts to local businesspeople; these are also part of the city ledger. Unregistered hotel guests may keep open accounts for entertaining clients, for example. All of the folios are held in a *folio well*, a device that holds the individual printed hard-copy guest folios and city ledger folios, or a bucket with the physical dimensions of the guest ledger and city ledger.

TABLE 8-3 Transactions Affecting the City Ledger	
Nonregistered Guest Activity	**Type of Transaction**
Food and beverage	• Deposit on upcoming function • Return of deposit due to cancellation • Charge for food and beverages • Payment for food and beverages
Business/entertainment	• Charge for food and beverages • Payment for food and beverages
Office and retail rental	• Rental charge • Payment of rental charge
Parking rental	• Parking charge • Payment of parking charge

The accurate and timely processing of all these accounts assists the front office manager in maintaining hard copies of guests' financial transactions with the hotel. These accounts are collectively referred to as the hotel's *accounts receivable*—what guests owe the hotel. The accounts receivable consist of two categories, the guest ledger and the city ledger.

Tracking a guest stay from initial reservation through checkout provides examples of the many charges and payments that affect the guest ledger (Table 8-2). Likewise, following the activities of the unregistered guest shows how city ledger accounts are affected (Table 8-3).

Posting Guest Charges and Payments

As mentioned earlier, processing guest charges and payments is referred to as *posting* (increasing and decreasing assets and liabilities). Posting adds or subtracts guest charges and payments to the guest's individual account. Again, the accurate and timely posting of guest charges and payments is important to maintaining accurate financial records, as the guest may decide to check out at any time during the day and will require an accurate statement of transactions at that time.

Posting charges and payments with a PMS greatly increases the accuracy of posting. Each of the PMS posting module options, listed in Figure 4-11, allows the front desk clerk to post the charges and payments a guest incurs during his or her stay. With relative ease, the guest's electronic folio can be updated at the time of purchase of goods and services. Figure 8-3 shows an electronic folio to which charges and payments have been posted with a PMS.

Point-of-sale

The point-of-sale option allows the front office computer to interface with computers in other departments. In a hotel, when the front office interfaces with the restaurant, the front office computer terminal accepts and automatically posts charges made in the restaurant (the point of sale) to a guest's folio. Any department (gift shop, recreational facilities, room service, and telephone) in the hotel that can serve as a point of sale (the place where a product or service is purchased) must be able to interface with the front office to post charges to the guest's account. This electronic transfer ensures the charge is posted to the guest folio promptly and increases the accuracy of the posting (see Figure 8-4).

Room and Tax

The room option of the posting module has been described as a blessing by front office employees who used to work with a mechanical posting machine. In a mechanical front office system, the desk clerk or night auditor physically removed each guest folio from its file, placed the folio into the posting machine, depressed the correct keys, removed the folio from the posting machine, and then refiled it. In a hotel with a PMS, the desk clerk

FIGURE 8-3   Posting charges electronically to a folio.

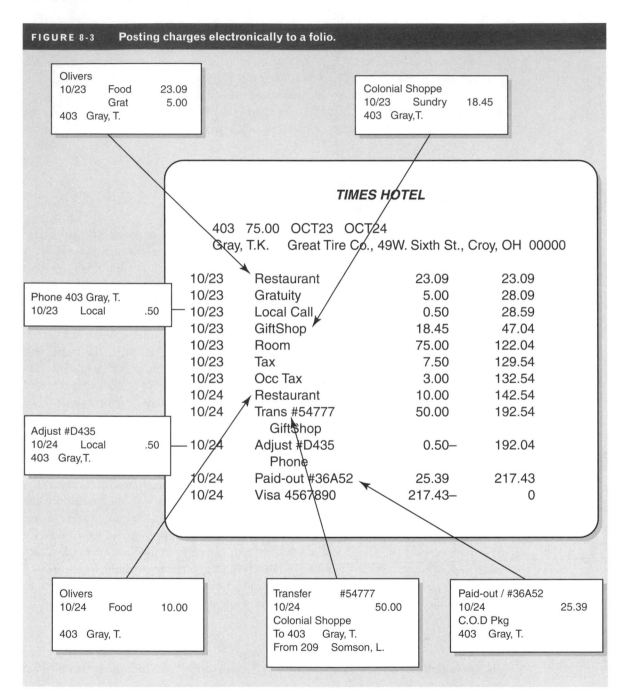

Olivers
10/23   Food   23.09
          Grat   5.00
403   Gray, T.

Colonial Shoppe
10/23   Sundry   18.45
403   Gray, T.

Phone 403 Gray, T.
10/23   Local   .50

Adjust #D435
10/24   Local   .50
403   Gray, T.

Olivers
10/24   Food   10.00

403   Gray, T.

Transfer   #54777
10/24   50.00
Colonial Shoppe
To 403   Gray, T.
From 209   Somson, L.

Paid-out / #36A52
10/24   25.39
C.O.D Pkg
403   Gray, T.

TIMES HOTEL

403   75.00   OCT23   OCT24
Gray, T.K.   Great Tire Co., 49W. Sixth St., Croy, OH 00000

10/23	Restaurant	23.09	23.09
10/23	Gratuity	5.00	28.09
10/23	Local Call	0.50	28.59
10/23	GiftShop	18.45	47.04
10/23	Room	75.00	122.04
10/23	Tax	7.50	129.54
10/23	Occ Tax	3.00	132.54
10/24	Restaurant	10.00	142.54
10/24	Trans #54777	50.00	192.54
	GiftShop		
10/24	Adjust #D435	0.50–	192.04
	Phone		
10/24	Paid-out #36A52	25.39	217.43
10/24	Visa 4567890	217.43–	0

FIGURE 8-4

When guests incur charges in the dining room, these are immediately posted electronically to the guest folios via the point-of-sale terminal. Photo courtesy of the author.

automatically posts charges to individual electronic folios by activating the room option. While the PMS is posting room charges, the clerk is free to do other tasks.

The tax option is often activated with the room option because most properties are required by state or local laws to charge and collect sales and occupancy taxes from guests. The tax option posts the appropriate taxes to the guest folio when the room charge is posted.

Transfers and Adjustments

The transfer and adjustment options enable front office personnel to correct errors in and make requested changes to the guest folio. The charges posted to a guest's electronic folio at times must be transferred to another folio, or adjustments to the amounts must be made. For example, a guest may discover that his or her hotel bill will be paid by a corporation in the city. The bill had been guaranteed with the guest's credit card. The front desk clerk must transfer the guest's charges from the folio in the guest ledger to the corporation's house account in the city ledger. Another guest may claim a charge for room service should have been charged to the person who was sharing the room. In this case, the front desk clerk adjusts (removes) the charge from one guest folio and transfers it to the other guest folio.

A guest may question charges for a phone call, movie viewing, or other services. The desk clerk can immediately adjust the account, depending on the authorized financial correction flexibility policy. This policy spells out the guidelines for a desk clerk to follow in adjusting a guest's account. For example, a guest may refuse to pay for a telephone call because it should have been posted to the folio of the guest who was sharing the room. If policy does not permit the desk clerk to authorize the adjustment, the front office shift supervisor or front office manager must be called to do so. It is important to remember that immediate correction of errors may influence a guest's perception of a hotel's service. The policy on authorized financial correction flexibility reflects the quality of service the hotel wants to deliver.

All of these transfers and adjustments can be made easily with a PMS. Also, the adjustments are at once reflected in all the guest and departmental accounts affected by the change, with very little paperwork. This system makes the night auditor's job of verifying the integrity of accounts much easier.

Paid-Out

The paid-out option is used to track authorized requests for cash paid out of the desk clerk's cash drawer. Desk clerks may be required to pay immediately for goods and services on behalf of guests, such as delivery of flowers, valet services, and COD (cash on delivery) packages. These charges are usually preauthorized by the hotel on behalf of the guest. The amount paid out can be charged to the guest's folio and reflected in the desk clerk's cash balance and the departmental account in one process. This saves the tedious effort of initiating a paper trail and also avoids the possibility of human error.

Miscellaneous Charges

The miscellaneous charges option is included in a PMS to allow the desk clerk to post charges atypical of the majority of hotel properties. If a hotel has, for example, a recreational facility that lacks a point-of-sale terminal, this option may be engaged. This feature can also be used to post miscellaneous charges to the city ledger accounts.

Phone

The phone option is included in a PMS for properties that do not have an interface with the call-accounting system. With the call-accounting interface, the charges for local and

FRONT-LINE REALITIES

A guest in the hotel has reviewed her account and says the person who was sharing the room incurred the $12.15 phone charges. The guest wants you to take care of this. How would you proceed?

long-distance phone calls, plus surcharges, are posted automatically. Without the interface, the desk clerk must manually post the phone charge on the electronic folio.

Display Folio

The display folio option permits the front desk clerk or other authorized members of the management staff to view a guest's electronic folio at any time. If a guest requests the current balance on his or her folio, the desk clerk can produce a hard copy of the folio with a few keystrokes. After the guest reviews the hard copy, he or she may indicate a certain charge is in error. This discrepancy can be resolved prior to checkout.

Reports

The reports option allows the front office manager to organize data in a way that is useful to the controller and the management team. The night auditor can cross-check departmental totals from the restaurant, phone service, gift shop, or recreational facility with the amounts charged to the guest folios. These data can be shared with department managers to provide feedback for evaluating marketing programs and cost-control efforts. Figure 8-5 illustrates the types of reports that can be obtained.

Transferring Guest and City Ledgers to Accounts Receivable

The debits and credits incurred by guests and future guests of the hotel are maintained as back office accounts receivable (monies owed to the hotel). Once the guest has received the goods and enjoyed the services of the hotel, then this financial record must be transferred to the master accounts receivable for the hotel. If a guest's folio shows a debit balance (an amount the guest owes to the hotel) of $291 and the guest wants to pay that off by charging $291 to his MasterCard, then the amount is transferred to the MasterCard accounts receivable.

Another type of transaction involves the *back office accounts payable*, amounts of money prepaid on behalf of the guest for future consumption of goods or services (sometimes referred to as *back office cash accounts*), such as when a guest deposits a sum of money for a future stay. For example, the personal check a guest sends to the hotel, dated February 5, for a stay on the following December 21 must be credited first to the hotel's back office accounts payable or back office cash account and then to the guest's folio. This amount of money is held for the guest's arrival on December 21. When the guest arrives on December 21, the guest folio is brought to the front of the folio well and activated on registration.

These examples demonstrate that the activities in the guest ledger and city ledger are not isolated. They are reflected in the back office account. The guest ledger and city ledger are temporary holding facilities for the guest's account. The back office accounts are the permanent arenas for financial processing.

FIGURE 8-5   Reports created with the posting module.

Olivers Restaurant 1/28 2,315.92

M	Total	Room CHG	V	M/C	JCB	DC
B	750.25	125.90	67.50	35.87	234.00	.00
L	890.67	25.00	124.50	340.00	150.00	75.00
D	675.00	235.00	56.98	75.00	221.75	125.00

GRAYSTONE LOUNGE 1/28 1,496.48

1.	780.09	121.00	.00	.00	45.00	.00
2.	456.98	75.00	35.80	87.30	89.60	75.40
3.	259.41	12.90	.00	.00	.00	.00

COLONIAL SHOPPE 1/28 1,324.72

1.	571.97	153.98	.00	76.43	121.56	.00
2.	752.75	259.93	82.87	83.76	25.71	.00

ROOM 1/28   4,529.56

TAX 1/28   452.95

ADJUST 1/28   66.04

OLIVERS	23.98	#X4567
OLIVERS	5.98	#X4568
PHONE	.50	#X4569
PHONE	.50	#X4570
OLIVERS	27.54	#X4571
PHONE	7.54	#X4572

PAID OUT 1/28   143.20

OLIVERS	45.00	#45A41-SUPPLIES
OLIVERS	12.00	#45A42-SUPPLIES
ROOM 701	32.45	#45A43-FLOWERS
ROOM 531	3.75	#45S44-COD
ADMIN	50.00	#45A45-SUPPLIES

PHONE 1/28   578.15

LD	450.61
LOC	127.54

Importance of Standard Operating Procedures for Posting and the Night Audit

Standard operating procedures for processing charges and payments are used for the night audit, which is performed to balance the day's financial transactions. The financial activities recorded in the guest ledger, city ledger, and various departments within the hotel must be processed accurately. It is not uncommon for a night auditor to spend many hours looking for a small or large dollar amount to correct a discrepancy in the accounts. Errors can often be traced to a front desk clerk who transposed a dollar amount ($35.87 entered as $53.87) or transferred a charge to an incorrect account ($20.50 valet charge posted as a $20.50 restaurant charge). However, it is difficult to detect if a desk clerk used an incorrect folio (room 626 instead of room 625). An experienced night auditor can usually pinpoint the error and resolve discrepancies caused by transposing figures or picking up incorrect accounts.

Because of the tedious yet vital effort required to resolve such errors, front office managers must thoroughly train front office personnel to process guest charges and payments correctly. The training program must include a statement of behavioral objectives, preparation and demonstration of detailed written procedures to follow when posting charges and payments, preparation and discussion of theoretical material that explains debits and credits, explanation of all related backup paperwork, clarification of the relationship of front office accounting procedures to back office accounting procedures, and delivery of hands-on training on the PMS. It is also recommended to include a motivational plan to encourage employees to succeed in accomplishing their personal and program objectives. Such training efforts pay off in reduced bookkeeping errors and better customer service.

Solution to Opening Dilemma

The night auditor should check paid-out slips with accompanying invoices from floral shops, dry cleaners, specialty shops, and the like, or receipts from suppliers, to determine if posting figures were transposed.

Chapter Recap

This chapter described procedures for processing guest charges and payments in a front office that uses a property management system. This process is based on basic bookkeeping concepts—assets, liabilities, debit, and credits—as they apply to the guest ledger and city ledger. Folios, transfers, and paid-out slips form a communication system that tracks the charges and payments from the various departments and guests. The interface of the property management system with the point of sale was presented as it affects the guest bookkeeping system. Transferring accounting data from the guest ledger and city ledger to the back office accounts was also discussed. The importance of adhering to standard operating procedures in processing guest charges and payments for the night audit was emphasized. The preparation of a training program for new front office personnel was cited as a way to ensure this goal is achieved. These operating procedures are essential to maintaining the integrity of the guest's bill and streamlining the hotel's bookkeeping process.

End-of-Chapter Questions

1. List some assets a student may hold. List some liabilities a student may incur. What differentiates the two?

2. In your own words, define the bookkeeping terms *debit* and *credit*. What power do they have in a bookkeeping context?

3. What forms are used in hotel departments and the front office to provide records of a guest's charges and payments? Describe each. What are the purposes of these forms?

4. What is an electronic folio? How would you describe this to a front desk clerk who just started to use a PMS?

5. What is the guest ledger? Give an example of something included in it. Describe how you would post a check for prepayment of two nights' room rate.

6. What is the city ledger? Give an example of something included in it. Describe how you would post a check for prepayment of a social reception.

7. Give examples of the financial transactions that may occur during a guest stay.

8. Give examples of the financial transactions in which the nonregistered guest may be involved.

9. If you are employed in a hotel that uses a property management system that interfaces with a point-of-sale department, describe the procedure for posting a guest charge or payment.

10. Why are the guest and city ledgers considered temporary holding areas for financial transactions? Where are such records permanently maintained?

11. Why is careful and accurate posting of charges and payments so important to the night audit? How can a front office manager ensure posting is done correctly?

CASE STUDY 801

Ana Chavarria, the front office manager, has just finished talking with Cynthia Restin, the night auditor, who has spent the majority of her shift trying to track down three posting errors totaling $298.98. Last Tuesday night, a charge of $34.50 was posted to the wrong department in the city ledger; on Wednesday night, a paid-out in the amount of $21.85 had no financial document attached to the paid-out slip; and on Thursday, a $250.00 prepayment on a social event was credited to a city ledger account as $520.00. Cynthia told Ana she has been at The Times Hotel for more than ten years and, in her experience, such mistakes are usually the result of improper training of new front desk clerks. Ana thanked Cynthia for the information and told her she would look into the matter.

Ana called Mary Yu, lead person on the first shift, into her office. Mary trained the new front desk clerks, Henry Yee and Tony Berks. Both Henry and Tony were good trainees and seemed to understand all the tasks involved in operating the property management system. Ana asked Mary to relate the procedure she used to train these new recruits.

Mary says she described the property management system to them and then let them post some dummy charges on the training module. Then she had them correct each other's mistakes. After they had practiced for 15 minutes, the front desk became very busy, and they had to turn the training mode off and activate the regular operating mode. Henry posted several paid-out charges and transfers. Tony was a little more reluctant to touch the machine, but after the coffee break, he wanted to try to post guest payments.

Ana realizes the development of a training program is her responsibility, and she has let that responsibility slip. How would you help Ana prepare an effective training program that teaches new front desk clerks why and how to post guest charges and payments?

CASE STUDY 802

Ana Chavarria, the front office manager of The Times Hotel, has gathered her staff at a meeting to discuss the current policy on adjusting guest charges. Several guests have completed and returned guest comment cards indicating requests for adjustments on their accounts were delayed.

Luis Jimenez recalls one guest had requested a $10.25 phone call be removed from his account because he did not make that call. Another guest wanted an $8.95 movie charge deducted from her bill because she did not watch the movie. Luis said he referred these guests to the front office supervisor on duty, which made both guests angry. The guests who were waiting in line for service were also annoyed.

Lavina Luquis had a similar situation, but she decided to just deduct a disputed $32.95 lunch charge without approval. The front office supervisor on duty reprimanded Lavina and told her, "All adjustments are handled by me."

Ana wants to update the hotel's policy on authorizing adjustment of guest accounts. Give her guidelines on dollar amounts that can be adjusted without the supervisor's approval, and describe some situations in which adjustments can be applied.

CASE STUDY 803

Ana Chavarria, the front office manager of The Times Hotel, is busy in her office answering emails from former customers. Several of them have questions on their folio about how billing charges were handled. Ana realized these are simple errors on the part of her new desk clerks, but she thought it had been resolved with the great training program that was developed several weeks ago. She included a statement of behavioral objectives, preparation and demonstration of detailed written procedures to follow when posting charges and payments, preparation and discussion of theoretical material that explains debits and credits, explanation of all related backup paperwork, clarification of the relationship of front office accounting procedures to back office accounting procedures, and delivery of hands-on training on the PMS. Everyone was "into the procedures." They seemed to understand all the concepts presented.

Do you have any ideas to assist Ana in making her training program a success?

Key Words

accounts receivable

assets

back office accounts payable

credit

debit

folio well

liabilities

paid-out slips

posting

revenue account

transfer slip

CHAPTER 9

Guest Checkout

OPENING DILEMMA

The general manager of the hotel indicated at the staff meeting today that the budget allows for the purchase of an additional module in the property management system. She suggests the guest history module might be just what the hotel needs to increase room sales. The general manager has scheduled a visit from the PMS vendor tomorrow and wants you (the front office manager), the director of marketing and sales, and the revenue manager to prepare a list of questions for the vendor to help determine whether the purchase of the guest history module is justified.

CHAPTER FOCUS POINTS

■ Organization of late charges to produce an accurate guest folio

■ Procedures necessary to perform the guest checkout

■ Transfer of guest accounts to the back office

■ Checkout reports available with a property management system

■ Guest histories

Guest checkout can be a time of confusion, short tempers, and long lines—a test of the patience of both the guest and the cashier. Think of the last time you checked out of a hotel. How did it go? Was the cashier courteous and hospitable? If not, were you angry because of his or her indifference? Always remember what it is like to be a guest. This simple approach will serve you well throughout your career in the hospitality industry.

This chapter assists you in developing a thorough understanding of the guest checkout process. It is not a difficult procedure to understand and implement; however, it does require planning to organize the details of this part of the guest's stay. The use of the checkout module of a PMS is discussed throughout the chapter. Recall from Figure 4-14, the checkout module, that the options available include folio, adjustments, cashier, back office transfer, reports, and guest history.

Organizing Late Charges to Ensure Accuracy

As you learned in earlier chapters, when a hotel utilizes all modules in the PMS throughout the guest's stay, charges for room, tax, food and beverages, valet, and other services are posted to the guest folio as they are incurred. In hotels that do not utilize a PMS or the checkout module at the time of checkout, *late charges*, or guest charges that might not be included on the guest folio because of a delay in posting by other departments, can result in substantial loss of income, as Table 9-1 indicates.

Failure to post telephone charges for local or long-distance calls made by the guest prior to checkout is another area where revenue may be lost. For example, a lodging property that fails to post 20 phone calls per day, at an average cost of 50 cents each, would lose $3650 per year.

Front offices with a property management system that can interface the posting module with the point-of-sale departments and the call-accounting system can post late charges easily. As soon as the charge is incurred at the point of sale or through the call-accounting system, it is posted to the electronic folio. Without this interface, the point-of-sale cashier must telephone the front desk clerk prior to the guest's checkout. The telephone operator and front desk clerk must have a good reporting system to record all phone calls. When a PMS is not used, the front office manager and other department managers should initiate a communication program for their employees that ensures the quick and accurate relay of last-minute charges.

TABLE 9-1 Revenue Loss Caused by Failure to Post Charges	
LOST BREAKFAST CHARGES	
Average number of charged breakfasts per day	100
Percentage of lost charges	× .03
Number of lost charges per day	3
Average check	× $5.00
Amount lost per day	$15.00
Days per year	× 365
Amount lost per year	$5475

Guest Checkout Procedure

If front office personnel collect and promptly post late charges, the guest checkout can proceed without bottlenecks. However, when the cashier or front desk clerk must call the restaurant, gift shop, and switchboard to verify charges, delays and disputes can occur.

The guest checkout involves the following steps:

1. Guest requests checkout.

2. Desk clerk inquires about quality of products and services.

3. Guest returns key to desk clerk.

4. Desk clerk retrieves hard copy of electronic folio.

5. Desk clerk reviews folio for completeness.

6. Guest reviews charges and payments.

7. Guest determines method of payment.

8. Guest makes payment.

9. Desk clerk inquires about additional reservations.

10. Desk clerk files folio and related documents for the night audit.

11. Desk clerk communicates guest departure to housekeeping and other departments in the hotel if necessary.

The objective of the checkout process is to process the guest's request for settlement of his or her account as quickly and efficiently as possible. The lodging establishment also wants to maintain a quality control system for both the guest and the hotel; posting errors can mean erroneous charges for the guest and lost money for the lodging establishment.

Throughout your career in lodging management, you will be called on to develop operational procedures. First, set your objectives and keep them simple. Accommodate guests and maintain necessary data to provide the lodging establishment with information for the income statement. The steps outlined for guest checkout show how easy it is to establish operational procedures when you keep these goals in mind. The narratives that follow elaborate on each step in the guest checkout.

Inquiring about Quality of Products and Services

When the guest arrives at the front desk to check out, the cashier should inquire about the guest's satisfaction with the accommodations, food and beverages, and miscellaneous services provided by the hotel (Figure 9-1). Cashiers should be alert to possible problems. Incidental comments about a cold room, low water pressure, leaky plumbing, or damaged furniture should be noted and passed along to the appropriate department head.

Because guests often do not verbalize complaints or compliments, all lodging properties should have guest comment cards available as an optional source of communication.
In many leading lodging chains, the chief executive officer answers these cards personally.
The general manager of an independent lodging property can provide a similar personal
touch by acknowledging negative comments. A good public relations program can be
enhanced by addressing minor problems experienced by the guest that might indicate lack
of concern. Also, concern for guest satisfaction affects the financial success of the hotel.

Retrieving the Room Key

Lodging properties that use a hard-key system must request the return of the hard key.
The security of the guest as well as the financial investment in the hard-key system man-
dates that this procedure be a part of the guest checkout. Guest security is jeopardized
if keys are lost or not returned. A 200-room property with approximately five keys per
room that must be constantly replaced finds that a great deal of money is spent to maintain the key supply. Some properties require a key deposit, returnable on checkout.

FRONT-LINE REALITIES

On checkout, a front desk clerk asks a guest if his accommodations were acceptable. The
guest says the heater in the room didn't work last night. Because the hotel has a 100 percent
satisfaction guarantee, the desk clerk is obliged to comp the room. If you were the front office
manager, what would you do to follow up on this incident?

The hotel with a PMS or an electronic key system can easily change the electronic code on a key for future entrance to the guest room. Although the initial financial investment in such a system is substantial, security is the objective in adopting this technology.

Retrieving and Reviewing the Folio

In a front office with a PMS, the cashier uses the folio option of the checkout module to retrieve the electronic folio by entering the guest's name or room number. A hard copy is printed for the guest.

The guest and the cashier should both review the folio. The cashier reviews the obvious charges: room fee and tax for the number of nights spent in the hotel (day of arrival through last night), incidentals (such as movie rental, personal phone calls, and purchases at the gift shop) paid for by the individual rather than a corporation, and the like. The cashier must inquire if late charges were incurred at the restaurant or other hotel department or if last-minute phone calls were made.

The guest must also be shown a copy of the folio for a final review. The front office manager should develop an empowerment procedure based on a list of tasks to perform if charges are questioned. Typical questions concern charges for phone calls not made, meals not eaten, gifts not purchased, flowers not received, laundry not sent out, or in-room movies not viewed. Using the list provided by the front office manager, the front desk clerk or cashier may adjust these charges up to a certain dollar amount. A thorough cost control procedure to track the total adjustments by each employee can help keep such adjustments in line. Large dollar amounts that are questioned by the guest should be referred to the front office manager. The adjustments option of the checkout module in a property management system can be used to make changes.

Empowerment is important to develop in staff members because many guests do question postings made to their accounts. Employees must learn listening skills that will enable them to discern just what form of satisfaction the guest is asking for. Employees should be encouraged to try several techniques to determine which will meet the needs of the guest within the financial and service limitations.

In-room Guest Checkout

Before proceeding with the guest checkout procedure, it is important to note the guest's option to use *in-room guest checkout*, a computerized procedure that allows guests to settle their accounts from their rooms (Figure 9-2). In some PMSs that feature in-room guest checkout, the guest can initiate the guest checkout the night before departing by following instructions located near the television set in the guest room. The guest can view a final version of the folio on the television screen on the morning of checkout. This expedites the process by alerting the front office to have a hard copy ready for payment. If the guest indicates he or she will pay by credit card or direct billing (bill-to-account), the guest need not stop by the front desk to check out. A control procedure is built into the PMS to prevent cash customers from using in-room checkout. A guest who is going to pay with cash has not established a line of credit with the hotel.

Determining Method of Payment and Collection

During registration, the guest indicates the method of payment he or she plans to use. Possibilities include credit cards, direct billing (bill-to-account), cash or personal check, traveler's checks, and debit cards. During checkout, the guest confirms the method of payment.

Credit Cards

Today's business and leisure travelers usually pay with a credit card. So-called plastic money has advantages for the cardholder as well as for the hotel. The cardholder is assured of instant credit to satisfy debts incurred. The extensive travel required of some business-people would make the almost constant requests for cash advances by corporate employees difficult to manage. The advantage for the lodging establishment is that payment is assured (less a discount paid to the corporation issuing the credit card). It is important to note that with the increased use and advances of computers in the business world, the reimbursement period can be reduced to zero—the hotel is immediately credited with payment. As these advances occur, the ready acceptance of credit cards will change.

The front office, in cooperation with the controller, usually establishes a priority system for accepting credit cards based on cash flow requirements and the effect of the discount rate offered. The average guest is probably not aware of the discount rate and may be willing to use whatever credit card the front desk clerk requests.

Processing a credit card in an automated hotel follows a standard procedure. The objectives of the procedure include accurate recording of the amounts of charges and tax, name (address and phone number of cardholder are optional), verification of the credit card dollar limit, and capture of fraudulent credit cards. The procedure includes the following steps:

1. Note the credit card expiration date.

2. Enter the approval of the charge amount on the PMS checkout screen.

3. Verify the credit limit available by using the credit card validator.

4. Allow the guest to review and sign the folio.

5. Check the guest signature on the folio against the signature on the card.

6. Give the card and a copy of the folio to the guest.

Once the procedure is developed, it must be followed to the letter, without exception. The fraudulent use of credit cards takes a great toll on the profits of the hotel. An incentive system for cashiers and front desk clerks can be built into the procedure for processing credit cards to encourage the capture of fraudulent cards. The small monetary reward is nominal compared to the cost of a hotel bill that may never be recovered. In addition, hotels should develop a procedure for retrieving fraudulent credit cards. The safety of front desk staff is extremely important in this procedure.

Bill-to-account (Direct Billing)

Hotel guests, both corporate representatives and private guests, may use the *bill-to-account*, a preauthorized account that allows guests to have their charges processed on a regular billing cycle without the use of a credit card (sometimes referred to as *direct billing*) to settle an account. Direct billing requires prior approval of the credit limit of an organization (corporate representatives) or an individual (private guest). Usually the corporation requesting direct billing completes an application for credit approval. The controller in the lodging establishment then performs a credit check to determine a credit rating and a credit limit. This *house limit* of credit, a credit limit set by an individual hotel, varies with the amount of projected charges and the length of time allowed for charges to be paid. The credit rating of the corporation in question plays a large part in assigning a credit limit.

The application usually lists people who are authorized to use the account, as well as authorized positions within the corporation. Identification cards with an authorization number are issued by the hotel. It is the responsibility of the corporation applying for credit to monitor the authorized use of the credit. The cashier must verify the identification of the corporate guest.

The bill-to-account option should be reviewed with an eye toward cost-effectiveness. Although the hotel does not have to pay a 3–8 percent discount rate to the credit card agency, the cost incurred by the controller's office (credit checks, billing, postage, collection of bad debts) must be considered. The question of cash flow—almost immediate payment from the credit card agency versus a four- to eight-week waiting period for corporate accounts—should also be considered. The marketing implications of direct billing deserve attention as well. The status conferred by this option may be desirable to corporate representatives and private guests.

The following procedure is used to process a bill-to-account payment:

1. Request corporate or personal identification.

2. Check to be sure the individual is authorized by the account holder to bill to the account.

3. Note the credit limit per employee.

4. Note red flags on the credit file due to nonpayment of bills.

5. Note authorized signature.

6. Enter charges into the point-of-sale terminal along with bill-to-account identification.

When this information is entered into the POS, it is also entered into an electronic folio in the city ledger of the PMS.

Cash and Personal Checks

When guests indicate during registration that they will pay their bills with cash or a personal check, the front desk clerk should immediately be on the alert. Such a guest may well charge everything during his or her stay (perhaps only one day in length) at the hotel and then exit without paying. Consequently, most hotels require cash in advance from guests who choose this method of payment, as the guest has not established a credit rating with the hotel. In addition, close monitoring by the night auditor and front desk clerks of the guest's charge activity is in order. Such guests are not allowed charge privileges at other departments in the hotel. In properties with a PMS, the guest name and room number are entered to block charges at point-of-sale areas. In a hotel without food and beverage, gift shop, and health club POS terminals, the front office must alert those departments that this guest has not been extended charge privileges.

To process a cash payment, the following procedure can be used:

1. Check the daily currency conversion rate when converting foreign into national currency. Take time to ensure the math is accurate.

2. Retain the amount tendered outside the cash drawer until the transaction is completed.

3. Maintain an orderly cash drawer, with bills separated by denomination.

4. Develop an orderly procedure to make change from the amount tendered.

5. Count the change out loud when giving it to the guest.

6. Perform only one procedure at a time. Refuse to make change for another bill of a different denomination if a previous transaction has not been completed.

7. Issue a receipt for the transaction.

Most lodging properties simply do not accept personal checks; the opportunity for fraud is too great. This policy often comes as a surprise to guests, who may protest this is the only means of payment they have. However, the hotel can use commercial check authorization companies and credit card companies that guarantee a guest's personal check.

The procedure for processing personal checks is as follows:

1. Request a personal-check-cashing card.

2. Refer to the list of persons who are not allowed to present checks as legal tender.

3. Compare the written amount of the check with the figures to be sure they match.

4. Note low-numbered checks. Low numbers may indicate a newly opened, unestablished account, and the check will require a supervisor's approval.

5. Request identification (a valid driver's license and a major credit card), and record the numbers on the back of the check. Compare the name and address imprinted on the check with a valid driver's license.

6. Compare the signature on the check with the requested identification.

7. Validate the amount of the check and the credit rating of the guest with a commercial check authorization company or credit card company.

Traveler's Checks

Traveler's checks are prepaid checks issued by a bank or financial organization; they have been an acceptable form of legal tender for many years. These checks are a welcome method of payment in the lodging industry. Traveler's checks are processed like cash. Proof of credit is already established, and the hotel pays no percentage of the sale to a credit card agency, as the guest paid a percentage of the face amount of the traveler's check to the issuing agency. However, checking proof of identification (a valid driver's license or major credit card) should be a standard traveler's check–cashing policy. The guest should sign the traveler's check in the cashier's presence, and that signature should be compared with the signature already on the check. The list of traveler's check numbers that are not acceptable, supplied regularly by the check-issuing agency, must be consulted to ensure the checks are valid.

Debit Cards

Debit cards, or check cards, are embossed plastic cards with a magnetic strip on the reverse side that authorize direct transfer of funds from a customer's bank account to the commercial organization's bank account for purchase of goods and services. Some examples of debit cards are MAC, NYCE, STAR, and PLUS. These are similar to credit cards in that they guarantee creditworthiness, against which the hotel charges the bill;

however, the payment is deducted directly and immediately from the guest's personal savings or checking account and transferred to the hotel's account rather than being billed to the guest on a monthly basis. Debit cards continue to gain in popularity as the use of credit cards becomes more costly to the guest. However, the concept of *float*, the delay in payment after using a credit card, may remain a more attractive benefit for some guests. Some debit cards have an embossed credit-card logo that indicates they are acceptable at places that accept that particular credit card and are processed through a credit card financial organization. Debit cards are processed similarly to credit cards.

To process a debit card payment, the following procedure is used:

1. Insert the debit card into the validation machine.

2. Have the guest enter his or her personal identification number.

3. Process the debit-card voucher as a cash payment on the guest folio.

Assisting the Guest with Method of Payment

Guests may find they are short on cash or are otherwise unable to pay their bill due to an expensive emergency, overextension of credit card limits, or theft. When these situations occur, the front desk clerk or cashier should be ready to offer the following services.

Money Wire

Western Union provides *money wire*, an electronic message that authorizes money from one person to be issued to another person; this service has been available to travelers for many years, with a fee charged by Western Union. This convenient service should be established as an option for a guest. The front office manager should develop and communicate a procedure that includes the phone number and address of the nearest money wire center.

Travelers Aid Society

The Travelers Aid Society was founded for the purpose of aiding the down-and-out traveler beset by an unexpected emergency in an unfamiliar city. The phone number and address of this organization must also be communicated to the front office staff as an option of payment. The Travelers Aid International website states its mission is "[t]o advance and support a network of human service provider organizations committed to assisting individuals and families who are in transition, or crisis, and are disconnected from their support systems."[1]

Auto Clubs

The auto clubs—AAA (American Automobile Association) being the best known—and private gasoline companies offer their members immediate cash advances in case of an emergency. Again, a listing of phone numbers of auto clubs for guest use not only helps the guest but ensures the lodging establishment will be paid.

The method of payment, in the end, can affect the hotel's bottom line. The preapproval criterion for credit card and debit card holders is an important requirement when a hotel is extending credit to a guest from check-in to checkout. The discount rate charged by the issuing agency, which takes a percentage of the gross charges, affects the income statement as well. It is important, however, to show concern for the guest whose circumstances have taken a turn for the worse (serious accident, theft, unexpected illness, etc.). The front office should be equipped to offer information on alternatives such as auto clubs and money wires; this can be perceived as a display of genuine hospitality.

International Currency Exchange

When an international guest presents a credit card for payment at checkout, the credit card issuing agency processes the payment according to the current exchange rate between countries. If a guest wants to pay in his or her national currency, the cashier must compute the exchange. The daily international exchange rate can be found by calling a bank or other financial institution or by reviewing the international exchange rates published in the *Wall Street Journal* in the Currency Trading section. Exchange rates for the U.S. dollar, pound, euro, peso, yen, and Canadian dollar are listed.

On January 1, 1999, the *euro* became the accepted currency for the following 11 member-states of the European Community: Belgium, Germany, Spain, France, Ireland, Italy, Luxembourg, the Netherlands, Austria, Portugal, and Finland. In January 2001, Greece adopted the euro, and in January 2002, euro coins and bills were introduced. The euro provides ease in traveling throughout Europe, as travelers need not exchange currency at each participating country.

The goal in computing the exchange is to determine how much of the international visitor's national currency is required to pay the bill in the United States. With that goal in mind, here is a simple procedure to follow. If a Canadian guest at a U.S. hotel wants to pay a US$500.00 hotel bill in Canadian dollars with an exchange rate of $0.80 (Canadian) to US$1.00, use the following formula to compute the exchange:

$$\frac{\text{US\$500.00}}{\text{Canadian \$0.80}} = \text{\$625.00 Canadian dollars required to pay the bill at a U.S. hotel}$$

If an English guest at a U.S. hotel wants to pay a US$500.00 hotel bill in pounds with an exchange rate of £1 to US$2.00, use the following formula to compute the exchange:

$$\frac{\text{US\$500.00}}{\text{£2.00}} = \text{£250 English pounds required to pay the bill at a U.S. hotel}$$

Another example is if a German guest at a U.S. hotel wants to pay a US$500.00 hotel bill in euros with an exchange rate of €1.687 to US$1.00, use the following formula to compute the exchange.

$$\frac{\text{US\$500.00}}{\text{€1.687}} = \text{€296 required to pay the bill at a U.S. hotel}$$

It is important to consider the float time of the international currency collected and presented to a bank for deposit in a hotel's account—that is, it will take several days or weeks before the currency is credited to the hotel's account. Also, a different rate of exchange may be in effect at the time of the currency exchange transaction. For example, a U.S. hotel may deposit £10,000 from an English tour group thinking it will receive US$20,000 (US$2.00 for each English pound), but three weeks later, when the transaction occurs, the exchange rate may be US$1.90 for £1. In this case, the U.S. hotel would receive approximately US$19,000 (10,000 × 1.9 = 19,000) instead of the US$20,000 originally computed at the time of deposit. To compensate for this, the hotel must consider adding a surcharge to the rate used that day as well as to cover a transaction fee charge by banks. For example, in the case in which a U.S. hotel anticipates receiving US$20,000 for a deposit of £10,000 based on an exchange rate of £1 for each US$2, it may be better for the hotel to use £1 for each $1.90 to cover a volatile exchange rate and a banking fee. The U.S. hotel would collect £10,526 ($20,000 ÷ 1.90 = £10,526) at checkout to compensate for the float time of the international currency.

Obtaining Future Reservations

Checkout, the last contact point with the guest, is the best opportunity to secure additional reservations. It is at this time the cashier or front desk clerk can best assist the marketing and sales department. The front office manager should develop a standard procedure for the front office staff to follow, which may include these steps:

1. At the beginning of the checkout procedure, inquire about the guest's stay. Maintain good eye contact and listen closely.

2. Ask if the guest will be returning to the area in the near future or if he or she will need a reservation for a property in the hotel's chain or referral group. If so, ask whether he or she would like to make a reservation for that visit. Because all the guest data are already on file, a confirmation of the reservation can be sent later. If the guest is in a hurry, the reservation staff can follow up later. Your role is to plant the seed of a future sale as well as to accommodate a guest.

3. Continue to check out the guest. Again, make eye contact. If the guest does not respond positively to the first inquiry, offer a departure brochure or directory that includes information about making additional reservations at the hotel's property or properties within the chain or referral group.

4. Bid the guest farewell.

5. Report to the shift supervisor any negative comments from the guest concerning his or her stay.

6. Process future reservations, or alert the reservation clerk to these requests.

This standard procedure should be part of the desk clerk's training program. As with other sales efforts at the front office, selling additional reservations at checkout should be rewarded through an employee incentive program. This procedure gives the front office personnel a basic structure to use in pitching the sale and accommodating the guest. The employee can adapt the pitch to his or her own style.

Filing Documents

The paperwork documenting the day's transactions must be in place when the night auditor's shift begins. Guest folios, transfers, paid-out slips, and the like must be filed according to a standard system. This may seem like a simple task, but at a busy front desk with many checkouts and check-ins, it is easy to misplace documents. Care must be taken to provide the night auditor with all the necessary proof of origination of charges and trail of payment options.

Relaying Guest Departures to Other Departments

It is essential that other departments be notified that a guest has checked out to ensure smooth operation of the hotel. The PMS allows the front desk clerk and the housekeeping employees to inform one another of guest departures, stayovers, room availability status, and other occupancy details as they occur. As mentioned earlier, once the electronic folio is cleared from active memory after checkout, the guest departure is indicated on all other modules of the system. The front desk clerk need not telephone the housekeeper to say room 203 is vacant; the housekeeper need not spend hours reporting room availability status to the front desk clerks. Backup phone calls are still made in situations where current information is needed from the maintenance department. The maid or houseman can inform the front desk clerk electronically of room availability status.

The food and beverage department should be informed of guests who have checked out; other departments, such as gift shops, recreational activity centers, and valet service, where guests can incur charges must be notified as well to prevent acceptance of unauthorized guest charges. A system for notifying other departments, perhaps not interfaced in the PMS, of guest checkouts should be a basic operating procedure of the front office.

The entire communication system between the front office and other departments is enhanced when employees care about doing their jobs right. Desk clerks should ensure that rooms showing a ready status are indeed available. Housekeeping personnel must report when rooms are ready to be occupied. Careful screening of job candidates and proper training, which includes an explanation of the importance of maintaining communication with other departments, are vital to smooth operations. When everyone works together, the guest is satisfied, the lodging establishment receives a fair return on its investment, and the employee's career opportunities are enhanced.

Removing Guest Information from the System

In hotels with a PMS, removing guest information requires closing the electronic folio. This deletes the guest name and room number from the electronic guest database and the call-accounting system. These data are stored for future processing by the accounting office (see the following section) as well as the marketing and sales department for developing guest histories (discussed later in the chapter).

Transfer of Guest Accounts to the Back Office

Some methods of payment require transferring folio balances to the back office for further processing. Credit card payments are processed and added to the master credit card account according to type (such as VISA or JCB). The controller maintains this account as accounts receivable. Bill-to-account charges must also be transferred to the back office accounts receivable. The controller processes the account according to standard operating procedures, which are handled electronically in a property management system. The back office transfer option enables the controller or front office staff to transfer accounts that require special handling or adjustments.

Checkout Reports Available with a Property Management System

The front office manager should review and analyze data produced during checkout. Most of this information is financial. The data can be grouped into categories as the front office manager desires; sorting options include method of payment and the respective amount, total room sales, total room count, and total room sales by type. Room status and occupancy availability can also be tracked. The number of guests who actually checked out versus the number who should have checked out can be compared. An analysis of guests who understayed or overstayed their reservations can be made. The reports option of the checkout module in the PMS allows the front office manager, director of marketing and sales, controller, and other department heads to review these statistics. Figures 9-3, 9-4, 9-5, and 9-6 are examples of reports available from this module.

FIGURE 9-3   Method of payment report option of a PMS.

2/15 Method of Payment

Type	Gross	Net
V	$ 456.98	$ 431.56
MC/	598.01	565.20
JCB	4125.73	3202.11
Direct bill	105.34	105.34
Cash	395.91	395.91
TOTALS	$5681.97	$4700.12

FIGURE 9-4   Room sales report option of a PMS.

9/22 Room Sales

Type	Occupied	Available	Sales	Guests
K	35	37	$2698.12	42
KK	50	50	2965.09	65
KS	10	15	1000.54	11
DD	45	50	2258.36	68
TOTALS	140	152	$8922.11	186

FIGURE 9-5   Room status report option of a PMS.

11/1—2:19 P.M. Room Status

DD	K	KK	KS
104 OCC	101 ON CHG	201 ON CHG	108 ON CHG
204 READY	102 ON CHG	202 ON CHG	109 READY
209 READY	103 ON CHG	203 OOO	205 READY
210 ON CHG	105 READY	206 READY	208 READY
211 ON CHG	106 OUT OF ORDR	207 READY	301 OCC
304 ON CHG	107 ON CHG	303 OCC	308 READY
309 READY	302 OCC	307 OCC	
310 READY	305 OUT OF ORDR		
311 READY	306 ON CHG		

FIGURE 9-6	Understay reservation report option of a PMS.				
	Week Beginning: 2/01				
	2/1	2/2	2/3	2/4	2/5
No. reservations	125	54	10	5	2
No. completed	125	50	7	3	1
Variation	0	4	3	2	1
Lost revenue	0	$480	$630	$480	$300
TOTAL LOST SALES:	$1890				

Guest Histories

Guest histories are marketing analyses of guests' geographic and demographic information that also provide information about guest activities while staying at the hotel. This analysis is simplified by the use of a PMS. The guest history option of the checkout module assists the front office manager in preparing reports of such data for the director of marketing and sales. The particulars of guest histories can also be obtained from registration cards, if the hotel still uses them, the electronic folio and the data from the reservation system in the PMS, or the Internet.

ZIP Code or Postal Code

The most useful part of the marketing data is the *ZIP or postal code*, an individual local postal designation assigned by a country. It provides the person who is developing marketing strategies with geographic indicators of populations who have tried the products and services of a particular lodging establishment. This geographic information can be matched with communications media, such as website, radio, television, and newspapers, available in that area and with demographic (age, sex, income, occupation, marital status, etc.) and psychographic (lifestyle) data. Matching website, radio stations, television stations, and newspapers to a group that constitutes the hotel's prime market, as well as developing well-structured direct-mail campaigns, can be a profitable marketing strategy. Defining the market for continued business is part of a sound business plan.

Developing Conventions and Conferences

The front office manager who reviews the registration cards and reservation cards for group affiliations finds data for potential development of guests by the marketing and sales department. Follow-up by the marketing and sales department to representatives of organizations that have stayed in the hotel may lead to the booking of future conventions and conferences.

FIGURE 9-7	Referral sources analysis option of a PMS.	
1/1–6/30 Guest History Analysis of Method of Referral		
Method	No.	%
Direct mail	300	19
Billboard	121	8
Reservation system	420	26
Local referral	89	5
Car radio	35	2
Newspaper	35	2
Website	600	38

The constant demand for meeting facilities does not just happen. Corporate clients that book facility space want to be assured all details will be handled professionally. Trust in a hotel begins with the hotel's establishing a good track record in handling the small details of hospitality—efficiency in processing reservations, registrations, and checkout procedures, and in the maintenance of clean and attractive facilities. This trust (along with a good room rate and adequate meeting space) increases room sales to small conferences.

FAM Tours

The guest history also provides information about the method of advertising that helped secure the reservation and registration (Figure 9-7). If guest histories reveal a large number of reservations originated with a particular travel or tour agency, then the marketing and sales department should maintain a strong relationship with that agency and develop relationships with other agencies within that point of origin as well. *Fam (familiarization) tours*—complimentary visits sponsored by the lodging property that host representatives of travel organizations, bus associations, social and nonprofit organizations, and local corporate traffic managers—can produce an increase in future room revenue. During these tours, representatives can see firsthand what the property has to offer.

Origination of Reservation

A lodging property with a 70 percent corporate client market might also want to review who makes the reservations for these business professionals at the corporate client's office. The administrative assistant, traffic manager, or executive secretary is probably the person who makes the reservations. If this is the case, the lodging establishment should put in place a program that encourages these people to call the lodging establishment for the reservation. Incentive programs that reward those who make a certain number of reservations over a specified period are an example.

Walk-in guests can also provide valuable marketing data. If guests indicate "the bill-board on Route 777N" was the means by which they learned about your hotel, you will have an idea about the cost-effectiveness of this type of advertising. If guests are being referred by the local gasoline station or convenience store, consider providing brochures and other information to these businesses. Perhaps complimentary dinners or escape weekends for the referral source personnel would be effective.

Frequency of Guest Visit

Data from guest histories concerning frequency of visits also reveals areas for follow-up (Figure 9-8). The frequent guest, defined as a person who stays at the establishment more than a specified number of times per month or year, might be offered a free accommodation as either a business or a personal guest. This person and his or her company should be entered into the database for follow-up with advertising promotions designed to attract that market segment.

FIGURE 9-8	Corporate guest data option of a PMS.	
	1/1–1/31 Guest History—Corporate Guest Frequency	
Corporate Guest	**Frequency**	**No. Rooms**
Anderson Corp.	1/4	10
Anderson Corp.	1/7	2
Anderson Corp.	1/15	5
Dentson Co.	1/5	9
Dentson Co.	1/23	1
Hartson College	1/4	16
Montgomery House	1/20	7
Norris Insurance Co.	1/14	50
Norris Insurance Co.	1/15	65
Norris Insurance Co.	1/16	10
Olson Bakery	1/18	10
VIP Corp.	1/2	10
VIP Corp.	1/9	10
VIP Corp.	1/25	14
VIP Corp.	1/26	17
VIP Corp.	1/28	5
VIP Corp.	1/30	23

Types of Room Requested

The guest history is useful in determining the types of rooms requested. Are rooms with two double beds requested more often than rooms with one king-size bed? Are rooms designated as nonsmoking being requested more often than rooms designated as smoking? Are suites with cooking facilities requested by corporate clients for long-term guests? Such hard, quantifiable data are what hotel owners use to make construction and purchasing decisions.

Room Rates versus Occupancy Patterns

Reviewing room rates can assist the controller and director of marketing and sales in forecasting profit-and-loss statements. The frequency with which certain price categories of rooms are rented indicates the price sensitivity of certain market segments. If price sensitivity is an indicator of room occupancy, then marketing programs that maximize profits in that area must be implemented.

Examining occupancy patterns helps the front office manager schedule personnel. In certain corporate market properties, the hotel may be full from Sunday through Thursday nights but nearly empty on Friday and Saturday. A lodging establishment with a large volume of tourist business on weekends experiences the opposite situation. The front office manager should schedule staff accordingly.

The guest history of the PMS checkout module gives the front office manager a sophisticated method of drawing on these data from a database of reservations and registrations. It is easy to group marketing patterns. The concepts already discussed help in developing readily available data.

Tracking Social Media

Application of social media such as LinkedIn, Facebook, Twitter, and Flickr provides an opportunity to capture users' email addresses and personal interests. In addition, if the origin of the hotel reservations from LinkedIn comes from a group of businesspersons within a certain occupational, sporting, or social segment, this may alert the marketing department to develop additional advertising opportunities.

Last Impressions of the Hotel

The front desk staff has the vital responsibility to create the guests' last impression of the hotel. All the great service opportunities afforded the guest throughout his or her stay can be shattered or advanced at the point of departure. Kind words, a speedy checkout, an offer for directions to the airport, and so on all let the guest know you care. For example, Marriott International, Inc., offers At Your Service®, which includes Internet resources for local weather reports, information on airport shuttle, and prior downloading of a future guest's email. All of these services allow guests to prepare for their visit—and, when checkout time arrives, a good opportunity exists for the front office staff to create that last impression that continues the display of hospitality.[2]

Solution to Opening Dilemma

The following list of questions to ask the vendor may help justify the purchase of the guest history PMS:

■ Does this module allow us to track registrations by ZIP code?

■ Can we match ZIP code and media indicated on registration, such as radio, television, newspaper, billboard, third-party website, central reservation, travel agent, and direct mail?

■ Can we print a list of guest business affiliations?

■ Can we print a list of persons who initiate the reservations for corporate clients?

■ Are we able to track frequency of individual guest reservations?

■ Is there a means of showing how many times our suites are rented versus how many times our standard deluxe rooms are rented?

■ Can that list of suite and standard deluxe room rentals be sorted by group, such as corporate, tourist, government, or commercial?

■ Can we track the number of denials we have had to issue because a certain type of room was not available?

■ Does this module show our occupancy patterns by week, month, and year?

■ How can I track social media applications such as LinkedIn, Facebook, Twitter, and Flickr?

Chapter Recap

This chapter introduced the concepts and procedures required to organize and operate a guest checkout system in a hotel. The importance of communicating late charges to the front office and of notifying point-of-sale areas about checkouts was discussed. The procedure for checking out a guest was reviewed, with attention given to the sales and hospitality aspects of the procedure. The chapter emphasized the importance of communication among the housekeeping department, the food and beverage department, and the front office to strengthen service and to ensure the profitability of the lodging property. The guest history, from which guest data are grouped and analyzed, was presented as an important source of marketing feedback.

End-of-Chapter Questions

1. Why should a front office manager be concerned about compiling a guest's late charges? Give an example of losses that can result if late charges go unpaid.

2. Why should a front desk clerk ask a guest who is checking out about the quality of products and services? Who needs this information?

3. Why is the retrieval of a room key so important to the guest? to the hotel?

4. Do you feel a guest should review the guest folio during checkout? Why?

5. If you have used an in-room guest checkout system while you were a guest in a hotel, describe the procedure you followed. Do you feel it was a convenience or a novelty?

6. Discuss the methods of payment available to the guest. Why does the hotel not consider these payment options financially equal?

7. Discuss the types of credit cards. Explain their advantages to the guest and to the hotel.

8. What does *bill-to-account* mean? What are the hidden costs of this method of payment?

9. Why is cash not an eagerly sought method of payment?

10. What is a debit card? How does it differ from a credit card?

11. Summarize the procedures to follow when accepting credit cards, bill-to-accounts, cash, checks, and traveler's checks as methods of payment.

12. A guest wants to pay her account of US$439 in Canadian dollars. How would you proceed?

13. How do you feel about obtaining a reservation at the time of checkout? What steps would you suggest to a front office manager to secure future reservations?

14. Why does the night auditor want all paperwork in order before beginning the night audit?

15. Why must the front office communicate a guest's departure to the point-of-sale areas not interfaced with a PMS?

16. Convert a guest's folio amount from US$395 to euros using an exchange rate of €1.592.

17. What types of guest account are transferred to the back office?

18. List the reports that can be generated by the checkout procedure and explain how they can assist management.

19. Discuss the role of the guest history in developing marketing strategies.

20. How would you suggest using Facebook to supplement guest history tactics in a hotel?

CASE STUDY 901

Margaret Chu, general manager of The Times Hotel, has received a phone call from the Service Feedback Agency, which she employs to provide feedback on customer service. The agent from this service said 6 of 15 former guests indicated a lengthy delay in checkout, the holdup was caused by a desk clerk who repeatedly called for the supervisor to clarify how to operate the PMS. On another point of service, none of the 15 former guests was asked to make a future reservation.

Ms. Chu calls Ana Chavarria, the front office manager, into her office to discuss this report. Ana finds the service feedback report disturbing and promises to rectify the matter. Later that day, she calls Vicente Ramirez, head cashier, into her office. She asks him to write a step-by-step procedure for checking out a guest, with particular attention to use of the PMS. She also calls Angelo DeSalo, head reservation agent, into her office and asks why no future reservations are being requested at the time of checkout. Angelo indicates the desk clerks are busy and just don't have time to request another reservation.

What steps do you think Vicente Ramirez will include in the procedure for checking out a guest? What suggestions can you give Ana Chavarria to motivate her desk clerks to ask for an additional reservation at checkout?

CASE STUDY 902

Margaret Chu, general manager of The Times Hotel, has returned from a meeting of the local hotel association. The head of the state government agency on international tourism made a presentation and asked the attendees to support the state's efforts to secure international visitors to the area. He said recent reports indicate foreign visitors to the state will increase by 25 percent in the next two years. The economic impact of this tourism could mean more than $100 million to the local economy.

Ms. Chu calls her hotel professor friend, Dr. Monica Blair, at the local university and asks if she has a student or two who might want to take on a project of outlining concepts to use in preparing a front desk staff for international visitors. The students would work with Ana Chavarria, front office manager.

Prior to visiting Ms. Chavarria, the students are instructed to prepare an outline focusing on the question "What does the international guest need to know to have a successful visit to our town?"

Help these two students develop a list of questions to ask in their meeting with Ana Chavarria.

CASE STUDY 903

The local hotel association in your area has called on your professor to ask a favor. They are forming a committee on social media and want a few of the professor's top students to serve on the committee. Several of their hotel association members are non-franchise owners of private hotels and do not know how to apply social media concepts such as Facebook, LinkedIn, and Twitter to reservations. There is a meeting in a few days. Provide three examples of how to use these social media to obtain more hotel guests.

Notes

1. Travelers Aid Interational, September, 2009, http://www.travelersaid.org/.

2. John Wolf, "Marriott Launches At Your Service® Pre-Arrival Planning Across Hotels Globally," January 1, 2005, www.hotelonline.com/News/PR2005_ 1stJan05_MarriottAtYourService.htm.

3. Cathy Keefe "New TIA Report Examines Emerging Inbound Markets," Travel Industry Association of America, 1100 New York Avenue, NW, Suite 450, Washington, DC 2005-3934, www.tia.org/Travel. December 2004. http://www. hospitalitynet.org/news/4021634.search?query=tia+report+examines+emerging +inbound+markets.

Key Words

bill-to-account   house limit

debit cards   in-room guest checkout

euro   late charges

FAM (familiarization) tours   money wire

float   traveler's checks

guest histories   ZIP or postal code

Preparation and Review of the Night Audit

OPENING DILEMMA

The front office manager has asked you to train a new night auditor. You are required to prepare an outline of concepts you will use in training. The outline is due tomorrow.

The hotel's financial management starts in the front office. Of course, this responsibility is shared with the controller's office, but it begins with the accurate and timely processing of guest accounts. This chapter addresses the assembling and balancing of all financial transactions in the guest accounts and hotel departments for each day of the year. This can be a time-consuming process for the night auditor, but it provides a balance of debit and credit entries to guest and *departmental accounts*, which include income- and expense-generating areas of the hotel (e.g., restaurants, gift shop, banquets) (Figure 10-1).

Importance of the Night Audit

The *night audit* is the control process whereby the financial activity of guests' accounts is maintained and balanced. This process tracks charges and payments (debits and credits) and the departmental receipts and charges on a daily basis. This working definition encompasses not only the mechanical proofing of charge and payment totals but also the further review of account activity by management. The front office manager monitors the credit activity of guests, projects daily cash flow from room sales, and monitors projected and actual sales for the various departments.

The night auditor provides a financial check on guest folios and departmental activities. Photo courtesy of the author.

Learning the night audit process can provide valuable information for someone who plans to continue in the hotel industry. It also gives the necessary objective overview to evaluate the hotel's financial activity. Students will become aware of the role of the general manager, as the night audit reviews all the financial activity that takes place in a hotel in one day. Based on that review, the general manager must determine how the night audit should be adapted to meet the expenses and profit goals for the accounting period. It also allows the general manager to see if marketing plans and operational activities have accomplished their stated profit goals. The night audit provides insight into how each department must be monitored to produce an acceptable income statement. It pulls together the plans and operations of a hotel every day, not just at the end of an accounting period. Ultimately, the night audit allows general managers to make good financial decisions based on current and cumulative data.

The Night Auditor

The night auditor has many responsibilities in addition to preparing the night audit report. This person also must check in and check out guests who arrive or depart after 11:00 P.M., process reservations, perform the duties of security guard, monitor fire safety systems, act as cashier for banquet functions, and perform the work of manager on duty. The night auditor acts as a communication link between the guest and hotel operations during the 11:00 P.M. to 7:00 A.M. shift. This is an important position.

The Night Audit Process

The night audit is *not* one of those reports that is put on the shelf and forgotten. Management uses it to verify the integrity of the guest accounts and to review *operational effectiveness*, which is the ability of a manager to control costs and meet profit goals. Therefore, accuracy is extremely important. Future hoteliers who want to comprehend the significance of the night audit should participate in the preparation of one. The following discussion of the preparation of the night audit will give you insight into the details of "where the numbers come from."

The six basic steps involved in preparing a night audit are:

1. Posting room and tax charges

2. Assembling guest charges and payments

3. Reconciling departmental financial activities

4. Reconciling the accounts receivable

5. Running the trial balance

6. Preparing the night audit report

This listing will guide you through the seemingly endless proofing of totals and cross-checking of entries, and will expedite the completion of the process.

The process presented in this chapter describes performing the night audit with a property management system. Learning the mechanical or hand method of doing the night audit, however, will help the front office manager understand the intricacies of following a paper trail of guest and departmental transactions. Undoubtedly, the modern method of performing the night audit on a PMS will be used, but you should also be familiar with its components up close and personal.

Posting Room and Tax Charges

After the night auditor reviews messages from other front office staff, reviews guests who checked out of the hotel, extends any guest stays, reviews all room rates, and prints a variance report, his or her first task is to post room and tax charges to all accounts. The PMS can easily post these charges to the electronic folios.

Assembling Guest Charges and Payments

The modules in a PMS (food and beverage, call accounting, gift shop, etc.) allow for ease in assembling guest charges and payments. The following is a typical list of point-of-sale departments for which income is reported:

- Restaurant 1 (breakfast)
- Restaurant 2 (lunch)
- Restaurant 3 (dinner)

- Room service 1 (breakfast)
- Room service 2 (lunch)
- Room service 3 (dinner)

- Lounge 1 (lunch)
- Lounge 2 (happy hour)
- Lounge 3 (dinner)
- Lounge 4 (entertainment)

- Valet
- Telephone
- Gift shop
- Spa and pool
- Parking
- Miscellaneous

Note how the restaurant, room service, and lounge paperwork is further classified by meal or function, to facilitate recordkeeping. General managers can review the income-generation activity of each of these departments when they are reported separately.

The guest charges option of the night audit module in a property management system can sort and total all departmental charges and payments posted to the electronic folios from the point-of-sale systems that interface with the PMS. These data are accurate as long as the person entering the charges at the point-of-sale terminal keys them in accurately.

Reconciling Departmental Financial Activities

The departmental totals option of the night audit module in the PMS report total sales by department, as shown in Figure 10-2. These totals are compared to posting information received from the point-of-sale system.

Another departmental total that must be verified is the cash tendered by guests at the front office. Hotels vary in their cash-processing policies. Some front offices process restaurant guest checks from cash customers or other departments in the hotel because management wants to centralize the cash transactions. In other hotels, this policy would

FIGURE 10-2   The departmental totals option of a **PMS** lists amounts generated by each department. Courtesy of Wyndham Reading Hotel, Reading, Pennsylvania.

Departmental Tools

Department	Amount
Room	
Tax	
Local Telephone	
Long-distance Telephone	
Paid-out	
Beverage	
Write-off Credit	
Restaurant Breakfast	
Restaurant Lunch	
Restaurant Dinner	
Lounge Beer	
Lounge Wine	
Lounge Liquor	
Restaurant Tips	
Restaurant Merchandise	
Restaurant Tax	
Room Service	
Room Service Tips	
Gift Shop	
Movie	
Vending	
Parking	
Dry Cleaning	
Newspaper	
Rollaway	
Gift Certificates	
Copies	
Faxes	
Stamps	
Adv. Deposit Refund	
Banquet Food	
Banquet Beverage	
Banquet Service Charge	
Banquet Wine	
Banquet Liquor	
Banquet Beer	
Banquet Meeting Rooms	
Banquet Tax	
TOTAL	

be a great inconvenience because of the distance of the restaurants, lounges, and gift shops from the front office. It also requires additional personnel to carry the guest checks with the cash or credit cards to the front office.

The cashier option of the night audit module in the PMS reports the amount of cash, credit cards, and coupons received and discounts processed during the shift, as shown in Figure 10-3. The total amount of cash received by each cashier issued a cash drawer must be verified against the total money deposited for that shift.

Reconciling Accounts Receivable

The city ledger is an accounts receivable held at the front office. As noted in chapter 2, the city ledger is a collection of guest accounts of persons who are not registered with the hotel. They have either received approval for direct billing privileges or paid a deposit on a future banquet, meeting, or reception. The night auditor treats these accounts just like the accounts on the guest ledger for registered guests. He or she must assemble the charges and verify their accuracy. The cash received from these accounts is reflected in the cashier's report.

The figures in a city ledger can be quite large. A hotel that promotes direct billing as a customer service may have outstanding guest debit charges of $10,000 to $50,000. The hotel may hold a *credit balance*, amounts of money it owes guests in future services, of $25,000 to $150,000 or more from deposits on future receptions and meeting room rentals. The controller of the hotel must closely watch the balances of these accounts to ensure effective cash flow management.

The *master credit card account*—an account receivable that tracks bank, commercial, private label, and intersell credit cards such as VISA, MasterCard, and JCB—is held at the front office. Depending on the size of the hotel, the services offered to the guest, and the speed of reimbursement from the credit card agency, this figure may also be quite large. It is not uncommon for a medium-size hotel to have an outstanding credit balance

FIGURE 10-3 The cashier's report maintains control of cashier activity. Courtesy of Wyndham Reading Hotel, Reading, Pennsylvania.

Cashier Report

Department	Amount
Front Desk	
Cash Received	
Write-Off	
Travel Agent Commission	
Checks	
Employee Discount Fee	
Credit Card Received	
MasterCard	
VISA	
Diners Club	
JCB	
Hotel Gift Certificate	
Restaurant	
Cash Received	
Credit Card Received	
VISA	
MasterCard	
Diners Club	
JCB	
Gift Certificate Redeemed	
Lounge	
Room Service	
Discounts	
Welcome Discount Coupon	
Banquets	
Cash Received	
Credit Card Received	
VISA	
MasterCard	
Diners Club	
JCB	
Allowances	
Total	
Deposit Summary	
Cash/Foreign Currency	
Other Payment Methods	
Deposits Subtotal	
A/R Total	
Paid Out	
Total Deposit	
Actual Deposit	
Over/Short	

of $30,000 to $50,000 at any one time. As checks are received from the credit card agency, this figure is reduced. It rises again when new charges are posted to a guest's folio. When the checks from the credit card agency are received, they are posted to the respective credit card's account receivable and a current balance is calculated. The city ledger and accounts receivable options of the night audit module of a PMS produce a report of the activity on the city ledger and master credit card accounts.

Running the Trial Balance

A *trial balance* (Figure 10-4) is a first run on a set of debits to determine their accuracy compared to a corresponding set of credits. The trial balance helps the night auditor focus on accounts in which charges may have been posted or reported incorrectly. For

FIGURE 10-4 A trial balance report lists the debit and credit activity of the front desk, receivables, and payables. Courtesy of Wyndham Reading Hotel, Reading, Pennsylvania.

Trial Balance

Front Desk Activity	Amount
Opening Balance	
Total Debits (Room and Tax)	
Total Credits (Various Methods of Payment)	
Deposits Transfer (Payments Collected on Banquets or Room Deposits)	
Closing Balance	

Advance Deposits (Current Amounts in System)	Amount
Opening Balance	
Total Credits	
Applied/Canceled	
Closing Balance	

Receivables	Amount
Opening Balance	
Total Debits (General Ledger Accounts of corporations and individuals)	
Total Credits (Various Methods of Payment)	
Closing Balance	

Payables	Amount
Opening Balance	
Total Debits (Travel Agent Fees Paid by the Hotel)	
Total Credits (Various Methods of Payment)	
Closing Balance	

that reason, it is important that the night auditor compare the departmental totals against transfers and paid-out slips for each department processed by desk clerks and cashiers.

Goal of Preparing the Night Audit Report

Now that all the financial data have been assembled, what do we do with the numbers? Students studying hotel front office management may ask, "Why should the night audit report be prepared?" It generates a massive amount of daily operational financial feedback that provides an immediate opportunity for managers to react and respond. General managers and supervisors must use the information to improve the situations that resulted from their efforts. The night audit report is key in maximizing the efficiency of a hotel. The daily figures regarding room occupancy, yield percentage, average daily rate, and revenue per available room (RevPAR) suggest opportunities to improve a slow sales period. Guests who demand an accurate folio complete with guest charges can be helped more efficiently as a result of this process.

As you begin your career in the hotel industry, take the opportunity to review the financial statistics generated by the night audit report. The result will be a capsule review of the importance of departmental financial activities and their role in delivering hospitality. This background will also give you with insight into the decision-making process, which, in turn, helps hotel departments adhere to their budgets.

Preparing the Night Audit Report

The night audit report is usually organized to meet the needs of a specific lodging establishment. Some general managers might require more financial data than others. Figure 10-5 is a sample of a night audit report of all financial activities of the day. You may want to note the columns headed "Budget" and "Goal." The budget figure is the target amount of sales planned for that day. The goal figure shows what percentage of the budgeted figure was actually achieved. If a larger amount was budgeted than was realized, then some part of the operation is not functioning as expected. Some hotel managers want a cumulative figure reported each day to gain a more comprehensive overview of the achievement of financial goals.

It is important that managers approach this report as a functional tool that provides daily operational financial data. Its major components may seem overwhelming when perceived as a whole. With experience, you learn to view this seemingly complicated document in separate parts, each of which provides feedback on daily operational performance. Daily review of the reported figures allows management the opportunity to be flexible in meeting financial goals.

FIGURE 10-5   Night audit report.

Night Audit	$ Actual	$ Budget	Date _____ Goal (%)
ROOM	4500.00	7500.00	60.00
TAX	450.00	750.00	60.00
Restaurant 1	750.00	825.00	90.91
Restaurant 2	1200.00	1500.00	80.00
Restaurant 3	2000.00	1500.00	133.33
TOTAL REST SALES	3950.00	3825.00	103.27
SALES TAX	197.50	191.25	103.27
Rest Tips 1	112.50	123.75	90.91
Rest Tips 2	180.00	225.00	80.00
Rest Tips 3	300.00	225.00	133.33
TOTAL REST TIPS	592.50	573.75	103.27
Room Srv 1	125.00	350.00	35.71
Room Srv 2	150.00	300.00	50.00
Room Srv 3	300.00	250.00	120.00
TOTAL ROOM SRV	575.00	900.00	63.89
SALES TAX	28.75	45.00	63.89
Room Srv 1 Tips	25.00	70.00	35.71
Room Srv 2 Tips	30.00	60.00	50.00
Room Srv 3 Tips	60.00	50.00	120.00
TOTAL ROOM SRV TIPS	115.00	180.00	63.89
Banq Bkfst	0.00	350.00	0.00
Banq Lunch	200.00	500.00	40.00
Banq Dinner	4300.00	6500.00	66.15
TOTAL BANQ	4500.00	7350.00	61.22
Banq Bkfst Tips	0.00	63.00	0.00
Banq Lunch Tips	36.00	90.00	40.00
Banq Dinner Tips	774.00	1170.00	66.15
TOTAL BANQ TIPS	810.00	1323.00	61.22
Banq Bar Lunch	125.00	200.00	62.50
Banq Bar Dinner	485.00	400.00	121.25
TOTAL BANQ BAR	610.00	600.00	101.67
ROOM RENTAL	200.00	250.00	80.00
Lounge 1	125.00	85.00	147.67
Lounge 2	780.00	950.00	82.11
Lounge 3	500.00	450.00	111.11
Lounge 4	600.00	575.00	104.35
TOTAL LOUNGE SALES	2005.00	2060.00	97.33

(continues)

FIGURE 10-5 (continued)			
Lounge Tips 1	12.50	8.50	147.06
Lounge Tips 2	78.00	95.00	82.11
Lounge Tips 3	50.00	45.00	111.11
Lounge Tips 4	60.00	57.50	104.35
TOTAL LOUNGE TIPS	200.50	206.00	97.33
VALET	350.00	250.00	140.00
Tele Local	110.00	125.00	88.00
Tele Long Distance	295.00	300.00	98.33
TOTAL PHONE	405.00	425.00	95.29
GIFT SHOP	212.00	350.00	60.57
GIFT SHOP SALES TAX	10.60	17.50	60.57
VENDING	125.00	100.00	125.00
SPA	450.00	500.00	90.00
PARKING	500.00	350.00	142.86
TOTAL REVENUE	20,786.85	27,746.50	74.92
Less Paid-outs			
Valet	120.00		
Tips	0.00		
TOTAL PAID-OUTS	120.00		
Less Discounts			
Room	0.00		
Food	25.00		
TOTAL DISCOUNTS	25.00		
Less Write-offs			
Rooms	75.00		
Food	15.00		
TOTAL WRITE-OFFS	90.00		
Total Paid-out and Noncollect Sales	235.00		
Total Cash Sales	4028.45		
Today's Outstd A/R	16,758.40		
Total Revenue	21,021.85		
Yesterday's Outstd A/R	75,985.12		
TOTAL OUTSTD A/R	92,743.52		
CREDIT CARD REC'D A/R	37,500.12		
Cash Rec'd A/R	5390.87		
BAL A/R	49,852.53	75,000.00	66.47

FIGURE 10-5   (continued)

ANALYSIS OF A/R

City Ledger	12,045.15
Direct Bill	3598.55
VISA	19,681.01
MasterCard	13,788.24
JCB	4939.03
Total A/R	54,411.98

BANK DEPOSIT

Cash	9419.32
VISA	22,967.98
MasterCard	11,687.05
JCB	2845.09
TTL BANK DEP	$46,191.44
AMT TR A/R	$16,758.40

ANALYSIS OF BANK DEPOSIT

Total Cash Sales	$4028.45
Credit Card Rec'd A/R	37,500.12
Cash Rec'd A/R	5390.87
	$46,919.44

Cashier's Report

	Actual Amount	POS Amount	Difference
Shift 1			
Cash	$907.25	$907.29	–$0.04
Cr Cd	29,750.67	29,750.67	$0.00
TOTAL 1	$30,657.92	$30,657.96	–$0.04
Shift 2			
Cash	$7884.81	$7883.81	$1.00
Cr Cd	7000.45	7000.45	0.00
TOTAL 2	$14,885.26	$14,884.26	$1.00
Shift 3			
Cash	$628.22	$628.22	$0.00
Cr Cd	749.00	749.00	0.00
TOTAL 3	$1377.22	$1377.22	$0.00
TOTALS	$46,920.40	$46,919.44	$0.96

Analysis Cash Report

Cash Sls	$4028.45
Cr Cd A/R	37,500.12
Cash A/R	5390.87
TOTAL	$46,919.44

(continues)

FIGURE 10-5 (continued)

Manager's Report

	Actual	Budget	Difference
ROOMS AVAIL	100	100	0
ROOMS SOLD	65	85	20
ROOM VAC	30	15	−15
ROOMS OOO	0	0	0
ROOMS COMP	0	0	0
OCC %	65.00%	85.00%	20.00%
DBL OCC %	15.38%	11.76%	−3.62%
YIELD %	52.94%	88.24%	35.30%
REVPAR	$45.00	$75.00	$30.00
ROOM INC	$4500.00	$7500.00	$3000.00
NO. GUESTS	75	95	20
AV. RATE	$69.23	$88.24	$19.01
RACK RATE	$85.00	$85.00	$0.00
NO-SHOWS	3	1	−2

Departmental Totals

Each department in the hotel is required to provide a daily sales report to the front office. These figures are listed and compared to the budget goal. General managers of hotels use these figures to determine the profitability of income-generating departments and the success of marketing programs.

Bank Deposit

Bank deposits are also part of the night audit. In large hotels, bank deposits are made several times a day to satisfy security concerns. The bank deposit includes both cash and credit card deposits. It is important to note that cash, business checks, and checks from credit card companies are received several times throughout the business day. After these are received and recorded, they are turned over to a cashier at the front desk for posting to the corresponding guest or city ledger account.

Accounts Receivable

The accounts receivable is an ongoing listing of outstanding amounts owed to the hotel. As mentioned in chapter 8, these potential sources of revenue are essential to positive cash flow. Managing and updating these accounts by reviewing them daily is a primary responsibility of the controller and general manager.

Cashier's Report

Some hotels run the traditional three shifts (7:00 A.M.–3:00 P.M., 3:00 P.M.–11:00 P.M., and 11:00 P.M.–7:00 A.M.) for cashiers. In larger hotels, several cashiers may work each shift. No matter how many cashiers work per shift, each is responsible for actual cash and credit card payments received; these are compared to PMS totals. The *cashier's report*, discussed earlier in the chapter, lists cashier activity including cash and credit cards and PMS totals; it is an important part of the financial control system of a hotel. The front office manager and the controller review this part of the night audit and look for discrepancies between the actual amount received and the PMS total. They also assess the cashier's accuracy.

Manager's Report

The *manager's report* is a listing of occupancy statistics from the previous day, such as occupancy percentage, yield percentage, average daily rate, RevPAR, and number of guests. Data such as these are necessary for monitoring the operation of a financially viable business. The general manager, controller, front office manager, and director of marketing and sales review these statistics daily.

Formulas for Balancing the Night Audit Report

The following formulas will provide you with an understanding of how to balance the night audit.

Formula to Balance Guest Ledger

total revenue
− **paid-outs and noncollect sales**
= **daily revenue**
− **total cash income**
− **today's outstanding A/R income**
= **0**

Formula to Balance Bank Deposit

total bank deposit
− **total cash sales**
− **credit card received A/R**
− **cash received A/R**
= **0**

Formula to Balance City Ledger

yesterday's outstanding A/R
+ **today's outstanding A/R income**
= **total outstanding A/R**
− **credit card received and applied to A/R**
− **cash received and applied to A/R**
= **balance of A/R**

Room and Tax

The *room sales figure* represents the total of posted daily guest room charges. The night auditor obtains this figure from the PMS by activating the *cumulative total feature*, an electronic feature that adds all posted room rate amounts previously entered into one grand total. This figure is only as accurate as the posting of daily room rates. If a desk clerk transposes figures, then the total room sales amount will be incorrect. Because a large portion of room income is considered profit, management watches this figure closely. The room sales figure is verified by the housekeeping report, which lists the occupancy status of each room according to the housekeeping department. The corresponding tax total is obtained by activating the *tax cumulative total feature*, which adds all posted room tax amounts previously entered into one grand total. This figure is necessary for tax collecting and reporting.

Total Restaurant Sales and Sales Tax

The *total restaurant sales figure* comprises all sales incurred at restaurants or food outlets in the hotel. Restaurant 1 may represent breakfast sales; 2, lunch sales; and 3, dinner sales. Or Restaurant 1 may represent all food sales from Restaurant A; 2, food sales from the pool snack bar; and 3, sales from Restaurant B. These figures are verified against the *daily sales report*, a financial activity report produced by a department in a hotel that reflects daily sales activities with accompanying cash register tapes or point-of-sale audit tapes from each of the restaurants or food outlets. The sales tax figure is also obtained from the daily sales reports.

Tips for Restaurant, Room Service, Banquet, and Lounge Employees

Tips paid out to service employees represent an important control feature. Not only is management required to report this amount to state and federal agencies, but also the tips may be paid out from the desk clerk's cash drawer or the restaurant cash drawer. In any case, tips charged to a guest's account on restaurant guest checks, tips paid immediately to service employees from the desk clerk's cash drawer on paid-out slips, room service guest checks, and charged tips on credit card vouchers are used to verify this total.

Room Service

Some hotels report room service sales as a figure separate from total restaurant sales. If a hotel has organized a special marketing and merchandising campaign to increase room service sales or feels careful monitoring of this potentially profitable service is necessary, the night auditor reports this figure. Room service 1 may represent breakfast sales only; 2, lunch sales; and 3, dinner sales.

Banquet Sales

Hotels with large banquet operations report the banquet sales figure separately from restaurant sales. These figures are a total of the guest checks, which tally the individual banquet charges. The night auditor also checks the daily function sheet to ensure all scheduled functions have been billed.

The general manager can use banquet sales figures to determine how effective the food and beverage manager is in controlling related expenses for this division. Banquet sales also indicate how effective the director of marketing and sales is in generating business. Banquet breakfast, banquet lunch, and banquet dinner figures are reported separately because they provide marketing information on which areas are successful and which could be more successful. The banquet sales figures (and the room sales figure) also provide information on the cash flow activity of the hotel. If the hotel has scheduled $25,000 of banquet business and $25,000 of rooms business for a weekend, it can meet various financial obligations due on Monday, depending on method of payment. The controller therefore watches room and banquet sales closely.

Banquet Bar and Total Lounge Sales

The sales figures for the banquet bar and lounge areas originate from the point-of-sale cash registers. The total sales figures from the outlets that serve alcoholic beverages are reported to the front office on a daily sales report after each shift. Each report is accompanied by the cash register tapes or audit tapes.

Sales figures from the lounges and banquets are reported separately because the food and beverage manager must determine how well cost-control efforts are maintained for that department, and the director of marketing and sales may want to research the success of certain marketing and merchandising campaigns.

Room Rental

The charges for room rental—not guest rooms but rather meeting and function rooms— are reported on special room rental guest checks. The night auditor cross-checks these guest checks against the daily function sheet to be sure the banquet manager charged room rentals to the appropriate guests. It is important to note that guest rooms can also be rented on a half-day rate for business meetings.

This figure is reported separately at hotels that charge fees for the rental of facilities when no food or beverage is ordered. For example, banquet rooms may be rented for seminars, meetings, demonstrations, and shows. Because room rental represents a potentially large profit area (especially during slow banquet sales periods), general managers want to know how effective the marketing and sales department is in maximizing this profit center.

Valet

Many hotels offer dry cleaning and laundry services. This feature must be closely monitored because the hotel pays cash to the off-premises dry cleaner or laundry service when the clothing is returned. These costs, plus a markup for hotel handling charges, are posted to the guests' folios. Some hotels maintain a valet or dry cleaning/laundry journal indicating valet tags, control numbers, processing dates, vendor charges, handling charges, posting activity, daily totals, and the like. Transfer slips are prepared to indicate the charges for valet service. The charges on these transfer slips are then posted to the guests' folios. The total of the transfer slips comprises the valet total for the night audit.

Telephone Charges

After the telephone industry was deregulated in the early 1980s, call accounting became standard practice in hotels. This allowed hotels to set individual *surcharge rates*, or rates for adding service charges for out-of-state long-distance telephone service. The telephone department became a profitable area in the hotel business. Because all phone calls are charged to the guest folio, an accurate accounting of the charges is necessary. In a hotel with a call-accounting system that interfaces with a property management system, this tally is obtained electronically.

Gift Shop Sales and Tax

The hotel gift shop prepares a daily sales report for the front office. Cash register tapes or point-of-sale audit tapes accompany the report. The general manager examines the financial activity of this profit center—another area in which cash flow potential is monitored. Recording the tax collected on gift shop sales and reporting this figure is a necessary accounting procedure.

Vending

Hotels that maintain their own vending machines monitor the daily collection of cash. If a facility has a large number of vending machines, the food and beverage manager assigns one person to collect and count the money and prepare a daily sales report. These reports provide the total sales figure for vending.

Spa

The use of health facilities at a hotel may be provided free to guests. However, other products and services—such as swimsuits, health-related products and equipment, the services of a masseur or masseuse, sports lessons, and rental equipment—are sold. These costs are usually charged to the guest folio. A daily sales report is prepared at each of the health/recreation facilities. Some hotels offer their health/recreation facilities to the general public for a fee. Transfer slips for charges to guest accounts for future billing in the city ledger provide a total against which total spa charges are verified.

Parking

A hotel that offers valet parking or parking spaces to guests and the general public acquires large amounts of cash during a business day. Cash, business checks, and debit and credit card payments are collected throughout the day for general parking, long-term business parking, and parking valet services. Guests in the hotel who are charged for parking services have this amount charged to their accounts. The parking garage manager prepares a daily report of the cash and charge activities for each shift. Supporting documentation, including parking tickets, cash register tapes, transfer slips, and monthly parking permit renewals, accompany the daily report. The night auditor prepares a summary total of this account from these reports.

Total Revenue and Total Write-Offs

The total revenue and total write-off figures represent all the cash and charge transactions for the day, reflecting all the previously reported figures. General managers compare the actual and budgeted figures to determine how well operations have met the financial goals of the hotel.

Throughout the business day, the front office manager authorizes paid-out slips (for valet service, tips, supplies, and the like), discounts (for rooms or restaurant charges, for example), and adjustments (room, telephone, and restaurant, for example) in the form of write-offs to guest accounts. The general manager maintains strict control over these figures. These amounts are verified with authorized paid-out slips and transfer slips.

Cash Sales and Accounts Receivable Balance

The total revenue represents both cash and charge guest sales. A separate figure is reported for total cash sales for the day. This figure represents the totals reported and received from the departmental daily reports and is required to justify the daily bank deposit.

Charge sales are reflected in the outstanding accounts receivable (Today's Outstd A/R). This is the amount that remains to be received from guests. Total paid-outs, total discounts, and total write-offs are subtracted from that figure. Today's outstanding accounts receivable figure is added to yesterday's outstanding accounts receivable (Yesterday's Outstd A/R) to obtain a cumulative balance of outstanding accounts receivable (Total Outstd A/R).

Credit Cards and Cash Applied to Accounts Receivable

Throughout the business day, the controller requests front desk clerks or cashiers to post business checks and cash received from credit card companies, direct billing accounts, and city ledger accounts. The charges from these groups were previously moved to accounts receivable. The checks and cash payments represent charges from previously held banquets, guest room rentals, and the like. The general manager of the hotel watches this figure to determine cash flow activity. Again, the outstanding balance of accounts receivable is updated.

Analysis of Accounts Receivable

The front office manager maintains an analysis of the accounts receivable balance that indicates the source of each account receivable—city ledger, direct billing, or various credit cards. (It is important to note here that city ledger accounts may have a credit balance but are maintained as an account receivable. For example, if a guest pays a $500 deposit on a future banquet, a credit balance is maintained on the account. When this credit balance is computed with other debit balances, a debit balance is realized.) The controller uses this information to track the *aging of accounts*, or the stage of the payment—such as 10 days old, 30 days overdue, 60 days overdue—and to operate an overdue payment collection program.

Bank Deposit and Amount Transferred to Accounts Receivable

The cash, credit card vouchers, and charges received during the business day from cash, charge, and accounts receivable transactions must be deposited in the hotel's bank accounts or transferred to the hotel's internal accounts receivable. The night auditor provides a summary of the components of the bank deposit. Bank deposits are made throughout the business day. Those individual totals make up the total bank deposit (TTL BANK DEP). Credit card totals are listed here because, in some circumstances, the credit card voucher is considered cash at the time of deposit. The cash and credit card totals deposited must match the total cash sales plus the cash received and applied to outstanding accounts receivable (Cash Rec'd A/R) minus total paid-outs. The total actual cash and credit card payments received, which are reported on the cashier's report, match the total bank deposit figure. The amount transferred to accounts receivable (AMT TR A/R) corresponds to today's outstanding accounts receivable (Today's Outstd A/R).

Cashier's Report

In hotels where the front desk clerk or cashier is responsible for proofing and collecting the departmental daily reports, the cash and credit card vouchers are added to the individual cashier's shift report. Also included in that report are the amounts of cash and credit card transactions received for application to accounts receivable. Each cashier's shift report is verified by departmental daily reports, cash and credit card vouchers, and accounts receivable cash and credit card transactions. These figures must be verified in the daily bank deposit.

The cashier's report also notes variances between actual totals and PMS totals. Usually, the hotel sets a policy regarding the liability of the front desk clerk or cashier for these variances. For example, if the actual amount collected is one cent to one dollar less than the amount obtained in the cashier's report, the front desk clerk or cashier is not liable for the difference. The front office manager should investigate amounts significantly larger than one dollar to see if such losses occur regularly. When the actual amount collected is more than the amount obtained in the cashier's report, the extra money is maintained in a house fund to compensate for undercollections. These amounts should also be investigated as to regularity and source. Substantial overages and shortages must be investigated for proper debiting and crediting of a guest's account.

Operating Statistics

The night auditor prepares the daily operating statistics for the general manager and the department directors. This summary reviews the day's activities and the hotel's success in meeting financial budget targets. Hotel general managers rely on these statistics as operational feedback mechanisms because they provide information on the need to modify existing operational procedures and offer insight into budgeting for future operational procedures. These figures become part of the hotel's historical operations record.

The rooms sold, rooms vacant, and rooms out of order are determined by assessing the housekeeping module (Figure 4-17) and the housekeeper's report (Figure 10-6). The number of complimentary rooms (rooms comp) is determined by reviewing guest reservations, registration cards, and electronic folios. A quick method used to determine occupancy percentage, double occupancy percentage, yield, average daily rate, and RevPAR is shown in Figure 10-7.

FRONT-LINE REALITIES

The PMS is down, and the night audit report must be prepared. How would you suggest the night auditor proceed?

FIGURE 10-6	The housekeeper's report verifies the number of rooms occupied on a particular night.

Housekeeper's Report   Date _____

Room	Status	Room	Status	Room	Status
101	O	134	OOO	167	V
102	O	135	O	168	O
103	O	136	V	169	O
104	O	137	V	170	O
105	V	138	O	171	O
106	V	139	O	172	O
107	O	140	V	173	O
108	O	141	O	174	O
109	O	142	O	175	O
110	O	143	O	176	O
111	O	144	OOO	177	OOO
112	O	145	OOO	178	OOO
113	O	146	O	179	O
114	O	147	O	180	O
115	O	148	V	181	V
116	V	149	V	182	O
117	O	150	O	183	O
118	O	151	O	184	O
119	O	152	O	185	O
120	O	153	O	186	O
121	V	154	O	187	V
122	V	155	V	188	V
123	V	156	V	189	V
124	O	157	O	190	O
125	O	158	O	191	V
126	O	159	O	192	V
127	O	160	V	193	O
128	O	161	V	194	V
129	O	162	V	195	O
130	O	163	O	196	V
131	O	164	O	197	O
132	O	165	O	198	V
133	V	166	V	199	V
				200	V

O: Occupied   V: Vacant   OOO: Out of order

FIGURE 10-7	These formulas offer an easy method for determining operating statistics.

Statistic	Method
Occupancy percentage	$\dfrac{\text{number of rooms sold}}{\text{number of rooms available}} \times 100$
Double occupancy percentage	$\dfrac{\text{number of guest} - \text{number of rooms sold}}{\text{number of rooms sold}} \times 100$
Yield	$\dfrac{\text{number of rooms sold} \times \text{average daily rate}}{\text{number of rooms available} \times \text{rack rate}} \times 100$
Average daily rate	$\dfrac{\text{room income}}{\text{number of rooms sold}}$
RevPAR	$\dfrac{\text{room revenue}}{\text{number of available rooms}}$ or hotel occupancy percentage $\times$ average daily rate

Room income for the day is obtained from the total room charges posted after a certain time in the evening (between 11:00 P.M. and midnight) and any half-day rate charges. The number of guests is provided by the PMS registration module. The number of no-shows is compiled by tallying the number of reservations with a confirmed no-show status. Not included in this figure are guaranteed reservations, which are processed with a credit card number regardless of whether the guest showed.

The preparation of a night audit report can be time-consuming. However, with a great deal of cooperation, planning, and organization, combined with the use of a PMS that interfaces with point-of-sale systems, the time can be greatly reduced. The accurate preparation of the night audit report yields an essential control and communication tool for management.

Daily Flash Report

The *daily flash report*, a PMS listing of departmental totals by day, period to date, and year to date, is useful to general managers and to department managers and supervisors. This report is reviewed daily to indicate how successful a department manager was in achieving sales the previous day. This tool is important in discussing strategies for the successful achievement of financial goals. Figure 10-8 illustrates the major components of a flash report.

FIGURE 10-8   **The daily flash report is reviewed each morning by the general manager and various department managers to determine the financial success of the previous day and current status in achieving other financial goals. Courtesy of The Abraham Lincoln - A Wyndham Historic Hotel, Reading, Pennsylvania.**

Daily Flash Report   Date _____

	Daily Totals	Period to Date	Year to Date
Revenue Types			
Room			
Telephone			
Food & Beverage			
Selected Departmental Totals			
Restaurant Breakfast			
Restaurant Lunch			
Restaurant Dinner			
Lounge Beer			
Lounge Wine			
Lounge Liquor			
Banquet Food			
Banquet Beverage			
Banquet Wine			
Banquet Liquor			
Banquet Beer			
Occupancy Totals			
Total Rooms			
Occupied Rooms			
Single Rooms			
Double/Plus Rooms			
Complimentary Rooms			
Day Rooms			
Group Rooms			
Transient Rooms			
OOO Rooms			
Occupancy %			
Average Daily Rate			
RevPAR			
Yield			
Arrivals			
Departures			
Stayovers			
6 P.M. No-shows			
Guar No-shows			
Walk-ins			
Arrivals Canceled			
Reservations Taken			
Reservations Canceled			

Reading the Flash Report

Here are insights into reading the Flash Report.

Room Sales—The general manager tracks these figures because they are the major source of income for the hotel. Because room sales provide the most profit, this is an important figure to watch daily. Marketing and sales also wants to know this figure, as does the front office manager.

Selected Departmental Totals for Food and Beverage—These figures are a primary concern for the general manager as he or she evaluates the effectiveness of the food and beverage manager and his or her staff. It is important to do this daily rather than weekly or monthly.

Occupancy Totals—These figures provide the general manager, front office manager, and marketing and sales personnel with feedback on the effectiveness of advertising in influencing patronage to the hotel. They provide bottom-line financial details of what works and what doesn't with regard to online and print-based ads, cold calls, and so on. When the daily totals fall below the projected figures, a group effort is needed to determine what steps should be taken to revitalize marketing.

Answering these questions may explain low occupancy: Why are OOO (out-of-order rooms) at such a high number? Did that have an effect on the low occupancy? Did the low arrival figure occur because of airline problems? Was the low yield caused by a group failing to meet its room quota? Are we not asking for credit cards to guarantee a room reservation? Experience in the hotel industry provides many opportunities for future hoteliers to gain insight by asking questions such as these.

When these questions arise, the general manager follows up with inquiries to the relevant departmental supervisor, such as the director of maintenance (rooms OOO); front office manager (airlines); marketing and sales manager (group room quota); and front office manager (reservations without credit card).

Reading the Night Audit

Here are insights into reading the Night Audit.

Room Sales—Check the budgeted and actual figures to determine if the sales efforts for the previous day were productive. If not, hold a brief meeting with the marketing and sales department to determine which strategies worked and which did not. Include the revenue manager in the discussion to provide feedback on rates and channels.

Restaurant Sales—Review the individual meal periods and determine if they met their goals. If the numbers are not up to the goal, ask the supervisor what factors (weather, quality of food, quality of service, competition, etc.) could have caused these results.

Room Service—Because this is a profitable area for the hotel, it should be reviewed carefully. Review the actual and budgeted numbers and determine what caused the difference. Perhaps room service should be actively marketed, compared to the silent marketing of a menu placed in the guest's room.

Banquet Sales—Again, this is a large profit producer for the hotel. However, this type of activity is planned many days and weeks in advance and should be reviewed accordingly. Sometimes unexpected events such as weather or mishap can occur that cause a cancellation. Management should also look at which type of meal is producing or not producing income. For example, if all the banquet income is coming from lunches, then there are opportunities for banquet sales in breakfast and dinner.

Banquet Bar Sales—Bar sales for lunch and dinner provide additional profit for the hotel. These too should be monitored as an opportunity for their inclusion in the meal occasion.

Room Rental—Room rental provides income for the hotel to pay heating, lighting, air conditioning, and other utilities. Therefore, every opportunity should be made to charge and collect this fee.

Lounge Sales—Lounges throughout the hotel are assigned a goal for the night, depending on their market. The general manager compares the actual with budget to determine if the staff at the lounge has done its job. If not, then a discussion should be held with the supervisor of the lounge and director of food and beverage.

Valet—This service is handled outside the hotel, and a fee is added to the guest's bill. This fee is basically profit for the hotel. The general manager should work with the front office manager to develop a marketing plan that ensures front desk staff promote this service to guests.

Telephone—Telephone charges are usually electronically posted to the guest's folio with the call-accounting module of the PMS. This figure allows the general manager to see how many dollars are collected. With the increased availability of high-speed Internet access in guest rooms, this dollar figure is worth watching because of the dollar investment in technology.

Gift Shop—When the gift shop is outsourced by the hotel to a third party, the hotel collects a certain percentage of the total gross sales. The general manager wants to know what gross sales are on this report. If the gift shop is operated by the hotel, the general manager wants to compare actual and budgeted sales and discuss marketing efforts with the gift shop manager.

Vending—If vending is outsourced, then the sales agreement that covers a daily, semiweekly, or weekly deposit is listed here. If vending is operated by the hotel, then the daily cash deposit is listed here. This is an easy target for theft, so the general manager must keep a close eye on the total produced by the vending machines in the hotel.

Spa—If the hotel spa is outsourced, the hotel collects a percentage of the total gross sales. The general manager tracks gross sales on this report. If the spa is operated by the hotel, then the general manager compares actual and budgeted sales and discusses marketing efforts with the spa's manager.

Parking—If the parking lot or parking deck is outsourced by the hotel to a third party, the hotel collects a certain percentage of the total gross sales. The general manager tracks gross sales on this report. If the parking garage is operated by the hotel, then the general manager compares actual and budgeted sales and discusses marketing efforts with the parking garage manager. Parking lots are expensive to operate, but they can also bring in money to the hotel.

Total Paid-Outs—This figure is usually low because not many people are authorized to receive money from the front desk clerk for emergency cash. Large amounts listed here on the night audit would indicate a problem!

Total Discounts—Some hotels have a 100 percent satisfaction pledge, and if this is the policy, discounts would be evident here. If the restaurant had to credit a guest's check for food, that too would be shown. Mistakes do occur, and they must be justified to provide feedback.

Total Write-Offs—This section of the night audit is reserved for writing off accounts (rooms and food) not being paid for by guests. These are usually guests of the hotel.

Total Paid-Out and Noncollect Sales—This is a total of total paid-outs, total discounts, and total write-offs; general managers must control this item so it doesn't get out of line.

Total Cash Sales—This figure represents non-credit sales. Usually it is low because the hotel operates mainly in credit sales. A high cash figure may be a red flag about guests who are paying cash and have not established creditworthiness and raise concerns about potential security problems for the hotel.

Today's Outstanding Accounts Receivable—This is the amount charged by guests on their folio from all departments.

Total Revenue—This figure is the total of all cash sales and charge sales for the day.

Yesterday's Outstanding Accounts Receivable—This number is large because of the delay in receiving actual funds from credit card companies. For example, when a guest charges a room-night on a credit card, there may be a five-day delay before the actual check or electronic payment clears the hotel's bank account. Until the time of the clearing, the controller maintains the balance of that guest's folio as outstanding. As a note of precaution, it must be monitored by the controller's staff to be sure the accounts are aged, especially those house accounts tended by in-house staff.

Total Outstanding Accounts Receivable—This is the sum of Today's and Yesterday's Outstanding Accounting Receivable. Again, this is a large number.

Credit Card Received Accounts Receivable—This figure tells the general manager how much money was applied to credit card balances and received in checks from credit card companies. Farther down on the page (Bank Deposit), an analysis indicates the credit cards to which this total was applied. As a control procedure, received checks are logged in by one person and then forwarded to a different staff person for deposit.

Cash Received Accounts Receivable—This figure represents cash received for application to credit card balances, etc.

Balance Accounts Receivable—This figure is the total of outstanding accounts receivable to the hotel—city ledger, direct bill, and credit cards. This figure is analyzed under Analysis of Accounts Receivable. These two totals must match.

Bank Deposit—This is a listing of cash and credit card deposits. The figure must match the Credit Card Received Accounts Receivable; this is a control feature. The accompanying Analysis of Bank Deposit provides the general manager with an overview of the sources of the funds deposited. Keep in mind that credit card sales do carry a discount fee and that this adds up over time.

Cashier's Report—This control report is included in the night audit to verify the totals of each cashier for cash sales, credit card sales, and sales applied to accounts receivable. The accompanying Analysis Cash Report summarizes these three areas. The totals must match the totals of each shift.

Manager's Report—This is a useful report for the general manger because it provides an overview of the staff's financial efforts of the previous day. This quick look or comparison of actual versus budgeted figures is also helpful for departmental managers.

Solution to Opening Dilemma

It is important to prepare a training outline that maximizes the front office manager's efforts to train the night auditor. The session can begin by explaining the objective of the night audit—which is to evaluate the hotel's financial activity—and that the night audit process monitors departmental financial activity. The outline should cover the major concepts of posting room and tax charges, assembling guest charges and payments, reconciling departmental financial activities, reconciling the accounts receivable, running the trial balance, and preparing the night audit report. The front office manager should explain the formulas used to balance the night audit: formula to balance guest ledger, formula to balance city ledger, and formula to balance bank deposit, as well as formulas to compute operating statistics. The night auditor must also know how to perform the duties of a front desk clerk—reservations, registrations, postings, and checkout.

Chapter Recap

This chapter demonstrated the importance of producing an accurate summary of the financial transactions that occur in a hotel on any given day. The components of the night audit were listed and described. These include posting room and tax charges, assembling guest charges and payments, reconciling departmental financial activities, reconciling the accounts receivable, running the trial balance, and preparing the night audit report. Also, the preparation of a night audit report and manager's report were illustrated, as was the daily flash report, and their management implications were discussed. The accurate preparation of the night audit report and follow-up on the data assembled allow the hotel's management team to adjust financial plans. A summary was offered of how to interpret the major components of the night audit.

End-of-Chapter Questions

1. Why does a hotel need to balance its financial transactions each day?

2. What is the night audit? What steps are involved in preparing it?

3. What is the manager's report? What does each statistic tell the general manager?

4. Why must the night audit be prepared systematically?

5. What is a trial balance? What information does it provide the night auditor?

6. Why must accounts receivable be included in the night audit? What do the accounts receivable comprise?

7. Discuss the importance of the night audit to the daily management of a hotel. Who reviews the night audit? Why would they be interested in these financial data?

8. If you were reading the night audit, which figure would assist you in determining whether or not the restaurant managers met their sales goals? How would you know the amount of money paid out on behalf of the food and beverage department on the previous day for miscellaneous grocery purchases? How would you know what total amount of money guests charged to their room folios yesterday? What figures represent the Total Outstanding Accounts Receivable?

9. Why should the accounts receivable be analyzed?

10. Why should the bank deposit and amount transferred to accounts receivable be listed on the night audit? What does each figure represent?

11. How can the front office manager control the cash in the front office cash drawer?

12. Assist the night auditor in preparing the operating statistics from the night of October 14: $20,000 room income; 306 rooms available; 211 room sold; 265 guests; and rack rate $147.

    a) occupancy percentage
    b) average daily rate
    c) RevPAR
    d) yield

13. Assist the night auditor in preparing the operating statistics from the night of October 15: $32,000 room income; 306 rooms available; 280 rooms sold; 300 guests; and rack rate $147.

   a) occupancy percentage
   b) average daily rate
   c) RevPAR
   d) yield

14. Assist the night auditor in preparing the operating statistics from the night of October 16: $38,350 room income; 306 rooms available; 295 rooms sold; 409 guests; and rack rate $147.

   a) occupancy percentage
   b) average daily rate
   c) RevPAR
   d) yield

15. Why is it important to prepare hotel operating statistics?

16. What use is the daily flash report to a general manager? to a front desk manager? to a food and beverage manager?

CASE STUDY 1001

The Times Hotel has collected the following data, which represent the financial transactions in the hotel today. Assemble this information into a night audit report, using the format shown in Figure 10-9 (a blank worksheet for you to fill in, which follows the data).

DEPARTMENTAL DAILY SALES REPORT

DATE _____

	$ Actual	$ Budget	Goal (%)
Restaurant 1	299.57	825.00	
Restaurant 2	500.00	1500.00	
Restaurant 3	1200.00	1500.00	
SALES TAX (rate = 5%)			
Rest Tips 1	45.00	123.75	
Rest Tips 2	75.00	225.00	
Rest Tips 3	180.00	225.00	
REST TIPS (rate = 15%)			
Room Srv 1	45.00	350.00	
Room Srv 2	200.00	300.00	
Room Srv 3	135.95	250.00	

CASE STUDY 1001

	$ Actual	$ Budget	Goal (%)
SALES TAX (rate = 5%)			
Room Srv 1 Tips	9.00	70.00	
Room Srv 2 Tips	40.00	60.00	
Room Srv 3 Tips	27.19	50.00	
ROOM SRV TIPS (rate = 20%)			
Banq Bkfst	0.00	350.00	
Banq Lunch	675.00	500.00	
Banq Dinner	3021.45	6500.00	
Banq Bkfst Tips	0.00	63.00	
Banq Lunch Tips	121.50	90.00	
Banq Dinner Tips	543.86	1170.00	
BANQ TIPS (rate = 18%)			
Banq Bar Lunch	85.00	200.00	
Banq Bar Dinner	587.25	400.00	
ROOM RENTAL	100.00	250.00	
Lounge 1	165.00	85.00	
Lounge 2	346.75	950.00	
Lounge 3	295.00	50.00	
Lounge 4	420.00	575.00	
Lounge Tips 1	16.50	8.50	
Lounge Tips 2	34.68	95.00	
Lounge Tips 3	29.50	45.00	
Lounge Tips 4	42.00	57.50	
LOUNGE TIPS (rate = 10%)			
VALET	45.00	250.00	
Tele Local	125.00	125.00	
Tele Long Dist	87.90	300.00	
GIFT SHOP	150.68	350.00	
SALES TAX (rate = 5%)	7.53	17.50	
VENDING	86.25	100.00	
SPA	211.00	500.00	
PARKING	397.50	350.00	
Paid-outs			
Valet	85.00		
Tips	0.00		
Discounts			
Room	0.00		
Food	15.00		

(continues)

CASE STUDY 1001 (CONTINUED)

	$ Actual	$ Budget	Goal (%)
Write-offs			
Rooms	0.00		
Food	122.89		
Total Cash Sales	2906.98		
Today's Outstd A/R	12,513.56		
Yesterday's Outstd A/R	43,900.11		
CREDIT CARD REC'D A/R	7034.76		
CASH REC'D A/R	2098.63		
BAL A/R	47,279.76	75,000.00	
ANALYSIS OF A/R			
City Ledger	3078.00		
Direct Bill	5901.00		
VISA	15,623.01		
MasterCard	15,540.45		
JCB	7137.30		
BANK DEPOSIT			
Cash	$5005.61		
VISA	$3532.98		
MasterCard	$1656.69		
JCB	$1845.09		

Cashier's Report

	Actual Amount	POS Amount	Difference
Shift 1			
Cash	$3754.21	$3755.21	
Cr Cd	5276.07	5276.07	
TOTAL 1	$9030.28	$9031.28	
Shift 2			
Cash	$1001.12	$1002.50	
Cr Cd	$1406.95	1406.95	
TOTAL 2	$2408.07	$2409.45	
Shift 3			
Cash	$250.28	$250.28	
Cr Cd	$351.74	$351.74	
TOTAL 3	$602.02	$602.02	
TOTALS	$12,040.37	$12,042.75	
Analysis Cash Report			
Cash Sls.	$2906.98		
Cr Cd A/R	7034.76		
Cash A/R	2098.63		
TOTAL	$12,040.37		

CASE STUDY 1001 (CONTINUED)

Manager's Report

	Actual	Budget	Difference
ROOMS AVAIL	125	125	0
ROOMS SOLD	60	85	25
ROOMS VAC	65	40	−25
ROOMS OOO	0	0	0
ROOMS COMP	0	0	0
ROOM INCOME	$4500.00	$7500.00	$3000.00
ROOM TAX	$450.00	$750.00	$300.00
NO. GUESTS	93	95	2
RACK RATE	$80.00	$80.00	$0.00
NO-SHOWS	1	1	0

BANK DEPOSIT		ANALYSIS OF BANK DEPOSIT	
Cash	$5005.61		
VISA	$3532.98	Total Cash Sales	$2906.98
MasterCard	$1656.69	Credit Card Rec'd A/R	7034.76
JCB	$1845.09	Cash Rec'd A/R	2098.63
			$12,040.37

FIGURE 10-9   Times Hotel night audit.

Night Audit   Date _____

	$ Actual	$ Budget	Goal (%)
ROOM	_____	7500.00	_____
TAX	_____	750.00	_____
Restaurant 1	_____	825.00	_____
Restaurant 2	_____	1500.00	_____
Restaurant 3	_____	1500.00	_____
TOTAL REST SALES	_____	3825.00	_____
SALES TAX	_____	191.25	_____
Rest Tips 1	_____	123.75	_____
Rest Tips 2	_____	225.00	_____
Rest Tips 3	_____	225.00	_____
TOTAL REST TIPS	_____	573.75	_____
Room Srv 1	_____	350.00	_____
Room Srv 2	_____	300.00	_____
Room Srv 3	_____	250.00	_____
TOTAL ROOM SRV	_____	900.00	_____

(*continues*)

FIGURE 10-9 (continued)

	$ Actual	$ Budget	Goal (%)
SALES TAX		45.00	
Room Srv 1 Tips		70.00	
Room Srv 2 Tips		60.00	
Room Srv 3 Tips		50.00	
TOTAL ROOM SRV TIPS		180.00	
Banq Bkfst		350.00	
Banq Lunch		500.00	
Banq Dinner		6500.00	
TOTAL BANQ		7350.00	
Banq Bkfst Tips		63.00	
Banq Lunch Tips		90.00	
Banq Dinner Tips		1170.00	
TOTAL BANQ TIPS		1323.00	
Banq Bar Lunch		200.00	
Banq Bar Dinner		400.00	
TOTAL BANQ BAR		600.00	
ROOM RENTAL		250.00	
Lounge 1		85.00	
Lounge 2		950.00	
Lounge 3		450.00	
Lounge 4		575.00	
TOTAL LOUNGE SALES		2060.00	
Lounge Tips 1		8.50	
Lounge Tips 2		95.00	
Lounge Tips 3		45.00	
Lounge Tips 4		57.50	
TOTAL LOUNGE TIPS		206.00	
VALET		250.00	
Tele Local		125.00	
Tele Long Distance		300.00	
TOTAL PHONE		425.00	
GIFT SHOP		350.00	
GIFT SHOP SALES TAX		17.50	
VENDING		100.00	
SPA		500.00	
PARKING		350.00	
TOTAL REVENUE		27,746.50	
Less Paid-outs			
Valet			
Tips			
TOTAL PAID-OUTS			

FIGURE 10-9   (continued)

	$ Actual	$ Budget	Goal (%)
Less Discounts			
Room			
Food			
TOTAL DISCOUNTS			
Less Write-offs			
Rooms			
Food			
TOTAL WRITE-OFFS			
Total Paid-out and Noncollect Sales			
Total Cash Sales			
Today's Outstd A/R			
Total Revenue			
Yesterday's Outstd A/R			
TOTAL OUTSTD A/R			
CREDIT CARD REC'D A/R			
Cash Rec'd A/R			
BAL A/R		75,000.00	
ANALYSIS OF A/R			
City Ledger			
Direct Bill			
VISA			
MasterCard			
JCB			
Total A/R			

BANK DEPOSIT

		ANALYSIS OF BANK DEPOSIT	
Cash		Total Cash Sales	
VISA		Credit Card Rec'd A/R	
MasterCard		Cash Rec'd A/R	
JCB			
TTL BANK DEP			
AMT TR A/R			

Cashier's Report

	Actual Amount	POS Amount	Difference
Shift 1			
Cash			
Cr Cd			
TOTAL 1			
Shift 2			
Cash			
Cr Cd			
TOTAL 2			

(continues)

FIGURE 10-9 (continued)

Cashier's Report

	Actual Amount	POS Amount	Difference
Shift 3			
Cash	_____	_____	_____
Cr Cd	_____	_____	_____
TOTAL 3	_____	_____	_____
TOTALS	_____	_____	_____

Analysis Cash Report

Cash Sls	_____		
Cr Cd A/R	_____		
Cash A/R	_____		
TOTAL	_____		

Manager's Report

	Actual	Budget	Difference
ROOMS AVAIL	_____	_____	_____
ROOMS SOLD	_____	_____	_____
ROOM VAC	_____	_____	_____
ROOMS OOO	_____	_____	_____
ROOMS COMP	_____	_____	_____
OCC %	_____	_____	_____
DBL OCC %	_____	_____	_____
YIELD %	_____	_____	_____
REVPAR	_____	_____	_____
ROOM INC	_____	_____	_____
NO. GUESTS	_____	_____	_____
AV. RATE	_____	_____	_____
RACK RATE	_____	_____	_____
NO-SHOWS	_____	_____	_____

CASE STUDY 1002

The Barrington Hotel has collected the following data, which represent the financial transactions in the hotel today. Assemble this information into a night audit report, using the format shown in Figure 10-10 (a blank worksheet for you to fill in, which follows the data).

DEPARTMENTAL DAILY SALES REPORT

DATE _____

	$ Actual	$ Budget	Goal (%)
Restaurant 1	500.00	475.00	
Restaurant 2	650.00	755.00	

CASE STUDY 1002 (*CONTINUED*)

	$ Actual	$ Budget	Goal (%)
Restaurant 3	1905.00	2100.00	
SALES TAX (rate = 5%)			
Rest Tips 1	75.00	71.25	
Rest Tips 2	97.50	113.25	
Rest Tips 3	285.75	315.00	
REST TIPS (rate = 15%)			
Room Srv 1	235.00	300.00	
Room Srv 2	120.00	250.00	
Room Srv 3	458.00	700.00	
SALES TAX (rate = 5%)			
Room Srv 1 Tips	47.00	60.00	
Room Srv 2 Tips	24.00	50.00	
Room Srv 3 Tips	91.60	140.00	
ROOM SRV TIPS (rate = 20%)			
Banq Bkfst	579.00	250.00	
Banq Lunch	2458.00	3500.00	
Banq Dinner	5091.00	7250.00	
Banq Bkfst Tips	104.22	45.00	
Banq Lunch Tips	442.44	630.00	
Banq Dinner Tips	916.38	1305.00	
BANQ TIPS (rate = 18%)			
Banq Bar Lunch	326.00	450.00	
Banq Bar Dinner	2987.50	3950.00	
ROOM RENTAL	725.00	1000.00	
Lounge 1	350.00	400.00	
Lounge 2	2104.00	2000.00	
Lounge 3	581.00	675.00	
Lounge 4	695.50	850.00	
Lounge Tips 1	35.00	40.00	
Lounge Tips 2	210.40	200.00	
Lounge Tips 3	58.10	67.50	
Lounge Tips 4	69.55	85.00	
LOUNGE TIPS (rate = 10%)			
VALET	210.00	350.00	
Tele Local	68.00	125.00	
Tele Long Dist	201.00	300.00	
GIFT SHOP	277.00	450.00	
SALES TAX (rate = 5%)	13.85	22.50	

(*continues*)

CASE STUDY 1002 (CONTINUED)

	$ Actual	$ Budget	Goal (%)
VENDING	121.00	100.00	
SPA	293.00	500.00	
PARKING	417.00	350.00	
Paid-outs			
Valet	132.00		
Tips	0.00		
Discounts			
Room	0.00		
Food	32.00		
Write-offs			
Rooms	0.00		
Food	87.97		
Total Cash Sales	2906.98		
Today's Outstd A/R	28,259.21		
Yesterday's Outstd A/R	57,880.11		
CREDIT CARD REC'D A/R 1	2091.50		
CASH REC'D A/R	322.65		
BAL A/R	70,525.17	80,000.00	
ANALYSIS OF A/R			
City Ledger	13,278.00		
Direct Bill	15,999.00		
VISA	25,623.01		
MasterCard	11,487.34		
JCB	4137.82		

BANK DEPOSIT		**ANALYSIS OF BANK DEPOSIT**	
Cash	$6429.63	Total Cash Sales	$2906.98
VISA	$7509.34	Credit Card Rec'd A/R	12,091.50
MasterCard	$2828.00	Cash Rec'd A/R	3522.65
JCB	$1754.16		
			$18,521.13

Cashier's Report

	Actual Amount	POS Amount	Difference
Shift 1			
Cash	$4822.22	$4822.50	
Cr Cd	9068.63	9068.63	
TOTAL 1	$13,890.85	$13,891.13	

CASE STUDY 1002 (CONTINUED)

Cashier's Report

	Actual Amount	POS Amount	Difference
Shift 2			
Cash	$1285.93	$1286.00	
Cr Cd	2418.30	2418.30	
TOTAL 2	$3704.23	$3704.30	
Shift 3			
Cash	$321.48	$321.48	
Cr Cd	604.58	604.58	
TOTAL 3	$926.06	$926.06	
TOTALS	$18,521.14	$18,521.49	
Analysis Cash Report			
Cash Sls	$2906.98		
Cr Cd A/R	12,091.50		
Cash A/R	3522.65		
TOTAL	$18,521.13		

Manager's Report

	Actual	Budget	Difference
ROOMS AVAIL	143	143	0
ROOMS SOLD	92	112	20
ROOMS VAC	51	31	−20
ROOMS OOO	0	0	0
ROOMS COMP	0	0	0
ROOM INC	$6500.00	$8200.00	$1700.00
ROOM TAX	$650.00	$820.00	$170.00
NO. GUESTS	100	160	60
RACK RATE	$95.00	$95.00	$0.00
NO-SHOWS	2	1	−1

FIGURE 10-10   Barrington Hotel Night Audit.

Night Audit   Date _____

	$ Actual	$ Budget	Goal (%)
ROOM	_____	8200.00	_____
TAX	_____	820.00	_____
Restaurant 1	_____	475.00	_____
Restaurant 2	_____	755.00	_____

(continues)

FIGURE 10-10   (continued)

	$ Actual	$ Budget	Goal (%)
Restaurant 3		2100.00	
TOTAL REST SALES		3330.00	
SALES TAX		166.50	
Rest Tips 1		71.25	
Rest Tips 2		113.25	
Rest Tips 3		315.00	
TOTAL REST TIPS		499.50	
Room Srv 1		300.00	
Room Srv 2		250.00	
Room Srv 3		700.00	
TOTAL ROOM SRV		1250.00	
SALES TAX		62.50	
Room Srv 1 Tips		60.00	
Room Srv 2 Tips		50.00	
Room Srv 3 Tips		140.00	
TOTAL ROOM SRV TIPS		250.00	
Banq Bkfst		250.00	
Banq Lunch		3500.00	
Banq Dinner		7250.00	
TOTAL BANQ		11,000.00	
Banq Bkfst Tips		45.00	
Banq Lunch Tips		630.00	
Banq Dinner Tips		1305.00	
TOTAL BANQ TIPS		1980.00	
Banq Bar Lunch		450.00	
Banq Bar Dinner		3950.00	
TOTAL BANQ BAR		4400.00	
ROOM RENTAL		1000.00	
Lounge 1		400.00	
Lounge 2		2000.00	
Lounge 3		675.00	
Lounge 4		850.00	
TOTAL LOUNGE SALES		3925.00	
Lounge Tips 1		40.00	
Lounge Tips 2		200.00	
Lounge Tips 3		67.50	
Lounge Tips 4		85.00	
TOTAL LOUNGE TIPS		392.50	
VALET		350.00	
Tele Local		125.00	
Tele Long Distance		300.00	
TOTAL PHONE		425.00	

FIGURE 10-10 (continued)

	$ Actual	$ Budget	Goal (%)
GIFT SHOP		450.00	
GIFT SHOP SALES TAX		22.50	
VENDING		100.00	
SPA		500.00	
PARKING		350.00	
TOTAL REVENUE		39,473.50	
Less Paid-outs			
Valet			
Tips			
TOTAL PAID-OUTS			
Less Discounts			
Room			
Food			
TOTAL DISCOUNTS			
Less Write-offs			
Rooms			
Food			
TOTAL WRITE-OFFS			
Total Paid-out and Noncollect Sales			
Total Cash Sales			
Today's Outstd A/R			
Total Revenue			
Yesterday's Outstd A/R			
TOTAL OUTSTD A/R			
CREDIT CARD REC'D A/R			
Cash Rec'd A/R			
BAL A/R		80,000.00	
ANALYSIS OF A/R			
City Ledger			
Direct Bill			
VISA			
MasterCard			
JCB			
Total A/R			

BANK DEPOSIT		ANALYSIS OF BANK DEPOSIT	
Cash		Total Cash Sales	
VISA		Credit Card Rec'd A/R	
MasterCard		Cash Rec'd A/R	
JCB			
TTL BANK DEP			
AMT TR A/R			

(*continues*)

FIGURE 10-10   (continued)

Cashier's Report

	Actual Amount	POS Amount	Difference
Shift 1			
Cash	_____	_____	_____
Cr Cd	_____	_____	_____
TOTAL 1	_____	_____	_____
Shift 2			
Cash	_____	_____	_____
Cr Cd	_____	_____	_____
TOTAL 2	_____	_____	_____
Shift 3			
Cash	_____	_____	_____
Cr Cd	_____	_____	_____
TOTAL 3	_____	_____	_____
TOTALS	_____	_____	_____

Analysis Cash Report

Cash Sls	_____		
Cr Cd A/R	_____		
Cash A/R	_____		
TOTAL	_____		

Manager's Report

	Actual	Budget	Difference
ROOMS AVAIL	_____	_____	_____
ROOMS SOLD	_____	_____	_____
ROOM VAC	_____	_____	_____
ROOMS OOO	_____	_____	_____
ROOMS COMP	_____	_____	_____
OCC %	_____	_____	_____
DBL OCC %	_____	_____	_____
YIELD %	_____	_____	_____
REVPAR	_____	_____	_____
ROOM INC	_____	_____	_____
NO. GUESTS	_____	_____	_____
AV. RATE	_____	_____	_____
RACK RATE	_____	_____	_____
NO-SHOWS	_____	_____	_____

CASE STUDY 1003

The Canton Hotel has collected the following data, which represent the financial transactions in the hotel today. Assemble this information into a night audit report, using the format shown in Figure 10-11 (a blank worksheet for you to fill in, which follows the data).

CASE STUDY 1003 (*CONTINUED*)

DEPARTMENTAL DAILY SALES REPORT

DATE _____

	$ Actual	$ Budget	Goal (%)
Restaurant 1	850.00	650.00	
Restaurant 2	1034.00	1200.00	
Restaurant 3	2896.00	3200.00	
SALES TAX (rate = 5%)			
Rest Tips 1	127.50	97.50	
Rest Tips 2	155.10	180.00	
Rest Tips 3	434.40	480.00	
REST TIPS (rate = 15%)			
Room Srv 1	456.87	500.00	
Room Srv 2	355.00	450.00	
Room Srv 3	760.75	1000.00	
SALES TAX (rate = 5%)			
Room Srv 1 Tips	91.37	100.00	
Room Srv 2 Tips	71.00	90.00	
Room Srv 3 Tips	152.15	200.00	
ROOM SRV TIPS (rate = 20%)	314.52	390.00	
Banq Bkfst	890.00	450.00	
Banq Lunch	1785.71	2500.00	
Banq Dinner	4951.76	7500.00	
Banq Bkfst Tips	160.20	81.00	
Banq Lunch Tips	891.32	1881.00	
Banq Dinner Tips	321.43	450.00	
BANQ TIPS (rate = 18%)	1372.95		
Banq Bar Lunch	508.75	350.00	
Banq Bar Dinner	1907.25	2500.00	
ROOM RENTAL	2000.00	500.00	
Lounge 1	495.00	500.00	
Lounge 2	2951.50	3500.00	
Lounge 3	724.75	450.00	
Lounge 4	805.00	750.00	
Lounge Tips 1	49.50	50.00	
Lounge Tips 2	295.15	350.00	
Lounge Tips 3	72.48	45.00	
Lounge Tips 4	80.50	75.00	
LOUNGE TIPS (rate= 10%)	497.63	520.00	
VALET	350.00	400.00	
Tele Local	85.00	150.00	

(*continues*)

CASE STUDY 1003 (CONTINUED)

	$ Actual	$ Budget	Goal (%)
Tele Long Dist	241.00	350.00	
GIFT SHOP	650.00	500.00	
SALES TAX (rate = 5%)	32.50	25.00	
VENDING	190.00	250.00	
SPA	293.00	650.00	
PARKING	627.00	750.00	
Paid-outs			
Valet	256.00		
Tips	0.00		
Discounts			
Room	85.00		
Food	46.95		
Write-offs			
Room	0.00		
Food	0.00		
Total Cash Sales	3759.32		
Today's Outstd A/R	36,851.24		
Yesterday's Outstd A/R	64,258.18		
CREDIT CARD REC'D A/R	22,681.15		
CASH REC'D A/R	5390.97		
BAL A/R	73,037.30	90,000.00	
ANALYSIS OF A/R			
City Ledger	14,671.05		
Direct Bill	12,784.09		
VISA	29,712.01		
MasterCard	10,254.81		
JCB	5615.34		
Total A/R	73,037.30		

BANK DEPOSIT		**ANALYSIS OF BANK DEPOSIT**	
Cash	$9150.29	Total Cash Sales	$3759.32
VISA	$15,685.26	Credit Card Rec'd A/R	$22,681.15
MasterCard	$4230.88	Cash Rec'd A/R	$5390.97
JCB	$2765.01		
			$31,831.44

Cashier's Report

	Actual Amount	POS Amount	Difference
Shift 1			
Cash	$6862.72	$6861.05	
Cr Cd	17,010.86	17,010.86	
TOTAL 1	$23,873.58	$23,871.91	

CASE STUDY 1003 (CONTINUED)

Cashier's Report

	Actual Amount	POS Amount	Difference
Shift 2			
Cash	$1830.06	$1829.83	
Cr Cd	4536.23	4536.23	
TOTAL 2	$6366.29	$6366.06	
Shift 3			
Cash	$457.51	$457.51	
Cr Cd	1134.06	1134.06	
TOTAL 3	$1591.57	$1591.57	
TOTALS	$31,831.44	$31,829.54	

Analysis Cash Report

Cash Sls	$3759.32
Cr Cd A/R	22,681.15
Cash A/R	5390.97
TOTAL	$31,831.44

Manager's Report

	Actual	Budget	Difference
ROOMS AVAIL	200	200	0
ROOMS SOLD	135	150	−15
ROOMS VAC	65	50	−15
ROOMS OOO	0	0	0
ROOMS COMP	0	0	0
ROOM INC	$10,500.00	$11,200.00	700
ROOM TAX	$1050.00	$1120.00	70
NO GUESTS	155	225	70
RACK RATE	$105.00	$105.00	$0.00
NO-SHOWS	4	2	−2

FIGURE 10-11   Canton Hotel night audit.

Night Audit   Date _____

	$ Actual	$ Budget	Goal (%)
ROOM	_____	11,200.00	_____
TAX	_____	1120.00	_____
Restaurant 1	_____	650.00	_____
Restaurant 2	_____	1200.00	_____
Restaurant 3	_____	3200.00	_____
TOTAL REST SALES	_____	5050.00	_____

(continues)

FIGURE 10-11   (continued)

	$ Actual	$ Budget	Goal (%)
SALES TAX	_____	252.50	_____
Rest Tips 1	_____	97.50	_____
Rest Tips 2	_____	180.00	_____
Rest Tips 3	_____	480.00	_____
TOTAL REST TIPS	_____	757.50	_____
Room Srv 1	_____	500.00	_____
Room Srv 2	_____	450.00	_____
Room Srv 3	_____	1000.00	_____
TOTAL ROOM SRV	_____	1950.00	_____
SALES TAX	_____	97.50	_____
Room Srv 1 Tips	_____	100.00	_____
Room Srv 2 Tips	_____	90.00	_____
Room Srv 3 Tips	_____	200.00	_____
TOTAL ROOM SRV TIPS	_____	390.00	_____
Banq Bkfst	_____	450.00	_____
Banq Lunch	_____	2500.00	_____
Banq Dinner	_____	7500.00	_____
TOTAL BANQ	_____	10,450.00	_____
Banq Bkfst Tips	_____	81.00	_____
Banq Lunch Tips	_____	450.00	_____
Banq Dinner Tips	_____	1350.00	_____
TOTAL BANQ TIPS	_____	1881.00	_____
Banq Bar Lunch	_____	350.00	_____
Banq Bar Dinner	_____	2500.00	_____
TOTAL BANQ BAR	_____	2850.00	_____
ROOM RENTAL	_____	500.00	_____
Lounge 1	_____	500.00	_____
Lounge 2	_____	3500.00	_____
Lounge 3	_____	450.00	_____
Lounge 4	_____	750.00	_____
TOTAL LOUNGE SALES	_____	5200.00	_____
Lounge Tips 1	_____	50.00	_____
Lounge Tips 2	_____	350.00	_____
Lounge Tips 3	_____	45.00	_____
Lounge Tips 4	_____	75.00	_____
TOTAL LOUNGE TIPS	_____	520.00	_____
VALET	_____	400.00	_____
Tele Local	_____	150.00	_____
Tele Long Distance	_____	350.00	_____
TOTAL PHONE	_____	500.00	_____
GIFT SHOP	_____	500.00	_____
GIFT SHOP SALES TAX	_____	25.00	_____
VENDING	_____	250.00	_____
SPA	_____	650.00	_____
PARKING	_____	750.00	_____

FIGURE 10-11   (continued)

	$ Actual	$ Budget	Goal (%)
TOTAL REVENUE	_____	45,293.60	_____
Less Paid-outs			
Valet	_____		
Tips	_____		
TOTAL PAID-OUTS	_____		
Less Discounts			
Room	_____		
Food	_____		
TOTAL DISCOUNTS	_____		
Less Write-offs			
Rooms	_____		
Food	_____		
TOTAL WRITE-OFFS	_____		
Total Paid-out and Noncollect Sales	_____		
Total Cash Sales	_____		
Today's Outstd A/R	_____		
Total Revenue	_____		
Yesterday's Outstd A/R	_____		
TOTAL OUTSTD A/R	_____		
CREDIT CARD REC'D A/R	_____		
Cash Rec'd A/R	_____		
BAL. A/R	_____	90,000.00	
ANALYSIS OF A/R			
City Ledger	_____		
Direct Bill	_____		
Visa	_____		
MC	_____		
JCB	_____		
Total A/R	_____		

BANK DEPOSIT		ANALYSIS OF BANK DEPOSIT	
Cash	_____	Total Cash Sales	_____
VISA	_____	Credit Card Rec'd A/R	_____
MasterCard	_____	Cash Rec'd A/R	_____
JCB	_____		
TTL BANK DEP	_____		
AMT TR A/R	_____		

Cashier's Report

	Actual Amount	POS Amount	Difference
Shift 1			
Cash			
Cr Cd	_____	_____	_____
TOTAL 1	_____	_____	_____
Shift 2			
Cash			
Cr Cd	_____	_____	_____
TOTAL 2	_____	_____	_____

(*continues*)

FIGURE 10-11 (continued)

Cashier's Report

	Actual Amount	POS Amount	Difference
Shift 3			
Cash	_____	_____	_____
Cr Cd	_____	_____	_____
TOTAL 3	_____	_____	_____
TOTALS	_____	_____	_____

Analysis Cash Report

	Actual Amount
Cash Sls	_____
Cr Cd A/R	_____
Cash A/R	_____
TOTAL	_____

Manager's Report

	Actual	Budget	Difference
ROOMS AVAIL	_____	_____	_____
ROOMS SOLD	_____	_____	_____
ROOM VAC	_____	_____	_____
ROOMS OOO	_____	_____	_____
ROOMS COMP	_____	_____	_____
OCC %	_____	_____	_____
DBL OCC %	_____	_____	_____
YIELD %	_____	_____	_____
REVPAR	_____	_____	_____
ROOM INC	_____	_____	_____
NO. GUESTS	_____	_____	_____
AV. RATE	_____	_____	_____
RACK RATE	_____	_____	_____
NO-SHOWS	_____	_____	_____

Key Words

aging of accounts

cashier's report

credit balance

cumulative total feature

daily flash report

daily sales report

departmental accounts

manager's report

master credit card account

night audit

operational effectiveness

room sales figure

surcharge rates

tax cumulative total feature

total restaurant sales figure

trial balance

CHAPTER 11

Managing Hospitality

OPENING DILEMMA

Upon check-in, a guest indicates the national reservation agent misquoted his room rate at $99 when it should have been $89 per night. The front desk clerk responds, "Sir, you will have to discuss that with the cashier when you check out in three days. I can only register you with the rate that was entered into the computer. What's $30 to a businessperson on a budget?"

The concept of *hospitality*, the generous and cordial provision of services to a guest, is at the heart of our industry. These services can include room accommodations, food and beverages, meeting facilities, reservations, information on hotel services, information on local attractions, and the like. Hospitality is a subjective concept, and the degree of hospitality a guest perceives has implications for the overall financial success of the hotel. Guests who feel they are not treated with respect or have not received full value for their dollar will seek out other hotels they believe will provide better hospitality. This chapter is intended to instill in you, the future hotel professional, a sense of responsibility for providing hospitality. As you prepare for a career in an industry that may differentiate its product by continual and efficient delivery of professional hospitality service, this material will serve as a primer for your development (Figure 11-1).

FIGURE 11-1

A well-informed hotel staff contributes to an enjoyable guest stay. Photo courtesy of iStockphoto.

This chapter was inspired by a book entitled *Service America!* by Karl Albrecht and Ron Zemke.[1] These management consultants were early proponents of the service concept in business. Their writings, as well as my own professional experience in hotels and restaurants, are the basis of this chapter. A chapter devoted to hospitality seems essential because the staff of the front office is often the only direct contact the guest has with hotel personnel. To emphasize the importance of quality a public relations article from the Greenbrier Hotel in White Sulphur Springs, West Virginia, stated the hotel hired a director of quality to pursue the five-star Mobil rating.[2]

Importance of Hospitality

Hospitality is an important consideration for both the guest and the hotel entrepreneur. Every guest expects and deserves hospitable treatment. Providing hospitality to meet guests' needs involves not only a positive attitude but also an array of services that make the guest's stay enjoyable. If the market the hotel serves is composed of business travelers, the staff will find their needs revolve around schedules and flexible delivery of hotel services. The business traveler may arrive late and leave early. The hotel restaurant must be organized to provide a healthy and quick breakfast. Wake-up services must be located within the room or provided by an efficient staff. The hotel should also offer office services, such as word-processing capabilities, advanced telephone systems, fax and photocopying facilities, computers, and Wi-Fi. The guest associated with a convention may want early check-in, late checkout, and a full range of hotel services. If the convention starts at noon on Tuesday, the guest may arrive at 9 A.M., wanting to unload and set up before the noon starting time. If the convention ends on Thursday at 3 P.M., the guest may want to retain occupancy of the room beyond the normal checkout time. While the guest is in the hotel, he or she may require flexible scheduling hours at the swimming pool, health club facilities, lounge and live entertainment, gift shops, coffee shop, and other hotel services. International guests may require assistance with using electrical appliances, converting their national currency into local currency, or interpreting geographic directions.

Success or failure in providing hospitality often determines the success or failure of the hotel. Capitalizing on opportunities to provide hospitality is essential. The failure to make the most of these chances directly affects the hotel's financial success, as Albrecht and Zemke make clear in *Service America!*

> The average business never hears from 96% of its unhappy customers. For every complaint received the average company in fact has 26 customers with problems, 6 of which are "serious" problems. Complainers are more likely than noncomplainers to do business again with the company that upset them, even if the problem isn't satisfactorily resolved. Of the customers who register a complaint, between 54 and 70% will do business again with the organization if their complaint is resolved. That figure goes up to a staggering 95% if the customer feels that the complaint was resolved quickly. The average customer who has had a problem with an organization recounts the incident to more than 20 people. Customers who have complained to an organization and had their complaints satisfactorily resolved tell an average of five people about the treatment they received.[3]

What do these issues of delivering hospitality to the guest mean to the entrepreneur? They emphasize that the guest who is not treated with hospitality (remember the definition of hospitality is subjective) will choose to do business with a competitor and may also influence others not to try your hotel for the first time or not to continue to do business with you. The entrepreneur who is aware of the competition realizes this negative advertising will severely affect the profit-and-loss statement. Albrecht and Zemke extended their concept mathematically. Let's examine the cumulative effects of poor service in the following example.

If a hotel does not provide the desired level of service to 10 guests on any given day, only 1 of the guests will bring the complaint to the attention of the hotel staff. If the complaint is resolved quickly, this person will almost surely do business again with the hotel. He or she will also have occasion to influence five people to use your hotel. On the other hand, the nine guests who did not bring their complaints to the attention of the hotel staff will probably not do business with the hotel again, and each of them may tell approximately 20 people—so a total of 180 people will hear their negative account of the hotel. If this model is extended to cover a whole year of dissatisfied guests, 68,985 people will have a negative impression of the hotel ([180 people told + 9 original dissatisfied customers] × 365 days), and 2190 will have a positive impression ([5 people told + 1 original satisfied customer] × 365 days).

The financial ramifications of so many people negatively impressed with your hotel are clearly disastrous. Hospitable treatment of guests must be more than just an option; it must be standard operating procedure. It is a concept that must be adopted as a corporate tenet and organized for effective delivery.

Managing the Delivery of Hospitality

It is not enough for the front office manager to decide the members of the front office staff should provide good service and display hospitality to guests. To provide satisfactory hospitality to all guests at all times, front office managers must develop and administer a *service management program*, which highlights the company's focus on meeting customers' needs and allows the hotel to achieve its financial goals. This program must be based on sound management principles and the hotel's commitment to meeting guests' needs.

Management's Role

Management may seem an odd place to start a discussion of delivering hospitality. After all, aren't the front desk clerks, switchboard operators, and bellhops the people who meet and greet guests and fulfill their needs at the front desk? Yes, these employees do provide hospitality directly, but managers must work behind the scenes to develop a plan that ensures employees' efforts are continuous and professional. For example, management may decide to implement one or two specific, immediate changes on learning a guest's needs were overlooked. Management may feel the negative impact of the rude, lazy, or careless employee has unnecessarily caused bad public relations. If a group of employees is not performing to management's standards, the cumulative effects of the group are perceived negatively by guests. This negative impression takes a toll in the long run. Although one or two directives may correct an individual guest's problems, the hotel will reap only short-lived gains. A comprehensive program aimed at meeting the needs of a hotel's prime market—guests who continue to do business with the hotel—is the foundation for long-term successful delivery of hospitality. This is what makes a hotel profitable.

Management's commitment to a service management program must be as integral to the organization as effective market planning, cost control programs, budgeting, and human resources management. In fact, service management is the most visible responsibility because it affects all other objectives of the hotel. Often the people in staff positions in hotels become so involved with their day-to-day paper shuffling and deadlines that they forget why they are in business. They may not mean to forget, but it happens all too often. Service management ensures a commitment to long-range effort by appointing someone within the organization to be responsible for developing, organizing, and delivering it. John W. Young, retired executive vice president of human resources at the Four Seasons Hotels and Resorts, tells us:

> We expect our general managers to respect the dignity of every employee, to understand their needs and recognize their contributions, and to work to maintain their job satisfaction with us—and to encourage their growth to the maximum extent their ability and desire allows. General measurement is based on detailed employee attitude surveys, conducted by an outside firm, as well as such factors as employee turnover [and] employee promotions, both within the hotel and to other hotels. Also specific people-related goals are set according to the hotel's needs or the manager's personal needs, and measured, e.g., implementing a planned change in response to concerns in an attitude survey.[4]

The front office manager usually supervises service management efforts. Other key department heads who supervise employees who deal with guests, such as the food and beverage manager and director of marketing and sales, rely on the organizational leadership of the front office manager. It is important to note that responsibility for delivering hospitality to the guest is always a part of the job of each department's supervisor or *shift leader*, the person responsible for directing the efforts of a particular work shift. The organizational efforts provided by the front office manager serve as the basis for a homogeneous plan for the hotel.

The owner and general manager must make a financial commitment to ensure the success of the program. An important component is motivating employees to deliver hospitality on a continual basis through incentive programs. *Incentive programs* are management's organized efforts to determine employees' needs and develop programs to help them meet their own needs as well as those of the hotel. Such programs reward employees for providing constant and satisfactory guest service and often involve money, in the form of bonuses, which must be budgeted in the annual projected budget. Incentives may involve the employees' choice of a monetary bonus, higher hourly rates, shift preference, or additional holiday or vacation days.

Mark Heymann, chairman and CEO of UniFocus, based in Carrollton, Texas, believes customer satisfaction and employee satisfaction (in hotels) should be considered simultaneously. He says, "Given today's extraordinarily tough labor market, dissatisfied workers don't stick around. So a happy staff is the key to happy campers." Mr. Heymann also reports on feedback from hotel property clients with UniFocus, saying, "Money is not the key driver when it comes to holding on to staff. It's the interaction with management and the environment."[5]

The daughter of an international guest approaches a front desk clerk and says her mother is experiencing chest pains. What hospitality opportunities are available to the front desk clerk?

The goal of every lodging establishment should be to extend the same degree of hospitality to the guest who arrives on a busy Monday morning and to one who arrives on a slow Saturday night. Management's ideological and financial commitment, along with the organizational efforts of the front office manager, will ensure both of these guests are treated equally.

The Service Strategy Statement

To produce an effective service management program, managers must devise a *service strategy statement,* a formal recognition by management that the hotel will strive to deliver the products and services desired by the guest in a professional manner. To accomplish this, management must first identify the guest's needs.

Those of you who have entry-level jobs in a hotel as bellhops, desk clerks, switchboard operators, table attendants, housekeeping attendants, or gift shop clerks may have some feel for what guests want. They want quick and efficient service. They want to avoid long

FIGURE 11-2

Owners and managers must commit financial resources and establish priorities for the operation of a successful service management program.
Photo courtesy of iStockphoto.

lines. They want to find their way easily around the hotel and the immediate vicinity. They want the products and services in the hotel to work. They want to feel safe and secure while residing in the hotel. If you use these observations as a basis for understanding guests' needs while they are away from home, you will be able to better satisfy them. John Young states, "Market research, internal guest comments and our regular employee attitude surveys all confirm that what has set and will continue to set Four Seasons apart from our competitors is personal service."[6]

As Eric Johnson and William Layton note, "It is only through the eyes of a customer that a definition of service quality can be obtained. Senior management cannot adequately determine what is desired at the customer level until a comprehensive evaluation of customer preference is established through a systematic consumer research study."[7] Thus, in addition to identifying *generally* what guests want, management should survey guests of the *particular* property to determine what services they expect and how they want them delivered. The general manager of the hotel may assign this task to the marketing and sales director, who may start by reviewing and summarizing customer comment cards, which are usually held on file for six months to a year. A review of the areas in which the hotel has disappointed its guests, like that shown in Figure 11-3, provides a basis for determining where to begin a guest survey. The problem areas identified from this study are then used

---

FIGURE 11-3   The report highlights areas of customer service and customer feedback.

The Times Hotel

CUSTOMER COMMENT CARD SUMMARY, SEPT.–DEC.

Product/Service	Sept.	Oct.	Nov.	Dec.
Overbooked	41	20	8	20
Slow check-in	50	31	12	25
Slow checkout	10	15	10	4
Room rate too high	10	7	9	8
Delay getting into room	35	12	18	5
Slow room service	90	3	3	10
Poor food in restaurant	6	10	2	8
Poor selections on menu	2	5	7	12
High prices on menu	2	10	10	20
Dirty room	3	4	8	15
Poor selection of amenities	—	—	5	—
Bedding insufficient	10	10	12	5
Lack of response from housekeeping	9	15	7	9
Rudeness from bell staff	1	—	5	—
Rudeness from dining room staff	1	—	10	—

FIGURE 11-4	This individual hotel guest survey asks guests for their opinions on delivery of service.

The Times Hotel

GUEST SURVEY

1. List and rate the services provided by the bell staff.

_____ excellent good fair poor
_____ excellent good fair poor

2. List and rate the services provided by the front desk.

_____ excellent good fair poor
_____ excellent good fair poor
_____ excellent good fair poor

3. List and rate the services provided by housekeeping.

_____ excellent good fair poor
_____ excellent good fair poor

4. List and rate the services provided by the food and beverage department.

_____ excellent good fair poor
_____ excellent good fair poor
_____ excellent good fair poor

as the focus of a simple survey form similar to that shown in Figure 11-4. Keep in mind that historical data provided by surveys is essential for building a plan on service management. However, managing the daily challenges of employee requests for improvement of service is always a responsibility of front-line employees, supervisors, and managers.

The survey may be administered by a member of the marketing and sales department at various times during the day. The resulting data, as well as that gleaned from comment cards, gives a general indication of what guests want. Sometimes pinpointing guest needs is not easy, because they change over time. In the example shown in Figure 11-3, speed of service delivery, high prices, poor selection of products, low-quality products, and rude personnel are problem areas. These areas, then, should be the focus of the service strategy statement, as they appear to be the primary guest concerns.

Ernest Cadotte and Normand Turgeon analyzed a survey concerning the frequency and types of complaints and compliments received from guests of members of the National Restaurant Association and the American Hotel & Motel Association (now the American Hotel & Lodging Association). They report:

The data seem to fall into a four-fold topology that compares how likely an attribute is to garner compliments versus the frequency of complaints.

1. Dissatisfiers—complaints for low performance, e.g., parking.

2. Satisfiers—unusual performance apparently elicits compliments, but average performance or even the absence of the feature will probably not cause dissatisfaction or complaints, e.g., atrium-type lobbies.
3. Critical variables—capable of eliciting both positive and negative feelings, depending on the situation, e.g., cleanliness, quality of service, employee knowledge and service, and quietness of surroundings.
4. Neutrals—factors that received neither a great number of compliments nor many complaints are probably either not salient to guests or easily brought up to guest standards.[8]

Albrecht and Zemke also identify general guest expectations as follows:

- Care and concern from service providers
- Spontaneity—people are authorized to think
- Problem solving—people can work out the intricacies of problems
- Recovery—will anybody make a special effort to set a problem right?[9]

Their conclusions add another dimension to the service strategy statement. In addition to wanting certain recognizable products and services delivered at a certain speed and level of quality, guests expect employees to accept responsibility for resolving problems. The guest should not encounter unconcerned staff or be bounced from employee to employee in order to have a problem solved. Management must develop a staff whose members can think and solve problems. This dimension to the service strategy statement makes the delivery of professional hospitality a challenge!

Developing the Service Strategy Statement

Once management identifies what guests want, it can develop a service strategy statement. The statement should include:

- A commitment to make service, from ownership and senior management on down, a top priority in the company
- A commitment to develop and administer a service management program
- A commitment to train employees to deliver service efficiently
- A commitment of financial resources to develop incentives for the employees who deliver the services

These directives serve as guidelines in the development of a service management program. More importantly, they force management to think of service as a long-range effort and not as a quick fix.

John W. Young states the service strategy of the Four Seasons Hotels and Resorts centers on offering

. . . exceptional levels of personal service. People are our most important asset. Each person has dignity and wants a sense of pride in what they do and where they work. Success in delivering excellent service depends on working together as a team and understanding the needs and contributions of our fellow employees. [We must] train and stimulate ourselves and our colleagues. [We must] deal with others as we would have them deal with us. [We must] avoid compromising long-term goals in the interest of short term profit.[10]

Here is one example of a service strategy statement:

The owners of fictitious The Times Hotel, management, and staff will combine forces to establish a Service to Our Guests program, administered by management and delivered by staff. Delivery of service to our guests is crucial to the economic viability of our hotel. The owners of the hotel will provide financial support to the people who deliver hospitality on a daily basis.

Here is another example:

The hotel, in its continual efforts to maintain a leadership position in the hotel industry, will develop a VIP Guest Service program. The administration and delivery of this program are essential to the financial success of the hotel. This program will include incentives and has received a priority budget line for this fiscal year.

These statements, however worded, convey the message from owners and management that a successful service management program depends on the support of all levels of management and staff.

Financial Commitment

Throughout the preceding discussion of service management, financial commitment from management was stressed. Managers who want to develop and deliver a successful service management program must allow adequate staff time to think through a plan and to develop methods to motivate their employees. Scheduling time for planning and strategy sessions can increase the labor budget. Determining and offering motivational opportunities also increases the financial investment. Often, lack of planning for these financial considerations impedes the desire to implement a service management program.

FRONT-LINE REALITIES

 A general manager has proposed a service management program to the owner of her hotel. The front office manager has developed a plan with a $10,000 budget that includes incentives for employees. The owner of the hotel likes the program but wants the budget scaled down to $0. The owner feels employees should be responsible for their own motivation. If you were the front office manager, how would you justify the budget in your plan?

Total Quality Management Applications

The previous discussion of developing a background for managing the delivery of hospitality is essential for adopting total quality management (TQM) practices, as discussed in chapter 2. Hotel owners and managers who fail to develop a clear service strategy statement and make a financial commitment to delivering hospitality experience extreme difficulty in applying TQM. TQM requires an immense commitment of labor to analyze guest and employee interaction, the reallocation of responsibilities and authority to foster an improvement in services, and a long-term commitment to learning a new method of management. Preparation for adopting TQM is a requisite for success.

HOSPITALITY PROFILE

Patrick Mene is the former vice president of quality for The Ritz-Carlton Hotel Company, LLC. That organization twice, in 1992 and 1999, won the Malcolm Baldrige Award, a prestigious recognition of excellence in overall performance, leadership, profitability, and competitiveness. After he graduated from college, Mr. Mene went to work as a management trainee at Hilton. He has also worked in hotel management positions at Hyatt, Westin International, Omni, Portman Hotel in San Francisco, and L'ErmitageHotels. He also has conducted a great deal of research, particularly on the teachings of Joseph Juran, a management specialist in quality planning, improvement, and control.

Mr. Mene states that competing for the Baldrige Award provided great feedback for the hotel. He explains the hotel was organized vertically; it is now organized horizontally to concentrate more on the critical processes that drive the company and to provide more employee empowerment. For example, a traditional hotel may have 30 departments, while the Ritz-Carlton has only four; each one is run by a horizontally organized team. One team focuses on the pre-arrival process (customer contact with the sales office; making reservations; planning meetings, conferences, and banquets),

one team focuses on arrival (laundry, housekeeping, front desk), one team runs the restaurant, and one team is responsible for banqueting. This horizontal structure creates a "leaner, linked, empowered organization."

Mr. Mene describes the managers in this type of organization as "coaches and advisers," while managers in traditional organizations are more "chief technicians and problem solvers." Mr. Mene reports that customer dissatisfaction has decreased. The new structure has resulted in fewer breakdowns and less need for rework. In the past, the hotel experienced problems with incorrect or late honor bar billings; guest rooms were always clean but were sometimes missing supplies; and, at times, when guests called for information or assistance, agents were not available and calls went unanswered. These problems have been dramatically reduced.

He states that quality management science is a new branch of knowledge. Traditional methods of management that concentrate on selling hard, raising prices, and forcing a profit cannot identify and eliminate waste. He adds that, in any hotel, 30 percent of expenditures are the result of quality failures and are unnecessary. He feels TQM is the most effective way to achieve revolutionary results.

W. Edwards Deming's principles of TQM[11] can be applied to front office management practices. Managers must focus on a distinct level of service at the front office. Managers and front-line employees must view the interaction between customers and service providers. A front office team develops a *flowchart*, an analysis of the delivery of a particular product or service, to illustrate what occurs after a customer has asked for a product or service. Analysis of this interaction by the group of people who deliver the product or service allows for suggestions for improvement. A key component of TQM is a commitment to continuous analysis of the delivery of guest services and to plans for improvement.

Developing a Service Management Program

Employee involvement in planning a service management program is as important as obtaining a financial commitment from owners to establishing such a program. Too often, when the employees are not included in the planning stages, they look at the final plan and remark, "This is ridiculous. It's not for me. Let the people in marketing and sales worry about it." In many cases, service is perceived as just another fancy concept proposed by management. Management must address this attitude from the outset. When employees are involved early, they are much more likely to buy into the program because they are already a part of it.

FIGURE 11-5

This **TQM team** is analyzing the delivery of a particular service to a guest. Managers and front-line employees provide an objective review. Photo courtesy of iStockphoto.com.

Guest Cycle

The front office manager responsible for developing an effective service management program, along with other department directors, should first look at the employees they supervise. Representatives from all job categories and shifts should be included on the planning committee. Planning by committee can be cumbersome (scheduling, planning meetings, incurring additional payroll, etc.), but it is most likely to lead to an effective program. It allows a drafted plan to be altered in the planning stages by those who must implement it and ensures clear, workable operational methods. It gives the employees time to adjust to the new concept, while developing adoption procedures. At each planning phase, employees learn how they will benefit from the program. This is a realistic way to focus management's efforts to promote this important concept.

Once the members of the planning committee are chosen, their first step is to analyze the guest's perception of the hospitality system:

> Visualize your organization as dealing with the customer in terms of a cycle of service, a repeatable sequence of events in which various people try to meet the customer's needs and expectations at each point. It may be the instant at which the customer sees your advertisement, gets a call from your salesperson, or initiates a telephone inquiry. It ends only temporarily, when the customer considers the service complete, and it begins anew when he or she decides to come back for more.[12]

Figure 11-6 illustrates the *cycle of service*, the progression of a guest's request for products and services through a hotel's departments. This outline is presented as a

FIGURE 11-6   This review of the cycle of services guests may encounter is the basis for developing a service management program.

Marketing
- Customer surveys (before and after stay)
- Advertising: billboards, direct mail, radio, television, print, Internet; incentive promotions, solo and with other hospitality organizations; social media

Reservations
- Toll-free numbers, fax, national reservation system (ease of access), Internet
- Telephone manner of reservationists
- Cancellation policy (reasonable restrictions)
- Credit card acceptance
- Accommodation availability (value and cost considerations)
- Complimentary services/products (value and cost considerations)
- Information on hotel shuttle and public transportation
- Social media

Registration
- Hotel shuttle and public transportation

FIGURE 11-6   Continued

- Greetings (doorman, bell staff, front desk personnel)
- Assistance with luggage
- Check-in procedure (length of time in line, ease of check-in with preprinted registration cards or self-registration machine)
- Room accommodations (value and cost considerations)
- Credit card acceptance
- Complimentary services/products (value and cost considerations)
- Room status/availability
- Information on other hotel services
- Cleanliness and interior design of lobby, elevators, room
- Operation of air conditioning, heat, television, radio, plumbing in room
- Amenities available
- Social media

Guest Stay

Other hotel departments:

- Food service department (menu offerings, hours of operation, prices, service level, ambiance)
- Gift shop (selection, souvenirs, value/price)
- Lounge (prices, entertainment, hours, service level)
- Room service (menu offerings, prices, hours of availability, promptness in delivery and pickup of trays)
- Valet service (pickup and delivery times, prices, quality of service)
- Housekeeping services (daily room cleaning, replenishment of amenities, cleanliness of public areas, requests for directions in hotel)
- Accommodation availability (value and cost considerations)
- Technology (business services, Wi-Fi, computers)
- Security (24-hour availability, fire safety devices, anonymous key blank and distribution, key and lock repair service, requests for directions in hotel)

Front office:

- Requests for information and assistance (wake-up calls, hours of operation of other departments, transmittal of requests to other departments)
- Telephone system (assistance from staff)
- Update of guest folio
- Extension of stay

Checkout

- Reasonable and flexible checkout time deadlines
- Assistance with luggage
- Elevator availability and promptness
- In-room video checkout
- Length of time in line
- Immediate availability of guest folio printout; accuracy of charges
- Additional reservations
- Social media

working tool for front office managers to use in analyzing the hotel services the guest encounters, not as a complete listing. It is important to remember these services are provided by the employees of the hotel. In developing a list for a specific hotel property, employee input is vital.

Another benefit of analyzing the cycle of service is that the process may reveal inefficiencies built into the system. Rectifying these will assist in delivering first-rate hospitality, as the following example, reported by Nancy J. Allin and Kelly Halpine of the quality assurance and training department at the Waldorf=Astoria in New York, indicates:

> While there can be many reasons to combine the positions of registration clerk and cashier, and many aspects were considered at the Waldorf=Astoria, the decision was driven by a desire to improve guest service where its impact is most obvious—at the front desk. Cross-trained employees speed the check-in and checkout process by performing both functions, as the traffic at the desk dictates. Registration clerks can cash checks and cashiers can issue duplicate room keys, in many cases eliminating the necessity of having the guest wait in two lines.[13]

Moments of Truth in Hotel Service Management

Central to the development of a guest service program is the management of what Albrecht and Zemke call *moments of truth*: "episode[s] in which a customer comes into contact with any aspect of the company, however remote, and thereby has an opportunity to form an impression."[14] Every time the hotel guest encounters some aspect of the hotel, he or she judges its hospitality. Guests who are told by a reservationist they must "take this room at this rate or stay elsewhere" will not feel hospitality is a primary consideration at this hotel. When a potential guest calls and asks to speak with Ms. General Manager and the switchboard operator answers, "Who is that?" the guest will expect the same kind of careless, impersonal treatment when (or if) he or she decides to stay at the hotel. The guest who is crammed into an elevator with half the housekeeping crew, their vacuum cleaners, and bins of soiled laundry will not feel welcomed. All these impressions make the guest feel service at this hotel is mismanaged.

These examples are only some of the moments of truth that can be identified from an analysis of the guest service cycle. Whether a guest considers an event a moment of truth or barely notices, it is a cumulative review of the delivery of hospitality. Albrecht and Zemke tell us guests each have a "report card" in their head that is the basis of a grading system that leads them to decide whether to partake of the service again or to go elsewhere.[15] If a guest is to award the hotel an A+ to the hotel's hospitality report card, it is essential that all moments of truth be well managed. This challenge is not to be viewed as an impossible mission but rather as an organized and concerted effort by owners, management, and employees. Keep this customer report card concept in mind as you develop your ideas about service management.

FRONT-LINE REALITIES

Shortcomings in providing guest services at the front office in The Times Hotel have become critical in one particular aspect—knowledge of special events in the local area. Guests have complained that front desk clerks do not give clear directions, estimates of travel time, information on timing of events, cost of admission, or suggestions for public transportation. Guests approach desk clerks and receive only a brief response to their questions.

The front office manager has decided to use total quality management principles to resolve this situation. The hotel has stated a commitment to service and a financial commitment to this goal. If you were the front office manager, how would you proceed?

Employee Buy-in Concept

As Albrecht and Zemke note, "in any kind of retail or service business, the factor that has the biggest effect on sales is the 'last four feet.' It's up to the people in the store to take over at the last four feet."[16] In other words, all the sophisticated marketing programs, well-orchestrated sales promotions, outstanding architectural designs, and degreed and certified management staff form only the backdrop for the delivery of hospitality. The front-line employee is *the* link in the service management program. He or she must deliver the service. This simple fact still amazes many people. How can front office managers ensure frontline employees deliver a consistently high level of service?

Albrecht and Zemke offer the following suggestions:

> To have a high standard of service, it is necessary to create and maintain a motivating environment in which service people can find personal reasons for committing their energies to the benefit of the customer. People commit their energies to the extent that what they do brings them what they want. What they want may be psychological—a feeling, a status, or an experience. Or it may be material—greenbacks are an excellent form of feedback. In any case the job of management is to engineer a motivating environment.[17]

John W. Young echoes their ideas: "The challenge is to motivate your employees to deliver the required level of service to your customers, and do it consistently. . . If we are to succeed in delivery of exceptional service, we have to convince every new employee of the benefit of 'buying in' to our philosophy and standards."[18]

In short, a consistently high level of service is provided only by employees who are committed to the service management program. This commitment is fostered by the hotel's managers. It is such commitment that allows the front desk clerk to tell the newly registered guest about the special musical combo group playing in the lounge or to ask how the traffic coming in from the airport was or to suggest consulting the concierge in the lobby for directions to points of interest in the city. Chapter 12 further discusses employee motivation; those concepts are crucial to the development and administration of a service management program.

Consider each employee in each hotel and determine how to stimulate his or her commitment to service. If money motivates employees, financial incentive programs that reward positive expressions of hospitality are in order. Employee stock ownership programs also provide an incentive for employees to realize financially the importance of delivering a consistently high level of hospitality. Other reward systems include preferential treatment in scheduling shifts, longer vacations, and extra holidays. Long-range rewards may include promotion opportunities.

Screening Employees Who Deliver Hospitality

Another factor to consider in developing a service management program is the employee character traits needed to provide hospitality. When candidates for front-line service positions are evaluated, interviews should be structured to screen out employees who are not able or willing to deal with the demands of guest service. Albrecht and Zemke offer these considerations for choosing front-line employees: "A service person needs to have at least an adequate level of maturity and self-esteem. He or she needs to be reasonably articulate, aware of the normal rules of social context, and be able to say and do what is necessary to establish rapport with a customer and maintain it. And third, he or she needs to have a fairly high level of tolerance for contact."[19] John W. Young notes:

The motivation process begins with the selection of employees, which is all-important. The average person applying for a job is interviewed by at least four people. When Four Seasons opens a property, every single employee hired is interviewed by the hotel general manager. First we look for people who are already motivated. Our compensation policies have been designed to support and reinforce our efforts in hiring, training, and development. We look on them not only as a motivator, but as a way of sending signals to our employees consistent with our philosophy and business strategy—almost as an employee communication program itself.[20]

Group discussions among the managerial staff help highlight the attributes of a person able to deliver hospitality. These discussions should lead to a rather informal procedure for screening employees. Questions that determine whether candidates display maturity and self-esteem, are articulate, possess social graces, and have a high level of tolerance for continued guest contact can be discussed in group settings. Managers who are aware of what they are looking for in employees are better able to secure the right people for the right jobs.

Empowerment

Empowerment—management's act of delegating authority and responsibility to *front-line employees*, those people who deliver service to guests as front desk clerks, cashiers, switchboard operators, bellhops, concierge, and housekeeping employees—is the bedrock of service management programs. The process of empowering employees requires front office managers to analyze the flow of guest services and determine how the front-line staff interacts with guests. Are there points of service at which a guest may request variations in the level of service provided? Might there be times when a guest questions standard operating procedures such as billing, guest room access, or room accommodations? Do front-line employees constantly inform guests, "I don't have the authority to rectify this matter. You'll have to see the manager"? If the review of the guest cycle reveals opportunities for delegating responsibility and authority, then empowerment should be exercised.

Adopting Empowerment into Front Office Management

Front office employees who are not accustomed to solving problems and are not treated as members of the management team may be reluctant to suddenly take charge and make decisions. Employees who have become comfortable with having their managers solve all the problems may see no need to change the established routine. However, it is becoming increasingly apparent to front office managers that a supervisory style that does not permit employees to be involved in the decision-making process will not be successful. The challenge to the front office manager, then, is to begin to introduce empowerment into the front office.

The analysis of the guest flow (described above) is the best way to start the empowerment process. However, this analysis must be performed by the front office manager in conjunction with front-line employees. If input from front-line employees is not included in the analysis, valuable data may be overlooked and an opportunity for employee ownership lost. The opportunity for employees to participate in the decision-making process ensures positive initiation of empowerment.

Parameters of Employee Empowerment

The authority and responsibility that underlie employee empowerment must be fully articulated and communicated to employees. If an analysis of the guest flow reveals opportunities for a guest to question a billing amount, then the billing amount must be discussed. If the amount in question is less than $5, do cashiers have the authority to credit the guest account for that amount? If the amount in question is less than $25, do cashiers have the authority to credit the guest account for that amount? What an amount over $25? Do cashiers have the authority to credit the guest account for that amount?

Along with setting parameters for employee empowerment is a management feedback system that provides information on cashier financial activity and guest satisfaction. For example, a cumulative tally as well as individual tallies of a front desk clerk's authorization of refunding charges that have been disputed by guests should be reviewed by front office managers. Financial totals that exceed the parameters of employee empowerment should be questioned.

FRONT-LINE REALITIES

A guest in room 284 calls the front desk and wants to order pizza from room service, but there is no room service menu in the guest room. The desk clerk relays the request to housekeeping, only to have the phone call go unanswered. Next, the desk clerk calls the restaurant and asks the hostess to call the guest and take care of the request. What underlying total quality management efforts are working in this situation?

Training for Empowerment

Employees need training to prepare for empowerment. Training sessions should address the feeling that management has not abandoned its responsibility by asking employees to resolve guest concerns. Employees may also experience anxiety in dealing with guests who are upset. Front office managers must develop flexible but relatively routine methods for employees to use to achieve a uniform delivery of service.

Training for empowerment begins by asking employees how they feel about providing guests with good service. Front office managers might ask employees how they think the hotel can make the guest feel most comfortable. Questions that pertain to employees' recent personal experiences at check-in or checkout may yield opportunities for discussion. Training continues with a list of empowerment policy standards that describe the authority and responsibility included in their job description. Employee-manager dialog about these standards helps clarify employee understanding and concerns and identify manager communication issues. The manager should demonstrate and have employees go over the use of empowerment policy standards. Managers should also hold follow-up training sessions that include reviews of employee performance and opportunities for employee feedback.

Training for Hospitality Management

Part of a service management program involves employee training to deliver hospitality. Just as managers discuss what they want in an employee, they decide what must be done to convey hospitality to travelers who are away from home. Of course, this discussion is not performed in isolation and requires input from employees. Using the guest service cycle (see Figure 11-6), the planning group determines what each front-line employee must do at each point to extend hospitality.

> The key to making training pay off is knowing what we want the trainees to be able to do when they have finished the program. An effective training process starts with a performance analysis. We must analyze the various jobs to be done in serving the customer well, and then spell out the knowledge, attitudes, and skills required of the person doing the job.[21]

You cannot take it for granted that the desk clerk knows to maintain eye contact with the guest during the check-in procedure while using a computer, that the switchboard operator knows to alert a security supervisor when a guest mysteriously hangs up in the middle of a call for information, or that a bellhop knows to check the operating conditions of the heating, ventilating, and air-conditioning unit and television when he or she brings the guest's luggage to the room. The expressions of hospitality must be identified so that each employee can be trained to convey them.

Evaluating the Service Management Program

Any program requires methods for evaluating whether the program has successfully achieved its goals. This chapter opened by defining hospitality as the generous and cordial provision of service to a guest. How do the owners and managers of a hotel know hospitality is being delivered?

Albrecht and Zemke base the development of a sound evaluation procedure on identifying the guest's moments of truth.[22] Figure 11-6 outlines the moments of truth in the guest service cycle. This outline can serve as a guideline for what should be evaluated. The more work done to identify the components of the guest service cycle for a specific hotel property, the more effective its managers and employees will be in evaluating service delivery. Specific desired behaviors can be identified and measured. For example, if part of the registration process depends on a prompt hotel shuttle van to pick up and deliver guests to the hotel, then complaints from guests about late or slow service tell the owners, managers, and employees that front-line employees are not delivering the necessary service correctly. Customer comment cards are one way hotel management and staff can receive feedback. However, not all satisfied or dissatisfied guests complete these cards. Owners, managers, and employees who are committed to a service management program must develop additional methods for determining guest satisfaction.

Another method that can be used to obtain useful feedback is to have front-line staff, such as a desk clerk, inquire about the guest's visit during checkout. Simply asking "Was everything all right?" is not sufficient. If the guest folio indicates the guest charged meals, beverages, room service, long-distance calls, or valet services, the front desk clerk should ask about the delivery of service for each: "Was your food delivered hot, on time, and removed from the hallway promptly?" "How did you enjoy the live entertainment in the lounge?" A method of communicating guest responses to the appropriate departments, which can rectify the errors or reward the front-line employee, completes the process of evaluating the success of a service management program. For example, a quick call to the manager on duty that relates the information received from the guest can assist in remedying a potential guest service problem.

An inquiry from the desk clerk at checkout provides feedback about service quality after the fact. Supervisors of the dining room, lounge, bell staff, housekeeping department, maintenance crew, and the like must develop communication procedures with their employees to monitor the guest's experience as it occurs. The host or hostess must develop sensitivity to a guest's reaction to menu items and prices; the bellhop must constantly be aware of the guest's needs for information, directions, or assistance with luggage; the housekeeping employee must be aware of the guest's needs for additional amenities, linens, or cleanliness of the public areas. All feedback must be communicated to the front-line employee for continuous improvement of service.

Follow-through

Vital to every service management program is the continued management of the program over time. In the hospitality industry, continued management can be difficult. A hotel operates every hour of every day, and innumerable jobs are involved in keeping it running smoothly and profitably. Managers can begin a service management program with the best of intentions, but too often it is dropped or neglected in the day-to-day flurry of operations. Albrecht and Zemke remind us that "isolated change and improvement programs tend to run their course and then to run downhill toward the performance levels that existed before the program. The difference between a program and continuous commitment is management."[23] Management is the key to implementing an effective guest service program. The commitment to hospitality is not a casual one; it requires constant attention, research, training, and evaluation. Only with this commitment can a hotel ensure hospitality every day for every guest.

Interfacing with Other Departments in Delivering Hospitality

One of the many benefits of employing total quality management is the participant's ability to understand fellow team members' job responsibilities. Teams whose members come from various departments in the hotel provide opportunities for insights into other employees' jobs. Sometimes the process of TQM can seem like a maze of charts, processes, interactions, and the like, which tends to confuse the uncommitted. But from the process rises a thorough understanding of how the guest moves through the hospitality system and of the jobs of the providers of these services. Participants in TQM come to realize the delivery of hospitality is not the responsibility of any one person. This may be a startling revelation to employees who feel alone in bearing the responsibility for guest satisfaction. TQM allows all participants the opportunity to see how employees from every departments share in the hospitality activity.

The "that's not my job" attitude is easy to adopt in a management system in which TQM is not used. Employees who feel they have distinct job duties within and between departments and are not paid to venture beyond them may contribute to the delivery of unacceptable service. Department managers who use TQM have the opportunity to prioritize service concepts and methods to deliver service with employees. This interaction gives managers and employees the occasion to air concerns about how restrictions resulting from narrowly written job descriptions affect their ability to provide service to the guest.

A typical TQM team assigns representatives from various departments to work on improving a particular guest service. For example, guests may complain there are not enough towels in a guest room. This complaint, especially after housekeeping has closed down for the evening, causes a reduction in guest satisfaction and additional work for the lone front desk clerk on duty.

At the outset, the answer may be to "just put a few more towels in each guest room." The controller of the hotel may see this as additional costs of inventory purchase and laundry. Housekeepers realize that excess supplies in guest rooms have a tendency to vaporize and result in an increase in costs. However, a team approach to this seemingly simple problem uncovers a list of possible solutions an individual employee might overlook.

FRONT-LINE REALITIES

 A guest in room 1104 has requested that housekeeping tidy up after a cocktail reception in his room. He is expecting additional business guests within two hours. He wants you to ensure the housekeeping department will respond within the next half-hour. What should you do?

A team of desk clerks, housekeepers, bellhops, servers, cooks, switchboard operators, cashiers, and supervisors reviews this particular service and how it is delivered. Objective analysis of the components of the service gives employees insight into how departments interact to accomplish their tasks. Brainstorming sessions identify possible improvements that can be debated by team members. Additional meetings find team members crystallizing concepts and gaining insights and respect for jobs performed by team members. The team may decide to have front desk clerks alert the housekeeping staff when more than two people check into a guest room. The housekeeping staff can then routinely bring additional towels. This decision not only solves the problem of guest dissatisfaction caused by too few towels but provides an opportunity for front-line employees to develop and deliver a guest service. It is no longer a front desk problem or a housekeeping problem but a *team* effort to produce a satisfied guest.

An example of a service management program is Hilton's Hilton Pride Program, which recognizes exceptional hotel performance and customer satisfaction. "The Pride Program reinforces our pledge to maintain exceptional levels of customer satisfaction while building pride in the workplace. This sense of pride enables us to create a level of service that brings our customers back," says Dieter H. Huckestein, executive vice president, Hilton Hotels Corporation, and president of the company's owned and managed hotel operations.

The performance criteria include the following items:

- Customer satisfaction tracking studies
- Guest comment card responses
- Mystery shopper evaluations
- Team member surveys
- EBITDA (earnings before interest, taxes, depreciation, and amortization)
- Room RevPAR
- RevPAR index
- Brand management and product standard"[24]

Delta Hotels [was] awarded the prestigious Order of Excellence, [2000 and 2007] the highest distinction conferred by Canada's National Quality Institute (NQI), in its Canada Awards for Excellence program. The award recognizes outstanding achievements in the areas of quality, customer service and a healthy workplace.

"From our front line to the heart of the house and to our leadership teams, each and every one of our 7,100 dedicated employees has been focused on quality since we began our journey in 1996," says Hank Stackhouse, president of Delta Hotels.[25]

Customer Relationship Management

Customer relationship management (CRM) is a system that allows hotel managers to integrate technology with support customer service techniques that lead to top-notch customer service. The technology that is so apparent in CRM must play a secondary role because one-on-one interaction with the guest continues to support reasons for return visits. Neil Holm, president of hypen, an information systems management company describes CRM as follows.

> Often referred to as a type of technology, CRM is first and foremost a business philosophy—a way to consistently treat your guests right. Technology is the enabler that helps get useful information into the hands of your management and staff so that they can more powerfully foster guest satisfaction and loyalty.[26]
>
> Haley and Watson list (1) guest recognition, (2) data capture and maintenance, (3) channel integration and consistency, (4) ranking and discrimination, and (5) two-way personalized dialogs as the five elements of CRM. Guest recognition on a routine basis is easy, but when the guest customer base is sporadic or international, then we need assistance with data on relevant information. This is where the computerized information of the guest's coffee or golf time preferences is important. Data capture and maintenance is essential to keeping this system working properly. Every time a guest indicates that something has changed, it should be reflected in the system.[27]

Solution to Opening Dilemma

An immediate response to correct this guest service situation is to have the desk clerk register the guest at $99 per night, discuss the situation with the supervisor after the guest leaves the front desk, and then have the front desk clerk call the guest to confirm the room rate. However, a more effective way to handle similar situations in the future is to work with the general manager and owner to develop a service strategy statement and obtain financial resources to support a service management program. Exploration and application of employee motivation and empowerment are necessary to make a service management program work. Total quality management teams will help employees determine tasks required to deliver service. New front office managers should not take the delivery of good service for granted. High-quality service is planned, not happenstance.

Chapter Recap

This chapter stressed the importance of delivering continuous high-quality service in hotels, as defined by the guest. Successful extension of hospitality starts with management's commitment to a service management program. Preparing a service strategy statement focuses the planning efforts of owners, management, and employees. Principles of total quality management provide managers with an opportunity to involve front-line employees in analyzing the components of delivery of service and methods to improve existing services. The development of the service management program requires the involvement of front-line employees, discussion of the guest cycle, moments of truth, employee buy-in, screening of potential employees, empowerment, training, evaluation of the service management program, follow-through, and interfacing with other departments in delivering hospitality. A long-term commitment to a successful service management program is necessary.

End-of-Chapter Questions

1. How important do you think hospitality is to guests in a hotel? If you are employed in a hotel, ask your manager how he or she feels about the importance of providing hospitality to guests.

2. How would you develop a service strategy statement? Why is this an important first step in managing the hospitality planning process?

3. Why should front-line employees be involved in the development of a service management program?

4. How would you apply TQM to a particular situation at your place of employment? What challenges do you think will be presented in the application of this management concept? What suggestions would you make to your manager to resolve these challenges?

5. If you are employed in a hotel, prepare an outline, similar to that in Figure 11-6, of the guest service cycle there.

6. What are "moments of truth" in a service delivery occasion? How can a front office manager identify them?

7. Why must an employee buy in to a service management program? What would you do to ensure employee commitment?

8. Discuss techniques that are useful in determining whether or not prospective employees have the attributes needed to extend hospitality.

9. Why is training an important component of the service management program? How could a front office manager begin to identify the skills needed for delivery of hospitality? If you are employed in a hotel, did you receive training in delivering hospitality?

10. How can a front office manager measure the effectiveness of a service management program?

11. Why is follow-through so necessary in the continued delivery of hospitality?

CASE STUDY 1101

The new owners of The Times Hotel have just boarded a plane at a city in Asia. Their stay in the Mandarin Hotel was superb. The attention to service was excellent, and they felt pampered. During the flight,

CASE STUDY 1101 (CONTINUED)

one of the owners reads an article in a popular magazine concerning the mediocre service in hotels in the United States. The article details the lack of concern for the guest in many properties, the high cost of hotel rooms, and the abrupt attitudes of the hotel staff. The owners realize many of the problems mentioned in the article can be found at The Times Hotel.

The next day, at the general staff meeting, the owners share their concerns with the management staff. As the group listens attentively, they cannot help but think, "We have heard this before—another idea from the owners that will make more work for our already overworked staff" However, this time the owners declare they don't know where to begin; they feel overwhelmed by the size of the problem. "Let's develop a plan," they suggest. All managers must do some research on this topic and return for a brainstorming session in two weeks.

The front office manager, Ana Chavarria, finds this a challenge! She has read some of the articles on service management in the trade journals and decides to do more research on the topic.

Through her reading, Ms. Chavarria learns there must be a financial commitment by the owners and a managerial commitment by the staff to make this work. If the employees become involved in the planning stages, it should work just fine. She thinks getting the cooperation of the employees will be easy if the owners pledge their financial commitment. She guesses the rest of the management staff will probably halfheartedly go along with the project—if it is forced on them.

At the scheduled brainstorming session, Ana outlines her findings. The owners are reluctant to incur additional expenses to motivate employees. They respond, "Let's find some more creative ways." The other managers suggest preparing posters with photos of employees who do a good job, placing names of employees who do a good job on the marquee, and placing a suggestion box in the employee lunchroom. Continued focus on the financial aspects distracts the group from discussing the content of a service management program. After two hours of futile effort, the owners decide to table the service management program.

If you were the front office manager, what would you have included in your presentation about developing an effective service management program?

CASE STUDY 1102

Ana Chavarria, front office manager of The Times Hotel, and Lorraine DeSantes, the hotel's director of marketing, learn their city will be hosting the next Olympic Games. The city council and the tourism board are planning to develop a program to ensure the delivery of high-quality service by all agencies, private and commercial, to the many guests. Individual groups (hotels, restaurants, public transportation, etc.) will meet and decide on a course of action. Margaret Chu, general manager of The Times Hotel, wants Ana and Lorraine to represent the hotel on the Hotel Hospitality Commission. Because the Games are several years away, there is ample time to involve various constituencies in developing a plan for implementation.

After a few meetings with the commission, the group feels it should break into smaller teams to discuss developing specific components of delivering high-quality service. Ana and Lorraine are heading the Service to the International Visitor planning team. What suggestions would you give Ana and Lorraine as they lead this team? Prepare an agenda for the team's first meeting.

CASE STUDY 1103

Ana Chavarria, front office manager of The Times Hotel, and Lorraine DeSantes, the hotel's director of marketing, are reviewing the statistics from a recent Customer Comment Card Summary. Things are looking challenging. Ana and Lorraine are friends, but they know they must come up with strategies to get a handle on why guest service isn't being delivered. What strategies would you suggest they utilize to make customer service a priority for The Times Hotel?

The Times Hotel

CUSTOMER COMMENT CARD SUMMARY, Week ending November 17, 200X

Product/Service	Nov.17.		
■ Overbooked	10	■ Slow room service	6
■ Slow check-in	5	■ Dirty room	7
■ Slow checkout	3	■ Poor selection of amenities	2
■ Room rate too high	8	■ Bedding insufficient	5
■ Delay getting into room	12	■ Lack of response from housekeeping	4
		■ Rudeness from bell staff	1

Notes

1. Karl Albrecht and Ron Zemke, *Service America!* (New York: Dow Jones–Irwin, 1985).

2. InterContinental Hotels Group, Total Quality Manager, ph.jobstreet.com/jobs/2005/3/default/20default/20/372616.htm, March 26, 2005.

3. Albrecht and Zemke, 6–7.

4. John W. Young, "Four Seasons Expansion into the U.S. Market," paper delivered at the Council on Hotel, Restaurant, and Institutional Education, Toronto, Canada, July 30, 1988; edited July 17, 2001, p. 29.

5. Cheryl Hall, "Data Crunchers at Irving-Based UniFocus Help Hotels Improve Customers Service, Maintain Employee Morale," *Dallas Morning News*, July 16, 2000. Reprinted with permission of the *Dallas Morning News*.

6. Young, 22.

7. Eric J. Johnson and William G. Layton, "Quality Customer Service, Part II," *Restaurant Hospitality* (October 1987): 40.

8. Ernest R. Cadotte and Normand Turgeon, "Key Factors in Guest Satisfaction," *Cornell Hotel Restaurant Administration Quarterly* 28, no. 4 (February 1988): 44–51.

9. Albrecht and Zemke, 33–34.

10. Young, 9–10.

11. Don Hellriegel and John W. Slochum, *Management* (New York: Addison-Wesley, 1991), 697.

12. Albrecht and Zemke, 37–38.

13. Nancy J. Allin and Kelly Halpine, "From Clerk and Cashier to Guest Agent," *Florida International University Hospitality Review* 6, no. 1 (Spring 1988): 42.

14. Albrecht and Zemke, 27.

15. Ibid., 32.

16. Ibid., 96–97.

17. Ibid., 107–108.

18. Young, 14, 35.

19. Albrecht and Zemke, 114.

20. Young, 25–26.

21. Albrecht and Zemke, 112–113.

22. Ibid., 139.

23. Ibid., 144.

24. Jeanne Datz, "Hilton Hotels Corporation Selects 16 out of More than 300 U.S. Hilton and Hilton Garden Inn Hotels for the 2000 Hilton Pride Customer Satisfaction Awards," Hilton Hotels Corporation, Beverly Hills, CA, April 16, 2001.

25. Sandy Indig, October, 2007, http://www.deltahotels.com/fr/about/press_view.html?id=207.

26. Neil Holm, "Understanding the Power of CRM," www.hotel-online.com/News/PR2003_4th/Nov03_UnderstandingCRM.html, April 7, 2005.

27. Mark Haley and Bill Watson, "The ABCs of CRM," www.hotel-online.com/News/PR2003_1st/Mar03_CRMHaley.html, April 7, 2005.

Key Words

customer relationship management (CRM)

cycle of service

empowerment

flowchart

front-line employees

hospitality

incentive programs

moments of truth

service management program

service strategy statement

shift leader

CHAPTER 12

Training for Hospitality

OPENING DILEMMA

Enrique Garcia, a hotel general manager, has heard the last complaint about his staff! He is tired of writing letters of apology and comping guest stays because of poor delivery of service. Recently, a guest complained that after he left the front desk area in his wheelchair, a desk clerk was overheard making an unkind remark. Two days before that, another hotel employee took 45 minutes to respond to a guest's request for assistance in moving a heavy box from his room to the lobby area, and that same person said it took 10 minutes to go through the check-in process. Mr. Garcia wants to contact an advertising agency to assist him in cleaning up the hotel's image.

Determining Employee Hospitality Qualities

Assessing personnel needs requires identifying the skills and character traits required to do a particular job. Frequently, the front office manager can recite a list of problems with front desk personnel but cannot identify their strengths. The ability to recognize positive traits—skills of present employees as well as skills a potential employee should have—helps not only in choosing the right candidate for a particular position but also in assigning tasks to employees that match their abilities. If you do not know the skills of your current staff and the skills future staff will need, you cannot assemble a staff that will meet your needs or make effective use of their skills.

Job Analysis and Job Descriptions

A front office manager should begin by preparing job analysis and descriptions of each position in a department. Identify the responsibilities and objectives of each and then consider the personal qualities, skills, and experience needed to perform those duties. For example, a front office manager may want front desk clerks to sell the more expensive suites or rooms and other services of the hotel. To accomplish this objective, an individual must have an outgoing personality or be willing to accept new responsibilities as a challenge or an opportunity to grow. The front office manager may wish the front desk clerks to be more efficient in handling clerical duties neatly and accurately. These qualities may be found in a person with prior experience in other clerical or sales positions. Previous experience outside the labor force—for example, as an officer in a service club or a community group—may indicate the person's leadership skills and ability to organize projects. These and other traits should be viewed as a complete package. The motivational concepts discussed later in the chapter will help a front office manager identify and develop an employee's positive attributes.

Positive Hospitality Character Traits

A front office manager must think about the character traits necessary to deliver hospitality on a daily basis. These traits include maturity, an outgoing personality, and patience as well as a willingness to accept constructive criticism. The employee should also feel comfortable selling, as he or she must promote the hotel's services.

Outgoing employees are able to seek out other individuals and make the initial effort to set a relationship in motion. Employees who are extroverts enjoy meeting guests and making them feel welcome. This is the type of employee who, in many cases, can turn a difficult situation into a challenge. For example, if a guest says there is no way he or she will be walked to another hotel—"After all, a guaranteed reservation is a commitment"—an outgoing person may be better at persuading the guest the alternative hotel will surely "meet your highest standards" rather than saying nothing at all.

Mature employees are able to assess the big picture and quickly analyze a situation before acting. Instead of reacting to a situation, this type of employee allows a guest to vent his or her concerns before offering a response. Mature employees also possess and exhibit patience in situations that require time to think or to carry out a request. Guests may be confused about geographic directions in an unfamiliar surrounding; a mature employee gladly repeats and offers written directions or sketches to allow the guest time to absorb the information.

Practicing Promotional Skills

Employees who possess a positive attitude about constructive criticism prosper and progress in a hotel career. All employees occasionally make errors in judgment and fail to meet standards. Employees who want to continue to learn seek a supervisor's insights into why a particular situation resulted from their actions.

Front desk clerks who are comfortable with practicing promotional skills are a great asset to a front office manager. This type of person accepts the challenge to sell products and services throughout the hotel and seek ways to meet or exceed sales quotas. This quality allows a front desk clerk to understand the total effort necessary to produce a profit for a hotel.

Screening for Hospitality Qualities

Composing questions prior to interviewing an applicant to determine if he or she has the personal qualities needed to fulfill a job's requirements is usually effective. The interview should have some structure but be flexible enough for both the interviewer and the applicant to freely express their concerns.

The front office manager begins to develop a list of questions based on the job description to guide the interview. He or she wants to determine if the candidate has an outgoing personality, patience, the ability to accept constructive criticism, and the ability to sell. These are only a few of the qualities for which a front office manager wants to screen in an interview.

An Outgoing Personality

The first question attempts to determine if the applicant is outgoing. Although observing the person during the interview gives some indication of how he or she deals with others, you could get more insight with this question: "Tell me about the last time you went out to dinner. What did you like about the host or hostess?" A response that indicates appreciation for a friendly welcome shows the candidate is aware of the concept of hospitality.

You have scheduled three job interviews for tomorrow. In the past six months, you have lost six front desk clerks. As a front office manager, how will you prepare for the interviews to ensure you choose the best employee?

Patience

To learn about the level of patience a job candidate possesses, ask a question such as "Tell me about your recent participation in an event (sporting, social, or work) at which you received less than what you had expected." For example, if you were a member of a sporting team that participated in a playoff and lost, how did you handle recovery? Or if a good friend of yours didn't get a job he or she was expecting, what did you have to say to him or her? A response that indicates that small details were overlooked but overall the experience was rewarding may indicate the person is willing to be a team player.

Ability to Accept Constructive Criticism

To assess a candidate's ability to accept constructive criticism, a question such as "At your previous job, how did your manager handle a situation in which you did not meet stated goals, showed up late for work, or didn't follow company procedure?" may be used. A candidate's response to this reflects how well he or she understands the reason for the reprimand; how the situation was corrected may indicate how the person accepts constructive criticism.

Interest in Selling

A question that allows a candidate to express his or her openness to soliciting donations for a charity assists an interviewer in understanding the applicant's desire to sell products and services for the hotel.

These questions do not guarantee the front office manager will choose wisely, but the effort will produce a more effective track record of screening for hospitality.

Developing an Orientation Program

The person hired to work in the front office is in a unique position. In no other department of the hotel is each employee expected to know the operations, personnel, and layout of the facilities of every other department. The front office employee is constantly bombarded with questions from guests and other employees concerning when a certain banquet or reception is being held, where key supervisors are, or how to find the lounge or pool area. The *orientation process* introduces new hires to the organization and work environment and is vital in giving them background information about the property. This program helps new hires become aware of the activities, procedures, people, and layout of the hotel. It is a critical first step in training new employees.

Of the utmost importance is ensuring the orientation is thorough and well designed. An employee who is given a brief introduction to the people who work the same shift, a quick tour of the guest rooms, and information concerning the time clock can hardly be expected to be competent. By the time orientation is complete, new employees should be able to answer guests' questions easily. If they don't have answers at their fingertips, they should know how to find them quickly. For example, if someone asks for the general manager by name and the new front desk clerk responds, "Who is that?" an inefficient and unprofessional image of the organization is conveyed. The new employee should know who that person is and how to reach him or her. Moreover, orientation should prepare all new hires to provide correct and complete information to guests, the general public, or other employees.

Orientation programs for front office employees differ from one establishment to another. However, the following outline can be used as a basis for a program for any establishment. This outline incorporates factors common to all properties, such as the economic position of the establishment in the community, an overview of the hotel, the employee handbook, the policy and procedure manual, and an introduction to the front office environment.

Economic Position of the Property in the Community

A new employee benefits from knowing how a hotel fits into the economic scheme of the community and the region. He or she may be impressed to learn, for example, that a particular hotel is responsible for 10 percent of the employment in the area. Information concerning the value of the tax dollars generated by employees, significance of the tourism market, number of conventions and subsequent guests who rely on the services of the operation, significant growth accomplishments, and other economic contributions not only reassure new employees they have chosen the right employer but also instill a sense of pride in the organization. These and other economic indicators help the new hire think of the employer as a well-respected member of the business community. Larger organizations can prepare a slide or multimedia presentation to demonstrate their commitment to the business area.

Overview of the Lodging Establishment

An overview of the lodging establishment includes the number of rooms (accompanied by a detailed printed handout of the layout), a list of services offered in the establishment, an organization chart of the staff in the various departments, and, of course, a tour of the property.

Guest Rooms   The guest rooms are an important part of the day-to-day activity of the front office staff. The sooner the employee is aware of the location and contents of the rooms, the quicker he or she feels comfortable with the job. Floor plans for each floor and a printed summary of the typical contents of the rooms are handy references the new person can review at a later time. For instance, if the odd-numbered floors have three suites and the even-numbered floors have study areas for businesspersons, including this information in the printed material assists in the training process.

Service Areas   The services offered by the hotel (restaurants, banquet facilities, room services, lounges, pool, athletics room, and gift shops) should be identified during the orientation program so the new employee can assist and direct guests. Listing the hours of operation for each department helps the new employee learn about the systematic operation of the hotel.

Organization Chart   The people listed on the organization chart should be pointed out to the new hires. These people and their lines of authority and responsibilities should be explained. This background information assists in decision making and communication of information to department heads. It also gives the new hire a sense of belonging to the group.

Tour of the Property   The overview of the lodging establishment is not complete without a tour of the property. This tour should include the guest rooms and guest room areas, major departments, and service areas such as restaurants, banquet rooms, gift shops, and recreational facilities. The tour can be informal yet specific in content. It allows the new employee to see the establishment both as a place of work and as a place of recreation for the guest. The tour also helps the employee understand the front office's relationship to the entire establishment.

Employee Handbook

The *employee handbook* provides general guidelines concerning employee conduct and is a valuable resource for new hires (Figure 12-1). In this publication, hotel managers describe many topics related to personnel issues, including:

- Pay categories
- Evaluation procedures
- Vacation time
- Personal days
- Holidays
- Paydays
- Use of controlled substances
- Social interaction with guests
- Resolving disputes with guests and other employees
- Insurance benefits
- Uniform requirements
- 401(k), 403(b) plans

FIGURE 12-1

All employees should be given an employee handbook or orientation folder. Photo courtesy of the author.

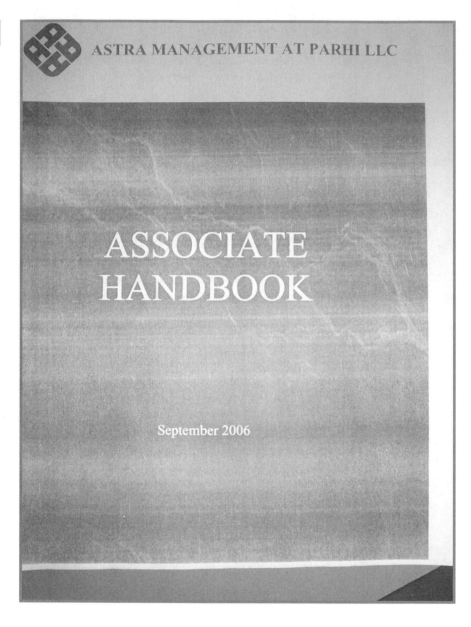

ASTRA MANAGEMENT AT PARHI LLC

ASSOCIATE HANDBOOK

September 2006

Sometimes candidates for positions at an establishment or new hires do not ask questions about these policies because they feel the employer may think them greedy, lazy, or overconcerned with a certain issue. On the contrary, these questions form the basis for a good employment contract. Employers should make the effort to discuss and explain their personnel policies.

Policy and Procedure Manual

The *policy and procedure manual*, also known as *standard operating procedures* (SOPs), outlines how the specific duties of each job are to be performed. This is another specific set of guidelines that is valuable for employee training. The policy and procedure manual addresses topics such as the following:

- Operation of the PMS and other equipment in the front office
- Reservations
- Registrations
- Posting
- Written and oral communications with guests and other employees of the hotel
- Checkouts
- Preparation of the night audit
- Safety and security measures

The front office manager who takes the time to develop these guidelines will have prepared a useful supervisory tool. Providing materials in writing to supplement the spoken training session allows new employees to review the skills they must master and to retain more of what they are taught.

Introduction to the Front Office Staff

The final segment of the orientation process is an introduction to the front office itself. This introduction prepares new hires for the training program that will follow. It familiarizes them with coworkers, equipment they will be using, personnel procedures, and interdepartmental relations.

New employees should be introduced to the current staff of front desk clerks, bellhops, telephone operators, reservation clerks, night auditors, supervisors, and others. A little planning on the front office manager's part is required to ensure the new employee meets the entire staff in the first few days. Saying a few words about the role of each employee during the introductions not only makes new hires feel more comfortable with their coworkers but also makes each current staff member feel like a special part of the team. Current staff members also appreciate meeting the new addition. This step is often overlooked, and new employees feel awkward for days or weeks.

Equipment Overview

The equipment in the front office should be described and shown to the new employee. Brief remarks about each piece serve as a reference point when needed skills are explained in detail during the training program. This part of the orientation program can be slowed somewhat to allow the new hire to become familiar with the equipment. The operator of the call-accounting system may have the new person pull up a chair to watch how calls are handled. The new employee may be encouraged to observe how a fellow desk clerk processes registrations and checkouts. The front office manager should assure the new employee that specific training will follow. This is a time for familiarization only.

The new employee should be shown how to check in for a shift on the PMS or the time clock. The location and timing of the posted schedule of shift coverage should also be indicated. The importance of reporting for duty on time and its effect on fellow employees should be explained at this time.

Interdepartmental Cooperation

Interdepartmental cooperation must be stressed during the introduction to the front office. This is an ideal time to establish the importance of synchronization among the housekeeping, maintenance, marketing and sales, food and beverage, and front office departments. The front office must take the lead in establishing good communications among departments. Because the front office is the initial contact for the guest, obtaining status reports, maintaining communications, and knowing the functions being hosted each day are the responsibilities of the front office staff. Overlooking trivial misunderstandings with other departments sometimes takes colossal effort, but the front office must keep the communication lines open. Guests benefit from and appreciate the work of a well-informed front office.

Administering the Orientation Program

Administering the orientation program requires planning by the front office manager. The front office is a hectic place, and there is much for the new employee to learn. Concern for the guests and the services and information they require must be a priority. A standard *orientation checklist* should be prepared that summarizes all items that must be covered during orientation; Figure 12-2 shows an example. The checklist ensures the new employee is properly introduced to the front office. It should be initialed by both the new employee and the orientation supervisor after the program is complete to verify that all policies were covered. Thus, no one can claim to be ignorant because there is written evidence the material was covered in the orientation program.

Selection of Orientation Leader

The orientation program should be delivered by a member of the supervisory staff or a trained senior staff member in the front office. This person must have the ability convey the attitude of the organization as well as the tasks of the employees. Whoever handles the orientation should not be on duty at the same time; it is impossible to explain so much about the property to a new employee while performing other tasks.

FIGURE 12-2 An orientation checklist is a useful tool that assists in providing a comprehensive orientation.

____ Economic position in community
____ Community geography
____ Printed floor plan of hotel
____ Visits to guest rooms
____ Hours for guest services
____ Organization chart
____ Explanation of key management personnel
____ Interdepartmental relations
____ Visits to:
  • Food and beverage areas
  • Housekeeping
  • Maintenance
  • Marketing and sales

  • Controller
  • Human resources department
  • Gift shop
  • Pool and athletics area

____ Sample restaurant menus
____ Employee handbook:
  • Dress code
  • Hygiene
  • Benefits
  • Pay rate
  • Paydays
  • Evaluation procedures
  • Vacation policy

  • Sick leave
  • Holiday policy
  • Drug and alcohol policy
  • Social interaction with guests
  • Schedules
  • Grievances

____ Policy and procedure manual
____ Coworkers in front office
____ Equipment in front office
____ Time clock
____ Fire and safety procedures
____ Training program

_____   _____
Orientation Supervisor/Date)   *(Employee/Date)*

FRONT-LINE REALITIES

In your new role as front office manager, you remember reading about the importance of an orientation program to new hires with disabilities, and you also remember the lack of an orientation experienced by a friend of yours with a disability. You want to organize a thorough orientation program and present it to the general manager. How would you proceed?

The orientation program helps the employer-employee relationship begin on the right foot. It introduces the workplace, guidelines and procedures, coworkers, and management staff to the new hire. The orientation program also introduces new employees to their work environment and encourages them to be a part of it.

Developing a Training Program

Training is an important management function, and it is required to develop and ensure high-quality performance.[1] In the hospitality industry, some hotel organizations take training seriously; others talk about it extensively but have no real program in place. Those that have developed, instituted, and continued to update their training programs consider them great assets in human resources management. They allow the management team to develop qualified employees who can perform jobs according to predetermined standards. A good training program reduces errors because all procedures are explained and demonstrated.

Planning and developing a training program for front office employees includes identifying the tasks performed by the front office staff, preparing step-by-step procedures for each task, determining who will train employees, administering the training program, and reviewing the steps in the training process.

Identification of Tasks and Job Management Skills

The tasks performed by each employee are usually identified in the job description. The job description is based on the job analysis (discussed in chapter 2), which lists, in chronological order, the daily tasks performed by the employee. For example, the front desk clerk performs the following tasks on the day shift:

6:00 A.M.	Enters start time with PMS.
6:05	Talks with night auditor about activities on the 11:00 P.M. to 7:00 A.M. shift; checks the front desk message book for current operational notes.
6:10	Obtains *cash bank*, a specific amount of paper money and coins issued to a cashier to be used for making change, from controller; counts and verifies contents.
6:30	Reviews daily report concerning occupancy rate and daily room rate.
6:35	Obtains function sheet (list of activities and special events, receptions, and the like) for the day.
6:37	Obtains housekeeper's report for the previous day.
6:40	Calls housekeeping and maintenance departments to determine the communications list (a log of unusual occurrences or special messages front office personnel should know about) from the previous shift(s).

6:45	Calls restaurant to learn specials for lunch and dinner.
6:50	Reviews expected checkouts and reservations for the day.
6:55	Checks out guests until 9:30 A.M.

All of the tasks identified in the job analysis must be broken down further into specific skills to build a sound training program. This may seem like a laborious procedure. It is! But the first step is always the most cumbersome. Using the job analysis for each of the jobs in the front office ensures that all tasks required to deliver hospitality to the guest are included in the training program.

Preparing Step-by-Step Procedures

Step-by-step procedures for each task help the trainee understand how to perform tasks correctly. This approach also helps the trainer prepare and deliver training sessions more efficiently.

If a hotel front office has a PMS, the operator of the computer terminal must learn to enter data or commands sequentially. *Documentation*, written instructions on how to operate computer software, accompanies all property management systems. Documentation can be used as a basis for developing the step-by-step training procedure for using the PMS, and it can serve as a model for preparing step-by-step procedures for other tasks. A step-by-step procedure to complete a guest checkout on the PMS might include the following:

1. Inquire about the guest's accommodations.

2. Enter the guest's room number.

3. Inquire about late charges.

4. Confirm method of payment.

5. Print a hard copy of the folio.

6. Allow the guest to review the folio.

7. Accept cash or credit card or bill-to-account.

8. Enter amount of payment.

9. Enter method of payment.

10. Enter department code.

11. Check for zero balance.

12. Give the guest a copy of the folio.

13. Inquire if additional reservations are needed.

14. Make farewell comments.

Each of these procedures can be subdivided as necessary. For example, as part of step 6, the new desk clerk could be trained to point out major sections of the folio and charges incurred so the guest is aware of all the charges that make up the total. The guest can then ask questions about any of the charges at once, rather than after the bill is produced, thus eliminating extra work for the controller's department.

Management Concepts

In addition to task performance, less tangible skills must be addressed in a training program for front office employees. Stress management, time management, and organizational skills are among the areas that should be discussed. Although these skills are often covered in seminar formats, they cannot be considered in isolation. They are better understood when integrated into the training program as a whole, so they can be applied to task performance. For example, the employee being trained to check out a guest should be made aware this process may occur under stressful conditions; he or she could face long lines, many guests questioning charges, and pressure from other guests to keep the line moving. Learning to remaining calm under these circumstances does come with experience, but the tenets of stress management will help even the new employee handle difficult situations. Self-control and concern for the guest's welfare are paramount.

Mastering time management is another important skill that enables employees to perform particular tasks at required times. For example, various departments regularly depend on front office employees to relay messages to guests and other departments; if the front office does not come through, a great deal of confusion results for all concerned. Organizational skills help employees deal with their workload systematically rather than jumping from one task to another without completing any of them. Completing paperwork promptly, rather than allowing it to mount into an intimidating pile, is one example of an organizational skill that can improve performance.

Steps in the Training Process

The recommended steps in the training process include preparation, delivery, trial and error, and follow-up.

Preparation: Get Ready

Behavioral Objectives: What Do You Want the Trainee to Do?

The trainer must plan the details of the training session. The first step is to prepare behavioral objectives for trainees. These objectives identify what trainees should know when the session is over and allow the trainees to achieve expected changes in behavior. They assist trainees in building their knowledge base as they develop skills. Behavioral objectives define what the trainee should be able to do, how effectively he or she should do it, and when the task should be complete. For example, a behavioral objective for a training session on guest check-in might be: "The trainee will be able to perform the guest check-in procedure for a guest with a prior reservation on the PMS with 100 percent accuracy in five minutes." This focuses the trainer on training a desk clerk to complete a check-in for a guest with a reservation, not a check-in for a guest without a reservation. The trainee must also have already mastered the step-by-step procedure for operating the registration module on the PMS. The goal of 100 percent accuracy in five minutes may be unrealistic to achieve during the actual training session because practice is required. The desk clerk must practice to achieve the speed.

Train the Trainer: The Trainer Must Be Ready.

In addition to preparing behavioral objectives for each training session, the trainer must know how to present the new skill to the trainee, relate the skill to other parts of the employee's job, review the presentation area and scheduling for the session, and supply ancillary materials, such as audiovisual presentation equipment and printed matter.

Presenting a skill requires the trainer to demonstrate the step-by-step procedure with the needs of the trainee in mind. This is not the time to show off how quickly the trainer can check in a guest. The trainer must be patient and consider the task from a beginner's point of view. First, the trainer must explain what the trainee is expected to learn. Next, he or she must repeat key instructions, particularly when demonstrating complicated equipment. The trainee must also be informed about where he or she can find assistance if help is needed (in printed instructions, with the user-friendly Help menu on the terminal, or from another employee). Trainers should always explain slowly and be sure the trainee understands all explanations as he or she goes along.

The trainer should also keep in mind what is best presented to trainees in various areas of the front office or hotel and at specific times of the day. Will the area be free of distractions and available for training? Is the time to present this skill better scheduled for the midmorning, early afternoon, or late evening? Training a new employee to use the PMS at the height of the morning rush almost guarantees failure. Of course, new employees must work under distracting and disorderly conditions, but during training they require a distraction-free, orderly area so they can concentrate on mastering skills.

The trainer should also be sure the materials needed to deliver the session are ready for use and in order. Have DVDs and CDs been ordered and received? Have they been previewed? Does the data/video projector work? Is the amplified lectern with microphone in working order? Has the video camera with tripod been prepared for use? Does the DVD on a cart work? Has the laptop with Internet connection been organized? Has the room been scheduled for the satellite reception, the use of telephone lines to send and receive video and audio impressions? Have *telephone initiation and reception agreements*, contracts between senders and receivers of satellite reception concerning specifications of the telephone call and who pays for the call, been set? Have the coordinates been set for the satellite dish reception? Has the printed material required for training and follow-up been duplicated? Are enough copies available? These preparations are essential to a professional presentation. They allow in-depth training to occur without interruption and provide the trainee with a means for review after the session is over.

Training Is a Communication Process: You Have to Help Them Think It Through.

Explaining how the skill being presented relates to other parts of the employee's job improves learning, enabling the trainee to understand how a particular task fits into the job as a whole. Trainees remember more when they understand why a task is important. Such explanations also teach new employees the importance of performing individual tasks correctly; this, in turn, forms the basis for a series of jobs. For example, encouraging front desk clerks to capture accurate information at the time of registration because the hotel marketing department uses that information for guest history to improve its marketing program will encourage them to feel they are participating in efforts to make a financial success of the hotel.

Delivery: Show Me

Adopt the Point of View of the Trainee: He or She Will Learn Better.

When demonstrating skills, the trainer must consider the presentation from the trainee's point of view. For example, present the skill with the trainee to your right or left so the trainee can observe as it is presented. The trainee who cannot see the skill being presented has a much harder time understanding and retaining it. If the trainee is left-handed, special presentation planning is required. Perhaps standing in front of the left-handed person for the presentation will allow him or her to reverse some of the items mentally. If the trainer is aware the trainee is left-handed (in a right-handed operation), training time and employee errors decrease.

Trainers' Communication Techniques: Master a Clear Presentation Style, Explain Jargon, and Present in Logical Steps.

The trainer must speak clearly and distinctly. Mumbling or talking too quickly only confuses the trainee. The trainer must consider not only what he or she says but also how it is stated. If the trainer's tone of voice implies the trainee is incompetent, he or she alienates the trainee. Instead, the trainer should encourage the trainee's efforts, offer praise when a skill is mastered, and always be patient.

Every industry has its own jargon. Trainees should learn hotel jargon during training. For example, *house count*, *no-show*, *sleeper*, *full house*, and *late arrival* are all terms used in the industry. Even if the trainee has previous experience at another lodging property, it is still necessary to review these terms to be sure he or she understands each term as it is used at the current establishment. For example, at a former job, the term *late arrivals* may have referred to guests who arrive after 9:00 P.M.; at the current establishment, however, *late arrival* may refer to anyone arriving after 4:00 P.M.

The presentation should be broken into logical, sequential steps. The step-by-step procedure that was previously prepared allows the front office manager to present the material in an orderly fashion. Trainees understand such straightforward instructions as "Press this key on the keyboard to activate the registration menu" more easily than they understand "Here is the registration menu...Oh, wait a minute. Let's go back to the reservation menu for a minute..." Printed material that outlines the procedure helps the trainee learn the skill with practice.

Relax as a Presenter: It's OK to Make Mistakes.

The trainer is encouraged to think out loud, explaining every step and its importance as the associated skill is demonstrated. The trainer might want to tell a story or two about how he or she performed at a first training session. The trainee can then logically follow the demonstration and feel more comfortable asking questions. This communication process also assists the trainer, who can observe whether or not the trainee is picking up on the skill. The more the trainee is involved in the process, the more likely learning will occur.

After training is complete, the front office manager should watch how the employee performs on the job. Skills performed correctly are a good indication the training was successful. Conversely, if the employee is confused or makes mistakes, it is possible a trainer wasn't stopping to make sure the trainee was following along. As is true of all skills, being a good trainer comes with experience.

Methods of Presentation

The methods a trainer selects to train an employee depend on the topic being presented. Clerical and computer skills are usually taught by skill demonstration and on-the-job training. Maintaining customer relations is usually handled with role-playing, videotaping and subsequent analysis of role-playing, or viewing and analyzing commercially prepared CDs and DVDs.

Skill Demonstration

In *skill demonstration*, the trainer demonstrates specific tasks required to complete a job. The trainer performs a task in a sequential manner and allows the trainee to practice while he or she is present to offer constructive feedback. These practice sessions provide great opportunities to build skills and confidence.

On-the-Job Training

On-the-job training occurs when the employee observes and practices a task while performing his or her job. This method is a mainstay of training in the hospitality industry. Planned training sessions must be incorporated into on-the-job training if this approach is to be successful. This method trains the new employee to perform tasks on an as-needed basis; the employee learns a skill only when he or she has to use it on the job. With this method, however, the demands of the business come first, and training takes a back seat. A consequence of failing to follow through is that the employee is never taught the correct procedures for performing a task. This means the ground on which a good training program is founded—planning, development, organization, delivery, and follow-up procedures—is undermined. The consequence is an employee who does not have all the skills necessary to do the most efficient job.

Role-Playing

Role-playing gives the trainee an opportunity to practice a customer service situation by acting out the role before actually being required to do the job. The front office staff members must often act as sounding boards for complaints and as problem solvers, even when the problem has nothing to do with the front office. Experience teaches that, sooner or later, every front desk clerk will have a customer with a guaranteed reservation when there are no vacancies, a customer who was given a key to a room that was not cleaned, or a customer who must wait a long time to gain admittance to a guest room. The options available for handling such situations are often not communicated to new employees. Only by trial and error do they learn to find accommodations at another hotel when the hotel is overbooked, to offer a sincere apology and provide another room to the guest who was sent to a dirty room, or to suggest a snack in the dining room or provide directions to the patio lounge to the guest who must wait an hour to get into a room. Role-playing allows the new employee to confront these situations before they actually occur. The goal is that when such situations really do crop up, the employee is able to act professionally and offer service with a smile.

If the hotel has the equipment to videotape employees, trainees can be taped during role-playing sessions. The tape can then be reviewed with the employee to provide feedback on his or her performance. The trainer can analyze the employee's eye contact, clarity of diction, talking speed, poise, manner of dress, and posture. This method is valuable in preparing new employees to handle the stress of a busy front desk or an irate telephone caller.

Commercial CDs and DVDs

Several commercially prepared training tapes are offered by the Educational Institute of the American Hotel & Lodging Association to front office managers to use in training front office employees. These dramatize customer service situations, enabling the new employee to see how other front office employees handle customer relations. The trainer should preview the tapes and prepare a list of discussion questions to be sure the employee understands the purpose of the tape and can apply on the job what he or she observes.

Trial and Error: Let Me Do It

At this stage of the training process, the new employee demonstrates the skill to the trainer, who observes the attempt and offers constructive criticism. Here, the trainer can use the behavioral objective to determine whether or not the employee is performing the skill according to desired standards.

The trainee should be encouraged to perform the procedure as often as necessary to master it and meet the objective. The trainer may note how much practice other employees needed to learn this particular skill; for example, saying "Many employees must practice this five or six times before they catch on and come up to speed" lets the trainee know instant mastery of the skill is not expected. The trainer should specify how long the trial-and-error period is likely to last. Additional training may be required.

The step-by-step training procedure is helpful to the trainee in learning to perform the skill. The parts of the skill demonstration that were confusing or fuzzy are clarified through individual effort.

Follow-up: Check My Progress

The trainer must follow up with trainees after the program is completed. This is a necessary final element in a sound training program. The trainer may develop a *training tickler file*, a database that keeps track of training sessions and alerts trainers to important upcoming dates for each new employee, listing the name of the training session, date of the session, comments, and date for follow-up. Figure 12-3 demonstrates how this management tool can be used. This type of information can be processed in a separate database program on the PMS or maintained in an index card file.

FIGURE 12-3 **The tickler files help the front office manager check up on employee training.**

Training File	Employee Name: _____
Session	Orientation Program
Date:	12/1
Comments:	Employee very enthusiastic; possible interest in reservationist position
Follow-up:	12/5 Show rooms again.
	12/6 Meet night auditor.
Trainer:	JB
Session:	Guest Check-in
Date:	12/6
Comments:	Rated 80%, 1st attempt on 12/6
	Rated 85%, 4th attempt on 12/9
Follow-up:	12/15 Check to see if flow has picked up.
Trainer:	JB

The follow-up completes the training session because it provides the feedback the trainee needs to meet the behavioral objective. It also assures management the skills necessary to deliver hospitality have been planned demonstrated, practiced, and mastered.

Administering a Training Program

Planning the training program includes making provisions for administering it. Many details must be coordinated. Accurate but flexible schedules for training sessions must be set and maintained. Content preparation and duplication of training materials must be completed promptly. Progress charts on employee training should be produced and displayed.

FRONT-LINE REALITIES

You have been asked by the front office manager of a local hotel to offer tips on training new employees at the front desk. What guidelines would you offer?

The responsibility for administering the training program rests with the front office manager. If this responsibility is delegated to an assistant in the front office or human resources department, details of administration must be discussed with that person.

Effective training for front office positions is not easy to apply in the hospitality industry. The constant flow of people at the front desk, registrations and special events, telephone calls, emergencies, vendor calls, and other demands require the front office manager to balance the needs of the moment with those of the future. However, if high-quality hospitality services and products are to be available, training procedures for new employees must be well planned and developed.

Cross-Training

Even the most basic training programs must make provisions for developing employee skills that are useful to the organization. The unpredictable nature of business volume and employee availability in the hotel industry calls for a versatile staff. *Cross-training*, which means training employees to perform multiple tasks and jobs, is vital. A front office staff member who is able to perform multiple jobs has rescued many a front office manager during a crisis (Figure 12-4). The front office manager who discovers that one front desk clerk and one telephone operator are unexpectedly absent on the same day can attest to the value of cross-training. If a bellhop knows how to operate the PMS and the reservationist is trained to use the switchboard, the day can be saved. However, cross-training will get a front office manager out of a tight situation only if he or she has planned for it. If cross-training is to be provided, it should be built into a job description and pay rate. Note, however, before planning for cross-training, that some labor unions prohibit the practice of assigning noncontractual duties; in this case, cross-training is not viable.

Developing a Trainer

Careful consideration should be given to selecting the individual who trains new employees. This person should have a professional attitude and provide trainees with a positive attitude and enthusiasm for their positions. The selected person should be in management or a senior staff employee. The trainer must also be well versed in all procedures pertaining to the employee's job and familiar with training methods.

Job Knowledge

Knowledge of performing tasks comes with practice after formal training. There is no substitute for experience. The trainee inevitably has questions about particular tasks,

Front-line employees should receive training in all areas of the hotel. Photo courtesy of iStockphoto.com.

and the trainer must be able to answer them accurately and completely. Answers are not always found in policy manuals and training handbooks; they are often learned only through hands-on experience.

Ability to Teach

The ability to teach is important. The trainer must be able to plan the session in a logical, incremental fashion. It is also critical that the trainer possess good communication skills. The training session may include demonstrations, discussions, and workshops. The trainer should be familiar with all front office equipment and know how to prepare printed instructions and how to operate audiovisual equipment. He or she should be familiar with the basic steps of the training process (discussed earlier in this chapter). Finally, trainers should try to empathize with the new employee, perhaps by recalling how inadequate they felt when they were new on the job. Patience is important, as is careful explanation. Trainers who give hurried explanations discourage questions and, as a result, end up with trainees who feel unprepared to do their jobs.

Professional Attitude

The trainer must have a professional and positive personal view that supports the organization's goals of providing high-quality services and products, maximizing profits, and controlling costs. A professional attitude is evident in the way an employee handles his or her job responsibilities: explaining a foul-up in a room reservation, helping a guest locate another department in the hotel, participating in programs to increase room rates, and controlling operating expenses. The desk clerk whose responses to these duties are

"This company always overbooks at this time of the year," "Follow the signs on the wall to find the restaurant," "I wouldn't help this place get higher room rates," and "Take an extra 15 minutes on your break—this place can afford it" does not exhibit a professional attitude.

Experienced managers are well aware of the skilled senior employee who has mastered the skills involved in a job, but holds a negative attitude toward the company or its management. It is best not to enlist the assistance of such employees in training new hires. Managers are responsible for molding attitudes, teaching skills, and passing knowledge on to their employees. Exposing new employees to an unprofessional, negative attitude during training undermines the purpose of the training sessions. The trainer should represent the company and demonstrate good employer-employee relations.

Training for Empowerment

The use of empowerment, discussed in chapter 11, must be taught to employees in training. The act of delegating authority and responsibility concerning specific tasks to front-line employees, empowerment is an essential element in operating an efficient front office. As part of the training program, a front office manager must specify the dollar amount within which an employee can credit a guest's folio without the intervention of the front office manager. The trainer must discuss this empowerment concept so the employee knows when the dollar amount and the guest's satisfaction are in harmony. Yes, at times the front desk clerk may have to stretch the dollar amount because of extenuating circumstances. However, a daily review of credits that allows an opportunity for employee explanation makes empowerment work for the guest, the employee, and the front office. According to Lawrence E. Sternberg, "Contemporary management thinking is that the greatest gains in efficiency, productivity, and guest satisfaction are generated by making improvements in the system. Those improvements are most likely to occur when employees are empowered to recommend and implement changes on their own."[2]

INTERNATIONAL HIGHLIGHTS

 Front office employees must be aware of the importance of greeting international visitors who require information about currency, local geography, or local time. They may be unfamiliar with smoking regulations, operation of dining facilities, or local customs. A training program for greeting international visitors includes trainee role-playing and employee sharing of relevant prior experiences. Sensitization of employees to the needs of international guests goes a long way toward ensuring hospitality.

Americans with Disabilities Act

The *Americans with Disabilities Act (ADA)* is a U.S. law enacted in 1990 that protects people with disabilities from being discriminated against when seeking accommodations and employment. There are two parts to this act: accommodations for people who are physically challenged and employment practices concerning hiring of them. Because the rhetoric of the law is still being reviewed in the courts, it is important to review employment practices and implications. Not only is it important to adhere to the principles of the law but also it is personally rewarding to employ an individual based solely on his or her talents.

> The ADA states that employers must make "reasonable accommodations" to the known disabilities of the person unless the employer demonstrates that this would constitute an "undue hardship." Section 1211 states that making "reasonable accommodations" includes making existing facilities used by employees readily accessible to people with disabilities and considering accommodations such as job restructuring, part-time or modified work schedules, reassignment, and provision of readers or interpreters.[3]

Current information on this important law can be obtained from state and U.S. legislative agencies as well as the Internet.

Front office managers must focus on the abilities of every job applicant regardless of physical challenge. Well-written job descriptions outline the specific tasks required to perform a job. These tasks provide the background for evaluating all job candidates. If a certain required task is physically impossible for an applicant to perform, then the front office manager should consult with the general manager on rearranging the work environment so the applicant can succeed. For example, if an applicant in a wheelchair applies for a job as a front desk clerk, initial reactions may be "It just won't work," "There's no room for the wheelchair," or "Too much movement is required between pieces of equipment." The front office manager should analyze how the physical work environment could be adjusted to meet the needs of this employee. Could pieces of equipment be clustered to provide easy access for an employee in a wheelchair? Could counter height be adjusted via a front desk that can be raised and lowered? All of this must be evaluated in terms of associated financial costs. But financial costs also must be evaluated against the costs of recruiting employees and paying for incentive programs, the expense of new trainee mistakes, and the like.

Training an employee with physical disabilities is no different than training any other new employee, in most cases. All the same methods are required. While the trainer may have to rethink the four steps involved in training, the opportunity to look at a familiar situation from another perspective may lead to improved routines for all.

The Marriott Foundation for People with Disabilities has made an exemplary effort in providing guidelines for working with people with handicaps and has developed a list entitled "Fears Versus Realities About Employing People with Disabilities."

The Marriott Foundation developed the list after interviewing employers and coworkers of young people with disabilities who participate in the Foundation's "Bridges... from school to work" program. "Bridges...from school to work" fosters the employment of young people with disabilities by facilitating paid internships for students with disabilities who are in their final year of high school. [Between 1989 and 2001,] Bridges...placed more than 5,000 students in paid internships with over 1,300 employers. Eighty-seven percent of the students completing the program have received offers of continued employment. "Finding meaningful employment can be hard enough for young people, not to mention young people with disabilities," said Richard E. Marriott, chairman of the Marriott Foundation. "By working with school districts and employers, the Foundation's Bridges program is helping these young people and their employers break through the 'fear' barrier and think in terms of 'ability' versus 'disability,'"[4] [Author's note: Since 1990, the Marriott Foundation has placed more than 10,000 young people with over 3200 employers in seven metropolitan areas.]

The seven "Fears Versus Realities About Employing People with Disabilities" are as follows:

1. Fear—People with disabilities need expensive accommodations.
   Reality—Often, no accommodation is needed. When necessary, most accommodations cost very little or nothing at all.
2. Fear—I'll have to do more work.
   Reality—Not true, especially when the abilities and skills of the individual are matched with the needs of the job. More effective matching up front will make disabilities largely irrelevant.
3. Fear—I'll have to supervise more.
   Reality—Most employees with disabilities do their jobs as well as, or better than, other employees in similar jobs, and often seem more motivated and dependable.
4. Fear—Turnover and absenteeism will be high.
   Reality—Studies show that employees with disabilities rate average to above average on attendance.
5. Fear—People with disabilities may not be able to do the job.
   Reality—Because people with disabilities often have to work harder to get the job they want and, therefore, appreciate what having a job means, they typically perform up to and beyond expectations. The key is effectively matching skills to job needs, focusing on ability.
6. Fear—People with disabilities need preferential treatment.
   Reality—People with disabilities neither require [n]or want to be treated any differently than employees without disabilities. What people with disabilities do need is an equal opportunity.
7. Fear—Will people with disabilities fit in?
   Reality—As part of a diverse workforce, employees with disabilities often bring unique life experiences, which can be a shot in the arm for the entire workplace.

FRONT-LINE REALITIES

The front office manager has a difficult time deciding which employee to hire. Mark and Tse have similar qualifications. Mark has two years' experience as a front desk clerk, but he was recently in an auto accident, which left him with a paralyzed right leg and dependent on a wheelchair for mobility. Tse has two years' experience as a salesperson with an electronics firm and expressed interest in learning all he can in the hotel business. How would you proceed?

Their perspectives on and approach to their jobs can be contagious, creating a positive ripple effect.[5]

Solution to Opening Dilemma

Although an advertising agency may be part of the answer to this hotel's image problem, the real problem lies with the people who are delivering hospitality. Determining the qualities required to provide hospitality in a hotel and screening job candidates for those qualities are essential to present an image that reflects the enthusiasm and professionalism of individuals who truly want to deliver hospitality.

Chapter Recap

If front office managers want to be sure their employees deliver hospitality, they must begin by hiring people with the character traits necessary to handle front office responsibilities. This chapter began with a review of those character traits—extroversion, maturity, patience, positive attitude toward constructive criticism, and an ability to sell. Finding these qualities in job candidates can be accomplished by developing interview questions designed to explore them. An orientation program is necessary to begin the process of training hospitality employees. An orientation checklist that tracks completion of the explanation of such matters as the economic position of the property in the community, an overview of the hotel's physical layout, services, and coworkers, and a tour of the property can be helpful. The orientation should also include a review of the employee handbook and policy and procedure manual. The new employee's introduction to the front office staff and general management staff completes the orientation. Administering an orientation program provides a check on the continual planning and delivery of this personnel function.

Training practices were also discussed. The front office manager should start by identifying tasks and job management skills required to perform an entry-level front office job. Preparing step-by-step procedures is necessary to assist the trainer in developing a training session. The four-step training process—get ready, show me, let me do it, and check my progress—assists the trainer in working through the details of the training session.

A discussion of methods of presentation included skill demonstrations, on-the-job training, role-playing, videotaping of role-playing, and commercially prepared CDs and DVDs. Administration of the training program is an essential element that allows the continual delivery of quality hospitality.

Cross-training of employees assists the front office manager in handling the daily formation of a front office team. Employees who are cross-trained in various tasks and jobs allow the front office manager to deliver service as required.

Developing a trainer is an important part of training for hospitality. The selection of a trainer should be based on a person's knowledge of the tasks and jobs, ability to teach, and possession of a professional attitude that represents the hotel.

Empowerment was discussed as an essential element in the training process that lets hospitality flourish.

A discussion of the Americans with Disabilities Act provided the background, concepts, and applications of this important U.S. legislation. It stressed the value of providing the opportunity for candidates with physical challenges to be offered employment and the benefits of hiring these candidates.

End-of-Chapter Questions

1. How does assessing personnel needs lead to a more efficiently managed front office?

2. How would you prepare to interview a front office job candidate? Develop a list of questions to use in interviewing an applicant for the position of front desk clerk.

3. If you are currently employed in the hospitality industry, describe the orientation you received. What would you add to the program if you were the manager?

4. If you are currently employed in the hospitality industry, describe the training you received. How does it compare with what was recommended in this chapter?

5. Prepare a mock training session on how to check a guest out of a hotel room. Where would you begin? Incorporate the four-step training method into your training session. Have a group evaluate your success in delivering the training session.

6. How do you feel about the concept of using the Internet as a 24/7 training resource?

7. How important is cross-training to operating a front desk?

8. If you were asked to choose a trainer, what qualities would you specify? Why are these qualities vital to the success of a training session?

END-OF-CHAPTER QUESTIONS 369

9. What does *empowerment* mean to you? Have you ever experienced empowerment on the job? How did you feel? How did the customer feel?

10. If you had the opportunity to hire a physically challenged job applicant as a cashier, what would you consider as a realistic assessment of the situation?

CASE STUDY 1201

Ana Chavarria, front office manager of The Times Hotel, is in the process of organizing an orientation program for new front office staff. As part of the program, she will introduce the front office equipment and associated paperwork. Further training on each piece of equipment will be scheduled at a later time.

She begins by listing and describing the functions of all the equipment. She also spells out how each piece of equipment relates to the overall function of the front office. Because most of her front office staff are relatively new (turnover is high), she decides she must deliver the orientation program herself.

Paolo and Brian have been hired at The Times Hotel as desk clerks. Paolo will start training on Monday at 7:00 A.M., and Brian will start on Monday at 3:00 P.M.

On Monday, a full house is going to check out by 11:15 A.M., and another full house will check in at 2:00 P.M. Ana greets Paolo at 6:45 A.M., but the PMS is malfunctioning and a switchboard operator has called in sick. After attending to these crises, she receives a request for 20 additional rooms for today. By 1:30 P.M., Paolo, who has helped out where he could, still has received no orientation. Ana feels that all is not lost—yet. Brian will be in at 2:45 P.M.

She will keep Paolo on for another hour and deliver the orientation program to both new hires at once.

Brian shows up at 2:45 P.M. ready to go to work. Ana takes both Paolo and Brian to the coffee shop and begins a brief orientation to The Times Hotel. Returning to the front office half an hour later, she finds a long line of people waiting to check in. She tells Paolo, "Check out on the time clock; I will catch up with you tomorrow," and asks Brian to work with the switchboard operator "until we get this mess straightened out."

At 5:00 P.M., things have calmed down, and Brian is eager to learn his way around the front desk. In desperation, Ana writes up a quick checklist and tells Brian to go to Kris, the switchboard operator, and Hoang, the front desk clerk, and have them explain how to operate the switchboard and the PMS registration module.

How does Ms. Chavarria's view of the orientation program compare to that presented in this chapter? What has she omitted from the program? How realistic is her scheduling of this orientation program? Is it possible to have a senior employee conduct the orientation program? Under what circumstances? Do you think Ms. Chavarria's turnover rate has anything to do with her approach to orientation?

CASE STUDY 1202

Ana Chavarria, front office manager of The Times Hotel, is participating on a team in her professional organization—Regional Hotel Administra-

tors (RHA)—to develop a procedure for screening candidates for front office employment that other front office managers will be able to use. A few of

CASE STUDY 1202 (CONTINUED)

the team members feel this procedure will probably end up being tossed out by the general membership because interviewing has so many variables.

Ana disagrees and says that if team members look at common characteristics of their successes and failures in hiring, they may be on the road to producing something really useful. Teresa Valquez, the representative from the RHA Southern Chapter, feels this might work, but she still thinks it is an overwhelming task. Steve Harp, the representative from the RHA Western Chapter, says, "We have to do *something*.

Our regional unemployment rate is so low we have a hard time finding employees, so our decisions have to be good ones." It seems there is sufficient energy in the team to begin planning to produce such a document. The group has elected Ana team leader, and she begins with a brainstorming session.

Play the roles of five team members—all front office managers—whose goals are to identify desirable qualities in employees that reflect the ability to deliver hospitality and to determine how to use that information in a screening interview.

CASE STUDY 1203

Jerry Smith is a potential front desk employee who has been recommended for employment by the local Employees With Assets (EWA). EWA is a nonprofit organization that works with potential employees who have physical and emotional disabilities under control. Jerry has been given a high emotional ability rating and would like work at the front desk; however, he is confined to a wheelchair. His caseworker indicates that someone from EWA will assist

in training. Jerry is able to work 4 hours a day, 3 days a week. His previous jobs were as a cashier in a grocery store, an attendant at a museum, and a greeter at a discount department store. He is very outgoing, and his previous employers all rated him highly.

How would you adapt your orientation and training program to fit Jerry into your front desk environment? into your hotel staff environment?

Notes

1. The content of this section relies on ideas found in *Supervision in the Hospitality Industry*, 4th ed., Chapter 6, "Developing Job Expectations" (New York: John Wiley & Sons, 2002), by Jack E. Miller, John R. Walker, and Karen Eich Drummond.
2. Lawrence E. Sternberg, "Empowerment: Trust Versus Control," *Cornell Hotel and Restaurant Administration Quarterly* 33, no. 1 (February 1992): 72.
3. J. Deutsch, "Welcoming Those with Disabilities," *New York Times*, February 3, 1991, quoted in John M. Ivancevich, *Human Resource Management*, 6th ed. (Chicago: Richard D. Irwin, Inc., 1995), 75.

4. Marriott Foundation, "'Fear of the Unknown' Invisible Barrier to Employ-ment, Says Marriott Foundation for People with Disabilities," Washington, DC, September 30, 1997; edited July 23, 2001. Copyright Marriott Foundation for People with Disabilities.
5. Ibid.

Key Words

Americans with Disabilities Act (ADA)

cash bank

cross-training

documentation

employee handbook

on-the-job training

orientation checklist

orientation process

policy and procedure manual

role-playing

skill demonstration

telephone initiation and reception agreements

training tickler file

CHAPTER 13

Promoting In-House Sales

OPENING DILEMMA

The food and beverage manager has spent several thousand dollars on a marketing study to determine the dining needs of in-house guests. The chef has rewritten each menu to reflect those needs. However, the bell staff and front desk clerks continue to recommend the MidTown Deli around the corner as "a nice place to get something good to eat any time of day."

CHAPTER FOCUS POINTS

■ Role of the front office in a hotel's marketing program

■ Planning a point-of-sale front office

As the hospitality industry grows more sophisticated, with greater concern for delivering high-quality services, maximizing sales in all profit centers of the hotel is important. Additional sales to current guests—in the form of future reservations, in-house dining, room service, lounge and entertainment patronage, gift shop purchases, and the like—assists in producing a favorable profit-and-loss statement. The front office plays a key role in promoting these sales, and the front office manager must develop and implement a plan to optimize the sales opportunities available to the front office staff. This plan includes focusing on areas for promotion; developing objectives and procedures, incentive programs, training programs for personnel, budgets, and tracking systems for employee feedback; and profitability.

The Role of the Front Office in Marketing and Sales

The front office is often seen as an information source and a request center for guests and hotel employees alike. Front office staff may need to field questions such as "Has the front office manager produced the room sales forecast yet?" "Is a block of rooms available for June 3 to 7?" "To which rooms is this seminar group assigned?" "Is someone on duty who can greet and provide information for the tourist group arriving this afternoon?" "Has the daily event board been set up in the lobby?" and "Has the daily message

FIGURE 13-1

Displays such as this one alert guests to in-house entertainment. Photo courtesy of iStockphoto.com.

been set on the great sign?" These are typical questions asked of the front office by other departments in the hotel. Answering them is a necessary part of any hotel's operations. Today, more than ever, hotel management demands a great deal of the front office.

In an article published in *Canadian Hotel and Restaurant*, Avinash Narula reports:

As market conditions have changed, the nature and importance of the functions performed by the front office have also changed from being an order-taking department to an order-generating or sales department. If one looks at the balance sheet of any hotel, it will become obvious that the major portion of the profits, on average 60 percent, come from room sales.[1]

Doug Kennedy emphasizes how the potential walk-in guest provides an excellent opportunity for a sale.

[T]he walk-in sales opportunity provides the hotel with some significant advantages over other distribution channels. For one, the sales person can visually evaluate the guests' needs and wants. Are they dressed as if on a business trip, or on vacation? What is their age? Are they traveling alone or with family? What is their level of commitment; do they park the car and walk in with luggage, or do they just run in to find out the price?

A second advantage is that the sales prospect can see the product firsthand and is able to formulate a first impression. (This is why it is critical for hotels to maintain curb appeal.) Another significant advantage in selling to walk-ins is that it takes more effort for the prospect to shop around. It's harder to get back in the car and drive down the road than it is to click on the next Internet link or to dial the phone number of the next property.

Kennedy continues with suggestions for securing a sale, such as connecting with the customer, offering options, describing room and rate options, and avoiding positioning last-sell or higher-rated options in the negative.[2]

This change in the nature of the front office's role, from a passive order taker to an active order generator, challenges the front office manager to review the front office staff's established routine. The front office manager must figure out the best way to direct the energies of the staff to support the efforts of the marketing and sales department.

The front office manager must first consider the attitude of the front office staff. These employees have been trained and rewarded for accurate performance of clerical tasks, playing a passive role in the sales of services. How easy will it be to transform them into active salespeople, persuading guests to purchase additional reservations, services in the dining room and lounge, or products in the gift shop? At the outset, most front office managers would say this is a tall order. Established, routine habits are comfortable and unstressful. However, the front office manager is a member of the management team and must interact with other managers as well as the employees as a plan is developed.

Lee Johnson is the director of corporate sales at Pier 5 Hotel and Brookshire Suites at the Inner Harbor in Baltimore, Maryland. After he graduated from Penn State Berks' associate degree program in hotel, restaurant, and institutional management, he worked in Reading, Pennsylvania, as a senior sales manager at the Sheraton Berkshire Hotel and as director of sales and marketing at the Riveredge.

Mr. Johnson relates the two primary ways in which he relies on the front office to do his job: communicating the needs of a group and operational issues. First, his office prepares a group resume of an incoming group that outlines the details of paying the bill, approvals of persons allowed to bill to master accounts, and descriptions of concierge service for the front office staff, as well as other details of the group's nature and needs. His department also prepares a banquet event order that summarizes the details of the event, such as location, time, and menu. Second, a "coaches meeting" is held early every day with department heads to discuss check-in and checkout patterns, storage requirements, and comment card review.

His department relies on the front desk staff to screen phone calls and channel them to the right person. This saves valuable time for the sales staff so they can spend their time selling instead of screening. Because it is on the front line of hospitality, Mr. Johnson relies on the front desk to deliver on promises made in sales negotiations. He also depends on the front desk staff to load accurate details of a group registration into the computer.

Mr. Johnson encourages students of hospitality management to keep their career options open and to investigate the many opportunities both in the front and the back of the house.

Planning a Point-of-sale Front Office

To be a *point-of-sale front office*, a front office staff must promote profit centers of the hotel. Planning includes setting objectives, brainstorming areas for promotion, evaluating alternatives, drawing up budgets, and developing an evaluation tool for feedback. Without a plan, a point-of-sale front office has little chance of success. The plan should be developed in consultation with hotel management, department managers, and front-line employees from various departments. Team members should be selected to assist in developing a workable, profitable plan.

Some of the goals Narula suggests for the front office as it adopts a sales department attitude include the following:

- Sell rooms to guests who have not made prior reservations.
- *Upsell* (encourage a customer to consider buying a higher-priced product or service than originally anticipated) to guests with prior reservations.
- Maintain the inventory of the product—that is, the rooms.
- Convey information to guests about other products available for sale at the

property—for example, food and beverages. The objective of the front office is to sell all available facilities at the hotel to the guests. Front office staff are probably the most important means of letting the guest know what services are available.

■ Ensure maximum revenue is generated from the sale of rooms by striking a balance between overbooking and a full house.

■ Obtain guest feedback.[3]

If we take these goals, as well as Narula's other goal of increasing communication between the front office and marketing and sales, then the planning can begin. Valuable information about the guest, essential for formulating an effective marketing strategy, can be conveyed by the front office staff. Changing market conditions require that such information be used by the marketing and sales division.[4] Based on this suggestion, we can infer that the marketing and sales department needs vital feedback regarding customer satisfaction with the availability of hotel products and services.

Set Objectives

The ultimate goal of a sales-oriented front office is an increase in revenue from room sales, food and beverage sales, and sales in other hotel departments. A front office manager who wants to develop a plan for a point-of-sale front office must set realistic objectives. What is it that he or she wants to accomplish? Should restaurant sales be increased by 10 percent, lounge sales by 15 percent, gift shop sales by 20 percent, or business center sales by 25 percent? Developing these objectives is carried out in consultation with the general manager and other department managers. The result of these consultations may be one realistic objective that states: "Increase profit center sales by 15 percent." This may be the objective for the next several months. A new objective is then planned for future months.

Brainstorm Areas for Promotion

When developing a program to increase front office sales activity, the front office manager, in conjunction with other department directors and employees, should identify as specifically as possible the hotel products and services to be promoted. Here is a typical outline of promotional areas:

I. Front office
  A. Reservations
    1. Upselling when reservation is placed
    2. Additional reservations during registration and checkout
  B. Rooms
    1. Upgrading reservation during registration
    2. Promotional packages
    3. Office rentals

      4. Movie library rental

      5. Computer games for children

   C. Office services

      1. Photocopies

      2. Dictation

      3. Typing

      4. Fax transmission

      5. Laptop computer rental

      6. In-room DVD rental

   D. Personal services

      1. Babysitting

      2. Shopping

      3. Bell staff assistance with luggage and equipment

      4. Concierge

         a. Theater/music/art tickets

         b. General tourist information

         c. Tours of the area

         d. Airline reservations

         e. Emergency services

         f. Information on local transportation

II. Food and beverage department

   A. Restaurants

      1. Special menu items of the day

      2. Signature menu items

      3. Special pricing combinations for diners

      4. Reservations

      5. Gift certificates

   B. Room service

      1. Meals

      2. Early-bird breakfast service

      3. Party service

      4. Snacks

      5. Beverages/alcohol

   C. Banquet service

   D. Lounge

      1. Specials of the day

      2. Special theme of the day

      3. Featured entertainer

      4. Promotional package

III. Gift shop

   A. Emergency items

      1. Clothing

      2. Toiletries

      B. Souvenirs

      C. Promotional sales in progress

  IV. Health facilities

      A. Swimming pool

         1. Availability to guests

         2. Memberships/gift certificates

      B. Jogging paths and times of organized daily group runs

      C. Health club

         1. Availability to guests

         2. Memberships/gift certificates

Evaluate Alternatives

Planning teams must determine which concepts produced in a brainstorming session warrant further consideration. This task is not always easy, but if the team refers to stated goals and objectives, then the job is much simpler. In this case, the overall purpose of the program is to maximize sales by the front office staff of front office, food and beverage department, gift shop, and health facilities products and services. The team must decide which area or areas will be most profitable to the hotel and its employees.

Devise Incentive Programs

During the brainstorming part of planning for a point-of-sale front office, the team should consider supporting incentives as an important part in the success of a sales program. The point-of-sale plan should include an *incentive program*, which entails understanding employees' motivational concerns and developing opportunities for them to achieve those goals. This encourages cooperation among the front-line employees who must implement the point-of-sale plan.

The front office manager is responsible for determining how each employee is motivated. Many motivational strategies require a financial commitment by management. These costs must be included as a budget line item. When the owner can see additional sales being created as a result of these programs, the idea of sharing some of the profit is more acceptable.

Motivation, or understanding employee needs and desires and developing a framework for meeting them, is an essential part of developing a point-of-sale front office. How does a front office manager discover what employees want? A number of theorists have explored this area; the theories of Douglas McGregor, Abraham Maslow, Elton Mayo, and Frederick Herzberg provide insight into what motivates employees to behave in desired ways (see Table 13-1). Once a front office manager knows what employees want, he or she must develop a means of meeting these needs in return for the desired behavior. The front office manager must work with the general manager and human resources department to develop effective programs that meet employees' needs. In this process, effective programs are defined by the employee.

TABLE 13-1	Theories of Motivation	
LOST BREAKFAST CHARGES		
McGregor	Theory X	Human beings have an inherent dislike of work.
	Theory Y	Work is as natural as play or rest.
Maslow	Satisfying individual needs	Used a triangle to indicate levels of human needs; the most basic needs of food, clothing, and shelter must be met before higher-level needs, such as self-actualization.
Mayo	Recognition of individuality in employees	Supervisors who recognize each employee as special will achieve greater results than supervisors who treat employees as a group.
Herzberg	Hygiene factors	The only factors that lead to positive job attitudes are achievement, recognition of achievement, responsibility, interesting work, personal growth, and advancement.

The objective of the sales incentive program for front office employees is to encourage the front office to promote products and services in various areas of the hotel, including the front office, the food and beverage department, the gift shop, and the health facilities. Each promotional area may be considered, or the front office manager might choose only a few areas—perhaps those that generate the most profit—as incentive targets. A few examples follow:

1. *Upgrading a reservation during registration:* If a desk clerk can sell a room package costing $95 to a guest who has a reservation for a $75 room, a percentage of that $20 increase in sales is awarded to the desk clerk.

2. *Selling a meal in the hotel's restaurant:* If a desk clerk successfully encourages a guest to patronize the hotel's restaurant, a percentage of the guest's check is rebated to the desk clerk. At the restaurant, when the guest presents the VIP Guest Card signed by the desk clerk to the waiter or waitress and receives VIP service, the desk clerk receives the rebate.

3. *Selling room service:* If a desk clerk succeeds in convincing a guest to use room service, a percentage of the guest check is rebated to the clerk. The guest presents a VIP Guest Card signed by the desk clerk to the room service person, which proves the sale was the result of that clerk's efforts.

Theories of Motivation

Douglas McGregor

Douglas McGregor theorized that management views employees in one of two ways. These theories are referred to as *Theory X* and *Theory Y*. Theory X states that the average human being has an inherent dislike of work and will avoid it if he or she can.[5] Theory Y states that the expenditure of physical and mental effort in work is as natural as play or rest.[6]

These two views of how human beings approach their jobs are vastly different. Theory X states that the supervisor must constantly expend direct effort to force the employee to do his or her job. Theory Y states that the employee brings to the job innate skills and talents the supervisor can develop through an effective administrative and communication network. Supervisors who give serious thought to these two views discover that sometimes they feel one employee works best under Theory X, another employee works best under Theory Y, and yet another requires a combination of Theory X and Theory Y. This is exactly the intent of McGregor's efforts. He wants the supervisor to look at each employee as an individual who responds to a particular type of supervision.

Abraham Maslow

Abraham Maslow theorized that an individual's needs can be categorized by levels of importance, with the most basic need being the most important. The hierarchy of needs he identified was:

Fifth level: self-actualization, self-realization, and self-accomplishment

Fourth level: self-esteem and the esteem of others

Third level: love, affection, and belonging

Second level: safety (security and freedom from fear, anxiety, and chaos)

First level: physiological (food, clothing, and shelter)

Maslow further theorized that individuals strive to meet the first level of needs before even considering the second, and so on up the ladder. The physiological needs of food, clothing, and shelter must be provided for (by the paycheck) before the employee can be concerned with safety, stability, and security. The need for love cannot be a concern until the individual has satisfied his or her physiological and safety needs.[7]

The front office manager can use Maslow's theory to identify the needs of individual employees and to design appropriate programs. If an employee's wages do not cover his rent, he will want this physiological need for shelter met and will find a tuition assistance program, for example, meaningless.

Through formal and informal communications, the employer should learn which needs are of greatest importance to each employee. Every employee has reached a different level in the hierarchy of needs, and it is important that supervisors recognize this. The front office manager should consider what levels of need each employee has met before attempting to provide for the next level.

Elton Mayo

Experiments conducted at the Hawthorne plant of the Western Electric Company in Chicago, Illinois, from 1927 to 1932 led Elton Mayo to conclude that supervisors who recognize each employee as special will achieve greater results than supervisors who treat employees as a group.[8] The employee who is recognized for special talents and skills will find this recognition an incentive to continue to do a good job. The front desk clerk who is recognized for his or her ability to sell additional services in the hotel may find this rewarding; it may fit into his or her career progression plan. This recognition may motivate the employee to duplicate the task in other areas and at other times.

Frederick Herzberg

Frederick Herzberg contends that factors such as "supervision, interpersonal relations, physical working conditions, salary, company policies and administrative practices, benefits, and job security are actually dissatisfiers or hygiene factors. When these factors deteriorate to a level below that which the employee considers acceptable, then job dissatisfaction ensues. The factors that lead to positive job attitudes do so because they satisfy the individual's need for self-actualization in his work."[9]

According to Herzberg, minimum hygiene factors must be set to prevent a nonproductive environment. He believes organizations that provide less than these create an atmosphere for dissatisfied employees. However, a truly productive organization requires improvement in the motivation factors: achievement, recognition for achievement, responsibility, interesting work, personal growth, and advancement. Herzberg questions whether, if a hotel provides five vacation days a year, that will be a motivational factor for a front desk clerk if all other hotels in the area also offer five vacation days to their front desk clerks.[10]

Applying Motivation Theories

Applying these motivational theories is a managerial challenge for the front office manager. It offers the opportunity to review the needs of the employees to establish a framework for day-to-day contact and incentive programs.

Maslow

The front office manager who reviews motivational principles learns that each member of his or her staff requires a different style of motivation. For example, Maslow's hierarchy of needs provides a way to determine motivational techniques based on level of need. The employee who works to be with people, the employee who is moonlighting to earn additional income for a family, and the employee who is working toward becoming a supervisor of the department each require different motivational strategies. Someone who works to maintain social relationships is not concerned with an additional 50 cents per hour; this person might be more motivated by knowing he or she can work the holiday shift. The person who is moonlighting is not motivated by health insurance benefits if his or her primary job provides that benefit. An additional 50 cents per hour, however, *will* motivate this person, as will the assurance of a specified number of scheduled work hours. The person working toward a supervisory position is not motivated by a better work schedule but rather the chance to be trained in all front office jobs or the opportunity to sit in on a general staff meeting.

Mayo

Mayo's work in recognizing the efforts of the individual gives the front office manager the opportunity to explore the connections among communication, satisfaction, and cost savings. A few words of encouragement about continuing to do a good job, an expression of personal concern about the employee's family or close friends, or recognition of an outstanding performance makes the employee feel special, even in a large hotel.

Herzberg

Herzberg offers the supervisor a different approach to motivation. He claims that the chance for self-actualization—personal growth and fulfillment—improves performance. While the employee needs an adequate salary, job security, benefits, and the like, these are expected to be present in the job. Anything less than what is expected causes dissatisfaction. Applying this theory requires the supervisor to analyze both the hygiene factors of a job and the opportunities for self-actualization it allows. What is the hotel providing that should be appreciated but is not? Why doesn't the company picnic or holiday party get the group together? The answers to these questions are at the crux of employee motivation.

Training Programs for a Point-of-sale Front Office

Another supportive concept to consider during the brainstorming part of planning is the training required to allow the successful delivery of sales techniques.

Train in Sales Skills

It is not safe to assume that all front office personnel are born salespeople; indeed, it is probably safer to assume no one is a born salesperson. The fear of rejection or of intruding on others when pitching a sale is far too real for many people. The front office manager must reduce this negative perception of sales by training and encouraging the staff; otherwise, the program is doomed to failure. The objective of training is to develop and teach employees methods to use to promote various profit centers of the hotel.

Develop an Attitude of Presenting Opportunities

The job of selling is more attractive if employees believe they are presenting opportunities to the guest. Front desk personnel who believe their suggestions are intended primarily to improve the guest's visit feel more comfortable with the idea of selling. Confidence in selling develops if the point-of-sale program is introduced gradually, promotion by promotion, giving employees a chance to try out various techniques. Incentive programs strengthen employees' commitment.

Let Employees Experience Hotel Services

An often overlooked but effective practice is to allow front office employees to experience the services and products they sell. Familiarity with and appreciation for the chef's specials, the luxury of an upgraded room, the equipment in the health club, the new merchandise in the gift shop, and the personal assistance provided by the concierge enable the employee to promote these areas knowledgeably and enthusiastically. Training concepts for each of the areas listed in the promotion target outline must be detailed. It is not sufficient simply to tell a front desk clerk to sell a higher-priced room to a guest with a reservation during registration. Employees should receive suggestions on what to say and when to say it; timing is an important part of the sales opportunity.

Use Role-Playing to Create Your Own Training Video

Using the video techniques discussed in chapter 12, such as taping role-playing episodes of the desk clerks promoting hotel products and services within the hotel to the guest,

FIGURE 13-2

Planning the taping of a training session will assist in developing a unique aid. Photo courtesy of iStockphoto.com.

A few of the senior desk clerks have expressed distaste for promoting future reservations at checkout. What do you think is the basis for their view? How would you handle the situation?

is an extremely effective training procedure. These episodes do not have to be elaborate. They need only highlight simple approaches to presenting opportunities that enhance the guest experience.

The front office manager who wants to use video as a training option must do a little homework first. Preparation for video training requires some thought as to just which skills and behaviors call for teaching or reinforcement. Discussions with the directors of other hotel departments (marketing and sales, food and beverage) provide a basis for promotional concepts. The front office manager should take an objective look at the salesmanship skills of the front office staff. How outgoing are they? How adept are they at recognizing the needs and wants of the guests?

The front office manager must then decide which specific promotional areas to highlight in the video. At the outset, he or she may want to choose one or two areas only. With these promotional areas in mind, the front office manager should write a script for the role-playing episode. It should include the specific behaviors or skills the employee is expected to master.

Producing the video involves scheduling a time that is conducive to shooting. Employee work shifts must be adjusted accordingly. Time for rehearsal must also be planned. The planning should take into consideration budgetary issues regarding the rental or purchase of a video camera and related equipment.

Budgeting for a Point-of-sale Front Office

The front office manager incurs costs in operating a point-of-sale front office, including expenses for implementing incentive programs, producing training materials, and planning time. These costs, while not overwhelming, should be anticipated. If all appropriate steps are taken, the income from increased sales should far outweigh the additional costs. The projection of sales and related expenses is useful when deciding which marketing ideas to explore.

Feedback

Evaluating the success of the front office staff in promoting other areas of the hotel is an important consideration in preparing a point-of-sale front office program. How can the front office manager know if the staff is using the sales techniques in which they were trained? How does the he or she determine how the staff feels about this program after the novelty wears off? How does the guest feel about being presented with all these alternatives? How financially successful is the program? Front office managers cannot tell exactly how effective the promotional strategy is, but they must make an effort to obtain as much feedback as possible from staff and guests. This information is valuable in planning future promotional ideas, incentive programs, and training programs. The objective of this part of the plan could be stated thus: "To develop feedback systems concerning employee performance, employee attitude, guest perception, and profitability."

Guest Test

The standard *guest test* is one in which an outside person (known as the *plant*) is hired by the hotel to experience hotel services and report the findings to management. This test enables the front office manager to evaluate the sales performance of the front desk clerk. If an unknown plant presents herself with a reservation and is greeted with "Yes, we have a reservation; please sign in," the front office manager knows the front desk clerk is disregarding the sales procedure. The front office manager should discuss with the employee why the procedure was not followed. Perhaps the goals of the employee have shifted from a larger paycheck to a more reasonable work schedule. Or maybe he or she forgot there was a choice of incentives for the job. Perhaps too many guests were responding negatively to the promotion, and the clerk gave up trying. This information may indicate unwanted goods or services are being targeted for promotion.

When hotel management designs guest comment cards, questions concerning alternative promotion targets should be listed. Choices offered by hotel staff, such as upgrading reservations or information received about restaurants, gift shops, additional reservations, or other areas of the hotel may be included. Answers will show whether suggestions were made and how they were received. There is always the chance guests will perceive an offer as pushy.

Financial Results

Another method for evaluating the program is reckoning the actual financial results. Were the anticipated profits outlined in the budget achieved? Use of a VIP Guest Card indicates to the restaurant manager that the guest was referred by the front desk clerk. Similar types of controls enable management to pinpoint the origins of room reservations, gift shop purchases, and other sales. A recordkeeping system must be established to reflect the amount of money awarded to front office employees as incentives to increase sales in targeted areas. The details of this recordkeeping system must be worked out with the department directors and the controller.

Planning a Point-of-sale Front Office—An Example

A typical session for preparing a point-of-sale plan might be as follows: The front office manager schedules an informal meeting with the director of marketing and sales, the director of food and beverage, and a few front-line employees from each of the respective areas. Prior to the meeting, she asks each team members to think of a few promotions they would like to stress in the next quarter. The food and beverage director begins the discussion by mentioning the following promotions that will run in the dining room:

1. Eat Wisely in January: Choice of entrée from the Eat Wisely lunch or dinner menu includes a free pass to the hotel health club.

2. Valentine Special in February: Dinner for two with choice of appetizer, dessert, or house wine at no charge.

3. Luncheon Special in March: Soup and salad bar free with entrée.

The director of marketing and sales wants to increase room sales during this quarter and suggests the following:

1. Increase convention bookings with I've Been There referrals.

2. Develop Weekend in the City packages.

After discussing these promotions, all team members agree the Eat Wisely menu and the I've Been There promotions should be the targets of front desk sales efforts. Incentives such as cash awards to front office employees for participation in Eat Wisely and I've Been There will be used. The team agrees that an in-house video should be developed to assist in training employees.

The front office manager schedules a time to shoot the training video, selects and schedules a few senior employees to be the actors, arranges for rental of a video camera and related equipment, and receives approval for the projected costs. After several days of writing and editing, the following script is ready:

Desk clerk: Good morning! Welcome to The Times Hotel. Did you have a pleasant trip to our city?

Guest: The airport was pretty busy, and getting a cab was unreal. Is it always this busy out here?

Desk clerk: At this time of year, there are usually several conventions in town. The city schedules extra public transportation, but sometimes delegates who arrive early get caught in the crunch. Do you have a reservation?

Guest: Yes, I'm Thomas Renton, with the Investment Group Conference. My reservation is for a room to be shared with Michael Dodson.

Desk clerk: Yes, Mr. Renton, I have a reservation for you, with departure scheduled for Friday, January 28. Mr. Dodson will be joining you tomorrow. All charges will be billed to Lawson Investment Firm, Inc. I have your room ready for you. Please sign the registration card.

Guest: Thank you. That certainly didn't take long. After that wait for a cab at the airport, I do appreciate this service.

Desk clerk: We appreciate your deciding to stay at The Times Hotel. Sir, I see from your reservation you are on the board of directors of the Investment Group Conference. Our marketing and sales department is pleased to provide you with this special weekend pass, good for room and meals on another weekend. Perhaps you will be able to return to see how our new convention hall is progressing. It's scheduled to open this summer. The general manager told us it will hold up to 10,000 delegates.

Guest: That sounds great. I'll have some free time later this month to use that weekend pass.

A budget for this plan includes the following revenue and expense categories. When the hard facts of projected revenues and related expenses are visualized, the plan becomes more concrete and realistic. Projected budgets that show how a small cash outlay can produce significant revenue are effective in convincing owners and senior management that a point-of-sale front office program is a realistic and potentially profitable concept.

TIMES HOTEL

SALES BUDGET—FRONT OFFICE

Anticipated Increase in Sales

10 lunches @ $20 = $200/day × 365	$ 73,000
15 dinners @ $50 = $750/day × 365	$ 273750
	136,875
5 room service @ $20 = $100/day × 365	36,500
5 room reservations @ $110 = $550/day × 365	200,750
5 gift shop referrals @ $20 = $100/day × 365	36,500
TOTAL	$410,625

Anticipated Increase in Costs

Incentives (cash awards for lunches, dinners, room service, room reservations, gift shop referrals)	$15,000
Management planning time	5000
Employee overtime for producing three videos	4000
Photocopies	300
Rental of video equipment	500

Hardware accessories	50
Purchase of DVD player and monitor	500
Miscellaneous	500
Subtotal	$26,850

Related cost of goods sold:

Food

$$\begin{pmatrix} \text{Lunches} & 136{,}875 \times 0.35 = 47{,}906.25 \\ \text{Dinners} & 273{,}750 \times 0.35 = 95812.5 \\ \text{Room service } 36{,}500 \times 0.35 = 12{,}775 \\ \hline & \$73{,}456 \end{pmatrix}$$

156,493.75

Room prep [$5 \times 365 = 1825 \times \$15 = \$27{,}375$]	$ 27,375
Merchandise	10,950
	$194,818.75

TOTAL [$\$26{,}850 + \$194{,}818.75 = \$221{,}668.75$] $ 221,668.7

ANTICIPATED PROFIT [$\$194{,}818.75 - \$221{,}668.75 = \$398{,}831.25$] $

The data the team gathers in deciding to use the two promotional concepts are also useful in deciding whether or not these ideas will produce a profit for the efforts involved. The incentives, training, and budgets developed support the operational efforts of the plan. Feedback mechanisms include the standard guest test, comment cards, and monitoring of the source of sales for both promotions.

Solution to Opening Dilemma

Recommending outside restaurants is common in many hotels. The reason is that front office employees have not bought in to the hotel's profitability goal. It is management's responsibility to include front-line employees in developing a point-of-sale front office. In this situation, promoting the hotel's restaurant facility becomes the focus of the point-of-sale. Front-line employees also should have the opportunity to decide which promotional programs will be most beneficial to the hotel and to each employee.

Chapter Recap

Front office management includes helping promote the overall profitability of a hotel. Developing a point-of-sale front office involves developing a plan of action, which includes setting goals and objectives, brainstorming areas for promotion, evaluating alternatives, discussing supportive areas for consideration such as incentive programs and training programs, projecting anticipated revenues and related expenses in a budget, and preparing feedback mechanisms. This simple framework for planning allows front office managers to gain a larger perspective on the issue rather than pushing forward with desperate efforts to produce sales.

A team of managers from various departments who select a few promotional strategies and explain them to the front office staff generate additional income. The front office manager is responsible for developing a plan for a point-of-sale front office that is the basis for a successful and continuous program. This plan must include goods and services to be promoted, objectives and procedures, incentive programs, training programs, budgets, and tracking systems for employee performance, guest response, and profitability. Students beginning a career in the hotel industry will find that promoting in-house sales is high on the front office manager's agenda for success.

End-of-Chapter Questions

1. Why is the front office often considered an extension of the marketing and sales department?

2. Is it possible to direct the energies of the front office staff to support the efforts of the marketing and sales department? Explain.

3. If you are employed at the front desk of a hotel, do you feel you are an extension of the marketing and sales department? Explain.

4. What is a point-of-sale front office?

5. How would you begin to develop a point-of-sale front office?

6. What are the major goals and objectives of a point-of-sale front office program?

7. Discuss the areas for maximizing sales opportunities outlined in the text.

8. How important are incentive programs to the operation of a point-of-sale front office? Give examples.

9. How would you go about developing a video program for training front office employees in sales techniques?

10. With a classmate, do a mock training session, using the video script in the text. Have several other students observe your performance. Ask them to react to what they learned. Do you feel this is what you want to convey to train an employee in a point-of-sale front office? Explain your answer.

11. Why is budgeting so important to the success of this program?

12. How do well-constructed feedback systems help the point-of-sale front office program? What should they cover? What do they tell management?

13. If you are employed at a hotel front office and the hotel has a website, discuss feedback options on the website.

CASE STUDY 1301

The message at the staff meeting of The Times Hotel was loud and clear: Increase sales! Ana Chavarria, front office manager, and other members of the management staff meet informally late that evening to brainstorm ideas for increasing sales for the hotel. Eric Jones, food and beverage manager, has brought along a copy of a recent hospitality publication that includes an article on increasing promotional efforts within the hotel as well as increasing marketing efforts outside the hotel. This concept gives Ana an idea: Maybe the front office employees, as well as other employees in the hotel, have ideas about promoting sales. Eric dismisses that thought, stating that management is the only group paid or trained to think. Frank Goss, director of marketing and sales, wants Ana to explain her idea further.

She feels the front office is a focal point for information for all guests. Maybe having her staff act as internal sales agents can increase sales in the hotel. She has a good rapport with her employees and feels they will give it a try. She is willing to put in the effort required to develop a plan.

How should Ana Chavarria proceed to develop an internal sales agents plan?

CASE STUDY 1302

Cynthia Restin, night auditor at The Times Hotel, has been discussing decreased sales in the restaurant with Lorraine DeSantes, director of marketing and sales. Ms. DeSantes recently developed a plan whereby the front office staff would start promoting restaurant sales. This plan was well thought out and even included an incentive plan in which all front desk clerks (several of whom are college students) would receive dental care.

Lorraine approaches Ana Chavarria, front office manager, and asks her, "What's the problem with your staff? Why aren't they pushing restaurant sales like we planned?" Ana asks Lorraine what plan she is referring to. Lorraine reminds her of the plan to increase sales in the restaurant with the assistance of her front desk clerks. Ana says she vaguely remembers her talking about this at a staff meeting, but there wasn't any follow-up.

What parts of Lorraine DeSantes's plan were missing? How would you revise her plan for reimplementation?

CASE STUDY 1303

The owners of the Times Hotel recently did a quick survey to determine why guests don't want to use in-house amenities such as fax machines, Wi-Fi, copy machines, room service, vending machines, restaurants, and so on. Some of the responses indicated the machines were in located in inconvenient areas and were not operating at times, but most of the responses centered on "Gee, I didn't know you had such things in the hotel." The survey was discussed at a recent staff meeting. Here are some of the comments from the staff members:

Eric Jones, food and beverage manager, says, "I am not surprised guests can't find the restaurants. The front desk clerks are always hiding in the back. Just the other day, I had to wait one minute to get some one's attention to wait on me—and I think

CASE STUDY 1303 (CONTINUED)

I am someone who does some work around here!" Thomas Brown, executive housekeeper, adds, "Last weekend, two guests asked the front desk clerk why the computer system wasn't working, and he responded, 'I'll make a note of it and get back to you in the morning.'" Yoon-Whan, executive engineer, begins his thoughts with, "Now let's take another look at the problem here. Some of these things are out of our control. For example, those vending machines are old. I have had a purchase order in for replacement with ten new ones—and I still haven't heard anything on my request. We shouldn't always blame the employees." Ana Chavarria, front office manager, responds "Thanks, Yoon-Whan, for seeing some good in those employees. They do try, but guests don't want to hear excuses. I get so frustrated with employees who don't try to see the guest's side of things. Employees fail to realize we are all in this together."

At this time, Margaret Chu, general manager, takes over and says, "I think we are at a crucial point in making suggestions on how to make our hotel more user-friendly to the guest."

Develop a discussion team to make suggestions to the Times hotel staff on what they should include in improving their situation.

Notes

1. Avinash Narula, "Boosting Sales Through the Front Office," *Canadian Hotel and Restaurant* (February 1987): 37.
2. Doug Kennedy, "Front Desk Training Is The Key to Capturing More Walk-In Business" June 2, 2009, http://www.hotel-online.com/News/PR2009_2nd/Jun09_FrontDesk.html.
3. Narula, 38.
4. Ibid.
5. Douglas McGregor, *The Human Side of Enterprise* (New York: McGraw-Hill, 1960), 33–34.
6. Ibid., 47–48.
7. Abraham H. Maslow, *Motivation and Personality,* 3d ed. (New York: Harper & Row, 1987), 15–22.
8. Elton Mayo, *The Human Problems of an Industrial Civilization* (New York: Viking, 1960).
9. Frederick Herzberg, B. Mausner, and B. B. Snyderman, *The Motivation to Work,* 2d ed. (New York: Wiley, 1967), 113–114.
10. Frederick Herzberg, personal communication with the author, June 1, 1989.

Key Words

guest test	plant
incentive program	point-of-sale front office
motivation	upsell

CHAPTER 14

Security

O P E N I N G   D I L E M M A

The general manager has been considering establishing an in-house security department. Security at the hotel has been outsourced in the past five years with minimal concern. However, with the recent media emphasis on the safety of both guests and employees, the general manager thinks it is time to prepare a plan of action to investigate the possibility of an in-house security department.

CHAPTER FOCUS POINTS

- Importance of a security department to effective front office management
- Organization of a security department
- In-house security department versus contracted security services
- Hotel law
- Room key security system
- Fire safety
- Emergency communication procedures
- Employee safety programs

The act of delivering hospitality is thought to occur naturally. However, throughout this text, delivering hospitality is discussed as a planned concept, complete with research on guests' needs, policy and program development, establishment and delivery of training programs, and follow-up information systems. Hospitality also includes providing a safe environment for guests, which requires a well-organized department to oversee and implement safety programs. The security department of a hotel is vital to delivering hospitality to guests. This department is responsible for establishing the details of the following systems:

- Guest and employee safety
- Room key security
- Fire safety systems
- Bomb threat action
- Emergency evacuation plans
- Employee safety training plans
- Emergency communication plans

These operational procedures are never really appreciated until a crime occurs or a disaster strikes a hotel. They are assumed to be in place but somehow take a back seat to accommodating guests' more immediate needs and meeting the financial objectives of the organization. The terrorist attacks of September 11, 2001, in New York City and Washington, DC, have affected security concerns like no other situation. Rolfe Winkler reports the following.*

> With hotels becoming an increasingly popular target for militant attacks in Asia and beyond, the issue of hotel security and appropriate travel precautions is growing in importance for business travelers and tourists. In the past year [2009], militants killed at least 54 people in a suicide bomb attack on Islamabad's Marriott hotel, 71 people in the siege of the Taj Mahal and Oberoi hotels in Mumbai, nine in a suicide attack on Peshawar's Pearl Continental, and seven in the bombings of Jakarta's Ritz Carlton and Marriott in July.[1]

National, state, and local safety codes and ordinances require the hotelier to provide a safe environment for guests. This chapter discusses safety awareness as it relates to the front office manager's job and how the front office helps provide this essential service to guests.

Importance of a Security Department

The front office is a hotel's communication center; it is the vital link between the hotel management and the guest. When a guest calls for assistance because of fire, illness, theft, or any other emergency, it is usually the front office that must respond. The staff on duty at the front office cannot leave and resolve the emergency because they must continue to provide communication services and process financial transactions. The security department staff must react with speed and efficiency to serve the guest.

The security department is often regarded as a passive department, acting only when called on. In reality, it is an active department, setting policies, organizing programs, and delivering training programs to promote guest and employee safety. The director of security is a trained professional who must ensure that a busy hotel filled with guests, employees, and equipment stays safe. One of the department's goals is to *prevent* emergencies through planning its services. Another goal, however, is to train all hotel employees to respond to emergencies.

The importance of security to a hotel is emphasized in the following *Hotel Security Report* article by Patrick M. Murphy, CPP, director of loss prevention services at Marriott International, Inc., Washington, DC, who reports on Marriott International's adoption of Crime Prevention Through Environmental Design (CPTED) in its chain of 1900 owned and managed properties worldwide:

> CPTED is part of a total security package. It can include anything and everything from the presence of security or loss prevention officers at a property to plans for protecting

the interior, lobby, and guestrooms; exterior and parking area; and the surrounding neighborhood. Its goal is to keep the criminals from breaking into any area of the property; it accomplishes this by subtly making the environment uncomfortable for them.

The hotel priority areas in CPTED include the following.

- Building entrances—When reviewing a property we look to see that all entrances are inviting, brightly lit, with no obstructing shrubbery. At night, side entrances should be restricted by use of card readers so that non-registered guests must pass through the lobby and past the main check-in desk.
- Hotel lobbies—They should be designed to be visually open, with minimal blind spots for front desk employees. Lobbies also should be designed so that persons walking through the front door must pass the front desk to reach the guestroom corridors or elevators.
- Guestrooms—These [electronic locking systems] create an environment where keys are automatically changed when a new guest checks in; locks also can be interrogated to determine the last person to enter the room.
- Guest amenities—Marriott designs its new properties with glass doors and walls to allow for maximum witness potential when providing swimming pools, exercise rooms, vending areas, and laundry facilities. Adding house phones in these areas makes it possible for guests to call for help if they feel uncomfortable or threatened by anyone.
- Exterior of the property—CPTED principles call for bright lighting at walkways and entrances. Traffic should be directed to the front of the hotel property to make would-be criminals as visible as possible. Entrances to the hotel grounds should be limited. Landscaping, such as hedges and shrubbery, can also create aesthetically pleasing barriers to promote the desired traffic and pedestrian flow.
- Parking—The preferred lighting is metal halide. High-pressure sodium should be avoided because it casts a harsh yellow light. The optimal parking lot or garage has one entrance and exit with well-marked routes of travel for both cars and pedestrians. Garages need to be as open as possible, encouraging clear lines of sight. Elevators and stairwells that lead from the garage into the hotel should terminate at the lobby level, where a transfer of elevators or a different set of stairs should be required to reach guestroom floors. Other CPTED features in the garage should include CCTV (closed-circuit television) cameras, installation of emergency call boxes, and painting the walls white to increase the luminosity of light fixtures while creating an atmosphere that is appealing to the eye.[2]

In today's *litigious society*, an environment in which consumers sue providers of products and services for not delivering those products and services according to expected operating standards, it is important to maintain a well-organized security department. The cost of a human life lost because of negligence or the financial loss due to a fire far outweighs the expense incurred in operating a security department.

The following case illustrates the expense that can result from security breaches:

Perhaps the most significant [of high-visibility hotel crimes] was the 1974 rape of singer/ actress Connie Francis in a Westbury, N.Y., hotel, which resulted in a much-publicized trial culminating in a multimillion-dollar verdict against the hotel. The case is still considered the industry's "wake-up call" in terms of legal liability.[3]

Organization of a Security Department

The security department of a hotel is organized like any other department. At the head of the department is the director of security, who is responsible for maintaining a safe environment for guests and employees. The security director needs personnel, technology, and a budget to operate a 24-hour control system for the hotel. Depending on the size of the hotel, there may be an assistant director of security who acts in the absence of the director and assists in the administrative and supervisory functions of the department. The director of security reports to and works with the general manager and interacts with each department director. Each of the shifts (7 A.M. to 3 P.M., 3 P.M. to 11 P.M., and 11 P.M. to 7 A.M.) is staffed with shift supervisors and security guards who are responsible for patrolling the grounds to watch the activities of the guests and employees and check on safety and security equipment. The number of people required to staff this department depends on the size of the hotel. Figure 14-1 is an organization chart of a security department for a large hotel.

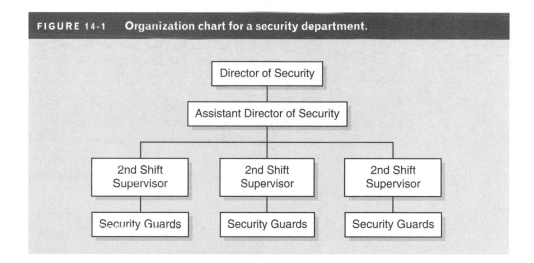

FIGURE 14-1   Organization chart for a security department.

Job Analysis of the Director of Security

The job analysis of a director of security outlines the administrative and supervisory tasks of this management team member. Active planning to ensure quick and effective reactions to problems and emergencies is the basis for successful job performance.

A typical job analysis is as follows:

8:00 A.M.	Reports to the hotel.
8:05	Discusses the activities of the previous night with the parking garage attendant.
8:15	Discusses the activities of the previous night with the security shift supervisor or security guard on duty.
8:30	Obtains notes concerning the activities of the previous night from the night auditor. Obtains the daily function sheet, which lists the events of the day.
8:40	Checks the audit report of fire and safety equipment located at the front desk.
8:45	Discusses the status of heating, ventilating, and air-conditioning equipment with the director of maintenance.
9:00	Meets with the security shift supervisor or security guards for the first shift to communicate activities and duties of the day.
9:30	Meets with the executive chef to be updated on special functions of the day and incidental activities in that department.
10:00	Meets with the housekeeper to discuss incidental activities in that department.
10:30	Returns to the office to review the daily security shift reports.
10:45	Updates the general manager on the status of security within the hotel and incidental departmental activities of importance.
11:00	Discusses the activities of the day with the restaurant manager.
11:30	Returns to the office to prepare the weekly schedule.
11:45	Responds to a call from the front office that a guest is stranded in an elevator. Assists maintenance in keeping order.
12:45 P.M.	Meets with the director of marketing and sales to determine the security needs for an upcoming high school prom and an insurance executives convention.
1:00	Returns to the office to work on the budget for the next fiscal year.
1:30	Lunches with the city fire marshal to discuss plans for renovating the sprinkler system in the new wing.
2:15	Meets with the front office manager to discuss the fire emergency and bomb threat action plan for front office personnel.
2:45	Meets with the security shift supervisors for the first and second shifts to discuss operational procedures.
3:15	Conducts a fire emergency training program for fourth- and fifth-floor housekeeping personnel.

4:15	Returns to the office to revise the fire emergency and bomb threat action plan for front office personnel.
5:00	Meets with the general manager to discuss the status of fire safety training in all departments.
5:30	Responds to a call from the front office that a guest has fallen on hotel property. Assists the guest with first aid and arranges for transportation to a medical facility. Completes an accident report. Assists the family of the guest in making arrangements for an extended stay.
6:00	Confers with maintenance personnel on the operational status of fire safety equipment.
6:15	Prepares a to-do list for the next day.
6:30	Checks with the banquet captain on the status of guests at scheduled banquets.
6:45	Checks with the lounge manager on the status of guests.
6:55	Checks with the front office manager on the status of guest check-in.
7:00	Checks with the garage attendant for an update on activities.
7:05	Checks with the shift security supervisor for an update on patrol activities.
7:10	Departs for the day.

This job analysis shows the security director to be involved with managing details concerning the whereabouts of people and showing a proactive concern for their safety. The job calls for constant interaction with department directors, employees, government officials, guests, and operational equipment. All of these tasks add up to a highly responsible position in the hotel. The following comment on hotel guest safety outlines the objective of a hotel's obligations to guests:

> The hotel is not the insurer of guest safety but it must exercise the care of a reasonable and prudent operator in protecting the guest. This duty extends to an innkeeper's obligation to protect guests from
>
> - negligent or deliberate acts of hotel employees
> - acts of other guests
> - acts by nonguests committed on the premises

FRONT-LINE REALITIES

 A guest calls down to the front desk indicating that her 6-year-old son has not returned from the vending machine area. He has been gone for 25 minutes. How should the desk clerk respond? What systems must be in place to ensure prompt, efficient action?

John Juliano is director of safety and security at the Royal Sonesta Hotel, Cambridge, Massachusetts. After earning a bachelor's degree in criminal justice, he worked in private security and then went on to work in hotels for the past 22 years.

Mr. Juliano feels a safe, secure environment is very important to travelers. He has been told by guests they feel as if they are at home when they stay at the Royal Sonesta Hotel; they want to feel as safe there as they do in their own house.

He is responsible for the day-to-day operations of the security department, including scheduling and management. He investigates incidents (theft, damaged property, etc.) and acts as a liaison with the hotel's safety committee. He is involved with employee training (CPR, airborne antigens, etc.); disseminates information on state, federal, and Occupational Safety and Health Administration (OSHA) requirements to supervisors; and helps implement new safety procedures.

Mr. Juliano says his job requires more in the way of management than operations. He develops protective/preventive measures to keep the hotel from experiencing security problems and liability lawsuits. He must be knowledgeable about local ordinances as well as state laws and OSHA regulations. Mr. Juliano's department is as involved with guest relations as the front desk, guest services, and the concierge are. He maintains a good relationship with the front office manager, to whom he provides informational guidelines. By following these guidelines, the front office manager and staff develop an understanding of what to do in certain situations. While Mr. Juliano does not interact with the front office manager every day, the front office manager calls him about situations that occur and asks for his feedback. Mostly he deals directly with guests or with a hotel employee when something goes wrong.

Failure to conform to the reasonableness standard in these three areas provides a liability risk for the hotel.[4]

The responsibilities outlined in the job description for the director of security may be assigned to other workers in some hotels due to budgetary reasons. The general manager in a limited-service property, for example, may assign the *crisis management* role of maintaining control of an emergency situation to the manager on duty. The administrative role may be shared with the assistant manager, reservations manager, or housekeeper.

In-House Security Departments versus Contracted Security

The events of September 11, 2001, as well more recent events of hotel bombing and seizing urged hotel operators to take the responsibility of guest security very seriously. However, general managers of hotels must determine how to make operating an in-house security department cost-effective. Operating a well-organized security department must be the primary concern when considering hiring an outside security firm. As the job analysis for the director of security indicates, there is more to the position than patrolling the halls and grounds of the hotel. *Foot patrol*—walking the halls, corridors, and outside property of a hotel to detect breaches of guest and employee safety—is an important feature of security, but it is a preventive measure, not an active means of organizing security. However, in some situations, a general manager is forced, for economic reasons, to consider the purchase of an outside service. Administrative and planning procedures for operating a security department are delegated to other department heads. The cost consideration must be weighed against planning and coordinating a safe environment for the guest and employee.

The hourly rate charged by the security service for *security escort service*, or having a uniformed security guard escort a hotel employee to a financial institution to make bank deposits, for performing regular hall patrol, and for maintaining surveillance of the parking garage may seem attractive compared to the annual salaries and administrative overhead associated with operating an in-house security department 24 hours a day. But more than cost must be considered. Who will work with the other department directors to establish fire safety and security procedures? Who will plan and deliver fire safety and security training sessions? Who will monitor fire safety devices? Who will work with city officials in interpreting fire and safety codes? Who will update management on the latest technology to ensure a safe environment? These and other questions must be answered if owners and management are committed to security.

If an outside security service is hired, the role of maintaining security is parceled out to department directors. The director of maintenance operates the fire safety and security equipment, maintains operating records of fire safety equipment and elevators, and reacts to hazardous situations. The general manager, if time permits, establishes a safety committee that responds to government guidelines and potential hazards. Each department director, if time permits, establishes security guidelines based on personal experience. Under these circumstances, safety and security become low priorities. The lack of coordination almost guarantees disaster when an emergency strikes.

The following excerpt discussing a hotel bombing in Jakarta, Indonesia, emphasizes the wisdom of adopting a proactive operational position on guest security. It encourages the need to share best practices rather than work alone.

As terrorism continues to pose a threat to soft targets such as hotels, as evidenced by the recent [2003] bombing outside the JW Marriott in Jakarta, security has never been more important. With this reality, global hotel companies are no doubt concerned with how to strike that delicate balance between security and guest convenience. Although this is an issue that hoteliers grapple with daily, many hotel companies continue to shy away from talking about their security procedures. Understandably, part of the issue is that hotels do not want to compromise their security by disclosing what measures they are taking. However, another issue is that hoteliers must learn to think of security as a positive rather than as a necessary evil.

"Our challenges far exceed appearing to be negative or painting doomsday scenarios," says Jimmy Chin, director of risk management, The Peninsula New York. "We need to hammer away at the message that something else can happen, and we

FIGURE 14-2

The security department in a hotel works closely with the front office manager. Photo courtesy of Pinkerton Security and Investigation Services.

need to address it and examine what steps we can take to either protect or respond to it. It should be positive because guests see us as a deterrent against possible crime and terrorism. Guests today expect to be protected. The hotel industry should be discussing security measures openly, sharing best practices instead of worrying about how it looks."[5]

Meeting the challenges of providing security for guests and employees requires a full-time approach. Part-time efforts to control crises in a hotel may be shortsighted. The following story shows the consequences of not providing adequate security.

The verdict against Hilton Hotels Corp. in the Tailhook case could have far-reaching implications for hotel liabilities in providing security for guests, according to hospitality legal experts. In this case, former Navy Lt. Paula Coughlin sued Hilton for failing to provide adequate security during the Tailhook Association convention at the Las Vegas Hilton in 1991. Jurors awarded Coughlin $1.7 million in compensatory damages and $5 million in punitive damages. Hilton claimed three security guards were adequate for the 5000 people at the event.[6]

Room Key Security

One of the responsibilities of the director of security is to establish and maintain a *room key control system*, an administrative procedure that authorizes certain personnel and registered guests to have access to keys for entrance to guest rooms and public areas. One court found that "as a general proposition, a guest has an expectation of privacy in his or her room and a hotel has an affirmative duty not to allow unregistered guests, unauthorized employees, and third parties to gain access to a guest's room."[7] Hotels have several options to offer guests that will protect their privacy, including traditional hard keys, electronic locks, smart card technology, and contactless electronic locks that use radio frequency identification (RFID).

Hard-key System

Hard-key systems consist of the traditional large key that fits into a keyhole in a lock; preset tumblers inside the lock are turned by the designated key. The hard-key system is less expensive than other lock systems at initial purchase. However, the costs of purchasing additional keys and rekeying locks must be considered over the long run. Also, reissuing the same key to guest after guest presents a security problem. Often, the guest fails to return the key at checkout. If a careless guest discards a room key or a criminal steals a key, guest safety is jeopardized. If regular maintenance and rekeying lock tumblers are not part of the preventive maintenance plan (and budget), guest security is compromised. While the hard-key system is the traditional method hotels have been using for many years, its cumbersome and costly maintenance indicates it should be replaced with advanced technology. This may be a slow process, but it will greatly improve guest, employee, and inventory safety. Economies of scale make the electronic key system an affordable necessity.

Electronic Locks System

The *electronic key system* is composed of:

> battery-powered or, less frequently, hardwired locks, a host computer and terminals, keypuncher, and special entry cards which are used as keys. The host computer generates the combinations for the locks, cancels the old ones and keeps track of master keying systems. The front desk staff uses at least one computer terminal to register the guest and an accompanying keypuncher to produce the card. An electronic locking system allows the hotel to issue a "fresh" key to each guest. When the guest inserts his or her key into the door, the lock's intelligent microchip scans the combination punched on the key and accepts it as the new, valid combination for the door, registering all previous combinations unacceptable.[8]

The electronic key system, smart card, and biometrics can be used for guest rooms as well as other areas of the hotel; they are an investment in guest security and safety. As each new guest registers, a fresh plastic key or appropriate electronic device is produced. The new combination for the guest room lock or public/storage area responds only to the new guest room key or pass key. This procedure almost guarantees guest and employee safety. The initial investment in these types of systems must be evaluated against over-all maintenance and replacement costs of a hard-key system and increased guest and employee security.

Electronic key access is one of many alternatives from which facility managers can choose. The system includes an electronically coded key and door controllers that can be easily programmed to recognize one or more codes. Since the electronic keys are assigned codes from one of several billion possible combinations, they are virtually impossible to duplicate.

High-end electronic access control systems can be equipped with numerous . . . features . . . [such as] recording who entered an area and at what time . . . [and can] link this information with a central computer, allowing facility managers to provide reports on the activities of thousands of users through thousands of doors. These reports are extremely helpful during the investigation phase of a crime incident. Access control systems also can be equipped with a panic alert that allows the individual to send a distress signal in the event they are being coerced to open the door.[9]

The following article describes an installation of SAFLOK MT™ locks at the Historic Westin St. Francis in San Francisco. The hotel has 1200 guest rooms and 28 meeting rooms.

The SAFLOK MT electronic lock is the company's flagship product. It has the ability to read three different types of keycard media: smart card, memory, and magstripe technologies. This multi-technical capability is a standard feature that SAFLOK provides at no additional charge. The lock stores a use-history of up to 5,900 entries.

The System 6000 operating program is a Windows-based system. Some user-friendly features include: point-and-click functionality, username and password protection to ensure that each user accesses the program with the rights assigned to their access level, lost or stolen key cancellation and replacement; customizable keycard programmability; and detailed system reporting. System 6000 also features the remote technical support feature that enables a SAFLOK technician to remotely access the property's system to rectify and troubleshoot any problem. For the property's security, this access is password-protected.[10]

Smart Card

Another version of the electronic key is the *smart card*, an electronic device with a computer chip that allows a hotel guest or an employee access to a designated area, tracking, and debit card capabilities for the guest. Bruce Adams reports the following on smart cards:

Keeping track of room access by hotel management has never been easier. Employees have smartcards that grant them access to different levels of security. The cards track what level of key was used, who was there, and create an audit trail that is easy to manage.

Beyond state-of-the-art locking and tracking capability, the smartcards serve as guest identification cards, which include the guest's name and dates of stay at Portofino Bay Hotel at Universal Studios theme park. "Their card functions as an ID card, which gives them special privileges at the theme park," [said Michael] Sansbury [regional vice president for Loews Hotels]. "Some of those benefits include front-of-line privileges at rides and events, early admission to the park and priority seating in restaurants." The smartcards also serve as charge cards at the hotel and park. "The smartcard is linked to the guest account in the hotel," Sansbury said. "The credit limit in the hotel is transmitted to the smartcard. Merchants at any shop or restaurant at Universal Studios can swipe the smartcard the same way they swipe a credit card. It works the same way as a credit card . . . If they lose their smartcard, it is very easy to invalidate," Sansbury said.[11]

Contactless Electronic Locks

Contactless locks in the form of wristbands, key fobs, and key cards have also been developed using *radio frequency identification (RFID)* as a form of electronic keys in lodging properties.

Suitable for hotel and resort applications, the Contactless 790 Electronic Lock from Kaba Ilco can read and write information to a variety of RFID [Radio Frequency Identification] credentials such as keycards, wristbands and key fobs. It features an ergonomically designed contactless reader. To gain access, guests and staff members simply present their keycards at the reader. An audit trail that specifies the date and time that each lock was accessed can be recorded on employee keycards.[12]

Another use of RFID is passing along the room key number via a cell phone.

Global electronic hotel lock provider SAFLOK™ announces its collaboration with OpenWays, a global provider of mobile-based access-management and guest-service solutions for the hospitality industry. Through this alliance, SAFLOK and Openways have developed an interface that enables SAFLOK locks to read a "key" that is delivered by an OpenWays–enabled cell phone.

This "interaction" between the two solutions enables the guest to securely receive his or her room number and room key via cell phone, thereby streamlining the check-in and checkout process by allowing the guest to bypass the front desk.

OpenWays interfaces with SAFLOK electronic locks regardless of the card technology being used. The solution interfaces with a hotel's PMS, CRS and CIS, and can facilitate mobile bookings and mobile confirmations, mobile upgrade offers, e-payment/e-ticketing vouchers, e-concierge, and more.[13]

Terence Ronson reports on an additional security measure—*biometrics*—that hotels are considering and some are using to control access.

Biometrics is the measurement of uniqueness of a human being, such as voice, hand-print, or facial characteristics. Some of you may have seen mock examples of such devices in James Bond movies, *Mission Impossible*, and *Star Trek*. Card-based access systems have been around for a long while; they control access using authorized pieces of plastic, but they do not track who is in actual possession of that card. Systems using PINs (personal identification numbers), such as ATMs (automatic teller machines) require only that an individual knows a specific number to gain entry. Who actually enters that code cannot be determined. Biometrics devices, on the other hand (no pun intended), verify who a person is by what they are, whether it's their hand, eye, finger-print, or voice. I expect hotels would be interested in fingerprint or hand-recognition access control systems—probably because of the cost and relative simplicity in which they can be implement[ed] into an existing operation.

For example, when captured, a fingerprint image is converted into a digital form by extracting a set of unique characteristics. The abstract data taken from the recording is then encrypted and stored in the database as a template, to be later used as a reference for comparison purposes.

Users are authenticated by extracting and comparing information derived from unique arches, loops, markings, and ridges of a fingerprint. This set of information, called *minutia*, is a mathematical representation captured as a series of numbers and relationships of the whorls and ridges of the fingerprint. No actual image of the finger-print is stored, ensuring privacy and security, the prime concern of users.[14]

Fire Safety

Hearing someone shout "Fire!" panics anyone who is unprepared to deal with this dangerous situation. Well-orchestrated safety procedures that are well managed at the onset of a fire can save the lives of guests and employees. The front office manager and the director of security must develop effective fire safety and evacuation plans as well as training programs for employees to ensure their effectiveness.

General Fire Code Requirements

Fire safety plans begin with the fire safety codes of the municipality where the hotel is located. These codes stipulate construction materials, interior design fabrics, entrance and exit requirements, space limitations, smoke alarm installation and maintenance, sprinkler system installation and maintenance, fire drill testing, fire alarm operation and maintenance, and the like. These extensive and detailed codes were developed to ensure guest safety. They may require extra financial investment, but they are intended to protect the guest and the occupants of the building.

Guest Expectations

Hotel guests expect, either consciously or unconsciously, to find a safe environment during their visit. Some guests may ask for a room on a lower level or inquire if the rooms have smoke alarms. However, most guests are concerned about other matters and do not ask about fire safety procedures. When the guest settles into a guest room, he or she may give a passing glance at the fire evacuation procedure posted behind the door. Some guests may even count the number of doors to the nearest exit. Is this enough? Will human lives be in jeopardy because guests' pressing concerns have caused them to place their safety in the hands of the management and employees of the hotel?

Fire Safety Plan

The front office manager who wants to take active measures to ensure guest safety must develop a simple fire safety plan, communicate it to employees and guests, and train employees and guests to handle a stressful situation. This includes the following commonsense elements:

1. Equip all guest rooms and public areas with smoke detectors that are tied to a central communications area.

2. Regularly test and maintain smoke detectors; keep up-to-date records of the tests, as shown in Table 14-1.

3. Install, maintain, and test fire alarms as required by local fire code regulations; again, keep up-to-date records of the tests, as shown in Table 14-2.

4. Constantly monitor smoke detectors and fire alarm systems, preferably at the front desk.

5. Prepare and post floor plans showing fire exit locations by area—public areas, work areas, and guest room areas (see Figures 14-3 and 14-4).

6. Tell employees and guests where the nearest fire extinguishers and fire alarms are located and how to evacuate the building. Instruct them in fire safety guidelines (Figure 14-5).

7. Develop a fire action communication procedure for front office personnel.

TABLE 14-1		Maintenance Records for Smoke Detector Tests				
401	12/1	OK	JB inspector	1/10	OK	JB inspector
402	12/1	OK	JB inspector	1/10	OK	JB inspector
403	12/1	bat. repl.	JB inspector	1/10	OK	JB inspector
404	12/2	OK	JB inspector	1/10	OK	JB inspector
405	12/2	OK	JB inspector	1/10	OK	JB inspector
406	12/2	OK	JB inspector	1/10	OK	JB inspector
407	12/2	OK	JB inspector	1/10	OK	JB inspector
408	12/2	OK	JB inspector	1/13	OK	JB inspector
409	12/2	OK	JB inspector	1/13	OK	JB inspector
410	12/2	OK	JB inspector	1/13	OK	JB inspector
411	12/2	OK	JB inspector	1/13	OK	JB inspector
412	12/2	OK	JB inspector	1/13	OK	JB inspector
413	12/3	bat. repl.	JB inspector	1/15	OK	JB inspector
414	12/3	bat. repl.	JB inspector	1/15	OK	JB inspector
415	12/3	OK	JB inspector	1/15	OK	JB inspector

JB = inspector's initials
bat. repl. = batteries replaced

TABLE 14-2	Maintenance Records for Fire Alarm Tests			
Floor 1, station A	4/10	OK		JB inspector
Floor 1, station B	4/10	OK		JB inspector
Floor 2, station A	4/10	OK		JB inspector
Floor 2, station B	4/10	OK		JB inspector
Floor 3, station A	4/10	OK		JB inspector
Floor 3, station B	4/10	OK		JB inspector
Floor 4, station A	4/10	OK		JB inspector
Floor 4, station B	4/10	OK		JB inspector
Floor 5, station A	4/10	no sound; repaired 4/10		JB inspector
Floor 5, station B	4/10	no sound; repaired 4/10		JB inspector
Floor 6, station A	4/10	OK		JB inspector
Floor 6, station B	4/10	OK		JB inspector
Kitchen	4/10	OK		JB inspector
Bakery	4/10	OK		JB inspector
Banquet A	4/10	OK		JB inspector
Banquet B	4/10	OK		JB inspector
Lounge	4/10	OK		JB inspector
Lobby	4/10	OK		JB inspector
Laundry	4/10	OK		JB inspector
Gift Shop	4/10	OK		JB inspector

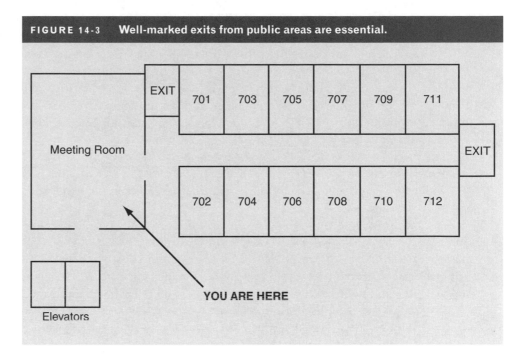

FIGURE 14-3 Well-marked exits from public areas are essential.

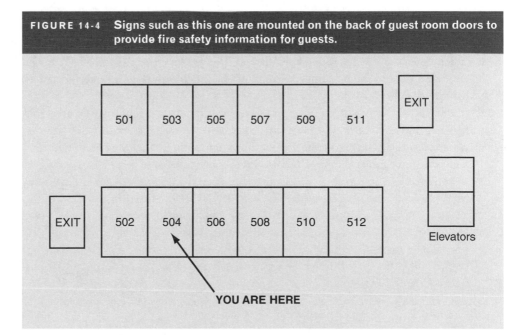

FIGURE 14-4 Signs such as this one are mounted on the back of guest room doors to provide fire safety information for guests.

FIGURE 14-5 Hotel fire safety procedures should be displayed in guest rooms.

1. When you check into any hotel or motel, ask for a copy of the fire procedures plan. If they do not have one, ask why.

2. Check to see if there is a smoke detector in your room. If there isn't, ask for a room that has one.

3. Familiarize yourself with the locations of the fire exits and count the number of doors from your room to the nearest fire exit. (If the corridor is smoky, you may not be able to see the exit, but you can feel your way along the floor.)

4. Get into the habit of keeping your key in the same place every time you stay at a motel or hotel so you'll always know exactly where it is. Then, if you have to leave your room, be sure to take your key with you. (If you cannot reach the exit, you may have to return to your room because of fire or smoke in the hallway.)

5. If you wake up and find your room is beginning to fill with smoke, grab your key, roll off the bed, and head for the door on your hands and knees. You'll want to save your eyes and lungs as long as possible, and the air 5 or 6 feet up may be filled with odorless carbon monoxide.

6. Before leaving your room, feel the door with the palm of your hand. If it is hot, or even warm, do not open it! If it is not warm, slowly open it a crack, with the palm of your hand still on the door (in case you have to slam it shut), and peek into the hallway to see what's happening.

7. If the coast is clear, crawl into the hallway, feeling your way along the exit side of the wall. It's easy to get lost or disoriented in smoke. Count the doors as you go.

8. Do not use an elevator as a fire exit. Smoke, heat, and fire may put it out of operation.

9. When you reach the exit, walk down the stairs to the first floor. (Exit doors are locked on the stairwell side, so you cannot enter any other floor.)

10. If you encounter smoke in the stairwell on the way down, the smoke may be stacking on the floors under it, and the stairwell may be impassable. Do not try to run through it. Turn around and go up to the roof.

11. When you reach the roof, open the door and leave it open so the stairwell can vent itself. Find the windward side of the building so you won't be caught up in the smoke. Then, have a seat and wait for the firefighters to find you.

12. If you cannot get out of your room safely, fill the bathtub or sink with water. Soak towels and stuff them under the door and between the cracks to keep the smoke out. With your ice bucket, bail water onto the door to keep it cool. If the walls are hot, bail water on them, too. Wet your mattress and put it up against the door. Keep everything wet.

13. If smoke does begin to seep into your room, open the window. (Keep the window closed if there is no smoke. There may be smoke outside.) If you see the fire through the window, pull the drapes down so they will not catch fire. Also, wet a handkerchief or washcloth and breathe through it.

14. DO NOT JUMP unless you are certain of injury if you stay in your room *one minute longer*. Most people hurt themselves jumping, even from the second floor—from the third floor, quite severely. If you're higher than the third floor, chances are you will not survive the fall. You would be better off fighting the fire in your room.

Sources: National Safety Council. Courtesy of Knights Inn. Cardinal Industries, Inc., Reynoldsburg, OH © 1989 Cardinal Lodging Group, Inc., management company for Knights Inns and Arborgate Inns.

Employee Training in Fire Safety

Providing training programs for employees on the locations of the fire exits, fire extinguishers, and fire alarms and on methods of building evacuation greatly increases the chances that all occupants will escape the building safely when necessary. After new and current employees are taught the locations of fire exits, extinguishers, and alarms throughout the building, supervisors can spot-check the effectiveness of the training with random questions such as "Where is the nearest fire exit when you are cleaning room 707? Where is the nearest fire extinguisher when you are in the bakery? Where is the nearest fire alarm when you are in the laundry?" These simple questions, repeated often enough, impress employees with the importance of fire safety.

Local fire departments or the director of security can train employees to use fire extinguishers. These informal training sessions should include operational procedures and information on applying the appropriate type of fire extinguisher. The time to start reading directions is not during the fire. These training sessions give employees confidence in their ability to handle an emergency.

Guest Instruction in Fire Safety

Often, instructing guests on fire safety is overlooked. They are at the hotel for a relaxing, enjoyable visit. But fire can strike at any time, even during relaxing, enjoyable visits. Inform each guest that all rooms are equipped with smoke detectors, that the nearest fire exit from any room is, at the most, four doors to the right of the room, that a fire extinguisher is located next to the elevator on each floor, and that a fire can be reported by dialing 0 for the hotel operator. Guests appreciate that the hotel cares about their well-being and that it has taken every precaution to ensure equipment is available and in working order.

Management may want to encourage guests to read the fire evacuation guidelines posted on the door of the guest room by offering enticing promotions. For example, on registering, the guest is informed of a special coupon attached to the fire evacuation plan located on the door. This coupon may be redeemed for a two-for-one breakfast special, a free cover charge in the lounge, a free morning newspaper, a discount in the gift shop, or some other incentive.

Accommodations for guests who are physically challenged should also be a concern for hotel managers. *Visual alarm systems*, flashing lights that indicate a fire or other emergency in a hotel room, should be installed to alert hearing-impaired guests. A report of the locations of physically challenged guests should be easy to retrieve from the PMS registration module in case of an emergency.

Fire Action Communication Procedure

The front office employees must take the lead in controlling the panic that may arise when a fire strikes. The fire communications training program developed by the front office manager must be taught to all front office personnel. If fire strikes during the middle of the day, more than one person will probably be available to assist in maintaining control of the situation. But if the disaster occurs at 10:30 P.M., there may be only one person on duty to orchestrate communications.

The communications procedure begins when a guest or an employee calls the switchboard to report a fire. Unfortunately, in many cases, time has already been wasted in attempts to extinguish the fire. Seconds are important in reporting the fire to the local fire company. At some properties, the fire company is immediately notified via the interface of the hotel's fire alarm with the municipal or private monitoring station. But front office personnel should never assume the fire company has been notified and should immediately call the fire station to report the fire. The call may duplicate an earlier report, but it is better to have two notifications than none.

After the fire is reported, security and management should be alerted. Guest and employee evacuation procedures must be initiated and organized. Established procedures stipulating who should be informed and in what manner, as well as who is to assist the guests and employees in evacuating, result in an efficient evacuation. The front desk clerk must produce a list of occupied guest rooms immediately. The rooms on the floor where the fire is reported and those on the floors immediately above and below the fire room are of vital importance to firefighters and volunteers who assist in the evacuation.

On arrival, firefighters immediately report to the front desk. They need to know where the fire is located and which guest rooms are occupied. Copies of the list of occupied rooms and special notes on whether the occupants are children or physically challenged aid in the rescue effort.

Front office personnel must remain calm throughout the ordeal. The switchboard will be active, with calls from inside and outside the hotel. Requests for information from the fire emergency crew and first-aid and rescue squads will be mixed with phone calls from the media and persons related to hotel guests. Switchboard operators should keep phone calls brief so the phone lines are open.

Security should not be forgotten during crises. Some people take advantage of such confusion to loot and pilfer. Cash drawers and other documents should be secured.

Each hotel must develop its own communications procedure for a fire. Each plan will vary based on the strengths of the employees in the front office. Training the staff with fire drills aids all employees in handling the emergency; everyone must be part of the drill, no matter how calmly they react to ordinary crises. Holding fire drills on each shift gives employees practice and is worth the effort.

The following stories highlight the importance of being prepared to react in an emergency situation:

[James T. Davidson, executive director, Training Services, Educational Institute] was working as a front desk clerk in Bermuda during the arson riots in 1976. Rioters set fire to the top floor of the hotel. [The hotel's] communications tower was on the roof and [it] lost communications within moments, even though [the hotel's management] thought [that it] had a fool-proof system. Several people were killed, including some guests who tried to use the elevator—it took them straight to the blaze. There was an emergency plan for evacuating guests, but no real plan for getting them a safe distance away from the burning building.

Years later, [he] was general manager of a property on the Seychelles Islands during two attempted coups d'état. A total curfew was imposed during both coup attempts, but the second was worse because it happened during the middle of the night when [the] staff was limited. For six days, [the hotel] made do with a staff of 13 for 300 guests and lived off the food that was at the hotel. The 13 staff members worked in just about every department at one time or another. [They] enlisted guests to help keep the hotel running, and most were glad to pitch in.

Each incident taught [him] the importance of planning and communications, and how essential it is to have regular emergency procedure drills.[15]

Even though these events took place before September 11, 2001 and the international security events of 2009, planning for a general disaster and communications within that disaster were and are still vitally important.

Emergency Communication

There are times when guests and employees must evacuate a building in a nonemergency situation. Although it is imperative that the building be emptied, evacuation is not as urgent as it is during a fire. Examples of such situations include a bomb threat, a fire in an adjacent building, a gas leak, or an electrical power outage. When these situations occur, an emergency communication system must be in place to ensure an efficient evacuation.

The director of security, in conjunction with the front office manager and civil authorities, should develop a plan for all departments. The role of the front office is essential in directing communications with guests and employees. The front office staff is responsible for alerting employees and guests that an emergency situation exists. The emergency communication plan should establish a *communications hierarchy*, or the order in which management personnel may be called on to take charge; emphasize cooperation between the hotel and civil authorities; and provide training.

The 1993 bombing of the World Trade Center provides a cautionary lesson in preparedness:

When disaster strikes, inadequate or incomplete preparation becomes painfully evident—and costly. These hard lessons became clear in the immediate aftermath of the

February 26, 1993, bombing of New York's World Trade Center, when the staff of the adjacent Vista Hotel reacted heroically to a very daunting situation. Loss of the facility's main telephone switch made it impossible to communicate with management and arrange emergency recovery services. Cellular phones could have fetched thousands of dollars apiece that day. Drawings illustrating how the hotel was built were not easily accessible, creating confusion among the rescue teams.[16]

Here is another incident of a more urgent nature:

A natural gas explosion tore through the [Embassy Suites Outdoor World at Dallas/ Ft. Worth International Airport] swimming pool maintenance room at 6:25 P.M., August 6, 2000, just four days after the hotel's opening, forcing guests to flee the property. Rapid response by the hotel's staff, led by GM Bill Bretches, as well as police, firefighters and paramedics, helped clear the property swiftly and minimize injuries. Two hundred fifteen of the hotel's 329 guest suites were occupied at the time of the explosion, with many of the guests in the property's atrium for the evening reception.

Guests were brought to the hotel's parking lot, where they were given water and clothing provided by Bass Pro Shops Outdoor World, a part of the hotel complex. Staff accounted for guests by matching names with the registration list. All guests, accompanied by Embassy Suites staff, were relocated within 90 minutes to nearby hotels.[17]

The following discussion of planning for effective emergency communication outlines the most important features of such a plan.

Developing the Emergency Communication Plan

The emergency communication plan is developed in cooperation with the director of security, the front office manager, and local civil authorities. These individuals are responsible for developing a plan to be used in the event of an impending life-threatening emergency. The plan must involve training staff and employees.

Emergency Communications Manager on Duty

The job description of each management position includes a task entitled "emergency communications manager on duty." This duty requires the person to act as the liaison between the hotel and the civil authorities. Each member of the management staff is trained in the responsibilities of the job.

The role of emergency communications manager on duty is assumed in the following order:

General manager

Assistant general manager

Director of security

Director of maintenance

Food and beverage manager

Banquet manager

Restaurant manager

Director of marketing and sales

Controller .

Housekeeper

Front office manager

Front desk clerk on duty

Night auditor

Responsibilities of the Front Office

On receipt of a call informing the hotel that the guests and employees are in danger, these procedures are to be followed (Figure 14-6):

1. Remain calm. Write down the name, phone number, affiliation, and location of the person making the call.

2. Immediately alert the emergency communications manager on duty to the impending danger. If main telephone service to the hotel is inactivated, use a cellular phone.

3. Inform the front desk clerk of the impending danger. Produce a room list of all registered guests in the hotel. Produce a list of all social functions in progress.

4. Alert the emergency communications leaders on duty in each hotel department. These people report to the front office immediately. Hold an emergency action meeting with the emergency communications manager on duty. The lists of registered guests and social functions in progress will assist in the evacuation.

5. The emergency communications manager on duty will advise you which authorities should be alerted.

   - Police department: 000–000–0000
   - Fire department: 000–000–0000
   - Bomb squad: 000–000–0000
   - Electric company: 000–000–0000
   - Gas company: 000–000–0000
   - Water company: 000–000–0000
   - Rescue squad: 000–000–0000
   - Red Cross: 000–000–0000
   - Owner of hotel: 000–000–0000
   - General manager: 000–000–0000

FIGURE 14-6

The switchboard operator plays a pivotal role in an emergency communication plan. Photo courtesy of the author.

6. Respond to phone inquiries as directed by the emergency communications manager on duty.

7. Remain at the front office to manage emergency communications until directed to evacuate by the emergency communications manager on duty.

Responsibilities of Other Hotel Departments

Delegating the task of emergency communications leader on duty to other responsible members of a department requires the following considerations:

- Each department director develops a hierarchy of positions to assume the responsibility of emergency communications leader.
- Each emergency communications leader on duty receives adequate training in the responsibilities of this job duty.
- Upon receiving information indicating that the hotel guests and employees are in immediate danger, immediately relay the information to the front office—dial 0.
- All emergency communications leaders on duty report to the front office for an emergency communications meeting. Directions are given for assisting guests and employees to evacuate.
- Employees on duty take direction from the emergency communications leaders on duty on assisting guests and employees in evacuating the hotel.

John Juliano, the director of safety and security at the Royal Sonesta Hotel in Cambridge, Massachusetts, mentioned his participation in the Security Directors' Network, a group of hotels that gather and share information on security issues. For instance, if an incident occurs at the Royal Sonesta Hotel involving a nonpaying guest, he fills out a report and emails it to the International Lodging Safety & Security–Boston Intel Network (ILISA), which then emails the information to 40–45 other hotels and law enforcement agencies in the greater Boston area. This is especially helpful when a person goes from hotel to hotel causing problems. For example, several years ago in Boston, a man went to several hotels and set off fire alarms (he actually set a fire at one hotel); when the unsuspecting and panicked guests ran from their rooms, he would enter and steal the guests' possessions. The network was helpful in tracking his actions. However, nine of ten times when he receives a request for information about a specific person, Mr. Juliano has no information to supply.

Training

The emergency communications managers on duty should receive ten or more hours of training in leading a crisis situation. This training must be documented, with two hours of refresher training every year.

Current employees receive two hours of training in emergency evacuation procedures. New employees receive training in emergency evacuation at the time of orientation. Refresher training, two hours every year, is required of all employees.

Employee Safety Programs

The hospitality industry is rife with opportunities for employee accidents. Behind the scenes are many people crowded into small work areas, busy preparing food and beverages and performing other services for the guests. The employees who are most in danger include those whose equipment is in need of repair, who work in areas that are too small, or who depend on other employees who are not attentive to the job at hand. The front of the house also provides opportunities for accidents. Employees and guests must use public areas that may be overcrowded or worn from continual use. To comply with hotel law, "the innkeeper must periodically inspect the facility to discover hidden or latent defects and then to remove or repair those defects. During the time prior to repair the innkeeper has a duty to warn the guests about the existence and location of the dangers."[18]

How does hotel management begin to develop guidelines for employee safety?

Employee Safety Committee

The best way to begin is to establish a *safety committee*, a group of front-line employees and supervisors who discuss safety issues concerning guests and employees. Front-line employees know the details of day-to-day hazards. They deal with the faulty equipment, traverse the crowded banquet rooms, work next to one another in poorly laid-out kitchens, process soiled laundry, push carts through busy public corridors, and hear guest complaints during checkout. Moreover, these people are part of the group that employee safety procedures are supposed to protect. Why not give them an opportunity to make their environment better? Although some employees do not want this responsibility, others will welcome it. With positive results, there may be a few more volunteers the next time.

Management is also a necessary part of the committee, not only because it is used to carrying out long-range plans but because it supplies the clout and support needed to implement the procedures.

Composition and Activities of the Safety Committee

The safety committee should include representatives from all departments in the hotel. If this is not possible, then co-committees for each shift might be an option. Management should convey the importance of the safety committee. Every comment received from the members is worthwhile and should be noted in the minutes of the meeting (Figure 14-7). Checklists with assignments for fact-finding tours, to be reported at the next meeting, should be distributed to begin the process. The meetings should not be mere formalities, quickly conducted with little thought about their content. At each meeting, the minutes of the previous meeting should be read and progress made in accomplishing goals should be reported. Members should see that the tiles in the laundry room, the leak in the stack steamer, and the worn rug in the lobby have been repaired or replaced as suggested.

Department Supervisors' Responsibility

Each department director must encourage a safety-conscious attitude. Management members can set an example by following safety procedures themselves when operating equipment, scheduling adequate staff during busy time periods, and following up on requests for repairs. If employees know you place safety first, they will also adopt that attitude.

FRONT-LINE REALITIES

 After slipping on debris while assisting a guest with his luggage, a front office employee shrugs off the injury, saying, "I needed a few days off anyway." Discuss the danger inherent in this type of employee attitude.

FIGURE 14-7   Minutes from a safety meeting keep participants on track.

Hotel Safety Committee Minutes 5/19

Members present:

A. Johnson, Housekeeping

S. Thomas, Housekeeping

L. Retter, Food Production

K. Wotson, Food Production

M. Benssinger, Front Desk

V. Howe, Front Desk

F. Black, Gift Shop

B. Lacey, Director of Security

T. Hopewell, Food and
   Beverage Manager

J. Harper, Banquets

T. Senton, Restaurant

M. Povik, Lounge

A. Smith, Maintenance

J. Hanley, Maintenance

D. Frank, Parking Garage

A. Gricki, Accounting

1. The minutes from the 4/12 meeting were read. M. Benssinger noted the minutes stated that Johnson Rug, Inc., was in the process of repairing the rug in the lobby. This was not the case at all. No one to her knowledge has repaired the seams on the rug. The minutes were corrected.

2. B. Lacey gave an update regarding progress on suggestions for improving safety, compiled at the 3/01 meeting.
   - The safety valves on the steam pressure equipment in the kitchen have all been replaced.
   - The electrical cords on the vacuum cleaners on the 11th and 15th floors have been repaired.
   - Five of the kitchen employees have been enrolled in a sanitation correspondence course. T. Hopewell is monitoring their progress.
   - The basement has been cleaned up, and excess trash has been removed. Old furniture that was stored near the heating plant has been removed and will be sold at an auction.
   - A new trash removal service has been selected. Regular trash removal will occur daily instead of three times a week.
   - The lights in the east stairwell have been replaced. Maintenance has initiated a new preventive maintenance program for replacement of lights in stairwells and the garage.
   - Three employees have volunteered to enroll in a substance abuse program. Their enrollment is anonymous to management and other employees.

3. M. Povik reported that the beer coolers are not maintaining the proper temperature. Several requests for service from the Gentry Refrigeration Service have been ignored. The director of maintenance will be informed of the situation.

4. A. Gricki reported that her efforts to reach Johnson Rug, Inc., to repair the rug have not been successful. The situation is dangerous. One guest almost tripped in the lobby yesterday. The director of housekeeping will be informed of the situation.

5. A. Johnson would like support from the committee to request the purchase of two training films on the correct procedure for heavy lifting and the proper use of chemicals. The committee agreed to write a memo to the general manager in support of this motion.

6. Members of the committee will meet at convenient times to do an informal safety survey of the maintenance department, housekeeping department, and kitchen. These surveys will provide feedback for department directors. All surveys are to be returned by June 1.

7. Meeting was adjourned at 4:42 P.M. Next meeting will be held June 10.

Safety Training Programs

Specific safety training programs should be developed by each department director. The directors review their departments to determine where safety training is needed. Security, equipment operation, sanitation, chemical use, transport of materials, and movement of equipment are areas to examine in compiling a program. The orientation program is the best opportunity for providing employees with safety training. Films, handouts, and booklets produced specifically to teach the safe way to perform a task reinforce on-the-job training and practice.

Regularly scheduled training sessions with notations of progress for use in the annual employee review are a necessity; otherwise, the employee gets the impression that management is showing that same old film again just to meet the insurance company's requirements. Safety training sessions should be scheduled when the employee is able to concentrate on the session and is not distracted by other duties. This may mean sessions must be scheduled before or after a shift, with additional pay. If management wants to enhance safety with training programs, then this must be a budget item. Planning for safety takes time and financial investment.

Solution to Opening Dilemma

The investigation of establishing an in-house security department could address the following topics:

- How are communications with public safety officials regarding safety issues handled?
- How are fire safety and emergency communication plans developed?
- Who is responsible for establishing and maintaining an employee safety training committee?
- Who is responsible for maintaining the integrity of the key system in the hotel?
- Who is responsible for the safe delivery of cash deposits?
- How are smoke detector and fire alarm tests conducted, and how are records maintained?
- Who conducts fire and emergency evacuation training and drills?
- How can all members of the hotel staff adopt a cautious attitude with respect to potential terrorist activities?

Chapter Recap

The costs of the security department are a vital expenditure. This chapter examined security as it relates both to the front office and to the overall objective of the hotel in providing a safe environment for guests and employees, especially in light of the

September 11, 2001 and recent international security disasters. The organization and operation of a security department, along with a job analysis of the director of security, were outlined to demonstrate the many facets of this department. The decision about whether to use an in-house security department or to contract outside security services should be based on ensuring the safety and security of hotel guests rather than on costs.

Both the front office and the security department are involved in room key security, which is easier to guarantee with electronic key, smart card, and contactless systems than it is with hard-key systems. Building evacuation requires that established procedures be in place and that both employees and guests receive instruction on how to react during a fire. An employee safety program should involve both staff and management and include a safety committee that addresses safety concerns on a regular basis and a training program for all employees. Emergency communications procedures should be developed, with a plan that involves management, employees, and civil authorities.

End-of-Chapter Questions

1. How does the security department interact with the front office? Give examples.

2. Visit a hotel with an in-house security department. How is this department structured? How many employees are needed to provide 24-hour coverage? What are the typical job duties of employees in this department?

3. Visit a hotel that contracts with a private security agency for security services. What services does this agency provide? How satisfied is management with the level and range of services provided?

4. Compare your answers to questions 2 and 3.

5. Contrast the level of security in a hotel that uses a hard-key system with that in a hotel that uses an electronic key or smart card system.

6. Discuss the features of a hard-key system.

7. Discuss the features of an electronic key system.

8. Discuss the features of a smart card system.

9. Discuss the features of contactless room security system.

10. What advantages do biometrics provide for guest and employee safety?

11. How can a hotel take a proactive stance on fire safety?

12. Why are testing and maintenance of smoke detectors and fire alarms so important?

13. Consider the fire safety procedures provided in guest rooms. How detailed do you think they should be? How can hotels encourage guests to read them?

14. Why is it important for management to include employees when developing safety programs?

15. Review the minutes of the safety committee meeting in Figure 14-7. What issues do you feel are top priorities? Which are low priorities?

16. What value do you see in preparing an emergency communications system to be used in a hotel?

17. Review the emergency communication plan presented in this chapter. What are its most important features?

CASE STUDY 1401

Ana Chavarria, front office manager of The Times Hotel, has scheduled an appointment with the director of security, Ed Silver. Mr. Silver has just learned that a nearby hotel, Remington Veranda, recently received a bomb threat that required the evacuation of all guests and employees. The situation caused a great deal of confusion and panic. Several employees were screaming, "Bomb! Bomb! Run for your life!" while other employees and guests were absolutely stunned and couldn't move. Although the bomb threat was of no substance, five guests and three employees had to be treated in the emergency room for shock and broken limbs caused by the crush to evacuate the building.

After reviewing the files in the security department, Ed Silver feels he and Ana should develop an emergency communication procedure to be sure the situation that occurred at Remington Veranda would not be repeated at The Times Hotel. Ana agrees; her prior experience at a hotel on the East Coast makes her realize the importance of such a plan.

Give Ana and Ed suggestions for developing an emergency communication plan.

CASE STUDY 1402

Cynthia Restin, night auditor of The Times Hotel, waited to see Ana Chavarria, front office manager, after her shift was over. She related a few incidents to Ana that occurred during her evening shift. She said she received a call from a guest in room 470 who said he had received a threatening call from someone at 1:45 A.M. Cynthia discussed the incident with the guest and said she would alert the security guard on duty. At 2:05 A.M., Cynthia called the guest to see if he was OK. He thanked her for her concern and said he was ready to retire for the evening.

At 2:35 A.M., a guest in 521 called Cynthia at the front desk reporting a loud noise coming from the room located below him. Cynthia alerted the security guard on duty and asked him to go to room 421 to investigate the situation. The security guard found

CASE STUDY 1402 (*CONTINUED*)

the door ajar and the room vacant. There was no sign of violence, and the guest's belongings were removed; everything looked like a normal self-checkout.

At 3:29 A.M., Cynthia noticed a green sports car circling the portico of the hotel. The driver stopped the car once and drove off after 15 seconds. Cynthia again alerted the security guard on duty. Ana asked Cynthia to stay a few more minutes and prepare a report of the three incidents for the file. She said she would be talking with Ed Silver, The Times Hotel's director of security, later, and she wanted to discuss the events with him. These incidents seem to have been increasing over the past several weeks, and Ana feels there could be some problem.

The discussion with Ed Silver was brief. He said he feels these incidents are no cause for alarm but that a training program for front desk personnel on safety and security procedures should be initiated. Ana indicated that similar situations have occurred in other hotels where she worked and were the beginning of larger problems for them. Ana said she wanted the local police department involved and agreed that a training program on safety and security procedures is critical.

What do you think of Ana's suggestion of involving the police? What major topics would you include in a training program on safety and security procedures for front office personnel?

CASE STUDY 1403

The director of security, Ed Silver, has requested a discussion of contactless locks for guest rooms as an agenda item for the next supervisors' meeting. Recently he attended a hotel exhibitor show that displayed several "really cool" options where guests could check in on their cell phones and didn't have to stop at the front desk. He said this would assist communication between housekeeping and security if a breach in security arises. Ed is really fired up and

wants to get a committee together to find out what this system costs and how soon The Times Hotel can get it installed!

Ana Chavarria, front office manager, has recently accepted you and two of your classmates as semester interns and wants you to research contactless locks. Develop an outline of product description, possible vendors, and the cost ranges.

Notes

1. Rolfe Winkler, September 25, 2009. Avoiding And Surviving Hotel Terrorism, http://www.reuters.com/article/idUSTRE58O1ZT20090925.
2. Patrick M. Murphy, "How Marriott Employs CPTED in Its Properties' Total Security Package," *Hotel Security Report* 19, no. 2 (Port Washington, NY: Rusting Publications, January 2001): 1–2.
3. Timothy N. Troy, "Keys to Security," *Hotel & Motel Management* 209, no. 20 (November 21, 1994): 17.
4. Mahmood Khan, Michael Olsen, and Turgut Var, *VNR's Encyclopedia of Hospitality and Tourism* (New York: Van Nostrand Reinhold, 1993), 585.

5. Mary Gostelow, "Security Challenge: In Today's Reality, Do Hotels Need to Take a Stronger Stand?" *Hotels*, October, 10, 2003, http://www.hotelsmag.com/archives/2003/10/gu-security-marriott-security-sheraton.asp.

6. Toni Giovanetti, "Looking at the Law," *Hotel Business* 3, no. 23 (December 7–20, 1994): 1.

7. *Campbell v. Womack*, 35 So. 2d 96 La. App. (1977), quoted in Khan, Olsen, and Var, 586.

8. "Securing Guest Safety," *Lodging Hospitality* 42, no. 1 (January 1986): 66.

9. Richard B. Cooper, "Secure Facilities Depend on Functional Design," *Hotel & Motel Management* 210, no. 9 (May 22, 1995): 23. Copyright *Hotels* magazine, a division of Reed USA.

10. Yvette Felix, "Historic Westin St. Francis Installs SAFLOK MT™ Locks" March 30, 2009, http://www.saflok.com/saflok/news/pr/historic_westin_stfrancis.aspx.

11. Bruce Adams, "A Few Hotels Are Reaping Benefits from Smartcards," *Hotel & Motel Management* 215, no. 12 (July 3, 2000): 62.

12. Access Control & Security Systems, 2008. "Kaba Key Contactless Electronic Lock," July 30, 2008, http://securitysolutions.com/new_security_products/Kaba-Contactless-Electronic-Lock/.

13. Yvette Felix, "SAFLOK™ Unveils Integration with OpenWays SAFLOK™ Introduces New Remote Access Technology at IH/M&RS 2009" November 9, 2009, http://www.hotel online.com/News/PR2009_4th/Nov09_SaflokOpenWays.html.

14. Terence Ronson, "Biometrics Lend a Hand to Hotel Security," February 2002, www.hotel-online.com/News/PR2002_1st/Feb02_HotelBiometrics.html.

15. James T. Davidson, "Are You Ready for an Emergency?" *Hotels* 28, no. 10 (October 1994): 20. Copyright *Hotels* magazine, a division of Reed USA.

16. Michael Meyer, "Girding for Disaster," *Lodging Hospitality* 50, no. 7 (July 1994): 42.

17. Stefani C. O'Connor, "Embassy Suites Hotel in Dallas Exhibits Exemplary Crisis Management Skills," *Hotel Business*, August 16, 2000, www.hotelbusiness.com.

18. Mahmood Khan, Michael Olsen, and Turgut Var, VNR's Encyclopedia of Hospitality and Tourism, 585.

Key Words

biometrics	hard-key system
communications hierarchy	litigious society
contactless locks	room key control system
crisis management	safety committee
electronic key system	security escort service
radio frequency identification (RFID)	smart card
foot patrol	visual alarm systems

CHAPTER 15

Executive Housekeeping

OPENING DILEMMA

The general manager of the hotel has requested that you come to his office to talk over last week's lack of efficiency in your housekeeping department. Your housekeepers have not met their quota of cleaning 18 rooms per day; they cleaned only 15.5 rooms per day. How are you going to respond?

CHAPTER FOCUS POINTS

- Importance of the housekeeping department
- Overview of a housekeeping department
- Relationship of an executive housekeeper to the general manager
- Managing a housekeeping department
- Role of chief engineer in a lodging property
- Managing maintenance interdepartmental communications
- Energy management
- The greening of the lodging Industry

Importance of the Housekeeping Department

Guests return to a hotel, in part, because of its cleanliness—not the initial advertising efforts of the hotel marketing department to attract guests with price, product, and service features. This basic operating concept therefore requires special consideration of how the housekeeping and maintenance departments fit into the marketing effort. The focus of this chapter is the executive housekeeper's management of the people, processes, communications, and interactions that affect guests' stay. These operational procedures have an enormous impact on the financial position of the hotel. Guests who have a negative first experience—a messy lobby, a dismal-looking bathroom, or worn bedding—will not be impressed; the possibility of a return visit is slight. Also, negative word-of-mouth advertising will become another problem to manage.

Additionally, this chapter addresses the well-organized, mutually dependent operational aspects of the housekeeping department and the maintenance department, the role of the chief engineer, communications between maintenance and housekeeping, energy management, and the greening in the lodging industry.

The following passage from an article in *Hotel Management* reflects on the importance of the housekeeping staff in providing an excellent visit for a guest.

The impact of the housekeeping function on the success of a hotel's operations cannot be underestimated. Although the staff providing this service do not necessarily interact directly with the public, the quality of their work is critical in shaping guests' memories of their stay. "Housekeeping is an important part of the guest experience," says Werner Knechtli, general manager at the Radisson SAS Hotel in Berlin. "Other things such as security are important, but what guests really want is to feel at home, to feel comfortable." Also, as guests become more selective about their accommodation, getting the basics of cleanliness, efficiency and friendly service right becomes more of a challenge. "Guests' expectations are higher now, particularly in terms of deadlines," observes Knechtli. "They want their rooms to be ready by the time they come back from breakfast." Despite the evolution of benchmark standards across the industry, the housekeeping function must be closely managed and constantly reviewed and improved.[1]

Barbara Worcester also writes about the importance of housekeeping to the guest:

Sheets, blankets, pillows, towels and shower curtains aren't just soft goods . . . If sheets are soiled, blankets are rough and scratchy, pillows thin and nonsupportive and shower curtains are moldy and stained, the entire image of the hotel is tarnished, and the guest most likely will not return.[2]

All of this focus on how the housekeeping department can ensure a return visit will also encourage a profitable financial bottom line for the hotel. Now let's review the organization of the housekeeping department.

Overview of a Housekeeping Department

The housekeeping department is usually organized with an executive housekeeper as its leader. This person's job, even in select-service properties, is usually rather standard. In full-service hotels, an assistant executive housekeeper with floor supervisors manages the duties of the room attendants (housekeepers or housemen). Also, in select-service as well as full-service hotels, additional housekeepers are assigned to clean and maintain public areas. The responsibility for operating the in-house laundry also falls to the housekeeping department. The staffing of this housekeeping subdepartment includes a supervisor, shift

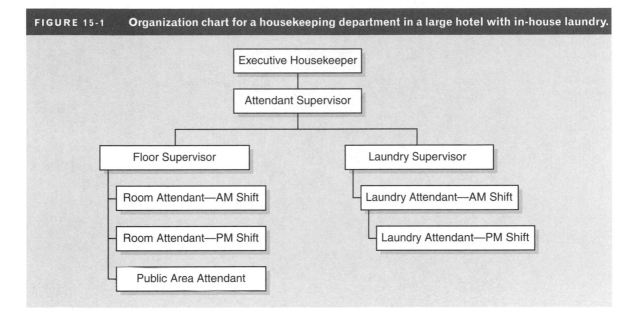

FIGURE 15-1   Organization chart for a housekeeping department in a large hotel with in-house laundry.

supervisors, and attendants. Figure 15-1 is an organization chart of a housekeeping department for a large hotel, while Figure 15-2 is one for a select-service property. Both properties operate an on-site laundry facility.

Shifts vary from hotel to hotel because of guest checkout times. Some executive housekeepers schedule a few room attendants from 7 A.M. to 3 P.M. and stagger the starting time of other room attendants depending on the size or nature of the group in the hotel. Laundry attendants may start earlier in the day, depending on whether there are banquet and restaurant linens that must be laundered or laundry held from a previous day.

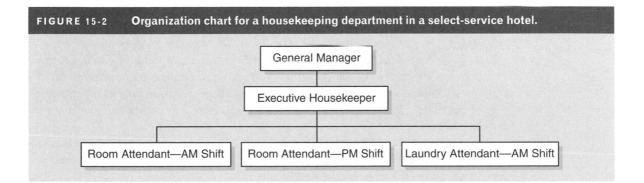

FIGURE 15-2   Organization chart for a housekeeping department in a select-service hotel.

FIGURE 15-3

Housekeeping staff provide essential components in guest service.

Relationship of the Executive Housekeeper to the General Manager

The executive housekeeper facilitates the work of the general manager by coordinating operational efforts that affect the customer satisfaction level—which, in turn, has an enormous impact on the financial position of the hotel. For example, when a group of businesspeople that represents $100,000 in gross sales to the hotel is pleased because the executive housekeeper's staff was able to provide quick turnaround service on room entry the day they arrived, keep the hallways free of room service trays, respond rapidly to requests for extra towels and toiletries, and maintain exceptionally clean bathrooms, then the executive housekeeper's staff can appreciate how important their role is in producing a profit for the hotel.

Throughout this text, the job analysis is used to trace the administrative and supervisory tasks of a member of the management team. The following job analysis portrays a typical day in the life of an executive housekeeper.

6:30 A.M.	Greets laundry staff; reviews banquet laundry; checks voice mail for call-offs
	Checks for room status to clean; assigns rooms to attendants
	Calls extra people if needed
6:50	Checks with front office for updated room status report; assigns rooms to attendants
	Conducts meeting with room attendants for announcements and five-minute stretching/exercising routines
	Lays out master keys by section and assignment sheets
7:00	Fills guest requests—toothbrushes, hairdryers, towels, cots
	Checks email
	Checks deliveries of guest soap, toilet paper, chemicals, coffee, paper, linen, etc.
	Visits with room attendants at workstations
7:45	Works on projects such as employee schedules and employee insurance
9:00	Meets with laundry supervisor to discuss purchase of new dryer
9:30	Attends staff meeting—discusses upcoming events, occupancy, successes, etc.
9:35	Attends meeting with general manager to discuss new advertising program and how housekeeping department will be involved
11:15	Meets with assistant executive housekeeper on employee motivation program
12:00 P.M.	Lunches with front office manager
12:45	Visits with room attendants to discuss condition of bedding
1:15	Meets with director of security to update a fire safety training session
2:30	Meets with front office manager to discuss recent comments on guest checkout
2:45	Prepares a to-do list for next day
3:00	Checks with front office manager on potential house count for tomorrow and next few days
3:15	Revises room attendant schedule for next day
4:00	Departs for the day

This job analysis indicates the executive housekeeper is focused on the small details of running a department yet at the same time is concerned with the department's interaction with others, such as the front office and security. The executive housekeeper realizes his or her department provides a service to the guest, and this service relies on good communication efforts with staff and departmental managers.

Marti Cannon, former executive housekeeper at the Reading Sheraton Hotel in Reading, Pennsylvania (now the Crowne Plaza Reading), graduated from the University of Nevada at Las Vegas in hotel administration; some of her favorite courses were in foods, gaming, and hotel entertainment. Some of the part-time jobs she held in college included front desk at the former Sands Hotel, inventory control, mystery shopper, and catering attendant in various Las Vegas hotels.

Her lodging career began with Marriott as the front desk manager at the 1000-room Los Angeles Marriott. She then traveled to New York and was promoted to the front office manager position at the 1800 room-Marriott Marquis. She traveled back to the West Coast and went to work for the San Antonio Marriott as the front office manager. As Marriott began to expand their brand, Ms. Cannon expanded her career and used her background to become the training manager for Courtyard by Marriott in Dallas, Texas. Not wanting to reject a challenge, she went into another segment of the hospitality business and operated her own private business for ten years—Cannon's Pub, an Irish pub in New York City. Her next move was back to the hotel business, but this time into the job of executive housekeeper at the 250-room Hotel Hershey in Hershey, Pennsylvania. She continued building her career as executive housekeeper at the 750-room Hyatt Regency in San Francisco and the 250-room Inn At Reading, located in Reading, Pennsylvania.

Ms. Cannon described her role as executive housekeeper in relation to the general manager as one that allows him to concentrate on issues of operating the hotel. The GM knows rooms will be clean and guests will be satisfied with them. If the housekeeping department were not run efficiently, then it would take away time the general manager needs for other projects, such as marketing the hotel.

While executive housekeeper, Ms. Cannon belonged to the International Executive Housekeepers Association (IEHA) and considered this organization a useful information source, particularly through its monthly trade journal, *Executive Housekeeping Today*. She also remained current by reading *Hotel & Motel Management* and *Laundry Today* and by logging on to the website www.hotel-online.com each day.

Some of the big issues she would like to emphasize to students who are considering executive housekeeping on their way to becoming general manager include knowing how to prepare budgets, costing payroll, and managing employees by motivating them, occasionally working with them on the job, and developing loyalty with them on a one-to-one basis.

Management of a Housekeeping Department

The executive housekeeper is a first and foremost a manager. This department, like any other in the hotel, requires the ability to plan, organize, control, direct, and communicate. There are many systems to develop, details to oversee, and people to supervise to ensure a well-run department. The job analysis shows a diverse array of staff members, department heads, and hotel procedures in the typical day of an executive housekeeper. In this section, we review topics that support management practices for executive housekeeping, including:

- Room assignment/workload
- Training
- Room inspection
- Outsourcing housekeeping activities
- Housekeepers report
- Communication—English as a second language
- Inventory control—linens, guest supplies, cleaning supplies, furniture
- Cleaning control
- In-house laundry versus outsourced laundry
- Occupational Safety and Health Administration
- Material Safety Data Sheets
- Going green
- Professional associations

Room Assignment/Workload

The number of rooms assigned to a *room attendant* has particular significance to the hotelier and general manager, the executive housekeeper, and the room attendant. The hotelier and general manager look at this number as a measure of effective use of human resources, daily income, and guest hospitality. The executive housekeeper views the number as an indicator of how efficient his or her staff is in meeting daily goals and providing guest hospitality. The room attendant views the number of rooms assigned to him or her as "the work of the day"—something that provides an opportunity to fulfill his or her biological, safety, and social needs as well as an expression of hospitality to the guest.

Determining the number of rooms a room attendant can clean during a day takes into consideration the design of the room, room furnishings, fabrics, number of people occupying the room, nature of the guests in the room, training provided for employees, and incentives. The usual number is between 15 and 20, depending on the hotel and its policies.

The method of assigning room attendants starts with the executive housekeeper or the assistant to the executive housekeeper retrieving the number of rooms occupied the previous night (let's say 180 rooms) from the PMS housekeeping module. This number is divided by the number of rooms assigned to each room attendant (let's say 18). This quotient equals 10; therefore, the schedule for the day is adjusted to reflect the need for 10 room attendants. An executive housekeeper could prepare a chart like that shown in Figure 15-4 to assist in this daily room assignment. However, room characteristics like those previously mentioned usually detract from the chart's usefulness.

FIGURE 15-4	Room attendant staffing requirement chart.	
No. Rooms in Hotel	Occupancy Percentage	No. Room Attendants Required
180	100	10.00
180	99	9.90
180	98	9.80
180	97	9.70
180	96	9.60
180	95	9.50
180	94	9.40
180	93	9.30
180	92	9.20
180	91	9.10
180	90	9.00
180	89	8.90
180	88	8.80
180	87	8.70
180	86	8.60
180	85	8.50
180	84	8.40
180	83	8.30
180	82	8.20
180	81	8.10
180	80	8.00

Note: Each room attendant is required to clean 18 rooms per day.

Technology is also used to assign room attendants with MTech's REX software.

REX [Room Expeditor] is a SaaS [Software as a Service]-based housekeeping application. Implementation of the software begins with a feed from the property-management system of rooms and reservation data, which coordinators quickly assign the rooms to each room attendant or multiple room attendants MTech President Luis Segredo explains, "Once the rooms are assigned and the day starts, room attendants are no longer given a list of rooms. Instead, they are given an iPod Touch," "After the attendant is logged in REX…REX analyzes a collection of variables about the rooms assigned to the room attendant." These variable include current PMS occupancy, VIP level of the guest, stay-over/checkout, estimated arrival time, room rush, room type, even physical occupancy."

From this information, REX ascertains the next most important room to clean, and it presents it to the room attendant. The room attendant has the option to start cleaning the room or declining for one of the following reasons: Service Refused, [Do Not Disturb] DND on the door, or guest asked to come back later.

"When the room attendant finishes cleaning the room, the housekeeping status is updated in the PMS. If the previous guest has left with his bags, REX will send a message to the front desk. It is that simple."[3]

Training

Training is an essential supervisory practice of the executive housekeeper. Each moment and movement of the staff is under the watchful eye of the guest, who wants hospitality, and the hotel owner, who seeks efficiency and safety. Robert J. Martin, in his text *Professional Management of Housekeeping Operations*, lists the following areas for skill training: bed making, vacuuming, dusting, window and mirror cleaning, setup awareness of the room, bathroom cleaning, daily routine of the worker, caring for and using equipment, and industrial safety.[4] These major areas provide focus points where time, labor, safety, and cost savings can be evaluated. Training should be viewed as an objective of a goal for delivering hospitality; a plan must be developed to carry out that objective. How can the executive housekeeper most effectively train his or her staff? The answer reflects such factors as time available, skilled people in the department to do the training, resources for purchasing DVD equipment and materials, room available in which to hold training sessions, etc. However, the underlying question is whether or not the hotel owner or general manager believes training will improve hospitality. If so, then the small financial investment in training will pay large rewards. Harry Nobles offers the following thought for executive housekeepers and their staff.

> Sir Winston Churchill is credited with saying "Truth is the first casualty of war." An applicable paraphrase for our industry might be "Training is the first casualty of bad economic times." Since less effective training often leads directly to a lower quality of guest service delivery, is this a loss you can afford?[5]

It is important to train both new and experienced employees. Training gives new employees the opportunity to strengthen skills brought with them, and it helps them adapt to their new environment. Training helps employees of all levels of experience take on new responsibilities with confidence, helping them to be more productive.[6]

Room Inspection

If training is properly managed in the housekeeping department, then the task of room inspection, a final review of the room to ascertain that all housekeeping tasks are completed and room furnishings are in order, can be approached with a positive management strategy. In some hotels, one person is appointed to inspect rooms in each area prior to releasing them to the front desk for occupancy. This person, usually a supervisor, goes to each room and inspects it for cleanliness, orderliness, and operational details. Although this system may work well in some hotels, executive housekeepers should consider having room attendants inspect their own work. This saves time and builds employee confidence. If a motivational system is built into this option, then it will probably work. All good plans incorporate an evaluation mechanism; examples include guest comment cards and front desk staff members who ask random guests at checkout for feedback on cleanliness of bathroom, bedding, proper working order of electronics, and so on.

Another department that works closely with housekeeping in producing hospitality is maintenance. The following article describes how one hotel chain combines the talents of the employees of both these departments to self-inspect guest rooms. An incentive program is built in.

At PMHS hotels, managers empower their housekeepers. In addition to cleaning supplies and fresh linen, housekeepers also carry a small yellow "Zero Defects" kit containing fresh light bulbs and batteries for remote controls, and a small screwdriver to fix a loose toilet seat. Although housekeepers never do major repair work, all are equipped with the necessary training that allows them to discern what repairs they are able to do, and what repairs need a work order.

Jim Lowe, Director of Facilities for PMHS, explains the logic behind Zero Defects. "During the half-hour that a housekeeper spends cleaning a room, he or she uses all of the appliances, remote control, air conditioner or heater, and the faucet."

To reward their housekeepers for taking a proactive stance, PMHS offers a bonus for every room that is inspected and found to have zero defects. The housekeeping department also receives a team bonus for every problem-free room. For every work order completed in a timely manner, maintenance technicians receive the same bonus.

One result of the Zero Defects program has been greater unity between the housekeeping and maintenance departments. "Instead of only communicating with each other by paperwork, our employees are free to consult one another and work together to make their jobs easier," explains Miller. "These departments are indeed the 'Heart of the House,' and the Zero Defects program really makes that clear."[7]

Outsourcing Housekeeping Activities

An option for executive housekeepers and general managers to consider is outsourcing housekeeping operations. This can involve guest rooms and/or public areas. Carol Kendrick offers the following concepts to consider.

Certain hotel functions are becoming more and more popular because of the cost-cutting aim of hotels. One function which could be considered as commonly outsourced would be housekeeping. How does outsourcing helps? Here are some of the advantages mentioned when outsourcing:

- Allows housekeepers to concentrate on the core competencies of their job, like delivering a well-kept house and keeping the areas maintained
- Allows flexibility of operations in terms of utilizing and rotating the manpower
- Offers specialized and expert guidance for the maintenance of different areas.
- Reduces staff problems in recruitment, training, allocation, appraisals, increments, and dismissals

These advantages would only work if hotels have proof that outsourcing would work for them and if they are also able to draw an outsourcing contract which they approve of.[8]

Werner Knechtli, general manager at the Radisson SAS Hotel in Berlin, a property with 115,000 room-nights per year, based on about 75 percent occupancy, offers the following insights of his experience with outsourcing the housekeeping function in a hotel.

"We employ one executive housekeeper, one assistant, seven supervisors and eight room attendants, but most of the room attendants are outsourced. Of course they are trained to our can-do attitude, our standards and our service philosophy."

The main advantage of this arrangement is the reduction of staffing costs. It allows hotels to pay room attendants on the basis of the work they do, which will change in response to occupancy rates.

It also guarantees that the job will be done, even if an individual worker is off sick. The task of supplying enough staff to cover the work becomes the responsibility of the service provider, not the hotel. It also eliminates the need to directly recruit employees for a function with a high staff turnover.

However, using outsourced staff also brings with it certain responsibilities. Knechtli acknowledges that constant monitoring is essential, though the benefits still outweigh the costs: "We check every room, and it must comply with our policy.

We also minimize the fluctuation in employees performing housekeeping duties, and we pay only for the number of rooms that are cleaned."[9]

Housekeeper's Report

The housekeeper's report was introduced in chapter 10. This report verifies the number of rooms sold on a particular night as well as rooms vacant and rooms out of order. This is an essential communication tool for the night auditor as he or she compiles the financial data for the current day's activities.

This report is compiled from the housekeeping status transmissions that are relayed to the front office throughout the day via the PMS or telephone calls, voice messages, text messaging, emails, electronic data submission, or, in some hotels, visits to the front desk to transfer the current housekeeping status. The executive housekeeper or his or her representative assembles data like that displayed in Figure 10-6. This function, provided by the executive housekeeper, is a safeguard in the accounting process.

Communication

English as a Second Language (ESL)

The hospitality industry has always provided individuals with an initial access to their careers. Working as a bellperson, front desk clerk, receptionist, or in the food service areas of the hospitality industry allows people to earn funds for furthering their academic career or supporting a growing family. The hospitality industry also attracts many people for whom English is a second language. Executive housekeepers are challenged to manage employees with limited English communication skills in areas such as issuing daily duties, training, and communication. How can these communication bridges be crossed with ease?

FIGURE 15-5	Spanish numerals—English phonetics pronunciation.
Spanish	**English**
Uno	Oo no
Dos	Dose
Tres	Trese
Cuatro	Quatro
Cinco	Sin co
Seis	Sais
Siete	See eight a
Ocho	Och oo
Nueve	New vea
Diez	De es

To begin with, the executive housekeeper may identify an English-speaking group leader with whom the minority feels comfortable and communicate with that person to develop a strategy with others in the group. The goals are to develop rapport and trust and to convey the importance of communication to the delivery of hospitality to the guest, job performance, and worker safety. The executive housekeeper also may acquire one of the English as a Second Language (ESL) resources on the market as a reference for the minority-speaking employees. Alternatively, or in addition, the executive housekeeper can develop training aids for phonetic pronunciation, such as that in Figure 15-5, using foreign language resources on the market.

Communication between Departments

Communication between the front office and the housekeeping department is vital to the delivery of hospitality to the guest. When room attendants complete their tasks, they must relay this information to the PMS. If their work is delayed—and, hence, the transfer of the information—then so is the delivery of hospitality. Review the following scenario to see how a small gesture made to fulfill a need for a group of guests caused great turmoil.

INTERNATIONAL HIGHLIGHTS

A regional conference of meeting planners whose clientele is international is scheduled to take place in your city. The general manager of your hotel, a member of the local visitor's bureau, agrees to host the event and requests her team to develop ways to show their welcome of international guests into the hotel. Some of the ways the executive housekeeper cites in his presentation are (1) making room attendants aware of international guests upon check-in, (2) assuring room attendants can speak at least two languages, and (3) asking room attendants to inquire if international guests need additional travel accessories to make their visit easier.

FIGURE 15-6

It's important for the executive housekeeper to have good communications with the front office manager and the general manager. Photo courtesy of the author.

Situation 1: Why Can't Room Attendants Get Those Rooms Cleaned More Quickly, or, If That Guest Asks One More Time...

It is a busy Tuesday morning at the front desk. The Rosebud Flower Association (350 guests) is checking out of the hotel. The Franklin Actuary Society (250 guests) is beginning to arrive for registration. Yesterday, the president of Rosebud, Jose Rodriguez, requested a late checkout for all his members because they had to vote on an important legislative issue. The president asked a desk clerk, Samantha (a new member of the front office staff), to approve the late checkout. Samantha, unaware of any reason not to grant this request, OK'd a 2:30 P.M. checkout time.

It is 11:15 A.M., and the front office manager is on the phone with the housekeeper asking why some of the rooms have not been released. The housekeeper assures the front office manager he will investigate the situation immediately and goes to the first, second, and third floors of the hotel to speak with the floor supervisors. They tell him there are DO NOT DISTURB signs on the doors of the majority of the rooms. One of the guests told the supervisor on the second floor he had permission to stay in his room until 2:30 P.M. When the housekeeper relays this information to the front office manager, a nasty exchange takes place concerning the delivery of professional hospitality.

It is now 3:15 P.M., and the hotel lobby is jammed with people checking out and checking in. Only about 20 percent of the rooms needed have been released by housekeeping. The food and beverage manager arrives and suggests to the front office manager that he announce the availability of the hotel coffee shop and lounge to the waiting guests. The front office manager feels this is a good idea but fears that, with such chaos, no one would hear the announcement. Therefore, he does not make the announcement.

At 7:20 P.M., the last guest is checked in. The front office manager breathes a sigh of relief and happens to notice a gift box addressed to Samantha, who opens it and reads the card out loud: "Extra thanks to you for your kind consideration." The front office manager reminds Samantha that gifts from registered guests are not encouraged. Samantha replies that this is from a former guest—"You know, that nice Mr. Rodriguez from the flower association. All he asked for was a late checkout time for his group."

Analysis

The miscommunication in this case was the fault of the front office manager. At some time during the orientation and training of new employees, the front office manager must communicate the policies, procedures, and limits of authority. Well-developed operational policies and procedures and documented training enable communications to flourish. For example, new employee orientation should include a discussion on the policy for communicating requests for late checkout to the supervisor on duty. An in-depth review of the clearance procedure the supervisor on duty must follow would further help the new employee understand the front office does not act alone. A decision made by one employee affects the work of many people. A typical review of procedures could include the following:

1. Consult with the reservations manager to determine the expected time of departure for the guests or groups of guests currently in the hotel and expected times of arrival of those who will be registering the next day.

2. Consult with the director of marketing and sales to determine if any special group requests concerning checkout times have been granted.

3. Consult with the housekeeper to determine the effect of a delayed checkout time on daily operations of the housekeeping department.

4. If the request for a delayed checkout time will conflict with another group's check-in time but the situation warrants approval of the request, ask the food and beverage manager to set up a special snack table in the lobby for guests unable to check into their rooms.

When the front office manager takes the time to explain the policies and procedures of the department, the new employee can think through situations rather than responding with a knee-jerk reaction. The delivery of service in a hotel requires the employee to meet the needs of the guests by exercising his or her authority and taking responsibility for conveying an atmosphere of hospitality.

Inventory Control

Inventory control is a major responsibility of the executive housekeeper. Linens, guest supplies, cleaning supplies, fixtures, and furniture all require attentive review for timely replenishment and replacement.

Linen Control

Linen control is based on a *par system*—an established level of inventory that provides adequately for service. The par system is established by the hotel general manager because linens are a major expense. For example, if the hotel decided to have a par of four (one set of sheets in the wash, one set of sheets on the bed, and two sets of sheets on the shelf ready for use) rather than a par of three (one set of sheets in the wash, one set of sheets on the bed, and one set of sheet on the shelf ready for use), the additional set of sheets could tie up several thousands of dollars each year in inventory. The same reasoning is applied to bath towels, bath mats, hand towels, face cloths, pillowcases, blankets, bedspreads, and so on.

Guest Supplies

Guest supplies, more commonly referred to as guest *amenities*—personal toiletries or care items—are another cost to the hotel that requires close attention because they support guest hospitality but are open to theft. Guests enjoy and appreciate the small bottles of shampoo, hair conditioner, lotion, soap, mouthwash, shoeshine cloth, mending kit, and other amenities. However, supplying these goods at a cost to the hotel of at least $1.50 per guest room per room-night and extending the math to a hotel with 250 rooms and an annual 65 percent occupancy, the expense rises to $88,968.75.

$$250 \times 0.65 \times 365 = 59,312 \text{ rooms} \times \$1.50 = \$88,968.75$$

Keep in mind that this is a *minimum*, and some hotels spend more. Not only is the hotel spending that amount of money on a guest service, but these types of products are easily removed from the premises by guests and employees from storage rooms and

FIGURE 15-7   Inventory requisition for amenities.

The Times Hotel Housekeeping Department Requisition

Attendant Name __I. Maid__   Floor # __2__   Cart # __4__

Amount	ITEM #	ITEM	SIZE
24	4530	Deod. Soap	1.5 oz
24	6309	Shampoo	2 oz
12	6555	Cond.	2 oz
6	9845	Sewing Kit	Small

Issued by __John Housekeeper__   Received by __I. Maid__

Today's Date __May 1__

FIGURE 15-8   Weekly inventory—guest supplies.

The Times Hotel Housekeeping Department
Inventory Sheet

Category: _____

ITEM #	SIZE	Beg. Inv.	+ Purch.	− End Inv.	Amt. Used	Price/Unit	Extension
4530	1.5 oz	3 cs	13	15	3	$40.00	$120.00
4535	1.5 oz	3 cs	7	6	4	$30.00	$120.00
4540	1.5 oz	2 cs	5	5	2	$45.00	$90.00

Counted by: L. Smith   Recorded by: D. Manager

Today's Date ___May 8___

housekeeper's carts parked in hallways during cleaning time. For these reasons, a workable inventory system must be initiated that ensures ease of use accountability. Figure 15-7 displays a simple inventory request, while Figure 15-8 displays a weekly inventory sheet.

Author's note: The definition of *amenities* has recently begun to include other guest room equipment such as the items cited in the title of this article dated February 15, 2005: "Hilton Garden Inn® Evolving with New Guest Room Amenities: 26" Flat Panel High-Def TVs, Ergonomic Desk Chair and New Technology Air Cell Mattresses."[10] The definition continues to expand as highlighted in this August 3, 2009, excerpt describing the amenities found in the opening of the Courtyard by Marriott in Buford, Georgia.

Guests have the following food and beverage options: the Courtyard Café, a breakfast restaurant; The Market, a 24-hour self-serve pantry; and the Center Court Lounge and Bar. The hotel features a lobby-level business library with individual workstations, ergonomic chairs, personal computers, complimentary high-speed Internet access, a printer, a copier and telephones. Other amenities include an indoor heated pool and whirlpool spa, a fitness center and an elegant fire pit in the outdoor area just off the lobby.[11]

FRONT-LINE REALITIES

One of the housekeepers asks you where she can obtain more information on a certain chemical included in a cleaning solution she uses for the bathroom tubs. Lately she has a rash on her forearm, and she thinks this cleaner is causing the rash. How would you assist the housekeeper in locating the information?

FIGURE 15-9   Requisition sheet—cleaning supplies.

The Times Hotel Housekeeping Department Requisition

Attendant Name ___I. Maid___   Floor # __2__   Cart # __4__

Amount	ITEM #	ITEM	SIZE
1	290	Window Cleaner Spray	12 oz
2	387	Tile Cleaner Spray Can	12 oz
1	6555	Spray Bottle 20 oz	24 o

Issued by ___J. Housekeeper___   Received by ___I. Maid___

Today's Date ___May 1___

Cleaning Supplies   Cleaning supplies for guest rooms include cleaners, disinfectants, and polishers for windows, tile, bathroom fixtures, office furniture, kitchen equipment, living room furniture, and so on. These may be purchased in 1-gallon to 5-gallon or larger containers for economy or in aerosol cans. The larger containers of the product are stored in the housekeeping department area, while the usable sizes for guest room cleaning are stored on the room attendant's cart. The product is dispensed into these smaller, more usable containers for the room attendants. Dispensing must be controlled by the executive housekeeper with a requisition and inventory sheet, as shown in Figures 15-9 and 15-10.

FIGURE 15-10   Weekly inventory—cleaning supplies.

The Times Hotel Housekeeping Department

Inventory Sheet

Category: _____

ITEM #	SIZE	Beg. Inv.	+ Purch.	− End Inv.	Amt. Used	Price/Unit	Extension
387	12 oz	5	13	15	3	$2.10	$6.10

Counted by: L. Smith   Recorded by: D. Manager

Today's Date ___May 8___

Fixtures

Fixtures of all types, makes, and sizes make the guest rooms, lobby, and public spaces the bright and inviting places that please the guest. However, all fixtures must be maintained in bright appearance and proper working condition. In some hotels, this is the responsibility of the housekeeping department. The light bulbs that go in the many lamps and chandeliers located throughout the hotel as well as the batteries that operate hand-held devices and smoke alarms (if the property is not electrically wired for such purposes) must be checked periodically to determine if they must be replaced.

With respect to light bulbs and batteries, a preventive maintenance program must be initiated to ensure guests' safety is at the forefront. For example, a room attendant may be assigned to go around regularly and check the level of energy in batteries in TV remote controls instead of waiting for a guest to call the front desk and ask for a replacement. These activities can be controlled through a computerized spreadsheet program that tracks the replacement trail of light bulbs and batteries for a particular unit. The dispensing of light bulbs and batteries requires control (requisition sheets and inventory sheets) similar to those used for dispensing guest room and other cleaning supplies.

Hotel basements are filled with used and worn-out furniture. These retired pieces represent the many inventory dollars that were spent furnishing a guest room. Each item in a room—pictures, beds, mattresses, headboards, desk chairs, tables, armchairs, desks, portable closets, televisions, computers, armoires—represents an investment by the hotel in a business venture. This pursuit requires control in maintaining them in like-new condition. Each piece of furniture should be cared for according to manufacturer's recommendation. This may be as simple as "Use a clean, damp cloth" or "Polish wooden surface with lemon oil polish as needed." A system should be developed that identifies each piece of equipment with its date of purchase, cost, location/relocation, refurbishing, and any other data the hotel wants to track. For example, if a hotel has a consistent group of business travelers, it may consider relocating the pictures on the wall periodically. Also, television sets have a certain life span; this should be tracked and the data used for developing budgets. Hotels should consider donations of used furniture to charitable organizations to assist in maintaining an organized, well-appointed inventory of furniture.

Theft Control of Inventory

Unfortunately, theft by guests and employees in the housekeeping department is commonplace. "The American Hotel & Lodging Association estimates that theft in hotel rooms—from towels to televisions—costs the lodging industry $100 million annually." Mark Snyder, senior vice president of brand management for Holiday Inn, says informal research estimates 560,000 towels are stolen per year.[12] This should not be accepted; rather, aggressive campaigns against theft should be developed. Small items from attendants' carts are an easy target for removal by guests passing in the hallway. Usually these carts are overloaded with items exposed for viewing. Perhaps placing tempting items in plastic see-through boxes would inhibit a passerby from picking them up.

More important than developing ways to control theft is for the executive house-keeper to calculate how much theft costs the hotel and then turn over the challenge to the employees. For example, if a particular hotel is experiencing a theft of $45,000 per year from towels, linens, toiletries, remote controls, toilet paper, tissue paper, light bulbs, batteries, televisions, and so on, the executive housekeeper could develop a committee to address this challenge. The plan might include incentives so a percentage of savings due to theft reduction is passed along to employees.

Cleaning Control   The mark of the housekeeping department is cleaning. Most housekeeping departments have one standardized routine for cleaning rooms and another for *deep cleaning*—a more thorough cleaning of furniture and accessories, windows, flooring, and walls. This process encompasses the guest rooms and the public areas. It requires a plan of communication with the front office manager to determine when occupancy will be low; with the maintenance engineer to identify scheduled repair dates; and with the food and beverage manager to identify down times in which empty banquet rooms can be deep cleaned. The plan is facilitated by a spreadsheet that outlines the room or area that must be deep cleaned and the specific sections of the room or area that need attention; the date is entered to maintain a continuous log of that particular deep cleaning activity. See Figure 15-11 for an example of a deep cleaning control log.

In-house Laundry versus Outsourced Laundry

Choosing how to provide clean linens, uniforms, and other fabric items for the hotel depends on several factors. According to Martin, planning an in-house laundry should include the following ten concepts: determination of needs; system definition and space allocation; equipment layouts; equipment selection, specifications, and budgets; detailed drawing and specification; equipment procurement and shipment coordination; installation scheduling and supervision; start-up, test, and demonstration; operator training; maintenance; and after-sale service.[13] These well-thought-out concepts are time-consuming but assure the executive housekeeper the in-house laundry will be operated correctly and efficiently.

FIGURE 15-11   Deep cleaning log.

The Times Hotel Deep Cleaning Log

Room	Rug Shampoo	Wall Wash	Wall Paint	Window Wash Outside	Grout	Mattress Turning Date
101	Jan. 10		Dec. 15	July 1	Dec. 1	April 5
102	Jan. 10		Dec. 15	July 1	Dec. 1	April 7
103	Jan. 13		Dec. 15	July 1	Dec. 5	April 9
104	Jan. 13		Dec. 15	July 1	Dec. 5	April 20
105	Jan. 13		Dec. 15	July 1	Dec. 7	April 23

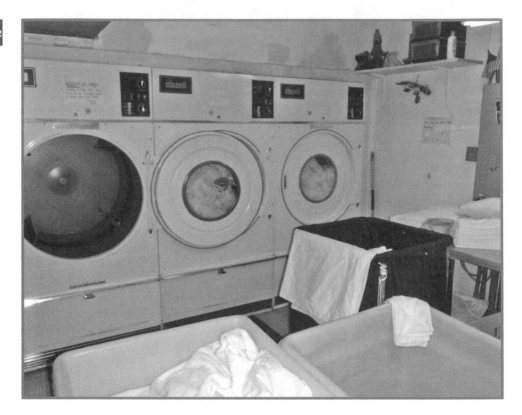

Why would a hotel consider outsourcing this function if it's going to be operated so well? Review the above list and note the required capital investment in equipment and replacement of that equipment; the cost of maintaining the equipment; the cost of personnel to operate the facility; the cost of training personnel; and the initial investment in linen and uniform inventory. On the plus side, the in-house laundry gives greater control of where and when the inventory will be laundered, stored, and ready for use.

Outsourcing laundry eliminates all the planning, with the exception of storage, for the hotel. There is no initial cash outlay for equipment and inventory, and no replacement cost either. Also, preventive and emergency maintenance of equipment is not a concern. However, some hoteliers still don't adopt the outsourcing opportunity because they feel they will lose control of their inventories through irregular pickup and deliveries and through sorting mistakes at the cleaning plant.[14]

Occupational Safety and Health Administration

The goal of the Occupational Safety and Health Administration (OSHA), in existence since 1971, is to send every worker home whole and healthy every day. OSHA carries out the following tasks, which are important in operating the housekeeping department:

- Encourages employers and employees to reduce workplace hazards and to implement new safety and health programs or improve existing programs.
- Develops mandatory job safety and health standards and enforces them through worksite inspections, by employer assistance, and, sometimes, by imposing citations or penalties or both.
- Establishes responsibilities and rights for employers and employees to achieve better safety and health conditions.
- Conducts research, either directly or through grants and contracts, to develop innovative ways of dealing with workplace hazards.
- Maintains a reporting and recordkeeping system to monitor job-related injuries and illnesses.
- Establishes training programs to increase the competence of occupational safety and health personnel.
- Develops, analyzes, evaluates, and approves state occupational safety and health programs.
- Provides technical and compliance assistance, training and education, and cooperative programs and partnerships to help employers reduce worker accidents and injuries.

If you are an *employer* covered by OSHA, you must:

- Meet your general duty responsibility to provide a workplace free from recognized hazards.
- Keep workers informed about OSHA and safety and health matters with which they are involved.
- Comply in a responsible manner with standards, rules, and regulations issued by OSHA.
- Be familiar with mandatory OSHA standards.
- Make copies of standards available to employees for review upon request.
- Evaluate workplace conditions.
- Minimize or eliminate potential hazards.
- Make sure employees have and use safe, properly maintained tools and equipment (including appropriate personal protective equipment).
- Warn employees of potential hazards.
- Establish or update operating procedures and communicate them to employees.
- Provide medical examinations when required.
- Provide training required by OSHA standards.
- Report within eight hours any accident that results in a fatality or the hospitalization of three or more employees.
- Keep OSHA-required records of work-related injuries and illnesses, unless otherwise specified.
- Post a copy of the *OSHA 200—Log and Summary of Occupational Injuries and Illnesses* for the prior year each year during the entire month of February unless otherwise specified.

- Post, at a prominent location within the workplace, the OSHA poster (OSHA 2203) informing employees of their rights and responsibilities.
- Provide employees, former employees, and their representatives access to the OSHA 200 form at a reasonable time and in a reasonable manner.
- Provide access to employee medical records and exposure records.
- Cooperate with OSHA compliance officers.
- Not discriminate against employees who properly exercise their rights under OSHA.
- Post OSHA citations and abatement verification notices at or near the worksite involved.
- Abate cited violations within the prescribed period.[15]

Material Safety Data Sheets

Material Safety Data Sheets (MSDS) —a listing of a product's chemical contents, relative hazards to users, and name and address of the producers—are a mainstay in the housekeeping departments of hotels. MSD sheets are available for employees to read in a readily available area. Each MSD sheet has specific requirements, including the following.

Each Material Safety Data Sheet shall be in English, and shall contain at least the following information:

1. The identity (product name) used on the label, and chemical and common name(s) of ingredients which have been determined to be health hazards, and which comprise 1% or greater of the composition, except carcinogens shall be listed if the concentrations are 0.1% or greater;
2. The chemical and common name(s) of all ingredients which have been determined to present a physical hazard when present in the mixture;
3. Relevant physical and chemical characteristics of the hazardous chemical (such as vapor pressure, flash point);
4. Relevant physical hazards, including the potential for fire, explosion, and reactivity;
5. Relevant health hazards, including signs and symptoms of exposure, and any medical conditions generally recognized as being aggravated by exposure to the chemical;
6. The primary route(s) of entry into the body;
7. The OSHA permissible exposure limit and ACGIH Threshold Limit Value. Additional applicable exposure limits may be listed;
8. Whether the hazardous chemical is listed in the National Toxicology Program (NTP) Annual Report on Carcinogens (latest edition) or has been found to be a potential carcinogen in the International Agency for Research on Cancer (IARC) Monographs (latest editions), or by OSHA;
9. Precautions for safe handling and use, including appropriate hygienic practices, protective measures during repair and maintenance of contaminated equipment, and procedures for clean-up of spills and leaks;

10. Appropriate control measures, such as engineering controls, work practices, or personal protective equipment;

11. Emergency and first aid procedures;

12. The date of preparation of the Material Safety Data Sheet or the last change to it; and,

13. The name, address and telephone number of the chemical manufacturer, importer, employer or other responsible party preparing or distributing the Material Safety Data Sheet, who can provide additional information on the hazardous chemical and appropriate emergency procedures, if necessary.[16]

The history of the MSDS is as follows:

On November 25, 1983, OSHA published the Hazard Communication Standard as 29 CFR Part 1910, adding §1910.1200. This initial standard applied only to Standard Industrial Classification (SIC) Codes 20 through 39. The requirement that manufacturers and distributors provide MSDSs to their customers became effective on November 25, 1985. The standard does not require a particular format for the MSDS but does specify what information must be included. Effective September 23, 1987, the requirements of the standard were extended to include ". . . all employers with employees exposed to hazardous chemicals in their workplaces."

In 1986, the U.S. Environmental Protection Agency (EPA) published the "Emergency Planning and Community Right-to-Know Act of 1986" and, in 1988, "Toxic Chemical Release Reporting: Community Right-to-Know." The use and distribution of MSDSs is an important part of these regulations. The "Toxic Chemical Release Reporting" regulation requires that MSDSs for chemicals requiring reporting by these regulations contain specific language notifying users that these chemicals are subject to these regulations. These and other EPA regulations have been promulgated under Title III C Emergency Planning and Community Right-to-Know Act of the Superfund Amendments and Reauthorization Act of 1986 (EPCRA).[17]

Americans with Disability Compliance

One part of the Americans with Disabilities Act (ADA) of 1990—adapting accommodations for people with physical challenges—should alert executive housekeepers to prepare their staff for compliance with this law and delivery of hospitality. Dr. Deborah T. Curtis has written a thoughtful article for executive housekeepers on this topic. Highlights of the article include:

The foremost rule must always be to treat every guest with respect and dignity. Speak directly to the guest, not to a companion. Just relax. People who are blind also say, "It's nice to see you."

Try hands-on training. Use a wheelchair to navigate through the hotel—or have one employee try to help guide another while one is blindfolded. If a guest has a guide dog, do not pet or play with the animal. It is performing a job and should not be distracted.

Training in the housekeeping department involves teaching housekeepers to leave guests' personal belongings precisely where they were found once the guestroom has been cleaned. The hand-held showerhead must be left hanging, furniture must not be repositioned, and hallways must be kept clear to allow movement.

If guests request a guide to get to their room, an employee should offer an arm or shoulder and provide verbal commentary while proceeding through the hotel. For example: "The elevator is 20 paces to your right. Your guest room is three doors past the elevator on the left. The key card slot is located two inches above the door handle."

Specific quantifiable directions are crucial to the visually impaired. Staff should explain where emergency exits are located relative to the guest's room and note the numbers to dial on the telephone to reach the front desk and other services. Be clear in terms of directions. Don't say "over there."[18]

Professional Associations

The American Hotel & Lodging Association's (AH&LA) Educational Institute (EI) offers a Certified Hospitality Housekeeping Executive (CHHE) program for executive housekeepers. AH&LA is headquartered in Washington, DC, for its 10,000 property members, and is prominent in supporting hoteliers with their operations, education, communications, and lobby efforts. The website for the AH&LA is www.ahla.com/index.asp, and the website for the EI is www.ei-ahla.org/.

The International Executive Housekeepers Association (IEHA), located in Westerville, Ohio, provides an opportunity for executive housekeepers to earn status in their profession as Certified Executive Housekeeper (CEH) and Registered Executive Housekeeper (REH). Its membership in 2010 was 3500 within 75 chapters internationally. The IEHA offers its membership *Executive Housekeeping Today* as their monthly trade publication and newsletter. Their website address is www.ieha.org/.

Role of Chief Engineer in a Lodging Property

The chief engineer or plant engineer, mentioned in chapter 2, is the person responsible for the operation and maintenance of the physical plant and who establishes an effective preventive maintenance program. This position encompasses some of the following duties: managing electricians, plumbers, heating, ventilating, and air-conditioning contractors, and general repair personnel; developing preventative maintenance and energy savings plans; interacting with all departments, in particular housekeeping and the front office, to maintain guest room optimal operational and access; and providing overall knowledge of building structure, equipment, and environment control.

Job Analysis

Let's review a job analysis of the chief engineer of a full-service hotel:

7:00 A.M.	Meets with the night auditor to review any equipment failures, heating/ventilation/air-conditioning problems from the previous evening.
7:30	Visits with the sales office to check on the incoming reservations for the day.
7:45	Greets the first-shift maintenance workers and discusses workload for the day. Prepares work assignments and talks about details of completing assignments.
8:15	Reviews the preventative maintenance plan and determines which goals will be accomplished today.
8:30	Meets with the executive housekeeper to identify potential problem areas of which the maintenance staff should be aware.
9:00	Returns to office to work on the planning document for a new elevator installation.
10:30	Checks with the chef to determine if a new dishwasher is working properly. Both of them schedule a time to develop a training session for food service employees to address additional questions they may have.
11:00	Stops by the front desk to ask staff if there are any emergencies from guests.
11:15	Works on a forecasting sheet for the coming week. Prepares preliminary schedule and anticipated payroll.
12:30 P.M.	Lunches with an architect to discuss floor plan for remodeling parking garage.
1:30	Works with the controller on budgetary targets for the next month. Receives feedback on budget targets from last month.
2:00	Meets with the general manager to discuss development of the next fiscal budget.
3:00	Greets the second-shift maintenance workers, relays operational information, and discusses workload for the day. Prepares work assignments and talks about details of completing assignments.
3:30	Works on energy-saving plan draft for presentation tomorrow at the Safety Committee meeting.
4:00	Responds to a request for help from a maintenance worker who needs assistance repairing a leaking toilet.
5:00	Checks with the banquet manager if the air conditioning is adequate for tonight's function.

5:30	Sends an email requesting a list of rooms to be placed out of order to front office manager and executive housekeeper for next week to have walls painted.
5:45	Reviews all work order request forms that were completed today.
6:15	Reviews preventive maintenance plan and determines which goals were met today.
6:45	Prepares to-do schedule for tomorrow.

This job analysis reveals the chief engineer is actively involved with the maintenance staff and the hotel staff. Planning, supervising, and communicating are essential aspects of this person's role in the management team.

Job Description

The following general job description summarizes the administrative and operational responsibilities of a chief engineer of a lodging property. Note, as you review the tasks found in this job description, refer to the previous section on job analysis.

Title: Chief Engineer
Reports To: General Manager

Planning

1. Coordinates preventative maintenance plan on all heating, ventilation, air-conditioning, and food service equipment safety.
2. Coordinates any repair orders from all departments such as guest rooms and food service.
3. Prepares budget for engineering department to include supplies and labor, etc.
4. Maintains cost control procedures on all costs associated with budget items.
5. Contributes to physical planning and development of property. Participates as active member of executive team.
6. Coordinates energy-saving plan for property. Involves hotel employees to promote an energy-saving attitude.
7. Coordinates room blocks and room repairs on a daily basis.
8. Cooperates with all national, state, and local laws affecting guests and employees with regard to safety and employment.

Supervising

1. Supervises work crew on daily tasks, prepares daily schedule, prepares work assignments, and assists crew members with tasks as needed.

Communicating

1. Communicates with various department heads in the lodging property concerning operational concerns such as equipment failures, heating/ventilation/

air-conditioning, marketing effects on property usage, housekeeping efforts to maintain green status, and food service operation equipment maintenance needs.

2. Communicates with employees in hotel to promote an energy saving attitude.

Perform these and other duties as required.

Technology

Technology is now available to assist the chief engineer in organizing and operating vital management services.

> Mintek Mobile Data Solutions, www.mintek.com, enables hotel owners and operators to manage five important processes: preventive maintenance, asset management, capital expenditure (CAPEX) planning, work orders, and document and contract management.
>
> This technology features opportunities to control a property's assets with a detailed database; to monitor scheduled inspections with a property management system; to enable anyone inside or outside of the engineering department of a hotel—engineers, housekeepers, general managers, [food and beverage] staff and others—to submit and monitor work orders via the browser-based system; to schedule work of the department; and to track important documents such as warranties, architectural designs, and maintenance contracts.[19]

Managing Maintenance Inter-departmental Communications

As noted previously, communication between departments is vital for delivering hospitality to the guest and creating a profit for the lodging property, and engineering is no exception. The chief engineer must take a proactive stance to manage communications with the maintenance, housekeeping, front office, food service, and marketing and sales departments. For example, a planned electrical outage to repair a major piece of equipment, such as an elevator, can affect the immediate daily activities of housekeeping staff, bell staff, and room service staff. Similarly, a plan to deep clean the rugs on several floors of a lodging establishment must be communicated well in advance to marketing and sales, food and beverage, housekeeping, and the front office, so they can plan for restrictions in available guest rooms and employee scheduling.

Disaster preparation was discussed in a previous chapter. The cooperation of the chief engineer with outside disaster officials is another example of vital communication.

Energy Management

A key concern of every executive housekeeper and chief engineer is their operating budget and the management of operating expenses, such as energy used for lighting, heating, and, air conditioning. Phil Sprague offers the following ideas on energy management in these areas. He urges the property manager to hire local lighting, mechanical, and electrical contractors to audit the hotel's lighting, heating, ventilating, air-conditioning equipment, and electrical equipment. In addition:

Energy-saving lighting retrofits have always been the most popular energy-saving projects for hotels, for obvious reasons. Insist that the contractor individually address the guestrooms, the corridors, the public space and the back-of-the house as separate categories. For example, the corridor operates twenty-four hours a day, while guestrooms operate on the average of four hours per day.

Typically, older [mechanical] equipment brings in an excessive amount of outside air which must be either heated or cooled. This includes areas such as bathroom exhaust from guest rooms, kitchen exhaust, and air handling units that close at the end of the work day.

Electric motors that are five horsepower or greater can easily [be] replaced with new energy-efficient electric motors that have a very good return on investment, especially motors in air handlers such as those that serve corridors and operate twenty-four hours a day.

The variable frequency drive allows the hotel to speed up or slow down a motor depending on the needs of the area that it serves. Slowing down a motor by just twenty percent provides a fifty percent reduction in energy consumption.

Sometimes it is necessary to install capacitors at a hotel's main electric vault to correct the Power Factor, a term used by utility companies to measure the efficiency with which each of its commercial customers uses electricity. An electric contractor can resolve the problem for less than $2000 and under a one-year return on investment.[20]

The Greening of the Lodging Industry

Businesspeople should reflect carefully on the responsibility to take care of environmental resources. This is not only a responsibility the organization owes future generations but also another opportunity to make profits for the organization. The money saved in laundry cleaning products, energy to operate washers, dryers, and other pieces of equipment in the laundry, water to launder bedding and towels, and labor in person-hours can add up.

Many hotels place a printed card on the pillow of an unmade bed asking guests to indicate their preference for bed making as an option. This can save many thousands of gallons of water, energy, and cleaning products per day if guests are inclined to participate with this program.

Ishmael Mensah reports, "Studies conducted by the International Hotels Environment Initiative (IHEI) and Accor revealed that 90% of hotel guests preferred to stay in a hotel that cared for the environment." He adds, "Cost savings seem to be the prime motivation for the increasing adoption of environmental management practices [energy and water] in hotels."[21]

FIGURE 15-13

Executive
housekeepers
work in
conjunction with
chief engineers to
find green clean
products to use in
the laundry.

In December 2007, a roundtable discussion of several lodging industry leaders gathered to discuss the future trends for 2008. At that discussion, Jim Butler, a hotel lawyer and business advisor specializing in creating solutions for hotel owners, developers, and lenders for Global Hospitality Group® of Jeffer, Mangels, Butler & Marmaro LLP, stated the year 2007 will go down as the year the hotel industry hit the tipping point on going green.[22] Since then, the greening of the lodging industry has taken on a product significance of its own for guests seeking value in their guest stay; investment and property managers searching for ways to manage costs; and chief engineers investigating ways to evaluate the effectiveness of front-line methods used in conserving water and electricity, and using ecological friendly products and promoting a healthy facility. David M. Green, president of Cre 8 Hospitality, an organization that specializes in consulting and training for the hospitality industry, offers easy steps for housekeeping managers to begin developing and implementing a green cleaning program.

Create your own green library with books, publications, websites, newsletters, etc.
Purchase green cleaning products by visiting www.GreenSeal.org and clicking on
    "Find a Certified Product/Service" [to] find product classifications for sanitation,
    cleaning and floor care products with information to clarify their intended use.

Use green paper/plastic products—check the website www.GreenSeal.org for standards.

Introduce green equipment by finding information on the Carpet and Rug Institute website, www.carpet-rug.org. This site will provide information about [the] Carpet and Rug Institute (CRI) Seal of Approval and Green Labeled equipment. By using certified equipment a hotel can increase the number of Leadership in Energy and Environmental Design (LEED) rating points it earns.[23]

It is to be noted that Marriott was the first [October 6, 2005] major hotel company in the U.S. with a LEED certified hotel—The Inn and Conference Center by Marriott at the University of Maryland in College Park. "LEED certification gives these hotels a 'green' stamp of approval that our customers recognize and look for," says Arne Sorenson, Marriott's newly appointed President and Chief Operating Officer and co-chair of the company's Executive Green Council. "Saving energy and reducing waste saves money and helps the environment—it's good for business and a key part of our growth strategy."[24]

Leadership in Energy and Environmental Design (LEED)

Here are highlights of the U.S. Green Building Council website, www.usgbc.org, concerning *LEED* certification.

LEED is an internationally recognized green building certification system, providing third-party verification that a building or community was designed and built using strategies aimed at improving performance across all the metrics that matter most: energy savings, water efficiency, CO_2 emissions reduction, improved indoor environmental quality, and stewardship of resources and sensitivity to their impacts.

LEED provides building owners and operators a concise framework for identifying and implementing practical and measurable green building design, construction, operations and maintenance solutions.

LEED is flexible enough to apply to all building types—commercial as well as residential. It works throughout the building lifecycle—design and construction, operations and maintenance, tenant fit out, and significant retrofit.

LEED promotes a whole-building approach to sustainability by recognizing performance in key areas:

1. sustainable sites (discourages development on previously undeveloped land; minimizes a building's impact on ecosystems and waterways; encourages regionally appropriate landscaping; rewards smart transportation choices; controls storm water runoff; and reduces erosion, light pollution, heat island effect and construction-related pollution);

2. water efficiency (more efficient appliances, fixtures and fittings inside and water-wise landscaping outside);

3. energy and atmosphere (monitoring energy use; efficient design and construction; efficient appliances, systems, and lighting; renewable and clean sources of energy generated on-site or off-site);

4. materials and resources (construction and operation phases/reuse and recycle);

5. indoor environmental quality (air quality, access to natural daylight, and improving acoustics);

6. locations and linkages;

7. awareness and education;

8. innovation in design; and regional priority.

LEED points are awarded on a 100-point scale, and credits are weighted to reflect their potential environmental impacts. Additionally, 10 bonus credits are available, four of which address regionally specific environmental issues. A project must satisfy all prerequisites and earn a minimum number of points to be certified. The following chart displays the ratings.

LEED for Commercial Interiors

Total Possible Points**	110*
Sustainable Sites	21
Water Efficiency	11
Energy & Atmosphere	37
Materials & Resources	14
Indoor Environmental Quality	17
*Out of a possible 100 points + 10 bonus points	
** Certified = 40+ points;	
Silver = 50+ points;	
Gold = 60+ points;	
Platinum = 80+ points	
Innovation in Design	6
Regional Priority	4 [25]

Solution to Opening Dilemma

This is a common question. The industry norm of 18 rooms per housekeeper per day can be maintained if proper training is implemented and maintained, adequate supervision and motivation are provided, and adequate tools and equipment are available. If any of these are missing on a daily basis, the overall picture will reflect the lapse.

Chapter Recap

This chapter focused on the executive housekeeper as the manager of many opportunities to provide hospitality to guests. The first section discussed how the efforts of the housekeeping department supplement the marketing efforts of the hotel. The organization of the housekeeping department for full-service and limited-service properties was described. The relationship of the executive housekeeper to the general manager was delineated with a job analysis that traced his or her typical day.

The next section of the chapter focused on the management of a housekeeping department. Topics included the significance of room assignment and workload of the staff to the hotelier, executive housekeeper, and employee. The method of assigning room attendants was also discussed, as was the importance of staff training. The key element of room inspection and how to organize this practice was presented. The housekeeper's report was presented as a crucial link in the hotel's communication chain. Communication in the housekeeping department with regard to the important aspects of English as a second language and communication between departments was offered. Inventory control of linens, guest supplies, cleaning supplies, fixtures, and furniture was presented with a focus on meeting goals of profitability and guest service. Inventory theft control was presented together with the suggestion that employees work to resolve the problem. The master plan for cleaning control or deep cleaning was described. A plan for developing an in-house laundry and a discussion of an in-house laundry versus outsourcing was included. Occupational Safety and Health Administration and Material Safety Data Sheets were presented with historical notes and a discussion of related administrative responsibilities.

The section on compliance with the Americans with Disability Act encouraged future executive hoteliers to prepare their staff with practical tips on delivering guest hospitality to people with physical challenges. Certification information offered through professional associations such as the American Hotel & Lodging Association's Educational Institute and the International Executive Housekeepers Association was presented.

Another section of the chapter focused on the role of the chief engineer, including a review of a daily job analysis, which assists in building a job description. Technology that supports organization and operation of a maintenance department was also used to highlight the role of the chief engineer. It was noted how skilled the chief engineer must be at developing good communications with other departments—housekeeping, front office, food service, and marketing and sales—to benefit the guest, hotel, and profit for the organization.

The executive housekeeper and chief engineer's duties with respect to managing energy were discussed. Highlights included energy audits for guest and public areas to control lighting, mechanical, and electrical devices. The final segment of the chapter featured the greening of the lodging industry, with emphasis on responsibility, economic, and operational details. Leadership in Energy and Environmental Design (LEED) certification was also introduced.

End-of-Chapter Questions

1. Mr. Jones is a corporate executive traveling on an expense account. He finds that his room has no extra towels, old socks are left under a chair, and the television remote batteries are dead. How does this reflect on the importance of the housekeeping department in the marketing plan of the hotel?

2. If you are employed in a full-service hotel, ask the executive director of the housekeeping department to outline the organization of the department.

3. If you are employed in a limited-service hotel, ask the executive director of the housekeeping department to outline the organization of the department.

4. What does the job analysis of an executive housekeeper tell you about his or her job?

5. How does the assignment of rooms differ to (1) a hotelier and general manager, (2) an executive housekeeper, and (3) a room attendant?

6. If you had to develop a list of skills in which to train a room attendant, what would you include?

7. What is your opinion of having room attendants inspect their own rooms? What built-in safeguards would you include to make the system work if you support it?

8. Why is the housekeeper's report so important to the night audit?

9. Do you think offering English as a Second Language (ESL) courses to housekeeping staff will help them perform their job?

10. Explain the par system for linen control. Do you think raising the par by one or two items will be a problem for the hotel?

11. How should guest amenities be controlled?

12. How should cleaning supplies be controlled?

13. What would you include on a computerized spreadsheet program to control the maintenance of the fixtures in a hotel?

14. How do you feel about including employees in developing a plan to decrease theft in a hotel? What incentives would you include to make this plan work?

15. What does the term *deep cleaning* indicate, and how do executive housekeepers organize it?

16. Discuss what to include in planning an in-house laundry.

17. Discuss the pros and cons of an in-house versus an outsourced laundry.

18. What are the main features of the Occupational Safety and Health Administration law of April 28, 1971?

19. What are Material Safety Data Sheets? If you are employed in a hotel, ask your executive housekeeper for a copy of one to bring to class.

20. What are some ways to comply with the Americans with Disability Act?

21. View the websites of the American Hotel & Lodging Association's Educational Institute and the International Executive Housekeepers Association to determine the requirements for their certification of executive housekeepers. What is your opinion of these requirements?

22. What does the job analysis of a chief engineer tell you about his or her job?

23. Search a website such as www.hotel-online.com to identify a software program that would assist a hotel chief engineer in operating his or her department.

24. Describe the importance of communication between a chief engineer and other departments in a lodging property. Give examples.

25. If you were assigned the task of controlling energy in a lodging property, where would you begin?

26. Jot down some ideas on what "greening of the lodging industry" means to you. Share them with another person in class. How would you establish one of these ideas where you work?

27. Review the information included in the text on LEED certification. How will it support positive growth for the lodging industry?

CASE STUDY 1501

Margaret Chu, general manager of The Times Hotel, asked Thomas Brown, executive housekeeper, to review the most recent display copy for the new billboard. Tom looked at the copy and said, "Margaret, what do you want me to say? I see our hotel, a bellman opening the door. And there is the caption—Our House Is Your House. And that's all." Margaret responded, "Tom, we put this billboard together to not only get people in the door of The Times Hotel but also to keep them here. Our marketing department tells me it is the cleanliness of the hotel that will bring them back. Guests want a room that is excep-tionally clean—no excuses. Tom, can you guarantee this? This billboard campaign is going to cost us over $25,000. That's a lot of money I am allocating in the budget this quarter. Our owners are depending on us to bring these corporate guests back for the second, third, and fourth visits!" Tom left the meeting with Margaret and decided he had to develop a plan to make his part of the advertising campaign work. He wanted to be sure his staff of room attendants would benefit from a plan for training and motivation. If you were the executive housekeeper, how would you proceed with such a plan?

CASE STUDY 1502

Thomas Brown, executive housekeeper of The Times Hotel, has been reviewing the last five quarterly reports on linen costs from the supplier, and he feels this cost is getting out of control. In addition, the supplier was unreliable over the busy convention season. Mr. Brown scheduled a meeting with Simon International Laundry Equipment in two days to discuss the possibility of an in-house laundry. What should he research prior to the meeting?

CASE STUDY 1503

Yoon-Whan Li, executive engineer of The Times Hotel, has been reading how several nearby hotels are applying for LEED certification. Margaret Chu, general manager of The Times Hotel, is also aware of those hotels and would like to investigate how The Times Hotel could become certified. Ms. Chu decided to organize a committee of the assistant general manager, executive housekeeper, front office manager, and food and beverage manager. She also wanted to include her two interns—you and your classmate.

Prior to the first meeting, she asked her two interns to prepare an agenda on what LEED certification is all about—the granting agency, levels of certification, and the point system. Prepare several bullet points and be prepared to discuss those concepts.

Notes

1. "Enhancing the Guest Experience," http://www.hotelmanagement-network.com/features/feature395/Hotel ManagementNetwork.com, December 1, 2005.

2. Barbara A. Worcester, "Sheets, Blankets, Pillows, Towels and Shower Curtains Are the Ambassador to the Hotel," *Hotel & Motel Management* (November 1998), http://www.hotel-online.com/SpecialReports1998/Nov98_Linens.html.

3. Alberto Santana, "Gaylord Opryland Expects $220K in Annual Housekeeping Savings, Better Guest Service Via MTech's REX," July 3, 2009, http://www.hotel-online.com/News/PR2009_3rd/Jul09_MTechGaylord.html 2009.

4. Robert J. Martin, *Professional Management of Housekeeping Operations*, 3rd ed. (New York: John Wiley & Sons, 1998), 142.

5. Harry Nobles, "Which Training Plan is Right for You?" June 9, 2009, http://www.hotel-online.com/News/PR2009_2nd/Jun09_HNoblesTraining.html, 2009.

6. Michael Hampton, "Optimizing New Employee Performance and Productivity or Getting New Hires Up to Speed Quickly," December 2003, www.hotelonline.com/News/PR2003_4th/Dec03_NewHires.html.

7. Jessica Wilbanks, "PM Hospitality Strategies Zero Defects Program Increases Unity Between the Housekeeping and Maintenance Departments," August 3, 2001, www.hotel-online.com/News/PR2001_3rd/Aug01_ZeroDefects.html.

8. Carol Kenrick, "The Outsoursing Weblog: Outsourcing Houskeeping Functions" December 26, 2006, http://www.outsourcing-weblog.com/50226711/outsourcing_housekeeping_functions.php 2006.

9. "Enhancing The Guest Experience" December 1, 2005, http://www.hotelmanagement-network.com/features/feature395/ hotelmanagement-network.com, 2005.

10. Agnes Sibal, "Hilton Garden Inn® Evolving with New Guest Room Amenities: 26" Flat Panel High-Def TVs, Ergonomic Desk Chair and New Technology Air Cell Mattresses," Hilton Garden Inn Brand Communications, February 15, 2005, www.hotel-online.com/News/PR2005_1st/Feb05_HiltonGardenInnEvolves.html.

11. Mary Beth Cutshall, "Hotel Equities Celebrates Grand Opening of the Courtyard by Marriott-Buford, Georgia," August 3, 2009, http://www.hotel-online.com/News/PR2009_3rd/Aug09_HECourtyard.html2009.

12. Cheryl Johnston, "Holiday Inn Wants Confessions, Declares Amnesty Day for Towel Snatchers," *Baltimore Sun*, Knight Ridder/Tribune Business News, August, 27, 2003, www.hotel-online.com/News/PR2003_3rd/Aug03_HITowels.html.

13. "Baring Laundry-Valet Profile," Baring Industries, 655 NW 122 Street, Miami, Florida, 33268, undated brochure. Quoted in Martin, 308–309.

14. D. E. Leger, "The Practice of Hoteliers Outsourcing Their Laundry Is Growing," *The Miami Herald*, Knight Ridder/Tribune Business News, March 29, 2004, www.hotel-online.com/News/PR2004_1st/Mar04_LaundryOutsource.html.

15. U.S. Department of Labor, Occupational Safety and Health Administration, *All About OSHA*, OSHA 2056, 2000 (Rev. ed.), 5, 6, 14.

16. Richard Gullickson, "Reference Data Sheet on Material Safety Data Sheets," May 1996, Meridian Engineering & Technology, Inc., http://www.msdssearch.com/msdshistory.htm.

17. Ibid.

18. Deborah T. Curtis, "ADA Compliant, But Ready?" May/June 2003, *The Rooms Chronicle®*, P.O. Box 2036, Niagara University, NY 14109-2036, Vol. 11, No. 2, 8-9.

19. Chris Kluis and Glenn Hasek, "Mintek Mobile Data Solutions Unveils New Website, Introduces Transcendent" May 2, 2009. Ideas & Trends, http://www.hotel-online.com/News/PR2009_2nd/May09_MintekWebsite.html.

20. Phil Sprague, "Hotel Energy Conservation Can Be Easy As 1, 2, 3" July/August 2008, *The Rooms Chronicle®*, P.O. Box 2036, Niagara University, NY 14109-2036, Vol. 16, No. 4, 10-11.

21. Ishmael Mensah, "Environmental Management Practices in US Hotels," May 2004, Cecil B. Day School of Hospitality Administration, Robinson College of Business, MSC 4A0310, Georgia State University, Atlanta, Georgia 30303, www.hotel-online.com/News/PR2004_2nd/May04_EnvironmentalPractices.html.

22. Jim Butler, "Hotel Industry Outlook 2008: A Roundtable Discussion Industry Fundamentals - Where have we been? Where are we going?" December 4, 2007, http://www.hotel-online.com/News/PR2007_4th/Dec07_RoundtableJMBM.html.

23. David M. Green, "Four Simple Steps for Housekeeping Managers Considering 'Going Green'" July/August 2008, *The Rooms Chronicle*®, P.O. Box 2036, Niagara University, NY 14109-2036, Vol. 16, No. 4, 16.

24. Stephanie Hampton, "Marriott International's Global Headquarters Building and 30 of its Hotels in Development Expected to Achieve LEED(R) Certification" May 9, 2009, http://www.hotel-online.com/News/PR2009_2nd/May09_MarriottGreen.html.

25. "Intro–What LEED Is" U.S. Green Building Council, 2009, http://www.usgbc.org/DisplayPage.aspx?CMSPageID=1988.

Key Words

amenities	LEED
room attendant	Material Safety Data Sheets (MSDS)
deep cleaning	par system

Glossary

access time: the amount of time required for a processor to retrieve information from the hard drive; recorded in milliseconds

accounts payable: financial obligations the hotel owes to private and government-related agencies and vendors

accounts receivable: amounts of money owed to the hotel by guests

aging of accounts: indication of the stage of the payment cycle, e.g., 10 days old, 30 days overdue, 60 days overdue

all-suites: a level of service provided by a hotel for a guest who desires an at-home atmosphere

amenities: personal toiletry items such as shampoo, toothpaste, mouthwash, and electrical equipment

American Hotel & Lodging Association: a professional association of hotel owners, managers, and persons in related occupations

American plan: a room rate that includes meals, usually breakfast and the evening meal, as well as room rental in the room rate

Americans with Disabilities Act (ADA): a U.S. law enacted in 1990 that protects people with disabilities from being discriminated against when seeking accommodations and employment

assets: items with monetary value

assistant general manager: a person in the hotel who executes plans developed by the corporate owners, general manager, and other members of the management staff

athletics director: the person responsible for supervising physical exercise facilities for guests

atrium concept: a hotel design in which guest rooms overlook the lobby from the first floor to the roof

average daily rate (ADR): a measure of the hotel staff's ability to sell available room rates; the method to compute the ADR is:

$$\frac{\text{room revenue}}{\text{number of rooms sold}}$$

back office: the accounting office of a hotel

back office accounts payable: amounts of money prepaid on behalf of the guest for future consumption of a good or service (also referred to as *back office cash accounts*)

balance sheet: an official financial listing of assets, liabilities, and owner's equity

bank cards: credit cards issued by banks, e.g., VISA, MasterCard, and JCB

banquet manager: a person responsible for fulfilling the details of service for a banquet or special event

banquet sheet: a listing of the details of an event at which food and beverages are served

bell captain: the supervisor of the bell staff

bell staff: people who lift and tote baggage, familiarize guests with their new surroundings, run errands, deliver supplies, provide guests with information on in-house marketing efforts and local attractions, and act as the hospitality link between the lodging establishment and the guest

bill-to-account: an extension of credit to a guest by an individual hotel; it requires the guest or the guest's employer to establish a line of credit and to adhere to a regular payment schedule

biometrics: an individual electronic measurement of the uniqueness of a human being, e.g., voice, handprint, or facial characteristics

blackout: total loss of electricity

blocking on the horizon: reserving guest rooms in the distant future

blocking procedure: process of reserving a room on a specific day

bottom up: a sales method that involves presenting the least expensive rate first

brownout: partial loss of electricity

bus association network: an organization of bus tour owners and operators who offer transportation and travel information to groups

business affiliation: chain or independent ownership of hotels

business services and communications center: guest services that include copying, computers, fax, etc.

call accounting: a computerized system that allows for automatic tracking and posting of outgoing guest room calls

cancellation code: a sequential series of alphanumeric combinations that provide the guest with a reference for a cancellation of a guaranteed reservation

cash bank: a specific amount of paper money and coins issued to a cashier to be used for making change

cashier: a person who processes guest checkouts and legal tender and makes change for guests

cashier's report: a daily cash control report that lists cashier activity of cash and credit cards and machine totals by cashier shift

Certified Hospitality Housekeeping Executive (CHHE): a certification for executive housekeepers offered through the Educational Institute of the American Hotel & Lodging Association

chain: a group of hotels that follow standard operating procedures such as marketing, reservations, quality of service, food and beverage operations, housekeeping, and accounting

chain affiliations: hotels that purchase operational and marketing services from a corporation

channel management: objective review of the most profitable marketing approach for guest rooms—central reservation system, GDS, third-party reservation system, toll-free phone reservation, travel agent, etc.

city ledger accounts: a collection of accounts receivable of nonregistered guests who use the services of the hotel

collective bargaining unit: labor union

commercial cards: credit cards issued by corporations, e.g., Diners Club

commercial hotels: hotels that provide short-term accommodations for traveling guests

commercial rates: room rates for businesspeople who represent a company but do not necessarily have bargaining power because of their infrequent or sporadic pattern of travel

communications hierarchy: the order in which management personnel may be called on to take charge in an emergency situation

company-owned property: a hotel that is owned and operated by a chain organization

complimentary rate (comp): no charge to the guest

computer supplies: paper, forms, ribbons, ink cartridges, and floppy disks needed to operate a computer system

concierge: a person in a hotel who provides an endless array of information on entertainment, sports, amusements, transportation, tours, church services, and babysitting in a particular city or town

conference call: a conversation in which three or more persons are linked by telephone

contactless locks: locks that use radio frequency identification (RFID) to control entry into guest, public, and work areas in a lodging property, e.g., wristbands, key fobs, and key cards

continental breakfast: juice, fruit, sweet roll, and/or cereal

controller: the hotel's internal accountant

convention guests: guests who attend a large convention and receive a special room rate

corporate client: a hotel guest who represents a business or is a guest of that business and who provides the hotel with an opportunity to establish a regular flow of business during sales periods that would normally be flat

corporate guests: frequent guests who are employed by a company and receive a special room rate

corporate rates: room rates offered to corporate clients staying in the hotel

CPS (characters per second): measure of the speed with which individual characters are printed

credit: a decrease in an asset or an increase in a liability, or an amount of money the hotel owes the guest

credit balance: amounts of money a hotel owes guests in future services

credit card imprinter: machine that makes an imprint of the credit card the guest will use as the method of payment

credit card validator: a computer terminal linked to a credit card data bank that holds information concerning the customer's current balance and security status

crisis management: maintaining control of an emergency situation

cross-training: training employees to perform multiple tasks and jobs

cumulative total feature: an electronic feature of a PMS that adds all posted room rate amounts into one grand total

current guests: guests registered in the hotel

cursor: a flashing point on a monitor that indicates where data can be entered on a computer screen

customer relationship management: a system that allows hotel managers to integrate technology to support customer service techniques that provide top-notch customer service

cycle of service: the progression of a guest's request for products and services through a hotel's departments

daily announcement board: an inside listing of the daily activities of the hotel (time, group, and room assignment)

daily blocking: assigning guests to their rooms on a daily basis

daily flash report: a PMS listing of departmental totals by day, period to date, and year to date that helps the manager determine the financial success of the previous day and current status in achieving other financial goals

daily function sheet: a listing of the planned events in the hotel

daily sales report: a financial activity report produced by a department in a hotel that reflects daily sales activities with accompanying cash register tapes or point-of-sale audit tapes

database interfaces: the means of sharing of information among computers

data sorts: report options in a PMS that indicate groupings of information

debit: an increase in an asset or a decrease in a liability

debit balance: an amount of money the guest owes the hotel

debit cards: embossed plastic cards with a magnetic strip on the reverse side that authorize direct transfer of funds from a customer's bank account to the commercial organization's bank account for purchase of goods and services

deep cleaning: a thorough cleaning of furniture and accessories, windows, flooring, and walls

demographic data: size, density, distribution, and vital statistics of a population broken down into, for example, age, sex, marital status, and occupation categories

departmental accounts: income- and expense-generating areas of the hotel, such as restaurants, the gift shop, and banquets

desk clerk: the person who verifies guest reservations, registers guests, assigns rooms, distributes keys, communicates with the housekeeping staff, answers telephones, gives information about and directions to local attractions, accepts cash and gives change, and acts as liaison between the lodging establishment and the guest as well as the community

direct-mail letters: letters sent directly to individuals in a targeted market group in a marketing effort

director of marketing and sales: the person who analyzes available markets, suggests products and services to meet the needs of those markets, and sells those products and services at a profit

director of security: the person who works with department directors to develop procedures that help ensure employee honesty and guest safety

discount rate: a percentage of the total sale charged by a credit card agency to the commercial enterprise for the convenience of accepting credit cards

discretionary income: the money remaining from wages after paying for necessities such as food, clothing, and shelter

disk drive: a place in the computer where data is stored or read; CD drive, hard drive, or key drive

documentation: printed or on-screen (monitor) instructions for operating hardware or software that accompanies a specific PMS

double occupancy percentage: a measure of a hotel's staff ability to attract more than one guest to a room; the method to compute double occupancy percentage is:

$$\frac{\text{number of guests} - \text{number of rooms sold}}{\text{number of rooms sold}} \times 100$$

ecotourists: tourists who plan vacations to understand the culture and environment of a particular area

electronic key: a plastic key with electronic codes embedded on a magnetic strip

electronic key system: a system composed of battery-powered or, less frequently, hardwired locks; a host computer and terminals; a keypuncher; and special entry cards used as keys

elevator operator: a person who manually operates the mechanical controls of the elevator

email: a communication system that uses an electronic network to send messages via computers

employee handbook: publication that provides general guidelines concerning employee conduct

empowerment: management's act of delegating certain areas of authority and responsibility to front-line employees

ergonomics: the study of how people relate psychologically and physiologically to machines

euro: the accepted currency for some European states: Belgium, Germany, Spain, France, Ireland, Italy, Luxembourg, the Netherlands, Austria, Portugal, Finland, and Greece

European plan: a rate that quotes room charges only

executive housekeeper: the person responsible for the upkeep of the guest rooms and public areas of the lodging property as well as control of guest room inventory items

express checkout: means by which the guest uses computer technology in a guest room or a computer in the hotel lobby to check out

extended stay: a level of service that attracts long-term guests by providing light food service and amenities, including a fully equipped kitchenette, spacious bedrooms, and living areas for relaxation and work

FAM (familiarization) tours: complimentary visits, sponsored by the lodging property, that host representatives of travel organizations, bus associations, social and nonprofit organizations, and local corporate traffic managers

family rates: room rates offered to encourage visits by families with children

fax machine: equipment for facsimile reproduction via telephone lines

fire safety display terminal: a device that ensures a constant surveillance of sprinkler systems and smoke detectors

float: the delay in payment from an account after using a credit card or personal check

floor inspector: a person who supervises the housekeeping function on a floor of a hotel

floor limit: a dollar amount set by a credit card agency that allows for a maximum amount of guest charges

flow analysis processes: the preparation of a schematic drawing of the operations included in a particular function

flowchart: an analysis of the delivery of a particular product or service

folio: a guest's record of charges and payments

folio well: a device that holds individual guest folios and city ledger folios

food and beverage director: the person responsible for the efficient operation of the kitchen, dining rooms, banquet service, room service, and lounge

foot patrol: walking the halls, corridors, and outside property of a hotel to detect breaches of guest and employee safety

forecasting: projecting room sales for a specific period

franchisee: a hotel owner who has access to a national reservation system and receives the benefits of the corporation's management expertise, financial backing, national advertising, and group purchasing

front-line employees: employees who deliver service to guests as front desk clerks, cashiers, switchboard operators, bellhops, concierge, and housekeeping employees

front office: the communication, accounting, and service center of the hotel

front office manager: the person responsible for leading the front office staff in delivering hospitality

full house: 100 percent hotel occupancy; a hotel that has all its guest rooms occupied

full service: a level of service provided by a hotel with a wide range of conveniences for the guest

function sheet: listing of the daily events in a hotel, e.g., meetings

general ledger: a collection of accounts the controller uses to organize the financial activities of the hotel

general manager: the person in charge of directing and leading the hotel staff in meeting its financial, environmental, and community responsibilities

gigabyte: 1024 megabytes of formatted capacity

gigahertz: a unit of frequency equal to 1 billion hertz; indicates computer speed

Global Distribution Systems (GDS): distributors of hotel rooms to corporations such as travel agents that buy rooms in large volume

going green: the responsibility to take care of the environment

group planner: the person responsible for securing guest room accommodations, food and beverage programs, transportation reservations, meeting facilities, registration procedures, tours, and information on sightseeing, while maintaining a budget, for group travelers

group rates: room rates offered to large groups of people visiting the hotel for a common reason

group travelers: people traveling on business or for pleasure in an organized fashion

gross operating profit per available room (GOPPAR): total revenue less the total departmental and operating expenses; it does not indicate the revenue mix of the hotel's property.

guaranteed reservations: prospective guests who have made a contract with the hotel for a guest room

guest folio: a form imprinted with the hotel's logo and a control number and allowing space for room number, guest identification, date in and date out, and room rate in the upper left-hand corner; it allows for guest charges to be imprinted with a PMS and is filed in room-number sequence

guest histories: details concerning the guests' visits, such as ZIP code, frequency of visits, corporate affiliation, or special needs

guest supplies: commonly referred to as *guest amenities* or *personal toiletries;* care items such as small bottles of shampoo, hair conditioner, lotion, soap, mouthwash, shoeshine cloth, or a mending kit

guest test: evaluation procedure in which an outside person is hired by the hotel to experience hotel services and report the findings to management

half-day rate: a room rate based on length of guest stay in a room—usually less than a full day

hard-key system: a security device consisting of the traditional hard key that fits into a keyhole in a lock; preset tumblers inside the lock are turned by the designated key

hardware: computer equipment used to process software, e.g., central processing units, keyboards, monitors, and printers

HITEC: an acronym for Hospitality Industry Technology Exposition and Conference, which features all the latest computer software for the hospitality industry

hospitality: the generous and cordial provision of services to a guest

hotel broker: a person who sells hotel room prize packages to corporations, sweepstakes promoters, game shows, and other sponsors

hotel representative: a member of the marketing and sales department of the hotel who actively seeks out group activities planners

house count: the number of persons registered in a hotel on a specific night

housekeeper's room report: a daily report that lists the occupancy status of each room according to the housekeeping department

housekeeping room status: terminology that indicates availability of a guest room such as *available, clean,* or *ready* (room is ready to be occupied), *occupied* (guest or guests are already occupying a room), *dirty* or *stayover* (guest will not be checking out of the room on the current day), *on change* (guest has checked out of the room, but the housekeeping staff has not released the room for occupancy), and *out of order* (the room is not available for occupancy because of a mechanical malfunction)

house limit: a dollar amount set by the hotel that allows for a maximum amount of guest charges

Hubbart formula: a method used to compute room rates that considers such factors as operating expenses, desired return on investment, and income from various departments in the hotel

human resources manager: the person responsible for administering federal, state, and local employment laws as well as advertising, screening, interviewing, selecting, orienting, training, and evaluating employees

incentive program: an organized effort by management to understand employees' motivational concerns and to develop opportunities for them to achieve both their own goals and those of the hotel

independent hotel: a hotel not associated with a franchise

in-house laundry: a hotel-operated department that launders linens, uniforms, bedspreads, etc.

inkjet: a printer that produces small dots printed with liquid ink on paper

inquiries/reports: a feature of the PMS that enables management to maintain a current view of operations and finances

in-room guest checkout: a feature of the PMS that allows the guest to use a guest room television to check out of a hotel

in-service education: courses that update a professional's educational background for use in current practice

interdepartmental communication: communication between departments

interfacing: the ability of computers to communicate electronically and share data

interhotel property referrals: a system in which one member-property recommends another member-property to a guest

International Executive Housekeepers Association (IEHA): a professional organization for executive housekeepers, located in Westerville, Ohio; www.ieha.org; it offers two certifications—Certified Executive Housekeeper (CEH) and Registered Executive Housekeeper (REH)

Internet: a worldwide network of computer systems that share information over high-speed electronic connections

intersell cards: credit cards issued by a hotel corporation, similar to private label cards

intradepartmental communication: communication inside a department

intranet: a computer network for in-house users that allows them to share timely operational information to conduct business

I/O ports (input/output devices): computer peripherals including keyboards, monitors, modems, mice, joysticks, light pens, printers, and trackballs

job analysis: a detailed listing of the tasks performed in a job—the basis for a sound job description

job description: a list of required duties to be performed by an employee in a particular job

keyboard: a standard or Dvorak-type typewriter-style keypad that allows a computer operator to enter or retrieve data

key drawer: a drawer located underneath the counter of the front desk that holds room keys in slots in numerical order

keydrive: a Universal Serial Bus (USB) flash drive storage device for storing data electronically

key fob: a decorative and descriptive plastic or metal tag attached to a hard key

keypad: a numeric collection of typewriter keys and function keys that allows the operator to enter numbers or perform math functions in a computer

laser: a printer that produces photo images on paper

late charges: guest charges that might not be included on the guest folio because of a delay in posting by departments

Leadership in Energy and Environmental Design (LEED) Certification: an internationally recognized green building certification system providing third-party verification that a building or community was designed and built using strategies aimed at improving performance across all the metrics that matter most: energy savings, water efficiency, CO_2 emissions reduction, improved indoor environmental quality, and stewardship of resources and sensitivity to their impacts

leisure travelers: people who travel alone or with others for visits to points of interest, to relatives, or for other personal reasons

letter-quality: a better type of dot-matrix print

liabilities: financial or other contractual obligations or debts

litigious society: an environment in which consumers sue providers of products and services for not delivering them according to expected operating standards

main menu: on-screen list of all the available individual programs (modules) included in a computer software system

maintenance manager: a staff member in a limited-service property who maintains the heating and air-conditioning plant, produces guest room keys, assists housekeeping attendants as required, and assists with guest safety and security

management contract property: a hotel operated by a consulting company that provides operational and marketing expertise and a professional staff

manager's report: a listing of occupancy statistics from the previous day, such as occupancy percentage, yield percentage, average daily rate, RevPAR, and number of guests

market segments: identifiable groups of customers with similar needs for products and services

marquee: a hotel's curbside message board, including the logo of the hotel and space for a message

mass marketing: advertising products and services through mass communications such as television, radio, and the Internet

master credit card account: an account receivable that tracks bank, commercial, private label, and intersell credit cards such as VISA, MasterCard, and JCB

Material Safety Data Sheets (MSDS): a listing of a product's chemical contents, relative hazards to users, and name and address of its producer

megabyte: 1024 kilobytes of formatted capacity, as in a computer memory card

message book: a loose-leaf binder in which the front desk staff on various shifts can record important messages

military and educational rates: room rates established for military personnel and educators

modem: computer hardware that allows for transfer of data over telephone lines; expressed in baud, or information transfer, rates

modified American plan: a room rate that offers one meal with the price of a room rental

moments of truth: every time a guest comes in contact with some aspect of a hotel and judges its hospitality

money wire: an electronic message that authorizes money from one person to be issued to another person

monitor: a color or monochrome television screen, associated with a computer, that enables the operator to view input and output data, control column width and line length of display, adjust height of character display, and control visuals

moonlighter: a person who holds a full-time job at one organization and a part-time job at another organization

motivation: investigation of employee needs and desires and development of a framework for meeting them

Murphy bed: a bed hinged at the base of the headboard that swings up into the wall for storage, e.g., a SICO brand wall-bed

needs analysis: assessment of the flow of information and services of a specific property to determine if proposed new equipment can improve the flow

night audit: the control process whereby the financial activity of guests' accounts is maintained and balanced daily

night auditor: a hotel employee who balances the daily financial transactions of guests, acts as a desk clerk for the night shift, and communicates with the controller

no-show factor: percentage of guests with confirmed or guaranteed reservations who do not show up

occupancy management formula: calculation that considers confirmed reservations, guaranteed reservations, no-show factors of these two types of reservations, predicted stayovers, predicted understays, and predicted walk-ins to determine the number of additional room reservations needed to achieve 100 percent occupancy

occupancy percentage: the number of rooms sold divided by the number of rooms available

Occupational Safety and Health Administration (OSHA): a U.S. federal government agency that oversees employee worksite safety

online: operational and connected to the main computer system

on-the-job training: a training process in which the employee observes and practices a task while performing his or her job

operational effectiveness: the ability of a manager to control costs and meet profit goals

operational reports: operational data on critical financial aspects of hotel operations

optimal occupancy: 100 percent occupancy with room sales that yield the highest room rate

optimal room rate: a room rate that approaches the rack rate

organization charts: schematic drawings that show management positions in an organization

orientation checklist: a summary of all items that must be covered during the orientation of a new employee

orientation process: the introduction of new hires to the organization and work environment, in order to provide background information about the property

outsourcing: provision of service to the hotel—for example, a central reservation system—by an agency outside of the hotel

outstanding balance report: a listing of guests' folio balances

overbooking: accepting reservations for more rooms than are available by forecasting the number of no-show reservations, stayovers, understays, and walk-ins, with the goal of attaining 100 percent occupancy

package rate: a room rate that includes goods and services in addition to rental of a room

paid in advance (PIA): guests who paid cash at check-in

paid-outs: amounts of money paid out of the cashier's drawer on behalf of guests or employees of the hotel

paid-out slips: numbered forms that authorize cash disbursement from the front desk clerk's bank on behalf of guests or employees of the hotel

par system: a level of inventory established that provides adequately for service

parking garage manager: the person responsible for supervising garage attendants and maintaining security of guests and cars in the parking garage

payback period: with respect to computer purchases, the expected time required for a hotel to recoup the purchase price, installation charges, financing fees, and so forth through cost savings and increased guest satisfaction; assists in the decision to install computers

percent occupancy: the number of rooms sold divided by the number of rooms available multiplied by 100

percent yield: the number of rooms sold at average daily rate versus number of rooms available at rack rate multiplied by 100

physical plant engineer: the person who oversees a team of electricians; plumbers; heating, ventilating, and air-conditioning contractors; and general repair people to provide behind-the-scenes services to the guests and employees of the lodging property

plant: an outside person hired by a hotel to experience hotel services and report the findings to management

point of sale: an outlet in the hotel that generates income, such as a restaurant, gift shop, spa, or garage

point-of-sale front office: a front office whose staff promotes other profit centers of the hotel

point-of-sale terminals: computerized cash registers that interface with the PMS

policy and procedure manual: publication that outlines how the specific duties of each job are to be performed

postal code: See ZIP code

posting: the process of debiting and crediting charges and payments to a guest folio

potential gross income: the amount of sales a hotel might obtain at a given level of occupancy, average daily rate, and anticipated yield

ppm (pages per minute): printing speed capability

predicted house count: an estimate of the number of guests expected to register based on previous occupancy activities

printer: computer hardware in dot-matrix, inkjet, or laser models that produces hard copies of output data in letter-quality or draft style in various print fonts, with printing speed being expressed in CPS (characters per second), number of characters per line, and pages per minute, and paper insertion being tractor-fed, single sheet, or continuous form

prior approved credit: use of a credit card to establish creditworthiness

private label cards: credit cards issued by a retail organization, such as a department store or gasoline company

processor speed: how fast a CPU (central processing unit) makes calculations per second; expressed in megahertz (MHz)

profit-and-loss statement: a listing of revenues and expenses for a certain period

property management system (PMS): a generic term for applications of computer hardware and software used to manage a hotel by networking reservation and registration databases, point-of-sale systems, accounting systems, and other office software

psychographic data: emotional and motivational forces that affect the use of a service or product by potential markets

rack rate: the highest room rate category offered by a hotel

real estate investment trust (REIT): a form of financing a real estate investment through a mutual fund

recreation director: the hotel employee in charge of developing and organizing recreational activities for guests

referral member: a hotel owner or developer with access to a national reservation system

referral property: a hotel operating as an independent that wishes to be associated with a certain chain; uses national reservation system

referral reservation service: a service offered by a management company of a chain of hotels to franchise members

registration card: a form on which a hotel guest indicates name, home or billing address, home or billing phone number, vehicle information, date of departure, and method of payment

reservation code: a sequential series of alphanumeric combinations that provide the guest with a reference for a guaranteed reservation

reservation referral system: a worldwide organization that processes requests for room reservations at member hotels

reservations manager: the hotel employee who takes and confirms incoming requests for rooms, noting special requests for service; provides guests with requested information; maintains an accurate room inventory; and communicates with marketing and sales

reservation status: terminology used to indicate the availability of a guest room to be rented on a particular night, e.g., *open* (room is available for renting), *confirmed* (room has been reserved until 4:00 P.M. or 6:00 P.M.), *guaranteed* (room has been reserved until guest arrives), and *repair* (room is not available for guest rental)

residential hotels: hotels that provide long-term accommodations for guests

revenue account: part of owner's equity

revenue management: a process of planning to achieve maximum room rates and most profitable guests (those who will spend money at the hotel's food and beverage outlets, gift shops, etc.) that encourages front office managers, general managers, and marketing and sales directors to target sales periods and develop sales programs that will maximize profit for the hotel

revenue manager: a management position that oversees room inventory and room rates through various marketing channels

revenue per available customer (RevPAC): reviewing dollars spent by customers in social areas of the hotel, such as restaurants, lounge, and gift shop

revenue per available room (RevPAR): the amount of dollars each hotel room produces for the overall financial success of the hotel, determined by dividing room revenues received for a specific day by the number of rooms available in the hotel that day

$$\frac{\text{room revenue}}{\text{number of available rooms}} \text{ or hotel occupancy} \times \text{average daily rate}$$

revenue potential: the room revenue that could be received if all the rooms were sold at the rack rate

revenue realized: the actual amount of room revenue earned (number of rooms sold $\times$ actual rate)

role-playing: acting out a role before actually being required to do the job

room attendants (housekeeping attendants): employees who clean and maintain guest rooms and public areas

room blocking: reserving rooms for guests who are holding reservations

room inspection: a final review of a guest room to assure that all housekeeping tasks have been completed and room furnishings are in order

room key control system: an administrative procedure that authorizes certain personnel and registered guests to have access to keys

room revenues: the amount of room sales received

room sales figure: the total of posted daily guest room charges

room sales projections: a weekly report prepared and distributed by the front office manager that indicates the number of departures, arrivals, walk-ins, stayovers, and no-shows

rooms forecast: the projection of room sales for a specific period

room status: information on the availability of entry to a guest room—reservation (open, confirmed, guaranteed, or repair) or housekeeping (ready, on change, or out of order)

rule-of-thumb method for determining room rates: guideline stipulating that the room rate should be $2 for every $1000 of construction costs

safety committee: a group of front-line employees and supervisors who discuss safety issues for guests and employees

sales associate: a hotel employee who books guests' requirements for banquets and other special events

sales indicators: number of guests and revenue generated

security escort service: having a uniformed security guard escort a hotel employee to a financial institution

select service: a level of service provided by a hotel with guest room accommodations and limited food service and meeting space

self-check-in process: a procedure that requires the guest to insert a credit card with a magnetic stripe containing personal and financial data into a self-check-in terminal and answer a few simple questions concerning the guest's stay; eliminates the need to check into the hotel at the front desk with the assistance of a hotel employee

service management program: a management program that highlights a company's focus on meeting customers' needs and that allows a hotel to achieve its financial goals

service strategy statement: a formal recognition by management that the hotel will strive to deliver the products and services desired by the guest in a professional manner

shift leader: the person responsible for directing the efforts of a particular work shift

single-sheet: a type of printer that uses single-sheet paper

skill demonstration: demonstration of specific tasks required to complete a job

sleeper: a room thought to be occupied that is in fact vacant

smart card: an electronic device with a computer chip that allows a guest or an employee access to a designated area, tracking, and debit-card capability for the hotel guest

software: computer applications that process data such as guest information and aid in financial transactions and report generation

social media: online social networks, such as Facebook, Twitter, YouTube, and LinkedIn, through which managers can reach consumers via a marketing plan

social networking: personal and professional groupings of people with a common interest in communicating via technology; examples include Facebook, Twitter, and LinkedIn

statement of cash flows: a projection of income from income-generating areas of the hotel

stayovers: currently registered guests who wish to extend their stay beyond the time for which they made reservations

surcharge rates: telephone rates for adding service charges for out-of-state long-distance telephone service

tax cumulative total feature: an electronic feature of a PMS that adds all posted room tax amounts into one grand total

telephone initiation and reception agreements: contracts between senders and receivers of PictureTel concerning specifications of the telephone call and who pays for it

telephone operator: the person who handles incoming and outgoing calls, locates registered guests and management staff, deals with emergency communications, and assists the desk clerk and cashier when necessary

tickler files: files used to prompt notice that certain events will be occurring

top-down: a sales method that involves presenting the most expensive rate first

total quality management (TQM): a management technique that encourages managers to look critically at processes used to produce products and services

total restaurant sales figure: total of all sales incurred at restaurants or food outlets in the hotel

touchscreen: a type of computer monitor that allows the operator to input data by touch

traffic manager: person who directs hotel guests to available elevators in the lobby

training tickler file: a database that keeps track of training sessions and alerts trainers to important upcoming dates

transfer slip: a form used to transfer an amount of money from one account to another while creating a paper trail

travel directories: organized listings of hotel reservation access methods, locations, and specific accommodations

traveler's checks: prepaid checks issued by a bank or other financial organization

trial balance: a first run on a set of debits to determine their accuracy compared to a corresponding set of credits

true integration: the sharing of a reservation database by a hotel's central reservation system and property management system

understays: hotel guests who arrive on time but decide to leave before their predicted date of departure

upsell: to encourage a customer to consider buying a higher-priced product or service than originally anticipated

visual alarm system: flashing lights that indicate a fire or other emergency in a hotel room

walking a guest with a reservation: offering accommodations at another hotel to a guest who has a reservation when your hotel is overbooked

walk-in guests: guests who request a room rental without having made a reservation

working supervisor: a person who participates in actual work performed while supervising

yield: the percentage of income that could be secured if 100 percent of available rooms are sold at their full rack rate

yield percentage: the effectiveness of a hotel at selling its rooms at the highest rate available to the most profitable guest

ZIP code: a local postal designation assigned by a country; also called *postal code*

Index